I0090820

revolutionary**Saints**

revolutionary**Saints**

Heidegger, National Socialism, and Antinomian Politics

CHRISTOPHER RICKEY

The Pennsylvania State University Press
University Park, Pennsylvania

LIBRARY OF CONGRESS CATALOGING-IN-PUBLICATION DATA

Rickey, Christopher, 1968–
    Revolutionary saints : Heidegger, national socialism, and antinomian
politics / Christopher Rickey.
    p.   cm.
    Includes bibliographical references and index
    ISBN 978-0-271-02397-7 (pbk : alk. paper)
    1. Heidegger, Martin, 1889–1976—Political and social views.
    2. National socialism.   3. Heidegger, Martin, 1889–1976—Religion.
    4. Religion and politics.   I. Title.

B3279 .H49 R5129 2002
193—dc21   2001041170

Copyright © 2002 The Pennsylvania State University
All rights reserved
Printed in the United States of America
Published by The Pennsylvania State University Press,
University Park, PA 16802-1003

It is the policy of The Pennsylvania State University Press to use acid-free paper
for the first printing of all clothbound books. Publications on uncoated stock
satisfy the minimum requirements of American National Standard for
Information Sciences—Permanence of Paper for Printed Library Materials, ANSI
Z39.48–1992.

To my mom

Contents

Acknowledgments

Like other ordinary mortals I rely upon the support of others to bring my projects to fruition. The kindnesses shown me during the preparation of this book included intellectual suggestions, copyediting, emotional encouragement during those inevitable depressions, arguments, the occasional kick in the pants, and sometimes just lending an ear to the latest idea in my head that was struggling to become clear. I am greatly indebted to my adviser, Michael Gillespie, for guiding and prodding me toward completion of a product that owes much of whatever positive qualities it can claim to his help. Ruth Grant, Rom Coles, Thomas Spragens, and Michael Moses also gave me valuable suggestions and advice along the way. This being the age of new means of communication, it seems timely to extend my thanks to people I have never seen and yet somehow feel I know, particularly Iain Thomson and Michael Eldred, from whom I learned much during our electronic discussions about Heidegger. I want to thank the John M. Olin Foundation for the support I received to finish this manuscript. My thanks go also to the people at the John M. Olin Center for Inquiry into the Theory and Practice of Democracy and the Committee on Social Thought at the University of Chicago, especially Nathan Tarcov and Stephen B. Gregory, for making my year smooth and productive. My family was a constant source of encouragement and affection over these years toiling far from home. Last and most, I thank my mother, to whom this work is dedicated, for her help, her support, encouragement, sympathetic ear, and for just being a great mother.

List of Abbreviations

Works by Heidegger

BDT   "Building Dwelling Thinking," in *Poetry, Language, Thought,* trans. Albert Hofstadter (New York: Harper & Row, 1971), 145–61.

BT   *Being and Time,* trans. John Macquarrie and Edward Robinson (New York: Harper & Row, 1962).

BwHB   *Heidegger-Blochmann: Briefwechsel 1918–1969,* 2d ed., ed. Joachim W. Stork (Marbach am Neckar: Deutsche Schillergesellschaft, 1990).

CLS   "Call to Labor Service (January 23, 1934)," in *The Heidegger Controversy,* ed. Richard Wolin (Cambridge: MIT Press, 1993), 53–55.

CT   *The Concept of Time,* trans. William McNeill (Cambridge: Basil Blackwell, 1992).

DL   "A Dialogue on Language," in *On the Way to Language,* trans. Peter D. Hertz (New York: Harper & Row, 1972), 1–54.

DSAH   "Declaration of Support for Adolf Hitler and the National Socialist State (November 11, 1933)," in *The Heidegger Controversy,* ed. Richard Wolin (Cambridge: MIT Press, 1993), 49–52.

EGT   *Early Greek Thinking,* trans. David Farrell Krell and Frank A. Capuzzi (New York: Harper & Row, 1984).

ET   "On the Essence of Truth," in *Basic Writings,* ed. David Farrell Krell (New York: Harper & Row, 1977), 113–41.

FBSD   *Zur Frage nach der Bestimmung der Sache des Denkens,* ed. Hermann Heidegger (St. Gallen: Erker, 1984).

FT   "The Rectorate 1933/34: Facts and Thoughts," in *Martin Heidegger and National Socialism: Questions and Answers,* ed. Günther Neske and Emil Kettering (New York: Paragon, 1990), 15–32.

G   *Gelassenheit,* 9th ed. (Pfullingen: Neske, 1988).

GA1   *Frühe Schriften,* ed. Friedrich-Wilhelm von Herrmann, vol. 1 of the *Gesamtausgabe* (Frankfurt a. M.: Klostermann, 1978).

GA3   *Kant und das Problem der Metaphysik,* ed. Friedrich-Wilhelm von Herrmann, vol. 3 of the *Gesamtausgabe* (Frankfurt a. M.: Klostermann, 1991).

GA4   *Erläuterungen zu Hölderlins Dichtung,* ed. Friedrich-Wilhelm von Herrmann, vol. 4 of the *Gesamtausgabe* (Frankfurt a. M.: Klostermann, 1981).

GA16   *Reden und andere Zeugnisse eines Lebensweges,* ed. Hermann Heidegger, vol. 16 of the *Gesamtausgabe* (Frankfurt a. M.: Klostermann, 2000).

GA19   *Platon: Sophistes,* ed. Ingeborg Schüßler, vol. 19 of the *Gesamtausgabe* (Frankfurt a. M.: Klostermann, 1992).

GA27   *Einleitung in die Philosophie,* ed. Otto Saame and Ina Saama-Speidel, vol. 27 of the *Gesamtausgabe* (Frankfurt a. M.: Klostermann, 1996).

GA29/30 *Die Grundbegriffe der Metaphysik: Welt—Endlichkeit—Einsamkeit,* ed. Friedrich-Wilhelm von Herrmann, vol.29/30 of the *Gesamtausgabe* (Frankfurt a. M.: Klostermann, 1983).

GA31   *Vom Wesen der Menschlichen Freiheit: Einleitung in die Philosophie,* ed. Hartmut Tietjen, vol. 31 of the *Gesamtausgabe* (Frankfurt a. M.: Klostermann, 1982).

GA33   *Aristoteles: Metaphysik IX,* ed. Heinrich Hüni, vol. 33 of the *Gesamtausgabe* (Frankfurt a. M.: Klostermann, 1981).

GA34   *Vom Wesen der Wahrheit: zu Platons Höhlengleichnis und Theätet,* ed. Hermann Mörchen, vol. 34 of the *Gesamtausgabe* (Frankfurt a. M.: Klostermann, 1988).

GA39   *Hölderlins Hymne "Germanien" und "Der Rhein,"* ed. Susanne Ziegler, vol. 39 of the *Gesamtausgabe* (Frankfurt a. M.: Klostermann, 1980).

GA45   *Grundfragen der Philosophie: Ausgewählte "Probleme" der*

"*Logik,*" ed. Friedrich-Wilhelm von Herrmann, vol. 45 of the *Gesamtausgabe* (Frankfurt a. M.: Klostermann, 1984).

GA50   *Nietzsches Metaphysik,* ed. Petra Jaeger, vol. 50 of the *Gesamtausgabe* (Frankfurt a. M.: Klostermann, 1990).

GA51   *Grundbegriffe,* ed. Petra Jaeger, vol. 51 of the *Gesamtausgabe* (Frankfurt a. M.: Klostermann, 1981).

GA52   *Hölderlins Hymne "Andenken,"* ed. Curd Ochwadt, vol. 52 of the *Gesamtausgabe* (Frankfurt a. M.: Klostermann, 1982).

GA53   *Hölderlins Hymne "Der Ister,"* ed. Walter Biemel, vol. 53 of the *Gesamtausgabe* (Frankfurt a. M.: Klostermann, 1984).

GA56/57 *Zur Bestimmung der Philosophie,* ed. Bernd Heimbüchel, vol. 56/57 of the *Gesamtausgabe* (Frankfurt a. M.: Klostermann, 1987).

GA60   *Phänomenologie des Religiösen Lebens,* ed. Mattias Jung, Thomas Regehly, and Claudius Strube, vol. 60 of the *Gesamtausgabe* (Frankfurt a. M.: Klostermann, 1995).

GA65   *Beiträge zur Philosophie: (Vom Ereignis),* ed. Friedrich-Wilhelm von Herrmann, vol. 65 of the *Gesamtausgabe* (Frankfurt a. M.: Klostermann, 1989).

GA79   *Bremer und Freiburger Vorträge,* ed. Petra Jaeger, vol. 79 of the *Gesamtausgabe* (Frankfurt a. M.: Klostermann, 1994).

GMW   "German Men and Women! (November 10, 1933)," in *The Heidegger Controversy,* ed. Richard Wolin (Cambridge: MIT Press, 1993), 47–49.

GS   "German Students (November 3, 1933)," in *The Heidegger Controversy,* ed. Richard Wolin (Cambridge: MIT Press, 1993), 46–47.

HCT   *History of the Concept of Time: Prolegomena,* trans. Theodore Kisiel (Bloomington: Indiana University Press, 1992).

HKBD   "Die Herkunft der Kunst und die Bestimmung des Denkens," in *Denkerfahrungen: 1910–1976,* ed. Hermann Heidegger (Frankfurt a. M.: Klostermann, 1983), 135–52.

ID   *Identity and Difference,* trans. Joan Stambaugh (New York: Harper & Row, 1969).

IM   *An Introduction to Metaphysics,* trans. Ralph Mannheim (New Haven: Yale University Press, 1959).

LH   "Letter on Humanism," in *Basic Writings,* ed. David Farrell Krell (New York: Harper & Row, 1977), 189–242.

LSU "Labor Service and the University (June 20, 1933)," in *The Heidegger Controversy,* ed. Richard Wolin (Cambridge: MIT Press, 1993), 42–43.

MFL *The Metaphysical Foundations of Logic,* trans. Michael Heim (Bloomington: Indiana University Press, 1984).

MHB "Metaphysics as History of Being," in *The End of Philosophy,* trans. Joan Stambaugh (New York: Harper & Row, 1973).

MWP "My Way to Phenomenology," in *On Time and Being,* trans. Joan Stambaugh (New York: Harper & Row, 1972), 74–82.

N1 *The Will to Power as Art,* trans. David Farrell Krell, *Nietzsche,* vol. 1 (San Francisco: HarperCollins, 1991).

N4 *Nihilism,* ed. David Farrell Krell, trans. Frank A. Capuzzi, *Nietzsche,* vol. 4 (San Francisco: HarperCollins, 1991).

NL "The Nature of Language," in *On the Way to Language,* trans. Peter D. Hertz (New York: Harper & Row, 1972), 57–108.

NSE "National Socialist Education (January 22, 1934)," in *The Heidegger Controversy,* ed. Richard Wolin (Cambridge: MIT Press, 1993), 55–60.

OM "Overcoming Metaphysics," in *The Heidegger Controversy,* ed. Richard Wolin (Cambridge: MIT Press, 1993), 67–90.

OWA "The Origin of the Work of Art," in *Poetry, Language, Thought,* trans. Albert Hofstadter (New York: Harper & Row, 1971), 15–87.

PMD " '. . . Poetically Man Dwells . . . ,' " in *Poetry, Language, Thought,* trans. Albert Hofstadter (New York: Harper & Row, 1971), 211–29.

PIA "Phenomenological Interpretations with Respect to Aristotle: Indication of the Hermeneutic Situation," *Man and World* 25 (1992): 355–93.

QCT "The Question Concerning Technology," in *The Question Concerning Technology and Other Essays,* trans. William Lovitt (New York: Harper & Row, 1977), 3–35.

SA "The Self-Assertion of the German University," in *Martin Heidegger and National Socialism: Questions and Answers,* ed. Günther Neske and Emil Kettering (New York: Paragon, 1990), 5–14.

Sl "Slageter (May 26, 1933)," in *The Heidegger Controversy,* ed. Richard Wolin (Cambridge: MIT Press, 1993), 40–42.

Sp   " 'Only a God can save us': *Der Spiegel*'s Interview with Martin Heidegger," in *The Heidegger Controversy,* ed. Richard Wolin (Cambridge: MIT Press, 1993), 91–116.

SR   "Science and Reflection," in *The Question Concerning Technology and Other Essays,* trans. William Lovitt (New York: Harper & Row, 1977), 155–82.

T   "The Turning," in *The Question Concerning Technology and Other Essays,* trans. William Lovitt (New York: Harper & Row, 1977), 36–39.

TI   "Martin Heidegger in Conversation (with Richard Wisser)," in *Martin Heidegger and National Socialism: Questions and Answers,* ed. Günther Neske and Emil Kettering (New York: Paragon, 1990), 81–87.

UNR   "The University in the New Reich (June 30, 1933)," in *The Heidegger Controversy,* ed. Richard Wolin (Cambridge: MIT Press, 1993), 43–45.

VA   *Vorträge und Aufsätze,* 6th ed. (Pfullingen: Neske, 1990).

W   "Words," in *On the Way to Language,* trans. Peter D. Hertz (New York: Harper & Row, 1972), 139–56.

WBP   "Vom Wesen und Begriff der Φύσις: Aristoteles, Physik B, 1," in *Wegmarken,* ed. Friedrich-Wilhelm von Herrmann, vol. 9 of the *Gesamtausgabe* (Frankfurt a. M.: Klostermann, 1976), 239–301.

WBW   "Schöpferische Landschaft: Warum Bleiben Wir in der Provinz?" in *Denkerfahrungen: 1910–1976,* ed. Hermann Heidegger (Frankfurt a. M.: Klostermann, 1983), 9–13.

WG   "Vom Wesen des Grundes," in *Wegmarken,* ed. Friedrich-Wilhelm von Herrmann, vol. 9 of the *Gesamtausgabe* (Frankfurt a. M.: Klostermann, 1976), 123–75.

WiT   *What Is a Thing?* trans. W. B. Barton Jr., and Vera Deutsch (South Bend, Ind.: Regnery/Gateway, 1967).

WM   "Was ist Metaphysik?" in *Wegmarken,* ed. Friedrich-Wilhelm von Herrmann, vol. 9 of the *Gesamtausgabe* (Frankfurt a. M.: Klostermann, 1976), 103–22.

WMe   "Einleitung zu 'Was ist Metaphysik?' " in *Wegmarken,* ed. Friedrich-Wilhelm von Herrmann, vol. 9 of the *Gesamtausgabe* (Frankfurt a. M.: Klostermann, 1976), 365–83.

WMn   "Nachwort zu 'Was ist Metaphysik?' " in *Wegmarken,* ed.

Friedrich-Wilhelm von Herrmann, vol. 9 of the *Gesamtausgabe* (Frankfurt a. M.: Klostermann, 1976), 303–12.

WN   "The Word of Nietzsche: 'God is Dead,'" in *The Question Concerning Technology and Other Essays,* trans. William Lovitt (New York: Harper & Row, 1977), 53–112.

ZS   "Zur Seinsfrage," in *Wegmarken,* ed. Friedrich-Wilhelm von Herrmann, vol. 9 of the *Gesamtausgabe* (Frankfurt a. M.: Klostermann, 1976), 385–426.

Introduction

Religion should accompany all the

doings of life like a holy music.

—Martin Heidegger, *Phänomenologie*

des Religiösen Lebens

There is no room for political philosophy

in Heidegger's work, and this may well be

due to the fact that the room in question

is occupied by gods or the gods.

—Leo Strauss, *Studies in Platonic*

Political Philosophy

This book concerns Martin Heidegger. It also concerns politics. Notwithstanding the numerous books, articles, conference papers, and talks on the subject, there is something strange about such a conjunction of Martin Heidegger and politics. The strangeness of this conjunction is, in fact, one of the central themes of this study.

Heidegger devoted no text to politics. He offered us no political science. In another sense, however, politics suffuses all his work. This can be, in part, because philosophy shares with political science the question "How should we live?" and Heidegger devoted his entire life to that question, which he called the question of being and which he understood as the question of how to be human, for only humans can raise and respond to the question of being. Already the strangeness of "Heidegger and politics" is evident, but if we are to follow the path, we must follow in Heidegger's footsteps. Heidegger conducted his political thinking, his great and sweeping critique of Western civilization and his insistent call to a higher kind of humanity, through the urgent pursuit of the question of being.

In this study, I will show why Heidegger conducted political philosophy in this way. I will show in detail how Heidegger's seemingly abstract metaphysical questioning is at heart a political and ethical undertaking. Lastly, I will show the consequences of Heidegger's path of political thinking.

The reader may justly fear that by "consequences" I mean to discuss Heidegger's ties to Nazism and that I am adding yet another book to the tiresome mud-slinging already in existence. I admit that Nazism will be a theme in this book too. One cannot talk about Heidegger and politics without mentioning Nazism. What I do wish to avoid is a facile polemic about Heidegger's involvement with the National Socialist movement, either a kind of *reductio ad Hitlerum* with respect to Heidegger's philosophy, or an unwarranted apology. The relationships between Heidegger the man and Heidegger the thinker, and between Heidegger's thought and his Nazi affiliation are quite complex and fascinating, and no honest study can reduce it to a polemic.

There is a reason, however, why I give the theme "Heidegger and Nazism" only one chapter in this book. This study is concerned with Heidegger and politics, and while Heidegger and Nazism is necessarily a constant companion to this concern, the central issue is broader. I wish to lay out Heidegger's answer to the question "How should we live?" If there is a connection between Heidegger's philosophy and Nazism, it must lie in that answer. If it was really no accident or error that Heidegger advocated National Socialism, it must follow as a consequence of his ideal of human being that originates in the question of how we ought to live. We cannot understand Heidegger and Nazism in a philosophically satisfactory way until we understand the political ideal that animates his entire work.

I thus propose to investigate Heidegger's political ideal of human being. What is its nature? What is its connection with the centerpiece of his philosophical thinking, the question of being? What are the political implications of the question of being? Only by considering these questions can one proceed to show the limitations, not only of Heidegger's politics, but of his political philosophy generally, for in the end, the lapses of one man, even a genius, are less significant than the principles he defends and with which he strives to make a claim upon us.

These and other questions lie behind my investigation of Heidegger's political philosophy. His deserved rank as a great thinker in the philosophic tradition, however, must be considered alongside the terrifying possibility that he was right about National Socialism. As shocking as that suggestion is to our moral sensibilities, our intellectual integrity obliges us to wonder whether national socialism represents *the* genuine answer to the question of how we ought to live. In thinking through this possibility, one gains an insight into the political possibilities beyond the modern, liberal society Heidegger wanted to overthrow.

Antinomian Politics

The inquiry into Heidegger's political philosophy must begin with an understanding of politics in the context of the whole human condition. Stated baldly, for Heidegger, politics was religion. This equation contributes to the strangeness of an inquiry into Heidegger and politics. One cannot leap directly from Heidegger to politics, but must pass through the question of religion. Religion and religiosity are the context for political life. In some sense, though, this is not so strange. Politics and religion have often been bedfellows because religion can also ask the question "How should we live?" Religion, understood broadly as the relationship between humans and the divine, was for Heidegger the central condition of human being. The question of how we ought to live (with each other here on earth) is answered in the answer to the question of how we ought to live (with respect to the divine).

It is his understanding of religion, however, that characterizes the peculiar nature of his politics. The peculiarity of his conception of the political lies in his understanding of authenticity, which rests upon a radically antinomian conception of religiosity. This antinomianism is central to the peculiar nature of Heidegger's political theology.

Antinomianism literally means "against the law." In a post-Reformation context it refers to a type of thought that strongly emphasizes the opposition Luther drew in "The Freedom of a Christian" between fulfillment through obedience to the law and fulfillment through grace, paralleled by the opposition between reason and faith.[1] What for Luther was a theo-

---

1. Martin Luther, "The Freedom of a Christian," in *Martin Luther: Selections from His Writings,* ed. John Dillenberger (New York: Anchor Books, 1962).

logical doctrine was quickly appropriated as a revolutionary political slogan. Political antinomianism renounces the violence and coercion inherent in secular politics in favor of a holy, Christian commonwealth bound together only by love and spiritual harmony. The basic antinomian social organization is the sect. The sect is the body of the elect who have been filled with God's grace. The political problem posed by the sect is its relation to members of the social whole who are not of the elect. On the one hand, the sect may feel a duty to bring the nonadherents to the correct path of salvation; on the other hand, it may forswear the coercion necessary to this public revolutionary project and withdraw into the private arena. These two poles of sectarian politics are the sole political possibilities offered by antinomian religiosity, which opposes law, reason, and works to spirit, faith, and grace.

Heidegger replicated these oppositions in his philosophy and his politics. His antinomian ideal of authenticity is a modern-day legacy of the theological-political currents of the radical Reformation. Heidegger's antinomianism leaves him caught between the two poles of sectarian politics: absolute tyranny on the one side, absolute noncoercion on the other. Only when one understands how his politics and philosophy are fundamentally shaped by a religious-theological framework can one understand how his thought offers so radical a departure from modern politics.

To understand Heidegger's proposed solution, it is necessary to see how he viewed the problem. Heidegger perceived the crisis of the Western spirit as a religious crisis and saw it as manifesting as nihilism understood as the death of God. This nihilism describes a threefold alienation: the human alienation from being, the human alienation from the divine, and the human alienation from an authentic community and thereby from his or her own self. These three elements of nihilism must be grasped together. The alienation of the self in modern society originates in an elemental alienation that manifests itself as a meaninglessness and the consequent loss of the sacredness that permeates a genuinely human existence.

Heidegger's aim was to heal the alienation inherent in modernity. Politically, this project demanded—as necessary for our authentic existence —a sacralization of the public sphere. This sacralization, however, was to ensue through a revolution in metaphysics. This revolution occurs only in and through the question of being, which opens a space in which the gods can appear. The question of being is thus no ivory tower pursuit, but instead the means by which Heidegger tried to incite "the great and long venture of demolishing a world that has grown old and of rebuilding it authentically anew" (*IM*, 125–26). The millenarian character of his politics is clear. Heidegger's politics are radical because they demand a deep-rooted and holistic solution to the problem of alienation.

In this manner, one could easily view Heidegger as an heir to the post-Kantian world in which reason is dirempted and fragmented within itself, and like many of Kant's heirs, Heidegger struggles to reunite a world torn apart. One can see parallels both to what Bernard Yack calls left Kantians and to right-wing religious, particularly Catholic, conservatives.[2] Whatever the parallels, one cannot assimilate Heidegger to either of these nineteenth-century camps. Unlike the left Kantians, Heidegger did not believe that conscious reason could heal the alienation of rationalism, and unlike religious conservatives, he had little faith in institutionalized religions in general and was actively hostile to the Catholic Church in particular, his own Catholic baptism and burial notwithstanding. His own critique of modernity was far more radical than either of these. It was a critique of both the rational critique of religion and institutional religion itself.

The best way to get to this intersection of religion and politics might be to turn to Max Weber. Weber, like many previous generations of German thinkers, was fascinated by the intersection of religion and politics. This fascination runs through his work, from his great works on the sociology of world religions to more subtle but still significant instances. For instance, the three ideal types of authority Weber introduces in *Economy and Society* are all kinds of religious organizing principles, even seemingly purely secular rational authority, as he makes clear in *The Protestant Work Ethic and the Spirit of Capitalism* that the seemingly purely secular rational authority in fact had a religious foundation. If he evinced a particular bent for the phenomenon of Protestant politics, it is only because that was most relevant to the development of capitalism, which was the decisive mold for modern society.

Much of Weber's sociology of religion consists in showing how religion is (or becomes) intertwined with the secular needs for organization, routine, stability, and what he calls everydayness. Religion, no matter how "otherworldly" its origins, is capable of accommodation with the world. This is true of both traditional and rational authority.

2. Bernard Yack, *The Longing for Total Revolution: Philosophic Sources of Social Discontent from Rousseau to Marx and Nietzsche* (Princeton: Princeton University Press, 1986); idem, *The Fetishism of Modernities* (Notre Dame: University of Notre Dame Press, 1997).

It is not true, however, of charismatic authority at least in its purest type. Charismatic authority rejects the world, organization, routine, stability, and "everydayness." It strives to meet the "spiritual" needs of humanity as opposed to its material needs. Although Weber never explicitly states it, it is hard not to suspect that charisma is, in this respect, religiosity *per se*. As such, charisma (or religiosity) has a strongly dislocative effect on society, since it rejects the very purpose of everyday social organization, the fulfillment of everyday human material needs. Indeed, Weber goes so far as to call charisma "the specifically creative revolutionary force of history."[3]

At some point, though, even a charismatic movement must make its peace with the world, for if man lives not by bread alone, he can still die from lack of it. Weber thus goes on to describe how charismatic authority becomes "routinized" and rationalized. The insurgency is tamed; the revolution becomes what it overthrew. This routinization can take many paths, some better able than others to maintain some small share of charisma. Churches, monasteries, and sects are three kinds of organized charisma. Although Weber describes this routinization of charisma in typically dry social-scientific language, one senses the loss involved, as if something great had become small. Charisma in its purest type is fleeting and ephemeral, but in these flashes of insurrection one glimpses the divine moment of the human.

For Heidegger, in such flashes of divinity lay the moment of human authenticity, *der Augenblick* when humans transcend their everyday existence to glimpse their fate and task in this world. Heidegger put this transcendent spirituality to practical use: the moment of vision was *phronēsis* or practical wisdom. Heidegger might have drawn on Aristotle to develop his account of human authenticity, but his underlying religiosity inflected Aristotle's practical categories into something quite other. In Heidegger, *phronēsis* became charisma, and politics became a revolutionary insurrection against the everyday.

Most interestingly for my comparison with Weber, Heidegger summed up inauthentic existence by the term "everydayness." The breaking out of everydayness by which Dasein becomes authentic he calls transcendence. The very way Heidegger structured Dasein's being follows the dichotomy

3. Max Weber, *Economy and Society*, ed. Guenther Roth and Claus Wittich (Berkeley and Los Angeles: University of California Press, 1978), 1117.

Weber outlines. This is not surprising, because from his earliest writings, Heidegger was concerned about the place (or lack of place) religion held in the modern world. The political problem of modern society was its godlessness, and Heidegger's lifelong task was to bring this problem to light and point toward how it could be overcome.

Heidegger's religiosity was uncompromising and thoroughly radical. As such, it gravitated to the purest type of charisma. It rejected all dogma and doctrine. It rejected mediation. It rejected organization and rule. It stood for inspiration, the sudden, the insurrection of the new, the revolutionary. When Heidegger in 1933 infamously declared "The Führer is now our rule and law," he was expressing a religious sentiment. As in Weber's ideal of pure charisma, Heidegger called for an unmediated community dedicated to the task established by a charismatic leader. Heidegger's ideal of the authentic polis was sectarian in the Weberian sense of a charismatic community of individuals, albeit one backed by a strong army. The radical nature of Heidegger's understanding of religion and the relationship between human being and the divine underlay his hostility toward modernity.

To give human existence meaning, Heidegger believed it was necessary to follow a path of spiritual commitment toward a sacralization the world. This path has two major segments: the first is an opening of a space in which the divine can manifest; the second is making this space public and political. Simply put, Heidegger's project aimed at a political community in which all activity is directed toward and receives its meaning from a divine source. In short, Heidegger was a radical sectarian. His predominant concern was finding and articulating an authentically religious stance toward the world. To a large extent this appears in his work as a sustained critique of the metaphysics underlying modern science, which he believed had both marginalized and co-opted the truly divine, leaving in its wake an inauthentic religiosity. His attempt to locate the authentic divine sphere beyond the principle of reason pushed his thought in radical theological directions: he rejected even the medieval synthesis of reason and revelation, as well as the important scientific, social, and political role natural reason played in medieval thought, in favor of the primacy of a radically free and ultimately groundless revelation.

The uniqueness of Heidegger's political theology lies in this odd combination of a mystical openness to divine revelation and a dedication to concrete action. The authentic human is a mystical revolutionary. This combination of mysticism and political action, odd in our day and age, has proved to be a stumbling block to understanding Heidegger's politics. Different interpretations emphasize one aspect of this combination or another without seeing the continuity. Many commentators are blind to the centrality of religion in Heidegger's thought. One group, represented by Ferry, Renaut, and Habermas, emphasize Heidegger's opposition to modernity without noting the theological context of this opposition; another group, represented by Gadamer and Kisiel, take up Heidegger's rejuvenation of Aristotelian practical wisdom apart from its transformation into divine revelation; Sartrean existentialism, so important for understanding deconstructionism's interpretation of Heidegger, took authenticity to be an atheist morality.[4] Overlooking the theological dimension to Heidegger's philosophy makes these interpretations suspect because it fails to grasp the overall meaning and importance of authenticity for Heidegger's political project.

There are other interpretations that are cognizant of the essentially religious meaning of authenticity, but for the most part they either ignore the political dimension to authenticity or fail to grasp the political meaning Heidegger believed inhered in his ideal. The root of this failure is the overdetermination of what constitutes religiosity in modern life. Heidegger's early students were certainly aware that Heidegger's ideal of authenticity drew from a religious wellspring, but they believed this wellspring to be a radically Lutheran and Kierkegaardian call to the individual conscience.[5] They read Heidegger as the exemplar of the archetypic modern religious

4. Luc Ferry and Alain Renaut, *Heidegger and Modernity,* trans. Franklin Philip (Chicago: University of Chicago Press, 1990); Jürgen Habermas, *The Philosophical Discourse of Modernity,* trans. Frederick G. Lawrence (Cambridge: MIT Press, 1987); Hans-Georg Gadamer, *Truth and Method,* trans. Joel Weinsheimer and Donald G. Marshall, 2d rev. ed. (New York: Crossroad Publishing, 1990); Theodore Kisiel, *The Genesis of Heidegger's "Being and Time"* (Berkeley and Los Angeles: University of California Press, 1993); Jean-Paul Sartre, "The Humanism of Existentialism," in *Essays in Existentialism,* ed. Wade Baskin (New York: Citadel Press, 1993). Although pervasive throughout deconstructionism, the specific figure I have in mind is Nancy. Jean-Luc Nancy, *The Inoperative Community,* trans. Peter Connor, Lisa Garbus, Michael Holland, and Simona Sawhney (Minneapolis: University of Minnesota Press, 1991).

5. Löwith, Gadamer, and Arendt all draw parallels between Kierkegaard and Heidegger. Another one of Heidegger's students, Hans Jonas, actually came quite close to making the connection I make, but while he connected gnosticism to existentialism (and thereby to Heidegger), in trying to explicate Heidegger's political behavior he agreed with Löwith's decisionist thesis. It remained to yet another German émigré, Eric Voegelin, to relate Jonas's analysis of gnosticism to the radical revolutionary movements, both fascist and communist, of our century. Jonas's and Voegelin's depictions of gnosticism resemble the antinomian nominalism I find in Heidegger's thought.

Stoic, the Pietist, whose divided soul matches the divided society of religious toleration.[6] For the modern Stoic, revelation calls to the individual conscience. Conscience is a private concern; indeed, it is because conscience is a private matter that toleration is a central principle of the modern state. This interpretation often stresses the apolitical nature of authenticity because it counsels withdrawal from society in order to preserve one's purity; some more recent readings have tried to show that this individualism is compatible with liberal politics.[7]

This overtly political and revolutionary aspect to Heidegger's religiosity stands in stark contrast to the usual quietist image of the mystical saint. Heidegger believed that revelation was communal, not individual. Indeed, the community is constituted by its shared participation in a particular revelation. The community has priority over the individual; indeed, the authentic self ceases to be an individual in the strict sense through participation in this revealed community. Heidegger's brazen attacks on liberalism and its key principles of individual freedom and toleration are thus not haphazard, but follow from his conception of the authentic self. Understanding Heidegger not as a Pietist but as a charismatic sectarian makes it clear that his politics was not some mysterious aberration, but followed directly from his antinomian conception of religiosity.

There is much discussion today of the "political," and some participants draw inspiration from Heidegger's thinking.[8] My investigation of Heidegger's thinking is intended in part to shed some light on this issue.

6. Hegel's analysis of the Stoic or unhappy consciousness in *The Phenomenology of Spirit* addresses Pietist religiosity in modern, bourgeois society. See also Gillian Rose, *The Broken Middle: Out of Our Ancient Society* (Cambridge, Mass.: Blackwell Publishers, 1992).

7. Arendt gives the exemplary reading of Heidegger as apolitical withdrawal. Hannah Arendt, "What Is Existential Philosophy?" in *Essays in Understanding: 1930–1954*, ed. Jerome Kohn (New York: Harcourt, Brace & Company, 1994), 163–87.Van Buren, Young, and Vogel all give liberal readings to authenticity; van Buren explicitly relates this liberalism to Heidegger's early Lutheranism. John van Buren, *The Young Heidegger* (Bloomington: Indiana University Press, 1994); idem, "The Ethics of *Formale Anzeige* in Heidegger," *American Catholic Philosophical Quarterly* 69, no. 2 (1995): 157–70; Julien Young, *Heidegger, Philosophy, Nazism* (New York: Cambridge University Press, 1997); Lawrence Vogel, *The Fragile "We": Ethical Implications of Heidegger's "Being and Time"* (Evanston: Northwestern University Press, 1994).

8. One increasingly commonplace postmodern trope is to distinguish the essence of the political from any concrete political position. According to this claim, concrete politics in the modern, bureaucratic world is dominated by technical and economic reasoning which conceals or even destroys authentic political action and relationships. Heidegger's critique of modern technology is well suited to this project; indeed, as I shall show, Heidegger himself

By looking at matters in this way, one frees oneself from the tiresome debate about Heidegger's Nazism to examine the broader, more vital issue of the viability of antinomian politics in general. Was Heidegger's engagement with National Socialism only the symptom of a failure in his most fundamental principles? Did the subsumption of politics to religion lead Heidegger to a monstrous or at least dangerously impractical politics? What is the nature of antinomian politics?

By addressing myself to these questions, I hope, not only to explain how Heidegger could support the Nazis, but also why he believed his principles were the only remedy for our modern situation. In Heidegger's thought one sees one of the great attempts to transcend the confines of modernity and tender a thoroughly radical alternative to modern politics. It may well be, however, that the remedy is worse than the disease. In a roundabout way, an examination of the depths and dangers of Heidegger's truly radical political philosophy may give one cause to reaffirm the legitimacy of modernity, liberalism, and the humanist politics of those who triumphed over tyranny in the Second World War.

Plan of the Work

In the first chapter, I concentrate on Heidegger's early work up to *Being and Time* in order to show how his early crisis of faith and his attempt to renew an authentic religiosity shaped how he raised the question of being. In particular, I demonstrate how Heidegger's rejection of the dominance of theory in modernity goes hand in hand with his ideal of a religious unity of feeling and intuition, and how this ideal guides the development of his hermeneutical phenomenology, in which authentic human existence comes from raising the question of being in a particular historical situation. I explicate how Heidegger appropriated Aristotle to this project, particularly the preeminent role he assigned to *phronēsis* or practical wisdom. I conclude by elucidating how Heidegger's religious ideal of authenticity trans-

---

juxtaposed technical and economic rationality to what he called the "essence of the political." Some more recent authors who have worked on this question include Mouffe, Lefort, and Dallmayr, as well as Nancy and Lacoue-Labarthe, whose conferences on the political in the early 1980s were collected in *Le Retrait du Politique* (recently translated into English with other related works as *Retreating the Political*). There is a new, ongoing series published by Routledge called "Thinking the Political" emblematic of this project; it includes Miguel de Beistegui's *Heidegger and the Political: Dystopias* (New York: Routledge, 1998).

forms *phronēsis* into divine revelation, which forms the basis of his revolutionary activism.

In the second chapter, I examine Heidegger's ethical ideal of authenticity in terms of his transformation of practical wisdom. Heidegger understood inauthenticity to be alienation from being and consequently authenticity as integration into being as a whole. A comparison with one of Heidegger's favorite thinkers, Meister Eckhart, reveals the mystical roots of this understanding of authenticity. Heidegger's mysticism, I argue, led him to embrace a new understanding of freedom as freedom for the revelation of being; in being free for being, one participates in the meaning of existence given by the revelation. By emphasizing the centrality of being-with or human sociality to human life, I show that this participation is communal, correcting a widely held misinterpretation of Dasein's irreducible individuality. The self becomes fully authentic only by participating in a communal revelation of being.

In Chapter 3, I investigate Heidegger's critique of modern technology and his related efforts to find an authentic meaning to work. Heidegger's growing conviction that human life is necessarily bound up with technology forced him to reconsider the disavowal of technicity in favor of *phronē sis* displayed in his earlier thinking. The necessary role of technology set Heidegger to work finding a way of thinking about technology and work that was compatible with his ideal of authenticity. I trace out how Heidegger exploited an ambiguity in the Greek origin of *technē*, from which he developed on the one hand an entire history of Western metaphysics and its nihilistic fulfillment in our modern technological society, and on the other hand a postmodern response to nihilism embodied in the phrase "poetic dwelling." Poetic dwelling, I argue, was Heidegger's reformulating of his earlier notion of authenticity to put authentic work in the service of a communal revelation.

Having laid the bases in the first three chapters for Heidegger's ideal of religious authenticity and its connection to communal life, I turn in the fourth chapter to the complex issue of Heidegger's complicity with National Socialism. In contrast to many previous commentators, I seek to focus on the substantive character of his "spiritual" national socialism and his political commitment to this ideal. In National Socialism, Heidegger thought he had found his political answer to the crisis of modernity: a worker's party dedicated to the service of the national community.

In the fifth and final chapter, I take up in more general terms Heidegger's political philosophy and his attempt to develop a politics that would be an alternative to modern political formations. In particular, I examine the political consequences of his antinomian conception of religiosity. I lay out the path that brought Heidegger to the conclusion that the alternative to rules and coercive power was the leadership principle. Leaders lead by virtue of their superior practical wisdom, which opens up a revelation of being for a people. A leader is successful as a leader only if the people take up the meaning of the revelation through self-will or self-responsibility. Without self-responsibility, there is only rule and tyranny. Heidegger's ideal politics is thus a leader-populism that is supposed to be an alternative to modern state formations. I argue, however, that in fact Heidegger's political regime was really a community of saints; his "leader" was not a man of great prudence or practical wisdom but a prophet or minister of a divinely ordained community. I thus show in conclusion that Heidegger's political ideal is founded on an apocalyptic vision of human existence and that this vision led him to advocate a revolutionary sectarian solution to political problems that was not merely monstrous in execution, but dangerous in principle.

| **Religiosity and the Meaning of Being**

Heidegger's quest to find a path beyond modernity began in a real sense with his crisis of faith in 1917; his postmodern ideal developed as a response to this intensely personal—yet in his own eyes also world-historical—distress.[1] In *Being and Time* Heidegger admits to having a "factical ideal" which motivated his project to renew the question of being (*BT,* 358). His early

1. Some commentators, such as Farias, locate the origin of Heidegger's Nazi proclivities in his conservative Catholic upbringing. Victor Farias, *Heidegger and Nazism,* trans. Paul Burrell (Philadelphia: Temple University Press, 1989). Although one can find antimodern sentiments in Heidegger's juvenilia, the links between these sentiments and Heidegger's later political activism are extremely tenuous; at most they demonstrate in some vague, unspecified way that Heidegger had long opposed modern nihilism. To adequately specify the nature of Heidegger's antimodern sentiments as they pertain to his Nazism, one must recognize two things: that his mature philosophy bears little relation to his works that predate 1917, and that his politics were revolutionary, not conservative.

students perceived this ideal to be the religious life. So Heidegger wrote to Löwith in 1921: "I concretely tactically labor out of my 'I am'—out of my spiritual, wholly factical heritage—milieu—life-contexts, out of that which is accessible to me from there as living experience in which I live . . . To this facticity of mine belongs—to state it briefly—, that I am a 'Christian theo*logian.*'"[2]

Later studies on Heidegger from Pöggeler's groundbreaking synthesis to recent major efforts from Kisiel and Van Buren have only confirmed the importance of the religious dimension.[3] Later in life Heidegger himself pointed toward his theological background as decisive for his path of thinking (DL, 10), but what was decisive in this heritage for his lifelong questioning of being? Generally in his late retrospectives he emphasized his Catholic origins: his studies with Carl Braig, the decisive impulse given by Brentano's study on the manifold meaning of being in Aristotle, and his own *Habilitationschrift* on Dun Scotus's theory of categories (MWP, 74–75). One could easily include his years of being funded by a Catholic stipend that required him to study Aquinas. Yet with this gesture Heidegger obscured the turns that set him on his path of thinking. Again in "My Way to Phenomenology," Heidegger says, "Thus I was brought to the path of the question of being, illuminated by the phenomenological attitude, again made uneasy in a different way than previously by the questions prompted by Brentano's dissertation" (MWP, 79). What is it that caused the question of being to be raised in a different way? From the passage quoted here, one would conclude that it was phenomenology, particularly the phenomenology of Husserl, that had brought Heidegger to this new path. This is partially true. Phenomenology would become decisive for how Heidegger

2. Martin Heidegger to Karl Löwith, August 19, 1921, in *Martin Heidegger and European Nihilism*, ed. Richard Wolin (New York: Columbia University Press, 1995), 236.

3. These studies, particularly Kisiel's, guided my interpretation in this chapter. See Theodore Kisiel, "Heidegger's Apology: Biography as Philosophy and Ideology," in *The Heidegger Case: On Philosophy and Politics*, ed. Tom Rockmore and Joseph Margolis (Philadelphia: Temple University Press, 1992); idem, *Genesis*; Otto Pöggeler, *Der Denkweg Martin Heideggers*, 3d ed. (Pfullingen: Neske, 1990); and van Buren, *Young Heidegger*. Also see the essays on the early Heidegger collected in Theodore Kisiel and John van Buren, eds., *Reading Heidegger from the Start* (Albany: SUNY Press, 1994). Safranski's and Ott's more biographical studies also proved very useful. Rüdiger Safranski, *Ein Meister aus Deutschland: Heidegger und seine Zeit* (Munich: Hanser, 1994); Hugo Ott, *Martin Heidegger: Unterwegs zu seiner Biographie* (New York: Campus, 1992); and idem, "Heidegger's Catholic Origins: The Theological Philosopher," in *Martin Heidegger: Politics, Art, and Technology*, ed. Karsten Harries and Christoph Jamme (New York: Holmes & Meier, 1994).

understood the question of being, but by itself it was not sufficient to have caused this change. For one thing, Heidegger was introduced to Husserl's work in 1910, almost a decade before this change occurred. For another, it is fairly clear that while he adopted some of Husserl's insights and attitude, his understanding of phenomenology differed significantly from that of his mentor. In fact, the change in the question of being that owed something to his understanding of phenomenology has an explicitly religious foundation; however, this foundation is not Catholic but rather a religiosity heavily influenced by Luther and the German mystics. This change in his understanding of the question of being can be traced to the previously mentioned crisis of faith that Heidegger suffered toward the end of the First World War, a crisis that led him to abandon his Catholic heritage and embrace a radical Lutheranism. By the time he had written to Löwith about laboring out of his life-context as a Christian theologian, he was no longer Catholic. This crisis of faith prompted by his conviction that there is a dire need to renew an authentically religious life that could not be satisfied within the confines of Catholic dogma led directly to his understanding of phenomenology and thus the path to renewing the question of being in this new and difficult manner. As Kisiel puts it: "One is hard put to find the slight allusions to his turn to a Protestant 'free Christianity' in 1917, let alone to atheism in 1929 and to a national folk religion of his own Hölderlinized invention in the 1930s. Yet these 'world views' are perhaps more influential on his turns of thought than his original Catholicism."[4]

The roots of the crisis include both personal and philosophical issues, although the two cannot be separated so neatly. In a letter written to a friend, Heidegger suggests that certain problems had "made the *system* of Catholicism problematic and unacceptable for me—but not Christianity *per se* or metaphysics, the latter albeit in a new sense."[5] The philosophical issue comes down to the meaning of the "system of Catholicism" and its relation to authentic religious life. The problem lies in the sense of "system." Belief systems alienate humans from their proper religious being because they are dogmatic and propositional. Dogmatic systems are universal and unchanging; they confront concrete historical living as alien forces, as collections of outdated beliefs whose real efficacy has been lost. The example that weighed most heavily on Heidegger was the Church's

4. Kisiel, "Heidegger's Apology," 21.
5. Martin Heidegger to Engelbert Krebs, January 9, 1919; quoted in Ott, *Martin Heidegger*, 106.

declaration that the teachings of St. Thomas Aquinas constituted the authoritative doctrine for present-day Catholics. The sense that truth can be expressed as a set of propositions valid for all times cuts humans off from authentic historical being and thus from access to God. How the Church thought of religious life, as a dogmatic system of propositions, made no room for the source of genuine religious meaning, which lies in the historicity of being human. An authentic relation to God can only be achieved when Dasein can achieve an authentic relation to itself. This is Heidegger's fundamental insight.[6]

To combat this double alienation, Heidegger searched for conceptions of religious life that were open to this foundational life element. He wanted humans to live in an undivided unity with the meaning of their existence, a unity he felt could be found in medieval life, both among the Scholastics and even more so among mystics such as Eckhardt. From Eckhardt it was only a small step to the early Luther, on whom Eckhardt had exercised considerable influence, and thence to nineteenth-century Protestants such as Dilthey, Kierkegaard, and Schleiermacher. In each case Heidegger appropriated them to his own task to find access to meaning in life, to maintain an authentic religiosity that held itself apart from the alienating effects of theoretical life. In particular, Schleiermacher's "Second Address on Religion," which sought to keep religion free from "alien teleologies," namely, science, exerted a strong influence on Heidegger's thinking in this respect.

Heidegger's own philosophical developments at the time show the direct influences of this Protestant turn. His new hermeneutical phenomenology, which found its initial expression in his first lectures after the war, took as its project the double task of deconstructing the theoretical life in order to lay bare the proper access to the "originary intentions" of life itself. In a thought experiment of stunning simplicity, Heidegger sought to find this access in "lived experience." In this experiencing, he both established an access to original meaning as environmental meaning (factical life-contexts) and related this meaning back to the experiencing I; it establishes both genuine meaning and an authentic sense of the self. In the most immediate case, this "lived experience" of things in their proper meaning occurs in our everyday work-world as we go about our business. Theory, understood as universally valid propositions, both "lives off" the genuine meaning gleaned in experiencing, in the sense of taking the life out of things by

---

6. In this Marion is absolutely correct. See Jean-Luc Marion, *God Without Being*, trans. Thomas A. Carlson (Chicago: University of Chicago Press, 1991).

denuding the experience of the meaning-giving grounds of our practical concerns, and in so doing also shuts off the genuine sense of one's self, because in objectifying our experiences so that they may be expressed in a universalizable proposition, the experiencing I for whom the meaning of the experience has meaning drops away.

As powerful and lasting an influence as this thought experiment exercised on Heidegger, he had already run up against a difficulty: theoretical experience was itself an experiencing, however cut off from authentic experience. The difficulty cropped up from the opposite side as well: all experience, genuine or not, was experienced through speech. Experiencing in and through speech is the literal sense of phenomenology, the speech that lets the phenomena come to presence for the experiencing self. One cannot oppose experience to theory, for theory is but one type of experience, that is to say, speech. In order to think through this problematic, Heidegger turned to Aristotle, particularly his account in book 6 of the *Nicomachean Ethics* of the so-called intellectual virtues, the modes of *alētheuein,* the ways of speaking that let something come to presence in its truth. Heidegger's appropriation of this theme enriched the ongoing project of hermeneutical phenomenology and the task of finding an authentic religious dimension separate from the alienating effects of theory. The modes of *alētheuein* disclosed a world in terms of the particular disclosing; this way of disclosing became in *Being and Time* the analysis of worldhood. Worldhood, however, was not a characteristic of a world, but of Dasein itself; thus *Being and Time* comprised an analytic of Dasein, an analysis of ways of being human. This dovetailed neatly with the religious project of finding genuine meaning in religious life, the religious way of being. He could make use of Aristotle's discussion of *alētheuein* to explore the authentic way of being human.

In this way the ontological investigation into the being of Dasein dovetailed with the "factical ideal" of religiosity. This factical ideal underlay the guiding motif developed in *Being and Time* between authenticity and inauthenticity. In authenticity commentators have generally seen the outline of an ethics or at least the basis for the subsequent development of one. For humans to be authentic, that is to be true to themselves, the being of the self must be authentically disclosed, that is to say, disclosed in such a way that being is thought appropriate to the human condition. The being proper to Dasein is the criterion for distinguishing which ways of disclosing of being, the modes of *alētheuein,* are authentic. Thus in his lecture course of 1924–25 Heidegger explicated the opposition between the inauthentic modes, chiefly *sophia* and the theoretical life, and the one authentic mode, *phronēsis,* which is the insight that brings forth the total situation for acting in the world.[7] *Phronēsis* was the authentic way to be Dasein because it disclosed being as what can be otherwise, and thus as possibility and temporality. *Sophia,* its highest counterpoint, disclosed that which was eternal, and so was inappropriate to the authentic understanding of Dasein. In this way Heidegger continued the theme of the inauthenticity of the theoretical life, but its counterpart was now *phronēsis,* the practical wisdom that guides action. Dasein was understood as authentic action.

Despite this turn to Aristotle's ethics to illuminate the question of being, Heidegger's understanding of authentic action is not classical, but instead thoroughly informed by his understanding of authentic religiosity. *Phronēsis* becomes "der Augenblick," the instantaneous moment of vision that clears the opening in which beings come to presence, the lightning flash of being which steers the whole. This understanding of *phronēsis* has profound consequences for Heidegger's political thought. Authentic action for Heidegger is revolutionary action. Action is a radical change in the experience of being which founds historical epochs based upon this understanding of being opened up in the moment of vision. Heidegger's understanding of being and time is determined by his underlying desire to renew authentic religiosity by posing in a radical way the question of the meaning of being.

From Religion to Phenomenology

The Crisis of Faith

We better understand today the path by which Heidegger came to the question of being. Between the *Habilitationschrift* and *Being and Time,* there stands a gap of eleven turbulent, formative, and productive years, known

---

7. What is surprising is that many of the luminaries who accuse Heidegger of having neglected politics and action—among them Gadamer, Strauss, and Arendt—attended this lecture. How all of them missed the equation between *phronēsis* and authenticity is a mystery to me. Even more ironically, Gadamer could later credit Heidegger's lectures on Aristotle with giving a decisive impulse to his own task of a hermeneutical theory of action, which he considered a necessary counterweight to Heidegger's own theories of authenticity. See for example, Hans-Georg Gadamer, "Heidegger und die Griechen," in *Hermeneutik im Rückblick* (Tübingen: J.C.B. Mohr, 1995).

to us until recently only through secondhand accounts by his students from this time, such as Gadamer and Becker. These accounts have been supplemented now by the painstaking researches of Ott, Sheehan, Van Buren, and above all Kisiel, and most importantly, by the ongoing publication of lecture courses from this period, which combined present a more complete picture than the one the older Heidegger draws in "My Way to Phenomenology." Missing from Heidegger's picture is the wrenching crisis of faith that caused him to abandon Catholicism. Missing is the headlong plunge into mysticism, free Lutheranism, and *Lebensphilosophie*. Missing is the enthusiastic appropriation of and confrontation with Aristotle. Missing are those steps that would lead him to designate hermeneutic phenomenology the authentic philosophy. Heidegger's path to the question of being was given decisive impetus by these missing elements broached in those eleven formative years.

Whatever the other psychological factors involved in his crisis of faith, this crisis, like that of Luther's, was produced in large part by a fundamental religious problem. What had become unacceptable for Heidegger was not Christianity or religion, but Catholicism, specifically the rigorous enforcement of dogma by papal encyclical. Heidegger wrote to a friend in 1919, "Epistemological insights applied to the theory of historical knowledge have made the *system of* Catholicism problematic and unacceptable for me—but not Christianity *per se* or metaphysics, the latter albeit in a new sense."[8] The opposition is not merely between Catholicism and Christianity, but between theoretical system and historical knowledge. A system was a form of theoretical dogma, shorn of any living spirit. In terms of Catholicism, the papal *motu proprio* of 1914 declared St. Thomas Aquinas to be the sole and absolute source of doctrinal authority within the Church. Without living spirit, these writings are mere propositions; and this *motu proprio* allowed no question about how these propositions arose in the first place, or how these propositions related to the medieval experience of God.

He aired the motivations behind his enterprise in the conclusion to the *Habilitationsschrift*. It was only at the end of a treatise on medieval theory of categories that he insisted, "History and its cultural-philosophical-theological meaning *must become a meaning-determining element for the*

8. Martin Heidegger to Engelbert Krebs, January 9, 1919; quoted in Ott, *Martin Heidegger*, 106.

problem of categories . . ." (*GA1,* 408). If not, a study of medieval categories (such as the *Habilitationschrift* itself) would "seem to be first of all a school concept rightly drained of color and not further meaningful" (*GA1,* 408). It acquires meaning only when we set it into its origin in the total medieval "world of experience," because it is "the conceptual expression of a determinate form of inner existence anchored in the transcendent primordial relationship of the soul to God as it was living in rare continuity in the middle ages" (*GA1,* 409). A theory of categories, the form of the epistemic system *per se,* was meaningful only as it grew out of an unbroken experience of the whole, that is, of the manifoldness of the living self and its relationship to God and world. Growing out of the living self, this relationship is historical. This relationship of self to God took its exemplary expression in medieval mysticism. It is a modern prejudice, Heidegger claimed, to oppose scholasticism to mysticism as one would oppose rationality to irrationality because the two belong essentially together in the medieval weltanschauung (*GA1,* 410).[9] Heidegger wanted to combine mysticism and scholasticism in such a manner that the two elements would function properly only together; he expressed this in the slogan "Philosophy as rationalistic structure [system!] cut off from life is *powerless,* mysticism as irrational experience is *aimless*" (*GA1,* 410). Authentic philosophy attempts to combine both of these elements; it must be historical experience (*Erleben*) which uncovers the rational aim in the experience itself. Only by this means can we overcome the one-sidedness of either pole, and come to experience a genuine connection with God. In particular, we can overcome the dangers of a theoretical system loosed from life that confronts each person as alien truth.

Heidegger waited until the final pages of his *Habilitationschrift* to let loose this barrage of Romantic *Lebensphilosophie.*[10] It has the unfortunate effect of reducing that which precedes it to a mere school exercise, because nowhere in the treatise does Heidegger analyze how Scotus's theory of categories relates to this overall medieval weltanschauung, or how his own exposition of Scotus's position arises in turn from his relationship to God.

---

9. Heidegger would repeat this from time to time later in life. It is of particular importance because as Heidegger well knew, many accused him of falling into mysticism. His lifelong task was to rethink rationality so that it would encompass both the particular in its particularity and the universal, although to do this he would have to rethink universality. His invocation of Hegel at the end is not accidental.

10. The epigraph for the conclusion is a quotation from Novalis (*GA1,* 399).

The slogan provided Heidegger with a direction for subsequent investigations (which would occupy the rest of his life), but in pursuing this direction, the tension with dogmatic theology became even greater. If being a Catholic in 1916 meant accepting the works of Aquinas as the absolute truth, it meant forgoing the historical, living element that was vital for the truth of these works. This is true in two related respects. First of all, 1916 is not 1270; the world is not the same. If meaning arises from its relationship to the world, then a statement will not have the same meaning from one time to another. Put more concretely, Aquinas's works meant something quite different to him (and his contemporaries) than they do to us, because they arose out of his historical philosophical labor, whereas they confront us as a systematic set of propositions. Aquinas arrived at his truth. For us to have the same experience of his truth, we must also arrive at his truth in a way that makes it our truth. To arrive at the truth so that it becomes a living experience as it was for Aquinas we must undergo the same philosophical labors he did, which means to pursue the same questions he did; it means that we must open ourselves to the questionableness of existence for ourselves and by ourselves.

This, in a nutshell, is the justification of the historical philosophizing Heidegger practiced. The history of philosophy must cease being a historiological acquaintance of the past as if it were something past, but instead become a historical confrontation with the tradition (*GA45,* 12, 41). In such a confrontation, we experience for ourselves the questioning that lie behind the answers given in the text. We must experience the questionableness of what is being questioned for ourselves before the questions can really matter to our being. This experience will point to the origin of the questioning itself in the world of the self which questions the truth of being. Historical philosophizing, the authentic intertwining of experience and reason, is thus radically opposed to theoretical systematization and dogmatic theology. Theory—either as dogma, mathematical science, or historiography —blocks off access to the origins of authentic existence. As this opposition became apparent to Heidegger, the "*system* of Catholicism" became increasingly unacceptable.

In the next several years Heidegger began the work of historical philosophizing that aimed to solve the problem expressed in the slogan "Philosophy as rationalistic structure cut off from life is *powerless,* mysticism as irrational experience is *aimless.*" His intent was to reintegrate reason into life, to find the meaning contained in experience. Foremost in the execution of this task was the destruction (*Abbau*) of the primacy of theory, an act that would free access to an authentic primordial layer of life from which theory was cut off. Heidegger called this access to a "referral back to a foundational level of life" "hermeneutic intuition," which coincides with the project of phenomenology. Deconstruction of the tradition was a necessary part of the positive project of hermeneutical phenomenology.

Heidegger took up the deconstruction of theory in reference to the "system of Catholicism," which had become unacceptable to him. The rejection of Catholicism was not, however, a rejection of Christianity. This opposition of Catholicism and Christianity signaled his newfound attraction to Luther.[11] In the final years of the First World War his attention turned increasingly to medieval mysticism, which influenced Luther and later the German Romantics, such as Schleiermacher, and the common roots of the Lutheran and proto-Protestant religiosity in Pauline literature (*GA60*, 310). Common to all of these was an intense sense of a personal experience with God without mediation of Church or theory (*BwHB*, 14). This intense personal experience that turned toward God made up the "original form of religiosity," which he now opposed to a dogmatic theology that remained dependent on the theoretical consciousness (*GA60*, 310). Heidegger found this original religiosity in the young Luther who railed in the Heidelberg Disputations against the *theologia gloriae* of scholastic speculation that sought to explain God from what is visible to human senses and reason in favor of a *theologia crucis*, a theology of the cross, that arises out of a fundamental humility before God's mystery. The key difference for Heidegger lay in the relation between reason and the divine; a theology of the cross maintained the radical insufficiency of purely

11. Van Buren's *Young Heidegger* takes up the Lutheran motives in painstaking detail. Van Buren's intent, apart from a historiographical analysis of Heidegger's early works, is to find a Heidegger more congenial to a sort of postmodern philosophy than the encrusted sludge of the later Heidegger. Hence the title, *The Young Heidegger*, is meant to parallel Lukacs's *The Young Hegel*, and echoes every attempt to find a more youthful, dynamic Hegel before he supposedly succumbed to world-weariness and absolutism. Even Heidegger's turn to Luther concentrates on the young Luther before "he himself fell victim to the burden of the tradition: there begins the encroachment of the *Protestant* scholasticism" (*GA60*, 282). It is clear that the Luther that interests Heidegger is the one who fought against scholasticism, whether Protestant or Catholic. As I will point out in a later chapter, however, what Heidegger understands as Luther's scholasticism is part and parcel of Luther's attempts to build a new church organized around his principles. The old Luther thus achieved a practical success that would ever elude Heidegger.

human reason to comprehend the divine, whereas a theology of God's glory sought to comprehend God's ultimate reasons within a unified system.[12] The *theologia gloriae* is identical with the system of Catholicism, which "shuts out a primordial genuine religious experience of values" and falls to "an entangled, inorganic, theoretically *fully uncleared,* dogmatic enclosure of propositions and proofs" that in the end sustains itself through police power *(GA60,* 313). The mystics were a countermovement to the dogmatizing influence of Church institutions *(GA60,* 314). Heidegger took up this Lutheran opposition by declaring authentic philosophy to be "humility before the mystery and grace-character of all life" *(BwHB,* 14). His new path of philosophy was infused with religiosity.

When philosophy frees itself from speculative impulses and returns to an authentically religious impulse, it will return the self to an authentic experience of life.[13] Heidegger takes up the distinction Schleiermacher made in "On the Essence of Religion" between religion and theoretical science, activities Schleiermacher assigns to two different spheres of existence. "Alien teleology and precisely the most dangerously confusing theoretical [must be] eliminated. It means 'to climb down into the innermost holiness of life,' there can be found the primordial relation of feeling and intuition. . . . It means to uncover a primordial region of life and accomplishment of the consciousness (or feeling), in which religion alone effects itself as determinate form of experience" *(GA60,* 321).[14] The undivided unity of feeling and intuition is found in the *"mysterious* moment of vision [Or if one wishes to be literal, moment of vision which is filled with mystery]" *(GA60,* 322).[15] In religion one finds the original relationship of

12. Heidegger maintains this distinction until the very end, even if he gives new names, e.g., thinking versus calculating or the questioning that is the piety of thinking versus the principle of reason, for Luther's opposition. See for instance, *ID,* 72. Also of great import is that the same distinction underlies Heidegger's understanding of poetry; what he calls poetic dwelling is to dwell in the mystery of the divine. I will go into this in more detail in Chapter 3.

13. German has two basic words for experience, *erfahren* and *erleben.* The latter is derived from *leben* "to live," and the "er-" is an intensifier; *er-leben* connotes "live intensively." *Erleben* and its cognate *Erlebnis* are the words Heidegger usually uses in this period, and its connection with *Leben* is intentional.

14. Much of this passage is a gloss of Heidegger's gloss of Schleiermacher. It is interesting that some of this terminology and manner of thinking appears in Heidegger's lectures on Aristotle, particularly the task of assigning the teleologies of the various ways of *alētheuein* to their proper place, which Heidegger there translates as "uncover," outlined in the sixth book of the *Nicomachean Ethics.* This is not surprising, given the fundamental unity of underlying motives in the development of Heidegger's early project.

15. This is the earliest passage I have found which connects *Augenblick,* usually a meas-

feeling and intuition which preserves the mystery of life, precisely the combination Heidegger wanted philosophy to become in contradistinction to its prevalent scientific rationalism. "The new life which we want, or that wants in us, has renounced being universal, i.e., false and flat (superficial)—its possession is originality—not the artificial-constructive, but rather the conclusiveness of total intuition" (*BwHB*, 15). This total intuition, which "wells up in blessed moments of vision," is thus found in the religious life (*BwHB*, 14).

Heidegger wished to emphasize the affective nature of experience which connects it with life, but he did not wish to lose sight of the meaning of this experience. As he noted in the conclusion to the *Habilitationschrift*, pure experience—he is referring to phenomenological intuition as described by Natorp and Bergson in particular—tends to fall into a broad, flat homogeneity of flowing sensation. Medieval intuition by contrast contains meaning because it has a determinate *telos*, that is, everything "flows" toward the God of biblical revelation. Heidegger believed he encountered a similar understanding of intuition in Husserl's *Logical Investigations*, with the important difference that the pregiven meaning toward which intuition was directed was not given by faith, but rather was contained in the directing intuition itself. Philosophy distinguished itself from theology not merely in its systematicity but also in not halting at a determinate understanding of that toward which it intends; theology must always begin and end with the certainty of faith, whereas philosophy remains open to radical questioning. As a philosopher, Heidegger was not particularly interested in proving the truth of biblical revelation, but rather in exploring how meaning and truth in general are derived from the intentional being of human existence. For Heidegger's studies, the "how" of human being, its manner of comporting toward the world as a whole, always takes precedence over the "what." Out of the "how" comes the particular "what" that is uncovered in its particularity as the situation in which historical Dasein finds itself. From this ordering Heidegger draws the peculiar but nevertheless consistent conclusion that "our experiential relation to God—that is primary, because it wells up graciously—is directive for the specific *religious* constitution of 'God' as a 'phenomenological object'" (*GA60*, 324). The "what" of God is derived from the experiential, intuiting "how" of the

---

ure of time, with *Anschauung*, intuition or sight. This connection becomes of central importance in *Being and Time*.

human being that relates to God. Phenomenology for Heidegger lays out the structure of this intuitional "how" of Dasein. In the first part of *Being and Time,* this task becomes the analytic of Dasein, which finds its unity in the intentional structure Heidegger calls *Sorge,* care.

What distinguishes theology from genuine religious life lies in the "how" of the comportment toward God. Theology is a theoretical science, which is its own peculiar type of intending, whereas religiosity has its own experiential type of intending. Both theology and religiosity direct themselves toward God, but how they are directed differs. In genuine religiosity God no longer stands before one as the object of theoretical seeing, but is experienced, that is, lived by the self. God is experienced as the "universum— the fullness of reality—in uninterrupted flowing and effecting; everything as part of the whole" (*GA60,* 321). But theology is a theoretical science and because theory is disconnected from life, theology cannot grasp the interconnectedness of each part of life, only pieces. Theory is at heart analysis, cutting up the whole into analyzable bits. For this reason, theory is "false and flat (super-ficial)" (*BwHB,* 15). Genuine religion, on the contrary, can experience the whole. Genuine religion is "the specifically religious intentional feeling relation of each content of experience to an infinite whole as the foundational meaning. . . . The specific experience leads back into the inner unity of life. Religious life is the constant renewing of this process" (*GA60,* 321–22). It is this connection of particularity and universality, experience and meaning, the self and the whole of which it is part, which is uncovered in the "*mysterious* moment of vision" (*GA60,* 322). Out of genuine experience arises the meaning of the whole. This meaning of the whole in its historical particularity is the intentional object of authentic religiosity. The intentional "object" of religion is in turn dependent on the way of intending specific to religiosity.

We are now in position to see how closely this understanding of religious being carried over into Heidegger's early phenomenological investigations. Religious life experiences the wholeness of existence as identical with the "inner unity of life" itself. This makes religious experience identical with "hermeneutical intuition," which is an experience that refers back to a "basic level of life" (*GA56/57,* 116–17). The close relation between these two ways of being is not surprising given the temporal proximity of these texts to each other (the notes on religious life date from 1918 and the first take on the task of hermeneutical phenomenology is the special "war need" semester of 1919). Phenomenology as Heidegger conceived it early on was an "Introduction to the Phenomenology of Religion," to give the title of the Winter Semester of 1920/21 lecture course. Heidegger was interested above all in finding the proper access to a way of intending that could experience the meaning of the whole. Indeed, his "Introduction to the Phenomenology of Religion" began as nothing other than an investigation of how one could talk about experiencing the meaning of the whole, a highly technical discussion of phenomenological method itself, which was broken off when non-majors complained to the dean that this course on religion had nothing to do with religion. Heidegger complied by turning to an exposition of several of Paul's epistles, but not before angrily telling his students that they would in all probability misunderstand the whole (GA60, 65). The non-majors can be forgiven for missing the point. Heidegger's intense relationship with phenomenology was mixed in his mind with his attempts to find the grounds for authentic religious life, but it requires knowing the specifics of his crisis of faith to see this. The religious motives became increasingly obscured by his phenomenological investigations, and were further obscured when Heidegger confronted Aristotle, but the motives were still there, lying behind all these labors. Although Heidegger himself avoided specific references to religion when discussing phenomenology, the specific religious background to his phenomenology should never be forgotten.

The Breakthrough to Phenomenology

The intentional aspects of religious experience—pretheoretical experiential comportment that gives access to an experience of the meaning of the whole—provide the backdrop to Heidegger's first postwar lecture course on phenomenology. Kisiel considers this course the true breakthrough to the themes of *Being and Time* and indeed beyond, and if we can also see the roots of this course in the notes for an abortive course on medieval mysticism, the introduction of terminology and themes in the War Emergency Semester marks a true gathering and condensation of thought that would propel Heidegger's thinking for years to come.[16]

16. It is hard in hindsight not to be excited when Heidegger declares that the world "worlds" and that this "worlding" of the world is nothing but the *Ereignis*, clearly foreshadowing the key word of his middle to late philosophy. See Hans-Georg Gadamer, "Die Religiöse Dimension," in *Neuere Philosophy: Hegel, Husserl, Heidegger*, vol. 3 of *Gesammelte Werke* (Tübingen: J.C.B. Mohr, 1987), 309, and idem, "Martin Heidegger's One Path," in *Reading Heidegger from the Start*, ed. Theodore Kisiel and John van Buren (Albany: SUNY

Heidegger had been influenced by Husserl and phenomenology before 1919, for he was struck by Husserl's *Logical Investigations* after having read it during his university years. What Heidegger found so decisive was Husserl's understanding of experience as a categorial act. The act of experiencing is not a flux of sensations devoid of meaning, but rather a composite of simple intuition and categorial intuition. "This means that concrete intuition expressly giving its object is never an isolated, single-layered sense perception, but is always a multi-layered intuition, that is, a categorially specified intuition" (*HCT*, 68). The talk of layers obscures to a certain extent the fundamental insight that Heidegger wants us to have: that experience is always categorial, in other words, that the categories of understanding are "in" the experience itself. A "categorially specified intuition" is simply an intuition in which the object that is intuited is intuited through categories. This categorially specified intuition is the primary level of experience. The specific target of this insight is the neo-Kantian and empiricist theory that sense impressions constitute the primary level of experience and that meaning comes only when the subject imposes structure and form, namely, categories, upon the disordered flux of sense impressions (*HCT*, 70). For Heidegger, the primary level of experience is already meaningful because it is categorial. There is no experience without categories; categories let objects appear as what they are.

Phenomenology is literally the science of phenomenon, which means the science of appearance. Because objects appear as what they are through categorial intuition, phenomenology is a study of how the categories make experience possible. As a study of the conditions of possibility of experience, phenomenology has a clear Kantian heritage, but Heidegger wanted to distinguish phenomenology from Kantian idealism, for he believed that categories are not found in a subject who imposes form upon matter, but

---

Press, 1994). In a very real sense Heidegger's "turn" is a return to a theme he had quietly dropped. It also underscores the fact that the linear conception of Heidegger's turns (first theme A, then theme B, then theme C, etc.) that underlies the dominant understanding of his "path of thinking" needs revision because Heidegger often reworked old insights. The older interpretation cannot be blamed for its reliance on available material. Although Pöggeler had access to some of the unpublished lectures from the early days, he does not mention the *Kriegesnotsemester*, and without knowing of the first phenomenological use of *Ereignis* in 1919, he was able to see its introduction in 1936 or so as a "progression" that overcame earlier deficiencies. This progressive schema overlooks the essential probing quality of Heidegger's philosophizing which truly has the character of *Holzwege*, paths that lead nowhere and double back on themselves, as Pöggeler himself has recognized. See the postscript to the third edition of *Der Denkweg Martin Heideggers*.

rather are "ideal constituents" which "manifest themselves in these acts" (*HCT,* 70). The unity of an experience is already in the experience itself; the task of the phenomenologist is to read off the structure of the unity that is manifest in the experience.[17] Ultimately, the task is to be able to make explicitly manifest the unity which gives meaning to the whole.

This understanding is already at work in his *Habilitationschrift* in the contrast he draws between a Bergsonian flux of experience and a medieval teleological experience which understands beings through the meaningfulness of the experience of God. God is the "primary transcendental," the center or unity of experience; God is the category of categories, the unity of the categories which gives meaning to the whole. This unity is the *universum* in Heidegger's interpretation of Schleiermacher subsequent to the *Habilitationsschrift*. In the subsequent lectures on phenomenology the *universum* is grasped as the "primordial something" (*Ur-etwas*) that makes experience possible. This primordial something is life. Thus God becomes understood as the living spirit who is manifest as the meaning of the whole in genuine religious living (*GA1,* 409). Because they aim at the same "object," the unity and meaning of the whole, to pursue phenomenology is already to live religiously.

The accord between genuine religiosity and phenomenology relies upon Heidegger's conviction that the theoretical life goes fundamentally astray in the way it tries to grasp the whole. In light of his conviction, Heidegger could not follow Husserl's own path to understanding experience even as he borrowed from it. In the War Emergency Semester lecture, Heidegger took up Husserl's demand that phenomenology be a "rigorous science" that hearkened "to the matter itself." Even in 1919, however, the younger colleague understood the matter differently (something Husserl did not realize until he read *Being and Time* years later). In particular, Heidegger could not accept Husserl's understanding of how to ground a rigorous, presuppositionless science. Husserl had followed in Descartes's footsteps by grounding absolute knowledge in the *cogito*. For Heidegger, this had two related consequences. First, it gave priority to the theoretical conscious-

---

17. To what degree Heidegger's project is Kantian is a difficult matter to sort out. His opposition to Kant on this point relies on a very psychologistic reading of the *Critique of Pure Reason*. Given this reading, Heidegger's understanding of the unity of being is closer to Aristotle than most post-Kantian philosophers. Since Heidegger uses the term "act" to signify the primary level of experience, however, he comes very close to an almost Fichtean understanding of the transcendental unity of apperception.

ness, and second, it overlooked the "being-character" of consciousness (a connection much clearer in German: *das* Sein*charakter des Bewußt*seins). We have seen that Heidegger rejected the priority of theory as an unliving type of comportment, and although he had not thematized it quite this way, the return to the experiential origins of knowledge meant to thematize the being of the "I" that thinks, or to put it another way, to thematize the "how" of the "I" which is constitutive for the "what" of any being. The particular "how" that interests Heidegger is the intentional "how" of Dasein, which points back to the "inner unity of life itself," which is the origin of genuine, living meaning. The rigorous science Heidegger wants is thus a "primordial science" (*Ur-wissenschaft*), whose "principle of principles" is to find the "primordial intention" (*Urintention*) of true life in general and the "primordial stance" (*Urhaltung*) of experience and life as such (*GA56/57*, 109–10). This originary science is enacted in a *hermeneutical intuition* that penetrates to a "foundational level of life." A truly rigorous science cannot be grounded in theory, but must return to the origins of theory itself in the pretheoretically experienced intentions of human being.

The phenomenological task is to bring into relief the unity of meaning found in experience. This unity is the unity of the categories taken as a whole. The meaning of the whole is manifest, even if only vaguely, in every experience. This whole forms the background, so to speak, within which each thing appears in its specific meaning. Things do not appear as such in themselves in isolation, but only within a relational nexus that, taken as a whole, constitutes the meaning of the whole.[18] This relational whole is what Heidegger calls the world, or what Husserl calls the lifeworld. Phenomenology wants to study the structure of the world as it appears to us in experience. Because the world appears in every experience, Heidegger directs our attention to how we experience things at the most primary level. In line with his antitheoretical stance, Heidegger will find this immediate level of experience in our everyday dealings with things. In this level of experience, we discover the world not as an object we examine, but as a surrounding world (*Umwelt*) to which we relate in dealing with it.[19]

---

18. From this point of view, Heidegger is directly opposed to nominalist ontology, which understands being as individual beings connected through efficient causality. Heidegger is more akin to Aquinas's or Aristotle's notion of an order of being.

19. The relationship between Heidegger and Husserl (and Heidegger's with phenomenology in general) is too complex to spell out fully here. While Marion is correct in seeing

Heidegger begins this return to experience in a thought "experiment" astonishing in its elegance and simple power. He asks his listeners present there in the lecture hall, "What do we experience when we experience?" As Heidegger, speaking in the first person, steps into the hall, he sees his rostrum. Does he see brown surfaces fastened together boxlike, on which he adds an additional, supplementary meaning "rostrum?" In no way, he insists; that is a deviation from the pure experience. In the experience, he experiences "rostrum" with a single stroke—a brown box which he uses in his lecture to hold his book and lecture notes as he speaks to his listeners in a university lecture hall. The experience which makes up the meaning of "rostrum," which makes it what it is, encompasses that whole. This whole in which I find myself "surrounds" me, as it were; it is the environment, in German the *Umwelt*, literally the around-world. This whole of the environment gives itself immediately to me in the act of experience. To experience is always to live in a meaningful relationship to things. This environmental meaning is the primary thing. This environmental world does not exist beforehand, but occurs in the experience itself. Heidegger uses the remarkable phrase "es weltet" (it worlds) for this experience. In pure experience, the world comes about, it comes about as the totality of meaningfulness in which I move and toward which I intend. This intentional meaningfulness exists even when that thing toward which I intend is wholly alien, that is, meaningless. The Senegalese (Heidegger's example) would not know what to make of a rostrum, but this not-knowing-what-to-make-of-it arises only out of the intentional nature of experiencing; it is only the one extreme of meaningfulness. All experiencing is intentionally "out toward something" (auf etwas zu). It intends toward the whole of meaningfulness which makes up the world (*GA56/57*, 71–73).

This "out toward" comes back to my self. In all experiencing I relate *myself* to something, and this experience gives itself immediately *to me*. Experience always brings with it an experience of the self; I experience myself as experiencing an "I am." This creates a problem with which epis-

---

Heidegger's ongoing criticism of Cartesian epistemology as an backhanded slap at Husserl's own Cartesian path, Held is also correct in seeing Heidegger's allegiance to the phenomenological project that tries to illuminate the horizon of meaning, in Husserlian terminology the "lifeworld," in Heidegger's, "being as a whole." See Jean-Luc Marion, "Heidegger and Descartes," in *Critical Heidegger*, ed. Christopher Macann (New York: Routledge, 1996), and Klaus Held, "Heidegger und das Prinzip der Phänomenologie," in *Heidegger und die praktische Philosophie*, ed. Annemarie Gethmann-Siefert and Otto Pöggeler (Frankfurt a. M.: Suhrkamp, 1989).

temology has long wrestled: what is the objectivity of my experience? Heidegger admits the problem. The experience of the Senegalese is as valid as his own, as any individual's experience (*GA56/57*, 72). The very "misunderstanding" of experience he indicated, empiricism, is itself an attempt to solve this problem of what in experience is objective. According to this theory, our basic experience is of sense impressions, at the root level patches of color or even different wavelengths of light, which our brain processes into a form to which the brain adds, through whatever miracle of habit, a word that is its meaning. There is a very necessary reason why this type of scientific understanding of experience came about. The objectivity of a true proposition is supposed to be universally valid, but of course everyone experiences differently. This is the problem of "perspectivism." What can be universal must thus be something common to each experience, but because each experience is individual, it must necessarily be abstracted from the experience. What precisely is abstracted out of the "objective" seeing is the experiencing I itself. When the I "sees" in a theoretically objective fashion, "*I* am indeed no longer" (*GA56/57*, 73). It is "lifted out" of authentic experience (*GA56/57*, 74). Here Heidegger introduces the dependence of theory on experience and its deficiency in regard to the latter. All knowledge begins in experience, but theory denudes experience of that which makes it experience, its relatedness to the experiencing self; it "lives off" (*Ent-leben*) the life out of lived experience (*Er-leben*). A truly rigorous science must stay true to the character of experience, which cannot lie in the objectivity of the experience itself.

Are we doomed to perspectivism or what is the same, endless and endlessly unsuccessful phenomenological descriptions of each individual experience? The problem of the logic of the phenomenon was the central question of phenomenology, and its proponents and opponents debated it vigorously. The problem lies in the articulation of the experience. If the experience is truly individual, how can anything be said about it without inventing a new language at each moment of experience for each individual experience? Heidegger was convinced nevertheless that it is possible to say something objective about experience. Following Husserl, he believes meaningfulness can be found in the intentional structure of experience. Intending includes both the "out toward something," the world, and the relating of this something back to the self. Making a Kantian move, he believes that this intentional structure can be analyzed to give formally objective ways that things are intended. In Kant's transcendental aesthetic, reflection on experience gives us the universal structures that make any experience possible, that it to say, time and space, and eventually the categories. Analogously, Heidegger will present the a priori formal structures of experience. Unlike Kant, however, the a priori structures of experience are not universal determinants of things, but ultimately "formal indications" which point to the "how" of any experience. The "how" of experience is based on the specific comportment of the self that experiences, the latter taken more broadly than the pure experience which we have been discussing. Heidegger compares the modern astronomical understanding of heavenly objects with that of Sophocles and finds them completely different in the "how" of their ways of experiencing (*GA56/57*, 74–75). The example he gives, although indirect, is clear enough. The modern astronomer sees in a sunrise (already the term is biased) the visual effects of the rotation of the earth around a stationary sun, whereas Sophocles sees beauty directed toward humanity. One is the modern scientific "how" of seeing, and the other is the poetic "how." When we indicate the "how" of experience, we are indicating not the "how" of the object but that of the experiencing self.

It is for this reason that genuine religion is a way of life, not theological dogma. Heidegger was convinced that it is only through a properly religious stance that the experiencing self is connected genuinely to the meaning of the whole, constituting an undivided unity of feeling and intuition. He was much more concerned with the how of our being which enables us to overcome our alienation from life than in justifying any particular understanding of life as superior to others; how something is done has a priority over what is done.

Even as Heidegger's phenomenology became less obviously influenced by religion, he still hunted for ways of understanding and getting at a type of comportment which is proper to being human. Heidegger believed he could find this in Aristotle, specifically in book 6 of the *Nicomachean Ethics,* where Aristotle analyzes the "*dianoetic* virtues." As the term "dianoetic" indicates, it is a *noēin* (perception), which includes a second factor, in this case, *logos,* speech; *dianoetic* indicates perception mediated through language (*GA19*, 59). Perception mediated through language is precisely the meaning of phenomenology, the speech of appearance or the appearing to us in speech. In Aristotle, Heidegger thought he had found the precursor to modern phenomenology.

To say that language "mediates" phenomena should not be mistaken to mean that there is a thing in itself which is mediated (distorted) by human cognition, but that a thing comes to appearance as it is uncovered in being spoken. "Uncovered" is how Heidegger first translated *alētheia*, the Greek word for truth.[20] In this way Heidegger could connect Aristotle and the Greeks with phenomenology's attempts to find the truth in phenomenological experience. The nature of truth is found in exploring how phenomena come to presence in speech, that is, how things are uncovered in their being. The various ways of coming to presence (and the verbal quality of being in the truth is vital to understanding how Heidegger understands truth) are the various ways of *alētheuein*, being uncovered, which takes the world out of its coveredness and exposes it to us (*GA19*, 17). *Alētheuein* "discloses" (*erschließt*) the world. *Alētheuein* shows itself in the first case in *legein*, speaking, which is the basic constitution of human being (*GA19*, 17). Human being is in the first case the disclosing of the world in and through speech. From the earlier War Emergency Semester course we know that "world" means the totality of environmental meaning given to me in my experience. In this way we can encounter a thing in its meaning. To encounter a thing in its meaning is to let it be seen "as" something, which in Greek is *apophasis*, which Heidegger calls "an uncovering which lets see." A thing "is" as it "as," if I can be permitted a lousy sentence. A thing appears "as" something in the Umwelt. As we know already, however, different worlds are possible, which means that a thing appears as something depending upon the world being disclosed; there are varieties of ways of disclosing a world of meaning that makes up the "as." As we have also learned already, the disclosing of the world varies according to the "how" of the being of Dasein. The modes of *alētheuein* correspond to the types of world-disclosing "hows." In book 6 of the *Nicomachean Ethics*, Heidegger found a discussion of the various "hows" of *alētheuein* which disclose the world.

Although much later Heidegger would recall his youthful introduction to Brentano's book on the manifold meanings of being in Aristotle as the decisive motive for taking up the question of being, in his renewed enthusiasm for Aristotelian metaphysics he recast ontology in the form of a

---

20. *Aufdecken, aufgedeckt.* As is well known, Heidegger translates *alētheia* with a variety of terms throughout the years. *Aufdecken* probably suggested itself because Heidegger was interested in the tendency of factical life to cover itself up. What is missing in this term is the privative, the "un-" found in Greek of which Heidegger would make so much later on. Thus the later translation "*Un-verborgenheit*" or "*Un-verborgene.*"

hermeneutics of life. It is striking that being almost never appears as a theme around the time of his crisis of faith and the phenomenology of religion, despite his affirmation that he wanted to do metaphysics other than in the Catholic manner. The hermeneutics of life occupies the place of honor, not the question of being. There is, however, an evident parallel between Heidegger's early phenomenology and Aristotle's metaphysics that must have eventually struck Heidegger: primary being serves the identical role in Aristotle's metaphysics that life does in Heidegger's phenomenology. Both are the conditions of possibility of experiencing things, the ultimate way in which things are understood as what they are. Thus the phenomenological task to appropriate the background structure of experience can easily appropriate Aristotle's project to grasp what makes out beings as such, which is to ask the question of being. Heidegger's mature phenomenology is explicitly understood as ontology, the study of beings and being. Since he is still concerned with human life, that is to say, acting, experiencing, suffering, living, Heidegger understands the question of being as the inquiry into human existence, in German, *Dasein.* Because the word for "being," *Sein,* is contained in the word for "existence," *Dasein,* to be concerned with one's living existence is to be concerned with being. Heidegger's early ontology, which is understood as an analytic of Dasein, is a direct descendant of his earlier phenomenology of life.

Worldhood and the Analytic of Dasein

The elements and strands of thought we have outlined thus far in Heidegger's early philosophy—intentionality, environmental experience, formal indication, the connection of speaking and appearance in which a thing appears "as" something, the emphasis on the "how" of Dasein—were slowly coming together into what would become Division One of Part One of *Being and Time.*[21] In fact, the bulk of this work can be seen as an expansion of the simple example of experiencing the rostrum that was found in the War Emergency Semester. To recall, this example began with the experience of the rostrum, in which the experiencing "I" was given the meaning of the rostrum as part of the totality of meanings found in the environment in which it found itself. The whole of experience consisted in

---

21. *Being and Time* was published in truncated form, consisting only of the first two of three planned divisions of part 1 and no part 2 at all.

a "simultaneous" dual movement, one directed out toward this whole which constituted the world and the other which related this disclosed meaning back to the experiencing self, which is itself "taken with" the whole of the experience. The importance of the last part is to emphasize that it is not the experiencing self that is primary, but rather the experiencing movement itself, which is intending. Evidence of different types of intentionality presents to us the problem of the "how" of intentionality. Heidegger enunciated all this in 1919.

This analysis of experience returned in expanded form in the analytic of Dasein. The use of Dasein marks Heidegger's new project of developing an understanding of being from the analysis of existence. This evinces itself in the first instance in the terminology contained in *Being and Time;* now everything is understood in terms of the being of human existence. Human life is always being something: being-with, being-by, being-in, etc. Taken as a whole, human life is always "being in the world."

Being-in-the-world is the primary setting for understanding the intentionality proper to human existence. The unity of Dasein is found in "care" (*Sorge*), which is the word Heidegger uses to designate the structure of intentionality. As caring, Dasein is in the first instance, "being-ahead-of-itself" (*BT,* 236). As Heidegger cautions, however, because Dasein is constituted as being in the world, being ahead of itself must be grasped more fully as "ahead-of-itself-in-already-being-in-a-world" (*BT,* 236). This constitutes the primordial structural whole of Dasein. The whole is the same as the dual movement that constitutes the whole of intentionality of the 1919 thought experiment.

Understanding intentionality as care has an important ramification that also comes out of that fecund experiment. One of Heidegger's chief goals was to displace theory from its preeminence as how things come to presence in their being. Husserl's theory of intentionality was a key ingredient toward achieving this goal, but it was not lost on Heidegger that Husserl used intentionality to buttress theory, not overthrow it. Caring overcomes this problem left by intentionality. Caring, as the term indicates (in German as well), means that something is of concern to the self; it relates that toward which it intends back to the self. This concern draws the self "out toward" what concerns it. That which is the concern of Dasein draws the self out. What the self is drawn "out toward," and equivalently that which draws it in, is the world. Being drawn in by the world means to be "in" the world. Caring means "being-in-the-world." Caring being-in discovers the world in its meaningfulness (*HCT*, 255). Because caring unites the "out toward" of intentionality with the relating of this back to the concernful self, which thus finds itself engaged meaningfully in the world, caring duplicates the primordial experiential quality of knowing Heidegger put forth in his experiment. Intentionality as Husserl developed it implies, as Heidegger points out, that the "ahead-of-itself" is that of a worldless subject with the concomitant problems in Husserl's phenomenology of the possibility of the subject transcending to the world and the reality of the world. Caring as being-already-in-the-world renders these problems nonsensical. Primordial knowing is found in the structure of care, which as in the 1919 thought experiment, is experiential intentionality of being-in-the-world.

Being-in-the-world, as Heidegger developed it in *Being and Time* also has its direct descendent in that useful little example. Dasein is always being-in-the-world. Being-in-the-world does not mean that Dasein exists as one individuated thing among all other things, the totality of which makes up the world. Being-in is not spatial, but relational. To be "in" something means to dwell in it, to be familiar with it, to be involved with it. We are "in" the world to the extent that we are involved with it, "in the sense of taking something into one's care, having it in one's care" (*HCT*, 158–59). The mode of care that cares for things in which it is involved is called concern (*HCT*, 294).[22] As in the earlier example, the primordial level of intentionality is found in the immediate familiarity with things. Likewise in *Being and Time* Heidegger begins with the nearest general example of involved familiarity with things, the working world. The analysis of going about one's work reveals both that our basic knowledge is being familiarly involved with things and that this involvement points to a for the most part unseen environment of meaning that makes possible our meaningful involvement at all. "Being-in-the-world, according to our interpretation hitherto, amounts to a non-thematic circumspective absorption in references or assignments constitutive for the readiness-to-hand [*Zuhandenheit*] of a totality of equipment" (*BT*, 107). This totality of connections of significance is what Heidegger calls a world. These connections derive from the structure of signification of being involved that is "for-the-sake-of-which." This structure points to an ultimate "for-the-sake-of-which," in

---

22. The connection is clearer in German: "care" is *Sorge* and "concern" is *Besorgen*, which has the connotation in German of managing something. With the publication of his lectures on Aristotle, we now know that Heidegger used *Besorgen* to translate the Greek *technē* (*GA19*, 22).

which the significance of a thing is grounded (*BT*, 182). Things in the world take on their significance through this world, and are thus understood or interpreted. Things are not taken as bare things, but come to presence only through the world: "It means rather that it is a *world which appresents* [*appräsentiert*] *a thing of the world*" (*HCT*, 190). The continuity with the earlier theme is evident, even down to deriving the theoretical attitude as a deficient sort of apprehending that can happen only when there is a break in the closed totality (a tool is missing or poorly designed for the task) which allows us to step back and regard the tool alone. As such, the tool is no longer a tool but rather a bare object without world, merely "present-at-hand" (*vorhanden*) (*BT*, 105–6).

The two types of being present point to the "how" that characterizes the coming to presence of a thing. Because things are appresented by the world in which they come to presence, to inquire into the "how" of things is to inquire into the "how" of the world. "When we ask about the phenomenal structure of the world, we are asking about the *how* of the being in which the entity we call the world *shows itself of itself as the encountered*, we are asking about the being of the entity which is encountered in the leeway for encounter granted by concern" (*HCT*, 169). This "how" is the worldhood of the world. When we recall Heidegger's long-standing commitment to differentiating ways of relating to the world, his next step should no longer be surprising. Contrary to what the word suggests, "worldhood" is in fact "understood not as a character of the being of the entity [world], but rather as the *character of the being of Dasein,* and only through it and along with it that of the entity!" (*HCT*, 169). The exclamation point indicates Heidegger's excitement at this turn. To study the world, we really need to study human existence. "To determine the worldhood of world is to lay open in its structure the how of the encounter, drawn from that encounter, of the entity in which Dasein is as being-in in accord with its basic constitution, in short to lay open the structure of the being of this entity" (*HCT*, 169). It should thus be clear why Heidegger insists that Dasein is not a "what," but rather a "how," a way "to be" (*Zu-sein*) (*HCT*, 153). This has always been one of the great stumbling blocks to understanding Heidegger's philosophy, for which he bears much of the blame, precisely for calling Dasein an "entity," as if it too were a thing.[23] It is rather an index of ways of being which Heidegger is indicat-

---

23. The confusion finds its clearest expression when Heidegger calls the object which *phronēsis* uncovers, Dasein itself, *praxis* or action (*GA19*, 146). Action is not a thing, except in the English phrase, "Action is the thing!" Oddly enough, this captures almost precisely

ing in their formality (the guiding presence of the formal indicative method he developed around 1920). To determine the worldhood of the world is to lay out in a "system" of formal indications the ways for Dasein "to be." This is precisely the analytic of Dasein, the first division of *Being and Time*.

Although Division One constitutes a thorough working through of intuition as first broached eight years earlier, there is still the matter of Division Two, where Heidegger lets loose the full arsenal of existential thematic which agitated intellectuals for many, many years. Death, conscience, resoluteness, the moment of vision, history: it makes Division One positively mundane. At the least, the title of the work should point to the deficiency of the first division; time is hardly mentioned there. This fact indicates even more clearly that Division One is really related to the early postwar lectures, where time plays little role. Although, as seen in the conclusion to the *Habilitationschrift*, Heidegger clearly wanted to establish the historical nature of human being, he did not connect this at a fundamental level with the analysis of experience and the facticity of life. Only later when studying Aristotle did he make his "ousialogical" breakthrough, the realization that time discriminated various types of being, to wit, eternal from "can be otherwise." What must have particularly struck Heidegger was that this distinction played a key role in book 6 of the *Nicomachean Ethics*, where Aristotle used this distinction of objects to classify the different types of *alētheuein*, the ways of disclosing the things—worldhood—which were distinguished in order to find the one most befitting proper human being.

Phronēsis, Being, and Time

The Question of the Meaning of Being

The task Heidegger accepts in *Being and Time* is to raise anew the question of being. The specific formulation of the question of being in this text is, What is the *meaning* (*Sinn*) of being? The meaning of being, like most of Heidegger's genitive expressions, has a twofold meaning: it can mean, on the one hand, how being makes sense (*Sinn*), how beings hold together as the meaning of the whole and, on the other hand, it can be a reference

---

the meaning Heidegger gave to the phenomenological slogan, "To the things themselves," for the "thing" that most concerned Heidegger was the nonobjective space or worldhood in which things show themselves as what they are.

to the meaning that belongs to being itself. This rather obscure formulation can be clarified in the following way. The analytic of Dasein showed that the meaning of beings derives from their embeddedness in a web of relationships of meaning that make up the world. This world, earlier explicated as the unity of the categories, manifests itself in each intentional act of understanding or experience. In the intending categorial act, beings appear to us *as* what they are. This intentional act is the source of meaning; it means to take a being as a meaningful something. Intentionality was understood to be care, which had the structure of being "out toward" the world. Meaning comes from this reaching out toward the world which reveals to us beings in their meaning.

This "out toward" movement of intention leads to Heidegger's understanding of meaning or sense as akin to a sense of direction. This in turn underscores why Heidegger turns to understanding the source of meaning, the direction of being, as how this intentional act intends; meaning, as already explicated, derives from the "how" of Dasein. "Thus a determinate *how* of the being of life, which here means: life, that 'is' *my* life, gives the direction of the connections of meaning [*Sinnzusammenhänge*]" (*GA60*, 242). Thus the theoretical "how" of existence directs the intentional act toward beings such that they appear as objects for theory; namely, as universally valid objects of scientific and, in the final analysis, mathematical knowledge; the pragmatic "how" of existence—and I leave "pragmatic" in its full ambiguous sense that combines work, action, and religious life, an ambiguity Heidegger was to labor hard to sort out—reveals things as tools for our work. Each type of intentional how reveals the meaning of being for that intentional act, for being, as Heidegger understands Aristotle, is that by virtue of which beings are revealed in their being, which Heidegger understands as the world, or the meaning of beings as a whole. This is the first sense of the meaning of being: the meaning of being is how beings are understood, taken, and revealed to us in the intentional act.

The second sense of the meaning of being flows from this understanding of the origin of determinate meaning. The priority of the "how," which can be understood through intentionality as the direction of the intentional act that takes something as something, points to the priority of the possible types of "how," the possible directions that intentional understanding can take. The second sense of the meaning of being is precisely that being means possibility, the possibility that being can take on many different meanings depending upon the how of Dasein. If being is the condition of possibility of beings, then at least one of the conditions is possibility itself.

Put together, the two senses of the meaning of being depict existence as a "choice" between possible paths which we can take. To take a path is to enact a possibility that determines, or rather is, the particular meaning of existence. The enactment of a possibility of existence is what Heidegger calls a resolution (*Entschluß*). Thus the latter part of *Being and Time* revolves around the structure of resoluteness, how Dasein is resolved upon a possibility of its existence.

The central feature of the structure of resoluteness is time. To enact a possibility is to bring it into being or actuality. To bring something into being from not-being indicates a change in being and thus the existence of time. Genuine temporality is bound up with and dependent upon being as possibility, for it is only in the change of being from possibility to actuality that time occurs. However, because the understanding of time, like the rest of the measures of being, depend upon the "how," time itself is not a constant, but depends upon the possibility enacted. The specific opposition Heidegger has in mind is that between the homogenous constant series of now-points as found in scientific measurement and a kairological understanding of time Heidegger appropriated from the early Christian and Augustinian understanding of time. In this latter sense of time Heidegger finds the authentic historical possibility of existence; humans are authentically historical insofar as the *kairos* occurs in resolution.

When Heidegger turned to Aristotle, he did so with the intention of finding a way to grasp the twofold sense of the meaning of being, specifically, with discovering a "how" of understanding being that could capture both senses of being: as specific direction and as possibility and thus time. He thought he had found it in Aristotle's explication of *phronēsis,* or practical wisdom. In a very real sense, Division Two of *Being and Time* is an appropriation of *phronēsis* as the way of authentically understanding the meaning of being. *Phronēsis* can capture both senses of the meaning of being because it takes being as that which can be otherwise, that is, possible, and is at the same time the enactment of this possibility as action in the world, as the sense-giving measure which directs our active being-in-the-world.

The appropriation of Aristotle and *phronēsis* to understand human existence does not, however, supersede Heidegger's religious concerns.[24] This

24. See for example, PIA, 372–73, where Heidegger ties together his proposed book on

can be seen in two ways. The simplest way is to note the peculiarity of turning to Aristotle's ethics to elucidate metaphysics. Heidegger gets at being only through a study of the "character" of human being, how we are. This again points to the priority of the "how" over the "what" of human being, how we live over any specific content of our beliefs; and I have already shown that at least for the early Heidegger, the most authentic way of life is the religious. Evidence that this remained true can be found in the way that Heidegger came again to the question of being. In his lecture course on Augustine, given the semester before he turned to Aristotle, he presents the Augustine's question, "I have become a question to myself," as in fact a troubling (*Bekümmerung*) over the *being* of the self (*GA60, 245*). The being of the self he understands as a determinate "how" of the being of life which gives the direction to the meaning of being (*GA60, 242*). Practical wisdom, as Aristotle presents it, is also the type of knowing that is concerned with the self; it aims at nothing other than the well-being of the actor. Putting Aristotle and Augustine together yields the insight that *phronēsis* is troubled by and thus seeks an answer to how one should be in order to live appropriately. From Augustine Heidegger gets the answer that the proper way to live, the authentic "how" of human existence, is "ultimately radical self-concern [*Selbstbekümmerung*] before God," in other words, how the self needs to be in order to find its path toward God (*GA60, 242*). Although practical wisdom need not be religious, for Heidegger, it means the path by which we come to relate ourselves to the divine, which means in the end, toward the mystery and grace-character of life, a mystery found in our relation to what he comes to understand as possibility. As we shall see in the next chapter, Heidegger ultimately understands practical wisdom not along classical lines, but rather in accordance with Meister Eckhart and the mystical tradition.

To express the central motive of Heidegger's project in a slightly different way, although the being of the world—being itself—depends *upon* how it is disclosed in the intentional act of understanding, Heidegger has a criterion for distinguishing which kind of disclosure is authentic. A disclosure is authentic when it discloses being as it is proper to human existence, which is to say when it rests on an understanding of being that recognizes

---

Aristotle with an investigation of both his positive and negative effects on Christianity. In Gadamer's words, "There is no doubt that it was Heidegger's old, well-attested concern with the originary Christian tidings that stood behind the Aristotle investigation." Gadamer, "Die Religiöse Dimension," 313.

that possibility and time are the horizons and ultimate conditions of being.[25] This criterion for distinguishing—and implicitly grading—ways of disclosing runs through all of his works from at least 1918 until the end of his life.

The implicit grading of the ways of disclosing being is the source of his "factical" ideal of Dasein and thus of the always manifest, often denied matter of the ethics of authenticity. In the concept of authenticity we come to where most commentators see the place of ethics in *Being and Time,* even if some do not find "authenticity" particularly ethical. As will become apparent in later chapters, I find Heidegger's concept of politics rooted firmly in his notion of authenticity, for authenticity is the criterion for distinguishing what is superior or better in human existence. Despite its seeming obviousness, however, the role authenticity plays in *Being and Time,* and thus what it means to be authentically human, is quite hard to pin down. That the meaning of authenticity is not self-evident is suggested by the fact that Heidegger believed that most people misunderstood it, including most of his students. Most of them interpreted authentic Dasein in a Kierkegaardian sense as being a resolute individual free from the grip of society. From this derives all those interpretations of Heidegger's decisionism, the belief that sheer commitment or resoluteness is all, or that from the radicalized individual no politics can result at all. This is wrong as a whole, even if paradoxically correct in parts.

Like many misunderstandings, it can be traced to ambiguities in Heidegger himself. What does it mean to be authentic? As commonly used, it can be summed up in Polonius's memorable phrase, "To thine own self be true." Unfortunately, Heidegger does not give an unequivocal definition of what it means to be a self. For the most part, we—and most of his students—take the self to be identical with the individual self who says "I am." As I will show in more detail in the next chapter, this is not what Heidegger meant by the term. From Augustine, Heidegger understood the self as questionable, a questionableness that ultimately must question its

---

25. How Heidegger knows what being "really" is remains mysterious in all his writings. In fact, if you take what he says seriously, it must remain mysterious because it is only a response to the gift of being as it gives itself to us in the question of being. In *Being and Time*, the "proof" of the correctness of his understanding of being is the genuine experience of death, which he claims is the proof of being's finitude and thus freedom. In actuality, his analysis of death already presumes what he wants to prove, namely that the soul is not immortal.

own being. The being of the self is disclosed along with all beings in the disclosure of being in resolution. That is to say, I understand the meaning of my existence only by understanding the meaning of existence itself, that is, the meaning of being as a whole. Who I am depends upon the meaning of being. As being-in-the-world, Dasein does not merely disclose a world from which it is removed, but discloses itself along with this disclosure. Every interpretation is also a self-interpretation. "in the manner in which Dasein in its world speaks about its way of dealing with its world, a *self-interpretation of Dasein* is also given. It states how Dasein specifically understands itself, what it takes itself to be" (*CT*, 8). Dasein catches sight of itself in its dealings with the world, it finds itself "disposed" in the world. This is the specific way it has a world and thus can be "in" the world. This way of having oneself and the world can be either authentic or inauthentic. Thus the motto of authenticity, to thine own self be true, really means, be true to being and the appropriate comportment that can reveal being as it really is. It means to be true to one's own being or nature. To be an authentic Dasein, to be true to one's self, means to understand oneself through *phronēsis* as a being that exists temporally, as something that can be otherwise and is thus in essence possibility. *Phronēsis* connects my self with the meaning of being because *phronēsis* not only reveals being as it authentically is but completes itself in action. Thus by virtue of *phronēsis,* I live in undivided unity with the authentic meaning of being. Perhaps the clearest way to express it is to say that my ontic authenticity depends on my ontological authenticity; my choice of "heroes" is authentic only if I have chosen my own essence, and that to choose my own essence authentically implies that I have simultaneously chosen a specific course of action.

Authentic Being

The "factical ideal" of an authentic sense of religious life inspired the turn to *phronēsis*. If we recall, the problem Catholicism posed Heidegger was the fact that it had become a theoretical system emptied of genuine historical meaning. This theoretical system of propositions and values confronts the self as an alien force both because it is theoretical in nature and because it does not account for the fundamentally historical nature of the self, but transposes a value system that had genuine meaning in one historical time into an epoch alien to it. The connection between these two points lies in the fundamentally ahistorical nature of theory, which understands itself as eternally valid for all historical times. The drive for objective validity which predominates in modern times meant to "live off" the source of genuine meaning which is the historical appropriation of this source to the self. Heidegger hoped to regain access to this source of genuine meaning which could guide historical action in the world. *Phronēsis* was the means to connect action and meaning in a genuine way such that the meaning would be related to the acting self as its own; the meaning disclosed would be meaningful for the self for its time. *Phronēsis* does this because as a way of "uncovering" it discloses the world, but as "practical wisdom" it discloses the world in terms of acting in the world. This way of disclosing the world is authentic because it discovers the authentic being of Dasein, which is being-possible and thus historical. *Phronēsis* unites the understanding of the good (practical wisdom) with the authentic historical nature of being human. It enables authentic acting in which action is guided by its own or proper understanding of the good (*GA19*, 136).[26] In this way, ethics acquires genuine meaning for the acting self. *Phronēsis* was the means Heidegger sought to employ in order to solve the problem of the emptiness of the system of values of contemporary Catholicism.

In order to explicate the being proper to humans, Heidegger turned to Aristotle's discussion of the dianoetic virtues in book 6 of the *Nicomachean Ethics* for a way of speaking that would connect an authentic character of the self with an authentic understanding of being as possibility. Since human life is fundamentally constituted by disclosing through speaking, the analytic of Dasein is fundamentally an index of how disclosing discloses the world of meaning. These ways correspond to the different types of *alētheuein—epistēmē, sophia, technē, phronēsis,* and *nous*[27]—which

---

26. One should bear in mind that by "the good" (*agathon*), Heidegger meant what is appropriate to the being of Dasein. Since Heidegger explicitly says that the good for human beings is something that can in each case be otherwise, he is maintaining the fundamental historical nature of goods (*GA19*, 136). In this sense, the *eu-* of *eudaimonia* should be translated as "well," since it is an adverb and refers to *how* something is done, rather than *what* the end is. See Michael Gillespie, "Martin Heidegger's Aristotelian National Socialism," *Political Theory* 28, no. 2 (2000): 147.

27. There are two others, but Aristotle does not discuss them. Heidegger eliminates *nous* by making the other four themselves types of *noein*, so he is left with four types to analyze. He does not think at any rate that humans are capable of *nous* in its pure form; all enacting of *nous* for human experience is mediated by speech, thus dia-noetic. He is quite cognizant that this is not Aristotle's own understanding and devotes a considerable amount of the lecture to showing that Aristotle is reflecting a Greek prejudice toward holding the highest human achievement to be godlike. See also Walter Brogan, "The Place of Aristotle in the

Aristotle enumerates. Thus *alētheuein* is how being is disclosed for human existence.

This connection bears more elucidation because it ties together several different threads that span many of Heidegger's works, especially his later writings on *alētheia* as unconcealment. *Alētheuein* is the verb that corresponds to *alētheia* or "truth." *Alētheuein* is the act in which a thing appears as it is; as such it is the equivalent of a categorial act that discloses the being of what is uncovered or unconcealed. The unity of the categories in the act of unconcealing is given by the type of unconcealing that takes place; thus being is disclosed or unconcealed one way for *epistēmē* (science) and another for *technē,* and yet another for *phronēsis.* Being is the unity of the categories by which a thing appears as what it is, the unity by which we take something *as* something. As the unity of the categories, being is equivalent to world. Heidegger's analysis of the modes of *alētheuein* are thus the same as the analysis of worldhood. As Heidegger understands the matter, *alētheuein,* being the act of unconcealment, is the act of bringing something out of its concealment into unconcealment. In being brought into unconcealment, a being is brought into the truth (*alētheia*). As unconcealment, *alētheia* is understood as the open region (*das Offene*) in which humans can encounter beings (ET, 127). Another term Heidegger used as equivalent to *das Offene* is "the clearing" [*Lichtung*], in the sense of a well-lit clearing in a dark forest. Beings can be encountered as what they are in *das Offene* because the open space itself directs how beings are disclosed (ET, 124–25). In this way, the act of unconcealing is the equivalent to what Heidegger in *Being and Time* called understanding, which is the articulation of something as something (*BT,* 192). This articulation is a sketch or project (*Entwurf*), which allows the entity to come to presence in its meaning; in its full designation, understanding is the sketch of being (*Seinsentwurf*).[28]

Development of Heidegger's Phenomenology," in *Reading Heidegger from the Start,* ed. Theodore Kisiel and John van Buren (Albany: SUNY Press, 1994).

This makes an interesting backdrop to Arendt's understanding of Heidegger. She always placed him among the pure thinkers, those whose thinking consists of the silent dialogue of the soul with itself, that being her Platonic understanding of the term "dianoetic" (Heidegger quoted that line from the *Sophist* in this lecture course which she attended). She even claims that the ideal of the self developed in *Being and Time* "follows as a consequence of Heidegger's making of man what God was in earlier ontology." Arendt, "What Is Existential Philosophy?" 180. This is clearly neither Heidegger's self-understanding nor his ideal.

28. *Entwerfen* and *Entwurf* are translated by Macquarrie and Robinson as "projection." The usual meaning of the word is to draw or sketch. I use "sketch" because *entwerfen* as

In the later text, even as I have often emphasized in this chapter, the openness varies depending upon the type of comportment, i.e., the way in which being is disclosed (ET, 124). This harks back to something from the lecture course on Augustine that I already cited, that a determinate how of the being of life gives the "direction" of the connection of meaning (*GA60*, 242). Thus *das Offene* as the directive for being is the first sense of the meaning of being I elucidated earlier, the specific meaning of being that makes up a world, the determinate sketch of being. In *Being and Time*, Heidegger understands the clearing or open space as the "there" of being (the "*Da*" of *Sein*; Da-sein). Thus to be Dasein, to be Da-sein, the there of being, means to be the clearing or disclosure of being itself (*BT*, 171). Although Heidegger's claim that Dasein is the world is sometimes taken as an extreme subjectivism, in the sense that the thinking subject is made the ground of being, Heidegger's rejection of the *cogito* and the Kantian correlate that the categories are found in the thinking self rather than in being means instead that as being-in-the-world, humans inhabit or participate in the "there" of being understood as the determinate directing meaning of being. Being, not the thinking subject, is the "agent," which must be understood carefully because being is understood as an agentless, unwilled, happening (the "Es gibt" as *Ereignis*).[29] I will discuss this in much more detail in the next chapter. For now, I want only to emphasize that Heidegger's discussion of the modes of *alētheuein* are his way of discussing how being can be "there" as the meaning of being.

Heidegger uses it has nothing to do with projecting things as by a slingshot, but with taking something as something, that is, seeing something as something, giving it shape and form; "sketching" is the enacting of understanding, articulating, interpreting, uncovering. If anything, it should be translated as "ob-jecting," to capture both the connection of the Latin and the German (both are "thrown off") and what is being "thrown off": the object, the thing, something as something.

29. The relation between thinking, subjectivity, and being plays an enormous role in Heidegger's own thought and thus in many interpretations of his thought, including his own self-interpretation. The complexity of the situation is such that Heidegger has been accused of extreme subjectivism (Levinas as an exemplar of this argument) and also of an extreme pre-critical positivism (Pippin, Rosen). See Emmanuel Levinas, *Totality and Infinity: An Essay on Exteriority*, trans. Alphonso Lingis (Pittsburgh: Duquesne University Press, 1969), 44–46; Robert Pippin, *Modernism as a Philosophical Problem* (Cambridge, Mass.: Basil Blackwell, 1991), 140–46; and Stanley Rosen, *The Question of Being: A Reversal of Heidegger* (New Haven: Yale University Press, 1993), 294–99. My own argument is closer to Rosen's and Pippin's, although I think Pippin misses the reason behind Heidegger's rejection of Kantian philosophy, the fact that in the end it alienates humans. Levinas's error stems, I believe, from his implicit equation of Dasein with Husserl's *cogito*, for it is only through this equation that his claim that the subject swallows up being makes sense. As I have shown, Heidegger had long since rejected the *cogito* as the basis of being.

The four modes of *alētheuein* are divided into two classes: *epistēmē* and *sophia* belong to the class of *epistemonokon*, which is the regarding of beings whose principle (*archē*) does not alter, whereas *technē* and *phronēsis* are classified as *logistikon*, which is the regarding of beings as "that which can be otherwise" (*GA19*, 27–28). More simply put, *epistemonokon* regards that which does not change or is eternal, whereas *logistikon* regards that which changes. The division is based on the being which is to be disclosed, and thus can be viewed as ways of appropriately gaining access to the being one wishes to investigate. Within each of these classes, the latter virtue, *sophia* and *phronēsis* respectively, are the highest excellences; thus *sophia* is higher than *epistēmē* and *phronēsis* is higher than *technē* (*GA19*, 30). The truly confusing part of these divisions as Heidegger presents them arises when it turns out that *sophia* is also the excellence of *technē*, which means that *technē* has within its kind of disclosing a tendency to become like *epistēmē* and depend upon *sophia* for its excellences.[30] In the final analysis, there is only *sophia* and *phronēsis* vying for attention.[31] The question Heidegger tackles, to sum up the first part of the lecture, is which virtue is most appropriate for disclosing Dasein, *sophia* or *phronēsis*. Because disclosing is itself a way of being of Dasein, the question really is, which is the appropriate or authentic way of being of Dasein. There is an intimate relation between an authentic understanding of Dasein and authentically being Dasein: when one *has* the one, one *is* the other. To give away the answer to the question of the choice between *sophia* and *phronēsis,* the answer is *phronēsis*. This results from the determination that Dasein is mortal and thus belongs with things that can be otherwise. In what could be termed Heidegger's own revelatory insight into what is, the distinction between *sophia* and *phronēsis* hinges upon the temporal element that makes up both; time discriminates between the nous of *sophia* (constant presence) and the nous of *phronēsis* (that which can be otherwise). The question of being belongs essentially to the question of time. Thus when we examine the "how" of *phronēsis,* which has as its object

---

30. This is precisely the root for the "technical" interpretation of the world that Heidegger finds at the root of modern metaphysics. It also points to a fundamental ambiguity within *technē* itself: because it tends to understand things either as changeable or as eternal, it can either provide access to proper human existence or cover up this access point and thereby misdirect existence onto inauthentic paths. More on this in Chapter 3.

31. See also Hans-Georg Gadamer, "Die Idee der praktischen Philosophie," in *Hermeneutik im Rückblick*, vol. 10 of *Gesammelte Werke* (Tübingen: J.C.B. Mohr, 1995), 240 n. 8. Gadamer almost certainly learned this point from Heidegger's course, which he attended.

praxis, action, we see how Dasein authentically is, and how this authentic being depends on the appropriation of the connection of time and being such that the being of Dasein is historical.[32]

Why is *phronēsis* authentic understanding? Heidegger realized that this identity was by no means self-evident, given that our tradition privileges theory and its ways of understanding, *epistēmē* and *sophia.* In the lecture in which he most thoroughly discusses *phronēsis,* Heidegger expended considerable energy to show that Aristotle was simply incorrect in identifying *sophia* and the way of life devoted to it (philosophy) as the highest human capacity, a situation which arose out of the Greeks' disposition to hold the eternal and divine as the highest.[33] To see why *phronēsis* is the highest, it is necessary to compare it to the other ways of uncovering. First of all, Heidegger dismisses *epistēmē* (science) out of hand as really derivative; not only does it not have access to Dasein, it does not even have access to the *archē* (principle) that guides its realm of being. *Technē* loses out because although it deals with things that can be otherwise, it does not concern Dasein itself; the producer does not consider himself while producing an object, but rather is absorbed in the production. Even if he steps back and regards himself technically as a worker, he has taken up one possibility of being without making explicit all of the possibilities he can be. *Phronēsis* is the excellence of *technē* precisely because it accounts for the whole being of Dasein. *Phronēsis* and *sophia* are the two excellences of being human, so the real contest comes down to these two. As he repeats on two different occasions in the lecture, *phronēsis* is superior to *sophia* as regards the understanding proper to Dasein because *phronēsis* considers that which "can be otherwise" while *sophia* considers the eternally constant and Dasein is not eternally constant, but mortally changeable. "The existence

---

32. Franco Volpi is essentially correct in seeing *Being and Time* as a "translation" of the *Nicomachean Ethics,* although as with all of Heidegger's "translations" one must always keep in mind his own agenda in appropriating a thinker. Division Two in particular found much of its direction in Aristotle, as will be made plain. See Franco Volpi, *"Being and Time: A 'Translation' of the Nicomachean Ethics?"* in *Reading Heidegger from the Start,* ed. Theodore Kisiel and John van Buren (Albany: SUNY Press, 1994), and idem, "Dasein as *Praxis:* The Heideggerian Assimilation and Radicalization of the Practical Philosophy of Aristotle," in *Critical Heidegger,* ed. Christopher Macann (New York: Routledge, 1996).

33. At this point Heidegger still identifies himself with philosophy, but the seeds are laid for his final thoughts on the "end of philosophy," which ends or finds its completion in science because as the love of (eternal) wisdom, philosophy runs together in the end with those ways of conceiving of being as eternal and not changeable. Only that activity he later names "thinking" can still conceive of being as presencing. Despite the change in terminology, the central issue, gaining access to the true changeable nature of being remains constant from early on until his death.

of man is not *aei* [eternal], not eternal; the being of man comes to be and passes away, it has its determined time, its *aion*" (*GA19*, 137; also 164). There is thus a close connection between being-possible, being mortal, and being historical. *Phronēsis* uncovers all these and in uncovering them, enacts them.

Authentic understanding uncovers the whole of Dasein. Dasein is essentially possibility. To uncover the whole that Dasein can be means to uncover all of the essential possibilities that define the limits of Dasein; it means to find Dasein's "utmost" possibility of being. The utmost possibility of Dasein's being is death (*BT*, 303). Death is the utmost because it is the possibility of the impossibility of possibility. Because *phronēsis* aims at the most extreme, the *eschaton*, it uncovers death as the utmost possibility of Dasein. Since *phronēsis* means not merely to speak about what it considers but to enact it in considering it, does this mean that *phronēsis* means to enact death, that is, to die? This conclusion is incorrect, but the care with which Heidegger skirts this issue points to the difficulties in his treatment of death. *Phronēsis* is one type of intentionality, that is to say, one type of care. Care is defined as "being-ahead-of-oneself-in-being-already-in." To be ahead of oneself means to anticipate, to "run ahead" of oneself toward what is intended. In *phronēsis,* we run ahead of ourselves to death; *phronēsis* is being-toward-death. However, the second half of the definition of care is vital. We do not run ahead to death as some possibility waiting for us at some indeterminate time in the future. This is the inauthentic understanding of death (*BT*, 301). Rather, we run ahead to death as something we already are. What Heidegger means is that we are mortal. In anticipating death, we come back to what we already are, which is to say mortal. Being mortal, it must be understood, is not a characteristic of a being which perishes, but a way of being toward death: "The uttermost 'not yet' has the character of something *toward which Dasein comports itself"* (*BT*, 293). It is for this reason that Heidegger calls being mortal "being-toward-death," and raises the possibility that Dasein can exist inauthentically toward death, despite the fact that it will die whether it takes up an authentic comportment to death or not. Being-toward-death means to take up one's mortality as one's ownmost, utmost possibility of being.[34] *Phronēsis* is authentic being-toward-death.

---

34. Heidegger much later expressed this thought in saying that we must "learn" to be mortal. This ability to learn to be mortal is also why humans "die" (*sterben*) and animals "perish" (*verenden*), for the latter cannot take up a being-toward-death (*BT*, 291; also NL, 107).

Being-toward-death is grounded in the anticipatory structure of care. Anticipation is directed toward something which is not yet present; this is its peculiar mode of making present. Heidegger brings up a way in which this making-present-of-that-which-is-not-yet structure of anticipation fails to truly capture being-toward-death as a possibility that one already is. The first belongs to *technē*, the "not yet" character of the *eidos* that guides production. When a housebuilder builds a house, he has a plan or idea of what a house is before he begins construction. This idea makes present the form of the house, which guides the actual production of the house. The actual house, though, is not yet present. Thus *technē* includes an anticipatory "not yet," the idea, which guides production. Producing, however, comes to an end when the work produced is finished. The completed house is the end of the production. The "not yet" disappears when production is completed or fulfilled; the house which during production was "not yet" is now presently finished and thus no longer "not yet." This "technical" understanding of the "not yet" commonly arises in contemplating death along biological lines, such as the ripening of a fruit, which in full ripeness "fulfills itself." In this sense, death is considered the fulfillment of life, that point when it reaches its end (*BT*, 288–89). Dasein, however, "is already its 'not yet'" (*BT*, 289). This is why Heidegger calls the end peculiar to death "being-toward-the-end," because it signifies that the "not yet" is always already present in the being of Dasein. Death indicates that the being of Dasein is shot through with this "not yet"; at the basis of Dasein is a "not." There is a nullity at the basis of the being of Dasein which is constitutive for Dasein. Dasein is being the basis of a nullity (*BT*, 329). The

---

Derrida presents an interesting critique of Heidegger's approach to death. Without following all of the implications Derrida draws (not the least the connection between death and language), I will bring out one important caveat to Heidegger's understanding of death. Heidegger has recourse to his understanding of authentic death as being-toward the impossibility of the possibility of being—death as such compared to other deficient understandings of death—for a very good reason: no one living has experienced their own death (the expression "near-death experience" sums this up nicely). The point Derrida raises is, How do we know this is death as such? How can we be certain that the death toward which Heidegger wishes us to comport ourselves is really the authentic understanding of death as such? Jacques Derrida, *Aporias*, trans. Thomas Dutoit (Stanford: Stanford University Press, 1993).

It is for this reason that I think we should understand Heidegger's analysis of death, against his own intentions, as a negative image of Kant's "proof" of the immortality of the soul: it is a postulate of practical reason. "By a postulate of pure practical reason, I understand a theoretical proposition which is not as such demonstrable, but which is an inseparable corollary of an a priori unconditionally valid practical law." Immanuel Kant, *Critique of Practical Reason*, trans. Lewis White Beck (New York: Macmillan, 1988), 127 (A220).

intersection of being and nothingness in Dasein is possibility.[35] Dasein is essentially possibility. We have already run into this earlier, but the analysis of death confirms what was said earlier. The sort of anticipatory care peculiar to *phronēsis* discloses to Dasein the nullity that lies in its own being.

Death is Heidegger's entree into the temporality peculiar to Dasein. There are three senses in which death indicates time. The first is that mortality indicates that time discriminates between the object of *sophia* and that of *phronēsis;* Dasein's mortality means that it belongs to time. The second is that Dasein's proper mortality points to Dasein's essence as being-possible. As it enacts a possibility, Dasein moves. This movement is the origin of time as a causal chain. Neither of these, however, covers any new ground. We are quite used to saying that humans exist temporally, that they exist from birth to death. We are also used to believing (only a few philosophers believe otherwise) that we are free to a certain extent and our actions cause a series of events to follow, but our present actions cannot change the past because time is unidirectional. This unidirectionality of a series of now-points is what Heidegger believes unites the tradition's understanding of time. Heidegger rejects that. He believes that death properly understood points to a sort of temporal existence unique to Dasein.[36]

Death is the "not yet" that "already is." Being-toward-death, the proper being of *phronēsis,* understands death in this way. *Phronēsis* has action as its object; it acts as it understands. Being-toward-death is itself the proper action of Dasein. As peculiar (or morbid) as that sounds, there is a good reason why this is so. By distinguishing between various understandings of "end," Heidegger is really distinguishing between possible ways of being-toward-the-end or *telos.* The two I identified earlier were the "technical" and "phronetic." These distinguish two different types of action, this in the broadest sense of being-in-the-world. To each belongs its peculiar understanding of time, which can be most clearly seen in how each regards an "end." *Technē* regards the "end" as *ergon* or work, the finished product; when the end is reached or the *telos* fulfilled, the action ceases. As Heidegger says following Aristotle, the end lies outside the action proper

---

35. Heidegger more than likely draws this understanding of possibility from Aristotle's discussion of potentiality in *Metaphysics* 1050b10.

36. It should be understood that Heidegger comes close to attributing to human existence that creation of time Christians reserve for God. The following analysis owes a great deal to Thomas Sheehan, "How (Not) to Read Heidegger," *American Catholic Philosophical Quarterly* 69, no. 2 (1995): 275–94.

(*GA19*, 41–42). *Phronēsis,* on the other hand, regards the end as inherent in action itself; at each "moment" of the action the end is already (*GA19*, 149). The *telos* of action is nothing other than action itself. Heidegger is following Aristotle's distinction found in *Metaphysics* 1048b 22–34, where Aristotle distinguishes between imperfect action and perfect or proper action. Aristotle's examples of imperfect action are building a house and losing weight. In both instances, the action is brought to a close when the end is achieved. We can distinguish grammatically the present tense, "I am building a house now" from the past tense, "I have built a house." His example of perfect action is seeing. In seeing, the two tenses merge, so to speak; in "seeing" something, I "have seen" something. This is a perfect action because the end, in this case having seen an object, does not bring the action itself to a halt, but persists in the action so long as the action continues. *Phronēsis* has action proper as its object. One can see how Heidegger models being-toward-death on action proper. The understanding of being-toward-death proper to *phronēsis* understands death, the end of Dasein, not as fulfillment of life, but as continuously inhering in the action itself. In being-toward-death, Dasein "is" as "having (already) been." This "having been" should not be understood as a past event, but as an already operative being, in Dasein's case, mortal. But Dasein is being-toward-death only anticipatorily; it runs ahead to its "not yet." In running ahead to its authentic "not yet," it "is" as "having been." This constitutes the temporality proper to Dasein. Because Dasein's temporalizing is the same as perfect action, Heidegger calls Dasein "authentic *praxis,*" which makes *phronēsis* the proper way of uncovering its being (*GA19*, 146; *MFL*, 183). Dasein exhibits the authentic unity of the three ecstases of time, the unity of past, present, and future. This unity of time that Dasein is precedes its division into the three ecstases, the point being that Dasein does not move within a flow of time between past, present, and future, but rather is the unity and direction of the flow of time itself. Being mortal does not merely mean that Dasein is finite or passes away like all things on this earth, but that it discovers an originary time proper to itself.

Dasein is thus not "in" time, but "as" time (*CT*, 20). Action proper temporalizes itself toward both the future and the past and unites them in the present as it acts. The "present" is not a now-point on some continuum, but the whole of the "stretching" between beginning and end. This is the temporality proper to human being which is exhibited in being-toward-death. It might be called "ontological" temporality. When one has secured one's being-toward-death, which means being-possible and being authentically temporal, one enters onto the authentic "how" of human existence which guides action in the world (*CT,* 12).

To briefly sum up the major points of the previous section, *phronēsis* is the authentic way of understanding Dasein because it grasps the being of Dasein as something that can be otherwise and is thus possibility. Possibility must be understood as the possibility of being one way or another, as if there is a moment in which we stand at a crossroads between paths that lead in different directions. To enact a possibility means to take one of the paths, to go off in a certain direction. The enactment of a possibility is thus the origin of meaning because in enacting a possibility we take a path that leads in a certain direction, which is the sense-giving directive, the way of the clearing in which we can encounter beings in their being. From this understanding of meaning as end or goal (*telos*) toward which the path as a whole leads comes the priority Heidegger assigns to the future among the three ecstases of time because humans are always "out toward" the end in anticipation. To say that humans are goal-oriented is as much to say that they are oriented to the future. Since goal-oriented behavior is characteristic of action or work, this aspect of Dasein as the enactment of a possibility is the final reason why Heidegger thought *phronēsis* to be the authentic way of understanding humans. Heidegger's understanding of being and time is oriented by the centrality of action, which he takes as the enactment of a possibility. The enactment of a possibility when one stands at the crossroads is what Heidegger called the resolution (*Entschluß*) in the moment of vision. *Phronēsis* lays bare the possibilities of one's given situation and so opens up a space for resolving upon one of those possibilities and so taking up a determinate direction that gives meaning to existence. As authentic action, the "moment of vision" temporalizes itself toward the future as the birth of history.

The Moment of Vision

Because it has action as its object, *phronēsis* uncovers the concrete situation in which action can act. *Phronēsis* cannot, however, be understood as a bare "seeing" of some situation; because it ends in action, its peculiar mode of uncovering is "right deliberation," that in deciding for one path or another, acts (*GA19,* 149). Deliberation uncovers the specific (*jeweilig*) possibilities of being in any given situation. It reveals these possibilities as the "facts of the case" according to which Dasein acts (*GA19,* 158). There are two levels involved in this uncovering of possibilities of being. One is the ontological, which we have covered; Dasein uncovers its being mortal and the temporality specific to it. It also uncovers the specific facts of the here and now which make up the situation. *Phronēsis* discloses both meanings of being, being as possibility and being as the specific here and now, the latter in terms of the former, that is, *phronēsis* discloses the concrete world in terms of the finite temporalizing that belongs to authentic Dasein. In this way Dasein comes to a "distinct and authentic disclosedness" (*BT*, 343). This disclosure is *bouleusthai,* deliberating, which comes to a close in a decision or resolution (*Entschluß*): "The Greek uncovering of the full situation ends in the authentic resolvedness to [*Entschlossenheit zu*] . . . in the taking-hold-of itself" (*GA19,* 150).[37] In *Being and Time,* resolution is similarly understood as *"precisely the disclosive projection and determination of what is tactically possible at the time"* (*BT*, 345). Resolution is thus the end movement of *phronēsis,* which as a type of speech, discloses or sketches a world. Because *phronēsis* as being-toward-death is the authentic way of disclosing, resolution is the enactment of authentic understanding.

Although it is not a bare seeing (*theōria*), *phronēsis* is a sort of "seeing" of the facts of the specific seeing, which Heidegger calls *aisthēsis,* "perception" (*GA19,* 160). Aisthēsis perceives the specifics of the case. The term Heidegger uses for "specific" is *jeweilig* or *jeweils,* which literally means "in each while," "at each time." The specificity has an explicit temporal character; it sees the "here and now." *Phronēsis* is the "beholding of the this-time" (*GA19,* 164). Heidegger continues, excitedly summarizing his analysis of *phronēsis* in a flourish: *"It is as* aisthēsis, *the glance of the*

---

37. I hyphenated "taking-hold-of" to indicate that the phrase does not mean take hold of oneself; the "itself" refers to the whole phrase (*im Zugreifen selbst*). Even here Heidegger uses "resolution" (*Entschluß*) interchangeably with "resolvedness" (*Entschlossenheit*). He continues this free and sloppy use in *Being and Time.* I will generally use "resolution" because the emphasis should be on the action, not on the psychological disposition of the actor. Heidegger warns us not to understand "resolvedness" psychologically, but this term strongly lends itself to this interpretation. Not the least of the unfortunate consequences is that Heidegger was understood (by Löwith among others) to mean that authenticity meant firm conviction; to paraphrase Nietzsche, a strong conviction hallowed any cause.

I believe Heidegger fell victim to a habit of his philosophical language. He often centers his discussion, in true philosophical manner, on the nature of the object of inquiry; we have encountered this most notably in his discussion of "worldhood" as a way of talking about the world. In the case of "resolvedness," resolvedness would be the nature of resolve. It so happens, however, that "resoluteness" is a normal word, unlike many other words which have the suffixes -ness or -hood attached to them. I think Heidegger wants to talk about the nature of a resolution, and for this reason uses the term "resoluteness."

eye, the moment of vision onto the specifically concrete that as such can always be otherwise" (*GA19*, 164).[38] *Phronēsis* is *der Augenblick*, the moment of vision (PIA, 381). It beholds the full situation, the full "there" of being (*BT*, 346). The moment of vision catches sight of and secures into truthful safekeeping the *archē* and *telos*, the "whence" and "for-the-sake-of-which" for that being whose *archē* and *telos* "can be otherwise" (PIA, 381–82). It understands the world it discloses temporally.

This disclosing of the world described in a "moment of vision" has a peculiar temporal character. First of all, as the beholding of the "here and now," it grasps that what is here and now can be otherwise, that it can change, because Dasein is essentially possibility. This means that there is a limit common both to resolution in general and the philosophy that uncovers the phenomenon of resolution. Among the facts of the situation which are discovered is the specific being of Dasein, which does not change, and so allows an "existential definiteness," whereas the specific worldly facts can change, meaning that there is an "existentiell indefiniteness" (*BT*, 345). In order to preserve both moments of resolution, the definite and indefinite, Heidegger devised the method of formal indications, which allows him to specify structures of Dasein which can enact themselves differently at different times. That is why Heidegger warns that the question of what Dasein resolves upon can only be answered in the resolution itself (*BT*, 345). Philosophy cannot give answers for all time, but must let each time come to its own answers. Only the actual resolution grounds an authentic ethics. This particular ethos goes back, if we recall, to his rejection of the system of Catholicism, which would impose through dictate and in the end police power an alien ethical system. It was alien because it denied the historical nature specific to ethics and human existence in general. Resolution overcomes this problem because the ultimate "for-the-sake-of-which" is immanent to the action which it guides. Resolution maintains the historicity of action from the other end by keeping in mind that the *archē* can be oth-

---

38. "*Sie ist als* aisthesis *der Blick des Auges, der Augenblick auf das jeweils Konkrete, das als solches immer anders sein kann.*" Missing in my English rendition is the connection between "*Blick des Auges*" and "*Augenblick.*" Curiously in her new translation, Joan Stambaugh translates *Augenblick* as "moment" in order to, as she says in the introduction, eliminate the mystical connotations in Macquarrie and Robinson's "moment-of-vision." Joan Stambaugh, translator's preface to *Being and Time*, by Martin Heidegger (Albany: SUNY Press, 1996), xvi. This is particularly curious because unlike the latter two, Stambaugh has access to this passage in the 1924/5 lecture, and so could have seen the emphasis Heidegger places upon the visionary aspect of the insight into the situation.

erwise, that resolvedness can resolve itself differently in different situations. In grasping the full meaning of the situation, resolution upholds the historical nature of action.

The second temporal aspect of the moment of vision concerns the "how" implied in the term. *Augenblick* is the "blink" of the eye, an instantaneous vision of the whole. Heidegger seems to have taken this understanding from Kierkegaard's use of *Augenblick* to translate the Greek *exaiphnes* in Plato as the "sudden" or the "instant."[39] The moment of vision is sudden in two ways: it is instantaneous and unexpected. It flashes up unawares, "like a thief in the night." Heidegger had cited this passage from 1 Thessalonians in his phenomenology of religion to show Paul's understanding of the temporality specific to Christianity. The "day of the Lord," that is to say, the "lighting" which grants vision to humans in this world comes unexpectedly; it is vain to predict it. Time is kairological. It occurs suddenly without reason. It "breaks into" the normal course of events and initiates a new time. Because a resolution discloses a world, the "it" that "breaks into" existence is the world itself. In/through this breaking in of the world the world "worlds," to recall the term Heidegger used in 1919. It is the happening of the world, the *Ereignis* of being as being "there," the "lightning flash" of being which steers the whole.[40] The moment of vision is an ecstatic glimpse, an epiphany. It is revelation.

This revelation in the moment of vision is, it should be remembered, *phronēsis*, practical wisdom. We have been concentrating up until now on distinguishing between systematic ethics and Heidegger's own attempts to circumvent the alienating problems of systematic ethics by reappropriat-

---

39. Heidegger himself cites Kierkegaard as the forerunner to this conception of the moment (*GA29/30*, 225; also his own explanation in *GA60*, 150–51). There he ties together *der Augenblick* with *kairos*. See also Otto Pöggeler, "Destruction and Moment," in *Reading Heidegger From the Start*, ed. Theodore Kisiel and John van Buren (Albany: SUNY Press, 1994). Krell claims that this understanding of time has its source in Aristotle's conception of change (*metabolē*) as presented in *Physics* 4.10–14. David Farrell Krell, *Intimations of Mortality* (University Park: Pennsylvania State University Press, 1986), 49–50. While this passage is consistent with Heidegger's understanding of time, I believe a more likely source is Augustine's notion of the creation, particularly of the new order of being created by the appearance (*parousia*) of Christ.

40. Heidegger had this last phrase of Heraclitus carved above the door of his mountain cabin. Toward the end of his essay, "The Turn," Heidegger writes, "The in-turning that is the lightning-flash of the truth of being is the entering flashing glance—insight [*Einblick*]. . . . In-flashing is the disclosing eventing [*Ereignis*] within being itself" (T, 45). "Insight" is one translation Heidegger offers for *phronēsis*.

ing Aristotle in a non-Thomistic fashion. Aristotle provided an ethical thinking that emphasized the situational, fluid character of ethics and politics and the concomitant necessary "lack" of absolute determinability of genuine ethical living. This sort of thinking would thus run counter to the Kantian determination of ethics as the application of the categorical imperative, operative at all times under all circumstances for rational beings. Indeed, Heidegger's lectures on Aristotle inspired a rebirth in Aristotelian ethics in German philosophy.[41] However, Heidegger's appropriation of Aristotle also provides a basis for comparing Heidegger with Aristotle. As is always necessary in examining Heidegger's interpretations, one must forswear simply declaring Heidegger's interpretations wayward for danger of missing the point. Heidegger was well aware that he was not presenting Aristotle exactly as Aristotle presented himself; he spends a considerable part of his analysis of book 6 explicitly trying to show that Aristotle did not stay true to his best insight. The point here is not to show that Heidegger was a poor interpreter of Aristotle, but rather to show the direction in which his reading leads in thinking about ethics.

When we say that someone has "practical wisdom" or is "prudent," we mean that the person has practical know-how, that they know their way around the world. The specific traits we attribute to practical wisdom indicate their Aristotelian roots. Practical wisdom is not theoretical knowledge; thus the figure of absent-minded professors, brilliant in their sphere of knowledge but utterly lacking in common sense about everyday details of living in the "real world." Practical wisdom is prudence, a grasp of when it is necessary to back down in a particular situation, to bend the rules as the facts of the case may indicate, to know, for instance, when honesty is not necessarily the best policy. Practical wisdom is flexible, cognizant that not everything can be subsumed under rules, cognizant that the good toward which action aims may require making exceptions. Nontheoretical, flexible, open to the specificity of the situation: these traits of our understanding of practical wisdom are the same as in Aristotle.

There is a clear sense in which Heidegger's view is similar. The resolution in the moment of vision is not theoretical in nature, it recognizes that

---

41. Particularly through Gadamer. In *The Idea of the Good in Platonic-Aristotelian Philosophy* and *Truth and Method* Gadamer develops a practical philosophy based in *phronēsis* opposed to a "technical" understanding of the good. Hans-Georg Gadamer, *The Idea of the Good in Platonic-Aristotelian Philosophy*, trans. P. Christopher Smith (New Haven: Yale University Press, 1986); idem, *Truth and Method*.

things can be otherwise, and it grasps the facts of the situation in its resolve. Resolution grasps the *telos* of action, which is to say, the end or purpose which is the good (*GA19,* 156). Heidegger's view here is similar to Aristotle's. The distinction between them lies in the nature of the moment of vision as revelation. The common understanding of practical wisdom is closely connected with experience, for it is experience that allows us to better recognize when and how to properly negotiate a particular situation. It is for this reason that adults govern in human society rather than children.[42] Aristotle emphasizes this point on several occasions when discussing practical wisdom: "There is also confirmation of what we have said in the fact that although the young develop ability in geometry and mathematics and become wise in such matters, they are not thought to develop prudence. The reason for this is that prudence also involves knowledge of particular facts, which become known from experience; and a young man is not experienced, because experience takes some time to acquire."[43] Experience is necessary to practical know-how. Experience is built up over time; we accumulate experience, and this accumulated knowledge enables us to make more precise distinctions in particulars.[44]

Whatever its other similarities to Aristotle, Heidegger's instantaneous lightning flash in which all becomes clear is definitely not accumulated experience. In fact, it overturns accumulated knowledge, which is built up on our everyday dispersion in its involvements in the world (*BT,* 441). Knowledge accumulates as it works within a paradigm that is accepted as self-evident by scholars and scientists, but at certain rare junctures in his-

42. We are familiar with distinguishing between thinking characteristic of children and adolescents and that of adults, although adults can act "childishly." When we think of typically "adolescent" thinking, we think of willfully maintaining one's opinion of right and wrong, of making absolute distinctions. As we acquire experience, our thinking "matures," so that we gain an insight into the alterability of the world. I recognize there is a counter-movement prevalent in our society that indeed holds the "childlike," synonymous with innocence and purity, as a standard against cynicism, which is always a possibility of maturation. This "childlike" quality is often connected with idealism. If I were to speak cynically, much of what we read in praise of the "childlike" is in fact the expression of cynical adults who look wistfully back at the time when they still believed in something as "silly" as ideals and the good.

43. Aristotle, *Nicomachean Ethics* (trans. Thomson) 1142a12.

44. For this reason Plato, quite like Aristotle, recommended that dialectics, the art of right distinguishing, be the last stage of education, suitable only for those over the age of fifty. This point is often lost on critics of the philosopher-king, who see Plato advocating the rule of a philosophical system, rather than practical wisdom. Gadamer's *The Idea of the Good in Platonic-Aristotelian Philosophy* is a useful corrective to this error.

tory a paradigm collapses and this same community shifts to a new paradigm. To use a distinction made famous by Thomas Kuhn, there are two kinds of science: normal science, which is the steady accumulation and extension of a paradigm, and revolutionary science, which is a sharp break from one paradigm to another. Almost forty years before Kuhn's book, Heidegger was articulating the same idea, but rather than focusing on paradigms of science, Heidegger was looking at shifts in the understanding of being which form epochs of being. The *Destruktion* of the metaphysical tradition was intended to reopen the question of being in all its questionableness by showing that the understanding of being that guides contemporary philosophy and by extension science is not self-evident. Only by this path would it be possible to enter into new understandings of being; the possibility that being has possibilities opens only when being becomes questionable, capable of taking on new answers, new paths, new worlds, new meanings. This is why Heidegger considers genuine thinking "a thinking that breaks the paths and opens the perspectives of the knowledge that sets the norms and hierarchies" (*IM*, 10). Genuine thinking is revolutionary.

The comparison with Kuhn makes manifest another deviation of Heidegger's understanding of *phronēsis* from the Aristotelian model: its rarity. The moment of vision is rare in two respects: first, that it occurs infrequently, and second, that it occurs only to a few (*IM*, 133). The rarity of its occurrence is based on its global nature: the birth of entirely new worlds, with new gods and new ways of grasping the direction of history, is a rare occurrence in human life. Although this rare occurrence of being alters worlds for a whole people, Heidegger believed that it occurs only to the few who thus become the leaders of a community founded upon this revelation of being (*GA39*, 99–100).[45] Because Aristotle believed that phronēsis accompanies all action, whether magnificent or menial, he does not draw such a vast distinction between grades of action, and although he does regard some people as more excellent in practical wisdom than others, Pericles for example, this excellence can be taught through experience because it lies in the nature of practical matters that general principles hold for most cases and situations. Although phronēsis is neither technical skill nor scientific knowledge, for Aristotle, experience gained in the course of practical life allows one to discern what must be done in any

---

45. I will discuss leaders in more detail in Chapter 5.

particular situation; each situation is a necessary combination of the particular and the universal.[46] For Heidegger, on the other hand, the situation is wholly singular: there is no connection between different situations, and so no knowledge that could pertain to any situation.

Invoking Pericles at this juncture is apropos because this revolution in the understanding of being has a manifestly political character. Revolutionary thinking is *phronēsis,* which is to say, action-guiding thinking. *Phronēsis* illuminates the ends toward which action aims as it enacts them. The end that it illuminates is the ultimate "for-the-sake-of-which," for action the good, which makes up the world as the connection of significance in which we move. The world is the "how" of being or the "there" of being, Da-sein; *phronēsis* illuminates the "there" of being as the ultimate end for the sake of which it acts. For *phronēsis,* the good and the particular "there" of being are identical. The *polis,* authentically understood, "is neither merely state, nor merely city, rather beforehand and really 'the site': the sites of the human historical stay of man in the midst of beings" (*GA53,* 101). In this site, this clearing of being, are "all of the relations of man to gods, to things, and to each other determined" (*GA53,* 102). A revolution in our understanding of being is also supposed to be a revolution in our politics, which involves a simultaneous revolution in understandings of the political and in concrete regime types which correspond to respective understandings of the political.[47] One should therefore never underestimate Heidegger's political intentions. Although it may often appear that he is engaged in some scholastic exercise concerning a highly abstract philosophical problematic, he himself believes his own commitment to thinking is the path to genuine political change because such a change is possible only on the basis of a change in being.[48] Viewed from

46. Gadamer points out that for Aristotle, correct political judgment can only be exercised by one who is a member of the polity, for only one who belongs to a polity can discern what is appropriate. This knowledge comes from accumulated experience gleaned through daily life of practical affairs. Gadamer wants to use this idea to uphold his notion that practical wisdom is embedded within a tradition, that is, that practical wisdom looks to the past for guidance. This is quite the opposite of Heidegger's future-oriented vision. Gadamer, "Die Idee der praktischen Philosophie," 241.

47. Also see Michael Gillespie, *Hegel, Heidegger, and the Ground of History* (Chicago: University of Chicago Press, 1984), 138.

48. He claimed after the war that his commitment to Nazism was guided by his long-held desire to reform the universities, as if he were some mere educational reformer. The truly radical nature of his aims can be seen only when one recognizes that he believes this reformation is possible only on the basis of new basic experience of being. Cf. *GA39,* 195–96.

the other perspective, a change in being will certainly mean a change in politics because being concerns being as a whole, our relationships to everything as well as each other, which certainly includes political relationships. *Phronēsis*, being the enacting in the world of a change in being, ties together the metaphysical and political aspects of revolutionary thinking.

Heidegger's radical revision of *phronēsis* led him to embrace radical politics. Because *phronēsis* illuminates being as a whole to the final and ultimate grounds of human existence, genuine political action will itself be the revelation of a new experience of being, and only such an ultimate experience of the whole of being can count as genuine politics. Thus, rather than valuing political leaders experienced in the necessary limitations of politics, Heidegger wants above all a leader who will change the whole metaphysical structure of Western society, for a genuine political leader is one who initiates a revolution in being. This demand for radical revolutions and abjuration of half-hearted measures led Heidegger directly to Hitler. One cannot truly recognize the philosophical extent of Heidegger's relation to Nazism without understanding how his revision of *phronēsis,* so central to his philosophy, demanded the most radical and extreme political action.[49]

One can see evidence for the political consequences of Heidegger's revision of *phronēsis* by comparing his radical revolutionary understanding to a passage in Aristotle's *Nicomachean Ethics*. Toward the end of book 6, Aristotle distinguishes genuine *phronēsis* from a closely related faculty he calls *deinotes,* or cleverness. Because cleverness is the ability to have insight in a particular situation, *phronēsis* implies cleverness, but is not identical to it. The difference is that cleverness can be used to either noble or ignoble ends, whereas *phronēsis* aims only at noble ends. There can be clever tyrants, but no tyrant can be truly phronetic. Aristotle concludes thus that "one cannot be prudent without being good."[50] *Phronēsis* is limited by the good. The merely clever person, on the other hand, is capable of anything. It is no accident that when Gadamer interprets this passage, he translates *deinos* as "uncanny," for he had before him Heidegger's famous translation of "human being" as *ton deinotaton,* the most uncanny being (*IM,* 149).[51] Gadamer's translation underlines the very different direction

49. I will cover Heidegger's connection to Nazism and Hitler more fully in Chapters 4 and 5.
50. Aristotle, *Ethics* 1144a30.
51. Gadamer, *Truth and Method,* 323–24.

Heidegger takes *phronēsis*, for in Heidegger's famous interpretation of the first chorus from Sophocles' *Antigone*, humans are *deinon* insofar as they become "pre-eminent in historical being as creators, as men of action" (*IM*, 152). These men of action create the structure and order that is the polis; the one who is uncanny carries out the revolutionary political action (*IM*, 152–53). In a Nietzschean vein, Heidegger insists that this revolutionary world-building activity makes the founders of states *apolis*, "without statute and limit," that is to say, beyond good and evil (*IM*, 152–53). Heidegger lifts and poetically amplifies Aristotle's understanding of *deinotes,* but in stark contrast to Aristotle, makes it identical to *phronēsis. Phronēsis* could not be revolutionary thinking if it were not without statute and limit, and it is precisely this unlimited characteristic that makes Heidegger's refashioning of *phronēsis* appropriate to a being for whom possibility is higher than actuality and consequently who is always oriented toward the future.

This revolutionary characterization of authentic thinking carries over into Heidegger's understanding of historical time. The path-breaking instant occurs as the event (*Ereignis*) of being. This path-breaking shift makes time discontinuous, that is to say, kairological. The "times" it forms are distinct epochs of being there. Heidegger contrasts this authentic sense of history with that of historicism or historiography. In this latter science, time is understood as homogenous, flat. This homogeneity allows historical science to be predictive along the model of the natural sciences, where the end is theoretically secured knowledge. The examples of this unfortunate Platonizing of history Heidegger brings forth are Windelband, Weber, and Spengler. In each case, historical epochs are typified so they can be formed into some sort of catalog of types; in Spengler's case, the types are arranged chronologically so that it is possible to predict the type toward which we are aiming (*GA60*, 394). This attempt to turn history into a science (*epistēmē*) blocks off our authentic relationship to historical time. We need to understand that history is not universal progress, but discontinuous breaks, that it is and consists in being broken up by revelations of being in the moment of vision, which temporalize themselves by uniting the past, present, and future as the "fate" toward which we tend.[52]

This concept of historical time clearly manifests the connection between the finitude of time and the origin of meaning. Time is "created" in the

---

52. History is temporalized along the same model that *phronēsis* temporalizes itself; the "fate" toward which we aim is in fact equivalent to death or the nothing which lies ever present in human life.

enactment of a possibility in the resolution, that is to say the sketch of being that is the meaning of being specific to the enactment provides the measure of time. The measure of time, as a measure, derives from the direction given by the enactment, that is to say, that it is directed toward an end. Having an end, time is finite (*endlich*). This finitude gives shape and form to historical time so that time appears as meaningful, a period of history determined by a paradigm, to use a Kuhnian expression. Only through the finitude of time can we recognize historical epochs, such as Western metaphysics, for epochs are the particular shape or measure of historical being. Each epoch is a specific revelation of being. Time is thus the horizon of being in two senses which correspond to the two senses of the meaning of being: time is the horizon of being in that being as possibility implies the historicity of being, that it can be otherwise and is subject to radical shifts in meaning, and finite time is the horizon of a specific enactment of being as a determinate and thus finite "there," which is the meaning of any particular epoch of being. The first is a "time" which is immeasurable and yet opens up a clearing for every measure—Heidegger's new understanding of the eternal, not in time, but not the unchanging—while the second is just that measure of time which is opened up.[53]

Every epoch and every new revelation of being is a response to the question of being, through which the null point of the crossroads of possibilities is reached; in terms of time, it is how humans open themselves to the eternal. To return to this crossroads of the question of being is what Heidegger calls repetition. Repetition is not by any means imitation in the sense of imitating the answer to the question of being of some past people, but of repeating the "how" of their questioning which begot the answers: "Only the 'how' can be repeated" (*CT*, 19).[54] It is only by repeating the "how" of past thinking, which means to repeat the course of *phronēsis* which is the thinking of being which can authentically temporalize

---

53. At this point I think Krell is correct in connecting change in the most general sense with the "instantaneous," which traditionally was held to be outside the time-series as such. Krell, *Intimations of Mortality*, 49.

54. Despite the fact that Heidegger consistently maintained that to go back to the Greeks does not mean to imitate their way of life, he is sometimes accused of this very thing. Bernasconi correctly points out that repetition and the tradition which it retrieves is grounded in the future, and so is at most a creative appropriation of history, along the lines of the sort of active historical interpretation Nietzsche commends in "On the Uses and Disadvantages of History for Life." Robert Bernasconi, "Repetition and Tradition: Heidegger's Destructuring of the Distinction Between Essence and Existence in *Basic Problems of Phenomenology*," in *Reading Heidegger from the Start*, ed. Theodore Kisiel and John van Buren (Albany: SUNY Press, 1994), 135.

itself, that I can discover our my time and situation as my fate. This sense of the necessity for repetition grew out of his break with the system of Catholicism that came to a head with the proclamation of Aquinas as the sole dogmatic authority for the Church. To recall, Heidegger believed that this proclamation confronted contemporary Catholics as an alien doctrine because it did not grow out of their own questioning, whereas for Aquinas and his contemporaries it held genuine meaning because it did grow out of theirs. The only way for twentieth-century Catholics to live with an authentic worldview was to repeat Aquinas's own questioning, his own quest for the meaning of existence; not the answers, but the questions. Only through recognizing the historical nature of existence and the source of genuine meaning can humans live genuinely ethically, which means to dwell in the abode of being (LH, 233). Repetition means to repeat essential possibilities of the past, which means to open ourselves for a new revelation of being which historicizes itself as the *kairos,* our situation.

The phronetic, kairological conception of being and time in *Being and Time* marks the maturation of the path of questioning set off by Heidegger's religious crisis during the final years of the First World War. His conception of historical action in the world fills out his early insight into the connection between meaning and history which is necessary to generate unalienated ethical living. Authentic religiosity as the path toward an unalienated existence metamorphosed into an analysis of practical wisdom as the way to authentically understand the being proper to humans. *Phronēsis* makes the end of action immanent in the action itself, and thus authentically connecting ideals and action. Unlike Aristotle, however, Heidegger understood practical wisdom through Christian categories that twist *phronēsis* into a revelation of being as a whole which breaks up the flat homogeneity of normal time. By understanding action as the free revelation of being, Heidegger understood the "how" of authentically being human, authentic action, in terms of the "how" of authentic religiosity, particularly, as we will now see in the next chapter, as fathomed in radical Lutheranism informed by a reading of German mysticism.

That religious "factical ideal" that motivates Heidegger's philosophy is summed up by his concept of authenticity. Authenticity means: to be true to oneself in the face of entanglements that lead one astray. By being lured into entanglements, the self becomes inauthentic and alienated from its true self. What this means concretely depends upon the conception of the self and the nature of the temptations. Heidegger's understanding of the authentic life grew out of his concerns to renew a genuine religiosity. He conceptualized inauthenticity as the alienation of the self from God, which is at the same time the loss of the unity of feeling and intuition that Heidegger hoped to recover through phenomenology; because it is alienated from God, the self is alienated from being integrated into the world. The first step upon the path to authenticity thus lies in discovering a divine region radically different than the one disclosed by theory and science. *Phronēsis* was to provide a path to this historical and antinomian God. The next step is describing the character of the integrated self given in the moment of vision.

His understanding of alienation and authenticity received its decisive bearing from Luther and German mysticism. Both Luther and mysticism in general are distinguished by their emphasis on inwardness (*Innerlichkeit*) as the path toward salvation and a genuinely ethical life. Inwardness can be understood as an ethics because it protects the purity of the soul from entanglements in the world; virtue comes to be understood as purity. The presumed coincidence of inwardness and ethical purity had a particularly profound impact on German religiosity in the wake of Luther's inward turn toward faith that constituted the freedom of a Christian. Whatever the political possibilities that can be discovered in this freedom, certainly one central reading has been to construe genuine religiosity as an inward turn to a care for the self that leads to an ethics of integrity and purity that itself coincides with an extreme individualism and renunciation of the compromises of politics. The ethics of religiosity have thus been taken to mean a renunciation of the public sphere and an inward turn toward care of the soul and thus toward God.

Because Heidegger understood authenticity as religiosity, his ethics of authenticity seems to replicate this traditional understanding of the opposition between religiosity and worldly entanglements. Authenticity means a care for the self in which the self pulled itself back together from out of the dispersions and disconnectedness of its involvements in its affairs in the world (*BT,* 441). Heidegger called how we become dispersed and thus alienated *das Man*. As first presented, *das Man* stands for the public sphere, and the manifold ways in which the public life corrupts Dasein's ownmost possibilities of existence. Because the self as lived by *das Man,* the "man-selbst," is opposed to the authentic self, being an authentic self, being genuinely religious, seems to be understood as withdrawal from the public sphere to one's authentic individual self. Authentic being-a-self seems to mean care for the inner self against the corruption of the self's dispersions into the public realm.

There is no doubt that for Heidegger, the ethics of authenticity as care of the self was substantially religious in character. However decisive Luther and mysticism were for his understanding of authenticity, though, he did not follow the traditional path of inwardness and purity through withdrawal from the world. First, for Heidegger, Dasein is constituted as being-in-the-world; authentically, Dasein is action in the world. Second, Dasein is constituted as being-with; there is no possible withdrawal from others because Dasein's own being is always only in and with others. Both factors weigh against the understanding of authenticity as inward purity. Even in its authentic existence, Dasein is being-with-others-in-the-world.

These factors and the questions they provoke require us to examine in more detail what it means to care for the self. In Chapter 1, I argued that Dasein's authenticity depended in the first instance upon correctly understanding its own being. For Dasein to be true to itself, it has to first understand its own being in the proper manner. From a proper understanding of its being, Dasein can then live in a manner appropriate to its own being. Heidegger's ethics thus depend upon his ontological project of raising the question of being. That ontology can be raised as an ethical project indicates how Heidegger treats authenticity as an ethical problem. Because Dasein can misunderstand its own being, it can be inauthentic.

Dasein's inauthenticity, then, must be understood as something like a false consciousness. As in other theories of false consciousness, Dasein is capable of living in this inverted world, thoughtlessly dwelling in this way of being without having an inkling that anything is out of the ordinary. Indeed, it is this very thoughtlessness that is the root of the inversion of human existence, for the thoughtlessness refers to the forgetting of the question of being. Only through posing the question of being is human existence exposed to the meaning of being, and so able to dwell authentically in the world. By failing to raise the question of being, Dasein loses itself in its inverted world. This loss of the self is understood as alienation, alienation from being. For Heidegger, inauthenticity is understood as alienation of the self from being and thus from its true self.

The famous rubric Heidegger ascribes to this alienating understanding of being is *das Man*. The chapter on *das Man* makes up one of the rhetorical high points in *Being and Time*. In the midst of difficult and often murky analyses of existential categories, it has a rapier thrust of directness into the falseness and alienation of our everyday social existence which captured the imagination of many in Heidegger's own day and continues to do so even in our own time. It is so straightforward and comprehensible that even the casual reader could hardly miss the point. In German, *das Man* literally means "one," the third-person singular impersonal pronoun. Living under the domination of *das Man*, Dasein is alienated into this flat, meaningless world. Heidegger speaks of the "dictatorship" of *das Man*, how its nearly absolute dominion levels and flattens Dasein. It is hard not to be moved by Heidegger's rhetorical flourish or not to be frightened by the picture of our existence he paints in such stark colors.

For this reason, *das Man* was—justly—taken as a critique of modern mass society. Just though this reception may be, it does not exhaust the manifold meanings and roles Heidegger assigned to *das Man*. *Das Man* is not just mass society, but it becomes an all-encompassing blanket term for our false understanding of being, which means that it stands opposed in each case to each authentic understanding of phenomenon, since this understanding reaches into every segment of our being. In many instances, it is difficult to see the connections between the various phenomena. The way past this seemingly random grouping of phenomena is to see *das Man* primarily as an inauthentic disclosure of being in which Dasein is dispersed and alienated into the world. Included in this way of disclosure are theory and science, public opinion (in modern mass societies), capitalism, common sense, curiosity, everydayness, and tradition. What each of these have in common is that they tranquilize Dasein into forgetting the question of being. *Das Man* is the symbol of alienation because in its various manifestations it closes off Dasein from the question of being.

Heidegger more generally called this alienation from the question of being "fallenness," which he understood as being absorbed into the world. In being absorbed into the world, Dasein busies itself with individual beings and forgets the question of being, which is the question of the meaning of the whole. Dasein can be true to its self only when it clears away the concealments and obscurities of its fallen absorption and is directed toward the meaning of the whole. Dasein is directed toward the meaning of the whole through *phronēsis,* the moment of vision in which the meaning of being is revealed in a sudden epiphany. In the resolution of the moment of vision, Dasein clears away its self-concealments, recovers from its fallen alienation, and is liberated.

As I showed in the previous chapter, Heidegger understood *phronēsis* in a far more radical manner than did Aristotle. I ascribed this radicality to the fact that Heidegger carried into his interpretation of *phronēsis* Christian categories of an authentic life. This impression is further underscored by construing liberation as the clearing away of Dasein's fallen condition caused by its absorption into the world of particular beings and its turning away from the meaning of the whole. This does not describe Aristotle; it describes Augustine and the whole Western tradition that grew up around Augustine's path to God. By turning away from the secular realm—signified by vanity, pride, and curiosity—and toward God, the pious person could open himself to the possibility of divine illumination and in some traditions, for a mystical union with God.

By this curious twist, Heidegger's understanding of the authentic self thus bears astonishing structural similarities to some Christian understandings of being a self. In particular, the parallels between Meister Eckhart's mysticism and Heidegger's authenticity are striking. As I pointed out in the previous chapter, Heidegger had long been fascinated by mysticism as a kind of genuine religiosity; he invokes it in the conclusion of his *Habilitationschrift,* and Eckhart in particular became an important figure for Heidegger around the time of his crisis of faith during the First World War.

For Eckhart, humans possessed in their souls the possibility for union with God. For the most part, however, humans are blind and deaf to this capacity. This oblivion to God has its cause in our absorption into the world of particular beings; as Heidegger would echo centuries later, in our absorption into the world we lose sight of the whole. In order to realize the divine capacity in the soul, humans must practice what Eckhart called *Gelassenheit* or releasement, so that the soul could be *abgeschieden,* or detached. Both *Gelassenheit* and detachment signify our detachment from the world or particularity itself; we are released from our attachments to particular beings and freed for God. Heidegger similarly discussed ways of detaching oneself from beings in order to turn to being: among the most important are deconstructive thinking, *Gelassenheit,* and anxiety. Heidegger's analysis of anxiety most closely duplicates the effects of Eckhart's practices. Anxiety, however, must be considered as one moment in Heidegger's efforts to raise the question of being; thinking belongs to the whole structure of the experience. For Eckhart, the soul in its state of detachment becomes united with God and so God is revealed to the soul, a revelation Eckhart describes as the birth of the Son in the soul. This divine revelation gives the person the true meaning of his or her existence, which can serve as a guide in daily life. In Heidegger's thinking, humans are the site of being's revelation, a matter described in a felicitous manner as the "Dasein in man." The Dasein in man is the Heideggerian soul. In anxiety, the human being becomes free from its attachments and so free for the breaking in of being into the world of beings as the "there" of being; this is the moment of vision, the revelation of being, the "event" (*Ereignis*) of being, as Heidegger later called it. Humans are Dasein insofar as they are the "there" of being, Da-sein. In the moment of authenticity, being ecstatically reveals itself as the meaning of the world. To be an authentic self means to be at one with this revelation of being, to be at one with a meaning of existence that is enacted as a specific historical epoch.

Although the parallels between Heidegger and Eckhart are striking, there are important differences. If Heidegger's mysticism radicalizes as it appropriates Aristotle's notion of *phronēsis*, it is still *phronēsis*, which means it is action in the world. Heidegger's epiphany of being, in stark contrast to almost the whole of the Western religious tradition, is not contemplation; it does not merely behold the eternal order of the cosmos. In Heidegger's thought there is no eternal order; each revelation of being gives birth to a new historical epoch defined by its particular order and meaning of being. Although this understanding of time and order is taken from a Christian understanding of divine revelation, it stands in direct contrast with the contemplative tradition, which exercised a dominant hold on Western religiosity. For a Christian mystic, the highest moment of being is seeing God face to face in a beatific vision. For Heidegger, this highest moment is *phronēsis* understood as authentic action in the world. To be an authentic self is to be the site of a revolutionary revelation of being that acts by founding worlds.

The dominance of contemplation in the tradition forms the backdrop of the second important distinction between Heidegger and mystics such as Eckhart. Contemplation is a solitary activity that requires withdrawing from the ordinary affairs of the world, sometimes even withdrawing entirely from human company, which is just one more distraction from finding unity with God. Mysticism is characterized as inwardness and inner freedom. For Heidegger, however, Dasein is characterized by outwardness; Dasein is always being-in-the-world. More fully, Dasein is always being-in-the-world-with-others. Being-with is part of Heidegger's authentic religiosity.

Because being-with is essentially constitutive of Dasein, Heidegger opposes individualism. Being-with is understood as participation in the open space in which things appear as what they are. In this participation, Dasein shares this open space, this medium, with others. As such, being-with really means being-in-common. Being-in-common is the ground for an authentic community in which each Dasein is a part of the whole in which it shares. Far from constituting a withdrawal from the public sphere, authentic Dasein is communal. Being a self means to participate in the communal meaning of being; it means to be part of and serve the nation (*Volk*). I am who I am, I am myself, only through my participation in the communal event of being that is opened by the question of being.

Das Man and Alienation

Heidegger broaches the theme of *das Man* by answering the question of "who" Dasein is when it says "I am." To recall from earlier, in the familiar experiencing of the world, I do not just experience things in the world but also relate this experience back to myself; in all experiencing there is also the experience of "I am," my being taken with the experience of the world. For this reason, all understanding is also self-understanding (*CT*, 8). In understanding the world, I understand myself. Thus who I am is bound up with the revelation of the meaning of being in the resolute moment of vision.

Who am I? I am I. As straightforward as this answer may seem, for Heidegger it instead opened up a Pandora's box of difficulties. When I say "I am," is it really self-evident "who" I am? This is the point Heidegger raised against Descartes, that he never questioned the being of the entity that says "I am," but accepted as self-evident that it is "I" who says "I am." Heidegger wanted to probe behind this. Am I really who I think I am? "Perhaps when Dasein addresses itself in the way which is closest to itself, it always says, 'I am this entity,' and in the long run says this loudest when it is 'not' this entity. Dasein is in each case mine, and this is its constitution; but what if this should be the reason why, proximally and for the most part, Dasein *is not itself?*" (*BT*, 151). Although phrased as a question, Heidegger clearly suspected that Dasein does not understand itself proximally and for the most part authentically. Dasein can deceive itself. It can (and does for the most part) misunderstand itself and thus becomes alienated for itself. Far from being self-evident, the "I" is a formal indication, capable of taking up several possibilities (*BT*, 152). These possibilities are the same as the possible ways of interpreting the world (which are also formal indications). Finding the authentic "who" of the "I" is at the same time to find the way of understanding concordant with the being of Dasein (*BT*, 367–70). This accounts for why Heidegger turned to the involved discussion of *phronēsis* in order to provide the criteria for distinguishing which way of being a self is proper to Dasein. In other words, I must first secure *what* I am, my being, in order that I can authentically determine *who* I am.

The possibility that I can be something other than my authentic self and yet still be a self is how Heidegger understood the phenomenon of alienation. Because the self is as such only in self-understanding, to be alienated is to understand oneself in terms of something that one is really not (*BT,* 368). Heidegger's concept of alienation is something like false consciousness. For this reason some commentators have drawn a connection between the early Heidegger and Lukács.[1] Perhaps a closer model for Heidegger's understanding would be Luther. Luther took the pope and late Scholasticism to be such diabolical threats to Christendom because they preached an interpretation of Scripture that deluded Christians into taking works seriously and turned them from their true salvation, which lay in faith alone. Luther sought to call the few who could still hear back to the true Word from out of their lostness. The interpretations of Scripture were paths to being Christian, but only one path led to true righteousness. The structural outline is almost identical for Heidegger: we resolve upon possible ways of understanding being, which in turn provide us with the possibility of being an authentic self wherein lies our salvation; if we choose the wrong path, we are lost.

Thus we return to the ethical significance of ways of being that I emphasized repeatedly in Chapter 1. In order to be an authentic self, it is necessary to find the path that leads to an authentic understanding of being, for it is only on this path that the authentic who of the self can be sought. To understand being incorrectly is to enact a possibility of being that leads the self astray. To be led astray, to be lost, is alienation. Alienation is enacting a possibility of being that does not correspond to the authentic understanding of being given by *phronēsis.* Alienation is in the first instance alienation from being. Heidegger understands this alienation concretely as the oblivion of the question of being, for it is only through posing the question of being that humans can first experience the questionableness of being

---

1. See, for example, Lucien Goldmann, *Lukács and Heidegger: Towards a New Philosophy,* trans. William Q. Boelhower (Boston: Routledge & Kegan Paul, 1977), and Jean Grondin, "The Ethical and Young Hegelian Motives in Heidegger's Hermeneutics of Facticity," in *Reading Heidegger from the Start,* ed. Theodore Kisiel and John van Buren (Albany: SUNY Press, 1994). Although there is little evidence that Heidegger had read Lukacs, they had some mutual friends, and it may be of some significance that both Lukacs and Heidegger can claim a common intellectual progenitor: Emil Lask.

that is the path to the historical enactment of an authentic and undivided experience of the meaning of being.

It is only from the perspective of the oblivion of the question of being and so the alienation of Dasein from its authentic being that Heidegger's famous invocation of *das Man* is comprehensible. *Das Man* is a blanket term that covers all of the ways in which Dasein loses its being and its authentic self; in *das Man*, Dasein is alienated. As a blanket term, *das Man* covers a wide variety of phenomenon seemingly only related by the fact that they are the negative to the authentic understanding of the structures of human existence; thus Heidegger's understanding of death, conscience, time, and history is counterpoised to an inauthentic understanding of each, which is attributed to the domination of *das Man*.[2] Some underlying causes for Dasein's alienation can be specified, however: they are science and custom. The first cause is clear; since *das Man* is a way of understanding being that is opposed to the authentic way, which is *phronēsis*, *das Man* is opposed to *phronēsis*, and thus is *sophia* or *epistēmē*, or in other words, theory. From the War Emergency Semester course we know that theory understands being as that which is universally valid. It is the universal element, its validity for each, that enables Heidegger to extend the meaning of *das Man* to the public realm or public opinion. From public opinion, which Heidegger analyzes as idle talk, Heidegger gleans the various misunderstandings of those phenomena he attributes to *das Man*; in this sense *das Man* is our everyday common opinion about matters in the world. These everyday understandings have been shaped and formed by the traditional understanding of these matters. However, the tradition has been formed by a series of genuine confrontations with the matters of thinking. In the everyday appropriation of these traditional answers, however, we no longer confront the matters in a genuine fashion, and so do not experience these matters authentically through the questioning itself.[3] In all these specifications of *das Man*, the object of Heidegger's ire

2. Because the connections among the phenomena are not carefully analyzed, Heidegger's later history of being as metaphysics, which does specify and unify the breathtakingly all-encompassing connections, is superior in most respects. I will cover this in Chapter 3. Since the unity of the history of metaphysics is found in the oblivion of being, there is a striking continuity in the issue between *das Man* and metaphysics.

3. I am uncertain whether everydayness really constitutes one of the causes of our alienation. My uncertainty derives from the question concerning the meaning Heidegger attaches to everydayness. If he means that everydayness is our everyday life (that of our daily work) which alienates because nobody dwells on the question of being while pounding a nail, then

is clear: contemporary life in all its configurations—modern social organization, capitalism, the domination of science, and the death of genuine philosophy as it forgets its proper (and leading) role as the path-breaking questioning of being. All of these confuse what I am and thus who I am.

In *Being and Time,* the question of "who" I am leads directly to the problem of *das Man. Das Man* is the "who" of everyday Dasein (*BT,* 165–66). Who is *das Man?* "Man" in German is "one." One does this, one does that. Who is "one?" As impersonal, the one is no one, no one in particular. It is "the '*nobody*' to whom every Dasein has already surrendered itself in being-among-one-another" (*BT,* 166). Under the sway of *das Man,* I am not truly myself, but understand myself in terms of *das Man,* which is to say, I understand myself impersonally. There is a close connection between the impersonal way of being and some of the other terms Heidegger uses in this chapter: "distantiality," "leveling down," "public sphere," and "averageness." What unites them all is that anything unique or idiosyncratic is removed so that what remains is by definition accessible to all. Experiences and understandings are leveled down or averaged out to what can be common to all, whose commonality makes up the public (*BT,* 165). I experience myself and the world in terms of what can be common, what is thus impersonal: "We take pleasure and enjoy ourselves as *one* takes pleasure; we read, see, and judge about literature and art as *one* sees and judges; likewise we shrink back from the 'great mass' as *one* shrinks back; we find 'shocking' what *one* finds shocking" (*BT,* 164).

The impersonal nature of everyday experience harks back to an idea from the 1919 War Emergency Semester course. In this course, Heidegger presents theory as objectifying all experiencing in order to arrive at universally valid statements; to objectify something means to make it valid for all. Because all experiencing proper is individual to the highest degree,

---

authenticity would be understood as an epiphany that we gradually lose when we return to the world. If this is the case, then everydayness would constitute a necessary and unavoidable alienating cause in human life. If, however, everydayness means commonsense opinions in twentieth-century society, then the alienating effect of everydayness is really the result of the more fundamental alienation caused by the domination of theory over our commonsensical understandings of being. In this case, a revolution in our experience of being will transform our everyday lives; we will hammer that nail in the service of the new revelation of the divine. This is the standpoint Heidegger adopts quite explicitly in the 1930s, and held to until the end of his life, albeit in a not so straightforwardly political form. In *Being and Time,* however, there is a deep ambiguity in the meaningfulness of work and the everyday world which Heidegger addresses later on, and to which I devote Chapter 3.

objectification must abstract the specificity of the experience in order to arrive at universality; it must abstract the personal "I" from the experience, leaving the impersonal "I" which establishes what is universally valid. "This grasping, establishing [literally, setting fast] as object in general, comes at the expense of the suppressing of my own I. . . . The I that establishes, *I* am no longer at all" (*GA56/57*, 73). In the theoretical way of experiencing the world, the personal I that I am disappears. *Das Man*, as the impersonal and universally accessible, is theory. As such, *das Man* is broader than it appears in *Being and Time*. *Das Man* holds sway wherever theoretical science dominates, wherever modern science determines what can be held to be true. Modern science understands truth to be that which is universally valid, and it extends this understanding of what can be true to all spheres of knowledge, including that which is usually understood as personal, for instance, taste or aesthetics. This drive can be seen in one of the earliest philosophies of aesthetic judgment, that of Kant, for whom a judgment about the beautiful must be disinterested and universally valid.[4] Modern science is thus not merely the investigation of natural phenomena, but the particular way in which truth is understood as a whole. It determines the truth of being, and thus being itself. This truth of being is impersonal. In this impersonal truth, one's own self is "lost" in *das Man*, "dispersed" in *das Man*, and "covered over" by *das Man*. A society dominated by *das Man*, that is to say, modern theoretical science, is thus an alienating society, alienating because I am alienated and abstracted from my authentic personal self.[5]

In the section on *das Man*, Heidegger has been taken to have criticized Weimar society. One can see now that his critique extends far beyond that one time and one place. It extends to everywhere modern science dominates, which is to say, to all modern society. In the section on *Das Man* Heidegger criticizes modernity itself. This is the point at which Heidegger's concerns intersect with those of a broader group, often leftist, who decry the alienation brought on by a capitalism fueled by the technological advances wrought by modern science. Heidegger rarely speaks directly

4. Ignoring for the moment the very important distinction Kant makes between subjective and objective judgments. Nonetheless, aesthetic judgments are understood as universally valid for subjects.

5. The connections Heidegger draws between objectification, modern science, and social alienation resembles the analysis of reification Lukacs presents in *History and Class Consciousness*.

about capitalism, although it is clearly an issue when he speaks about society being governed by the demand for maximum efficiency (QCT, 15), but he clearly is in accordance with a diffuse concern for the increasing rationalization of modern society, a concern given paradigmatic formulation in the darker hints of Max Weber, who in turn provided the conceptual apparatus for a vast array of sociological studies of modern society, and whose darkest hues were best brought out in Adorno and Horkheimer's *Dialectic of Enlightenment*. We cannot speak of direct influence, but rather an affinity of concerns with reason, science, technology, and human well-being. These affinities have led some on the Left to appropriate Heidegger as one of their own.[6]

While this connection between technology and modernity would become much more explicit in Heidegger's later writings on technology, it is barely implicit in *Being and Time*. In *Being and Time* itself, the connection between theory and society occurs through *das Man* understood as the public. Because *das Man* is a way of understanding being from which "everyday Dasein draws its pre-ontological way of interpreting its being," we should understand the public as public opinion (*BT*, 168). The real "dictatorship" of *das Man* is revealed in how "we take pleasure and enjoy ourselves as *one* takes pleasure; we read, see, and judge about literature and are as *one* sees and judges" (*BT*, 164). The reference a few lines earlier to newspapers as information services indicates the prevalence of the "media" as the medium through which we inhabit the world (*BT*, 164). The "aver-

6. Mörchen and Dallmayr are two who tried to connect Adorno and Heidegger at this level. See Hermann Mörchen, *Adorno und Heidegger: Untersuchung einer philosophischen Kommunikationsverweigerung* (Stuttgart: Klett-Cotta, 1981), and Fred Dallmayr, *Between Freiburg and Frankfurt* (Amherst: University of Massachussetts Press, 1991). Similarly Zimmerman came to Heidegger from Marcuse. Michael Zimmerman, *Contesting Earth's Future: Radical Ecology and Postmodernism* (Berkeley and Los Angeles: University of California Press, 1994), 4. At a broader level of concern with the rise of the administered society, one could include the postmodern Heideggerians such as Schurmann, Nancy, Lacoue-Labarthe, and Derrida, as well as, in her own peculiar way, Arendt. The affinities extend even to those who would never consider themselves to have anything to do with Heidegger. I am thinking of Habermas, whose dislike and scorn for Heidegger is well known, but whose project of finding a communicative reason that cannot be reduced to technical purposive rationality finds an exact parallel with Heidegger's own attempts to do likewise. See, for example, Jürgen Habermas, *Toward a Rational Society: Student Protest, Science, and Politics*, trans. Jeremy J. Shapiro (Boston: Beacon Press, 1970). It would take a separate study to really study the similarities and differences, but suffice it to say here the crux of the comparison would be who bests separates communicative from instrumental rationality; Habermas's own squabbles with postmodernism, Lyotard in particular, hinge in no small part on this very claim.

ageness" of the media derives from its necessity to make valid for each in the same way so that each can represent any other (*BT*, 164). In this universal validity of public opinion, "everything gets obscured, and what has thus been covered up gets passed off as something familiar and accessible to everyone" (*BT*, 165). This description of the public as information service indicates that the public is not sociality *per se*, but rather Heidegger's understanding of modern mass society and the domination that mass media exercises over our understanding of the world. The averageness of the media derives from its mass characteristic in its effort to be valid for as many people as possible. As such, its logic is that of capitalism, a parallel which crops up earlier in Heidegger's distinction between craft-oriented and machine-oriented manufacture, where the latter for production purposes creates a general model rather than tailoring each shoe specifically for the wearer. Because Heidegger's description relies implicitly on a specific historical situation, that of late modern capitalism, *das Man* in the sense of the public does not necessarily apply to every social organization or to sociality in general, but to any social situation in which "everything that is primordial gets glossed over as something that has long been well known" (*BT*, 165).

The connection between public opinion, language, and common everyday understanding gets taken up in a more general way in Heidegger's discussion of "idle talk," another characteristic of *das Man*. Idle talk is our everyday way of talking about things, our average discourse about beings in which there is contained a disclosure, no matter how vague, of being (*BT*, 210–14). Heidegger equates this everyday way of talking with gossip (*BT*, 212). Elsewhere he says, "Catchwords and catchphrases are indices of idle talk, which is a mode of being of Dasein in *das Man*" (*HCT*, 272). The reason idle talk belongs to *das Man*—why they are in fact identical, to judge from the common language used to describe them—is that language falls to being available to everyone, its being "leveled down" to "averageness" in our everydayness. Idle talk is how Heidegger describes how we talk about something without ever getting at the heart of the matter; because idle talk never gets at the heart of the matter, idle talk is equivalent to the public correctly identified as public opinion, but now with the implication of being everyday common sense (*BT*, 165, 213). Like the public, idle talk closes off and discourages any new inquiry into the heart of things (*BT*, 165, 213).

The source of our everyday opinions on matters is tradition. When we speak, we use words, significations, and meanings already there for our disposal; this is the sense of the "familiarity" that characterizes our dwelling in the world. For the most part, we use words habitually, almost unconsciously, as they are handed down to us. This is why we use the term "learn" to describe how we "pick up" a language. The language is there before us (*BT*, 211). This understanding of language stands behind his startling proposition: "We do not have language, rather language has us, in the absolute and right sense" (*GA39*, 23; but compare *BT*, 208). Language speaks us. Put more prosaically, we understand the world—and that means simultaneously ourselves—in terms of how language articulates. Because language articulates on the basis of a built-up reservoir of meanings, language is primarily traditional (*BT*, 211). Traditions are founded and modified when something original gets expressed, but this originality quickly falls off into commonplace sayings, clichés, and trite expressions. We speak of experiences (and ourselves) in terms of past experiences of other times. Because we do this thoughtlessly, however, we live through this understanding without ever genuinely experiencing the matter the traditional answer speaks of. When tradition becomes idle talk and everyday public opinion, Dasein is closed off from the matter and indeed closed off such that this closing off suppresses new questions.[7]

It should now be clear why *das Man* comes under such heavy and sustained fire: *das Man* suppresses the question of being. By suppressing the question of being, *das Man* suppresses the only path by which Dasein can authentically experience the meaning of being. By closing off the experience of the meaning of being, *das Man* is the source of our alienation.

Our alienation from being is peculiar in that *das Man's* dominion is "inconspicuous" (*BT*, 164). Because the public understanding seems obvious to all, no one realizes that they are living so inauthentically. This is an understanding of tyranny that is even more perniciously hidden than those tyrannies attacked by Marx, Tocqueville, and Weber, for at least for these analysts of modern society, humans know that something is wrong, even if the cause is hidden; in Heidegger's public world, no one realizes that anything is the matter, at least as far as Heidegger is concerned.[8]

7. This same structure of understanding comes up again in Heidegger's understanding of how metaphysics, in the very giving of its answer, forgets the question of being that made metaphysics possible in the first place. Metaphysics is the idle talk of being. Cf. WMe, 370.

8. This theme appears in the later Heidegger as the problem of our "needlessness," which is modernity's inability to experience the innermost questionableness of existence (*GA39*, 134; *GA79*, 55–57).

This inconspicuousness means that our being in the world is character-ized by a certain heedlessness or thoughtlessness that Heidegger calls our absorption in the world. The example Heidegger gives early on is our state of mind when busy at work on a particular task; we go about our busi-ness in a peculiar thoughtless state of mind we recognize as habit. Heidegger expands upon this phenomenon to arrive at a general absorp-tion into the world that is characteristic of our alienated being. We are absorbed into, and thus lived by, the understanding of the world given in *das Man*. Because this understanding is governed by idle talk, this absorp-tion into the world is characterized by a thoughtlessness with regard to the question of the meaning of being, that is, to the question of the meaning of the whole. We are absorbed into particulars and do not step back to reflect upon the whole in which our particular task is situated. This absorp-tion is what Heidegger more generally calls Dasein's "fallenness," which characterizes our everyday being in the world and encompasses idle talk, ambiguity, and "versatile curiosity" (*BT*, 219–22). Particularly in this last instance of fallenness one can see quite clearly the Augustinian roots of Heidegger's understanding of fallenness, even if Heidegger does put it in a modern, Nietzschean context in *Being and Time*, as a rootless historical cosmopolitanism (*BT*, 222).[9] In curiosity one is ensnared by a constant stream of particular events and things, and thus gains only a superficial knowledge of each. The superficiality is nothing other than understanding the particularity without understanding the connection of each to the whole. Fallenness is living among particulars without ever raising the issue of the meaning of the whole, that is, of being.

In the section on fallenness, Heidegger explicitly calls fallenness, in which Dasein "*has lost itself,* and in falling, 'lives' *away from itself,*" alienation (*BT*, 222–23). To lose oneself means that one's being is no longer an issue for Dasein; to be fallen into the world means that the question of being has been forgotten (*BT*, 222–23; *LH*, 212). Thus our alienation by *das Man* can be called our fallen absorption into the world; in both cases, we are alienated from the question of being.

9. The Nietzschean context I allude to is Nietzsche's criticism of the modern historical consciousness presented in "On the Uses and Disadvantages of History for Life." Friedrich Nietzsche, "On the Uses and Disadvantages of History for Life," in *Untimely Meditations,* trans. R. J. Hollingdale (New York: Cambridge University Press, 1983). The Augustinian background to the theme of curiosity can be seen in his 1922 lecture on Augustine, which was then adapted to his understanding of Dasein's "Ruinanz," the forerunner to fallenness, in subsequent lectures. For more on this issue, see Kisiel, *Genesis,* and David Farrell Krell, *Daimon Life: Heidegger and Life-Philosophy* (Bloomington: Indiana University Press, 1992).

Heidegger will subsequently occupy himself with finding ways of breaking through this fallen and alienating condition so that we can repeat the original condition, which is the question of being from which we can appropriate an authentic meaning of being. The Augustinian manner in which he understood alienation as absorption into the world of particularity determines the path by which Dasein can overcome our alienation in order to dispose of all fugitive self-concealments and pull itself back from its fallen dispersal among its particular affairs of being in the world (*BT,* 357, 441). Only by overcoming particularity can Dasein transcend beings to the meaning of being itself. The transcending occurs in the moment of vision of resolution in which the meaning of being breaks through the crust of our everyday lives and breaks open an open region that is the meaning of being understood as the truth of being. Humans can overcome their alienation from being when they let the revelation of being occur and become the open region, the "there" of being. How this can occur will be more closely examined in the next section.

On Being Human: The Dasein in Human Beings

In the previous chapter I showed how *phronēsis* and action came to signify Dasein's authentic potential for being itself. It became clear by the end that despite the use of Aristotelian categories, Heidegger understood action far differently than the more pragmatic Greek. This difference lies in certain categories Heidegger adopted from his Christian background. As in the Christian understanding of revelation, the real action for Heidegger belongs not to humans, but to being: being is free, being plays, being opens itself to human experience. In this opening, being addresses itself to humans, whose place is to respond to this address and by responding, let being be. Humans can never bring about on their own the event of being; it opens itself *to* humans. The human relation to being can be captured by a word Heidegger sometimes later in his life used: *das Brauch. Brauch* comes from the verb, *brauchen,* which means both to use and to need. Being both needs and uses humans; it fact, in needs humans insofar as they are to its use, namely, a tool. Thus Heidegger calls humans a "tool of being" (*GA39,* 62). This relationship is echoed in the parallel understanding of the structure of address and response; in order to address, the addresser requires an addressee or the address falls on deaf ears.

Turning a deaf ear to the address of being is the same as being alienated from being. Being can address itself to humans, but if no one hears it, it cannot take place (*sich ereignen*). In order to let being occur, humans must open themselves to this call. Opening oneself means to clear out the clutter that prevents us from hearing the call of being at all. This clutter is our fallen absorption into beings. Only when we free ourselves from these entanglements can we hear and respond to being, and only in responding to being are humans truly human, that is to say, Dasein. That humans can turn a deaf ear to being means that humans are not always Dasein, understood in a specific sense as the authentic revelation of being. As humans respond to the question of being, being "events"; it opens itself as the world in which humans exist. As such, humans are the place where the event of being takes place. In this event of being, humans exist as Dasein, that is, they stand out in the openness of being. In being Dasein, humans let being occur. To heed the call of being is to let the "Dasein in man" occur (*GA3*, 226).

With this felicitous phrase, Heidegger clearly shows his Christian roots. The "Dasein in man" is analogous to the soul, for the soul is in the Christian and particularly mystic tradition the place where God addresses himself to humans. It will pay to examine more closely how Heidegger appropriated this tradition, specifically in the work of Meister Eckhart. Eckhart is very similar to Heidegger on two vital points I have been raising in this chapter. First, humans must first free themselves from their attachments to particularity and so open themselves to being or God. Second, once the soul is free from particularity and turned toward what is not a being, the soul can become the place where God can be born. This openness to God is *Gelassenheit*, an Eckhartian word that Heidegger famously used in two essays, "Gelassenheit," and "Towards the Discussion of Gelassenheit." By examining how Eckhart put these elements together, one can quite clearly see the structural parallels in Heidegger's own thinking and thereby gain a better grasp of how humans overcome their alienation by becoming the site for the revelation of being in the moment of vision.

Eckhart on Detachment and Letting-be

In Heidegger's thought, our absorption into the world of particular beings means that we forget the question of being, or forget the "ontological difference," the difference between being and beings. By forgetting the difference between being and beings, humans are alienated from their authentic being, which is their capability of being the "there" of being.

Something similar is at work in Eckhart's mysticism, which surely accounts for some of Heidegger's attraction to Eckhart. One must bear in mind the limitations of this similarity. Eckhart was a believing Christian; his mysticism is how he sought to live the best Christian life. His popular works, the sermons and instructions that have come down to us, were intended to teach those with no direct access to the Vulgate proper Christian virtues. Even the most generously Christian reading of Heidegger must recognize that his Christianity was quite peculiar in that it retained the form and rejected the substance; none of the Christian virtues survive Heidegger's adaptation. This difference is due in large part to different understandings of God. For Eckhart, the divine was one and unchanging; for Heidegger, the divine was one but the origin of change. This critical difference enabled Heidegger to adopt the form of Eckhart's mystical path to God while making this path the origin of the historical revelation of being. This central difference necessarily limits the extent to which one can appropriate Heidegger to an Eckhartian mysticism; Heidegger appropriated the form of mysticism to entirely different ends.[10]

Notwithstanding these qualifications, the formal similarities between Heidegger and Eckhart make an examination of Eckhart worthwhile for understanding Heidegger. Eckhart, like most mystics, was something of a negative theologian. For Eckhart, being is God. As pure being, God is not any particular being; indeed, God is excluded from or is the negative of any particularity and multiplicity. Multiplicity is a category that pertains only to beings. So God is called the "simple" or the "one," which simply means that God as being is not a being.[11] As such, God is the nameless. To further underscore this point, Eckhart sometimes made a distinction between the Godhead (*Gottheit, divinitas*) and God (*Gott, deus*). The latter refers to the persons of the Trinity or the names of God, whereas the former is the unity of the names that lies concealed behind the names. The use of the term *Gottheit* indicates the direction in which Eckhart is heading. The suffix "-heit" is how German indicates the nature or essence of something; thus *Gott-heit* signifies the essence of God as a being or name,

---

10. In their excellent studies comparing Heidegger with mysticism, both Caputo and Sikka point out this limitation, which is attested to in the titles to their books ("elements" and "forms"). See John D. Caputo, *Mystical Element in Heidegger's Thought* (New York: Fordham University Press, 1986), and Sonya Sikka, *Forms of Transcendence: Heidegger and Mystical Theology* (Albany: SUNY Press, 1997).

11. In German, simple is *einfach*, which points to the obvious connection with "one" (*ein*). Particularly later in his career Heidegger often played on several *ein-* words—*ein, einfach, einfalt, einheit*—to indicate being.

and this essence is pure being. Eckhart was pointing to the truly divine God (*göttliche Gott*) who is not to be confused with any particular name that this divinity may have.[12] In common with his Scholastic brethren, Eckhart understood this negative God to be free, for he is free from all names and determinations. The truly divine God is free from determinations; God is nothing, but this nothing in particular is precisely being.

Eckhart understood God to be the ground of beings. He is their ground insofar as beings have being and thus share in being, namely, God. God is the One, so consequently, God as the ground of beings is the unity of all that is, or to understand it in Aristotelian terms, God is the unity of the categories. That beings "have" being is not, for Eckhart, a result of their creation; the implication of this is that once created, beings have their own being or substance, which is to some degree independent of God. Rather beings "have" being in the same manner as the air "has" light; only as long as the sun illuminates the air does it have light. This image in particular is close to Heidegger's own understanding of being as the clearing in which beings are illuminated and can thus appear as what they are, and also being as the one or the unity of all that is (*EGT,* 70–71).

The more significant point I want to develop, however, is how Eckhart conceives the connection between God and humans. The connection lies in the soul. According to Eckhart, the soul's hidden ground is the "little spark" which is the spark of the divine. Like most Dominicans, and unlike the Franciscans, Eckhart understood this spark as reason or intellect. However, he did distinguish between this reason which is capable of perceiving the naked essence of God or being from other capacities of the soul, such as sensation, will, and discursive reasoning, that is, reasoning from axioms. These other faculties are concerned with beings; sensation perceives beings; these sensations are the cause of desire, which the will attempts to satisfy through deliberation. The other "higher" reason, the spark in the soul, shares in the divine reason; it is the presence of God in our soul. The soul and the presence of God are unified. Eckhart wrote, "Wherever God is the soul is, and wherever the soul is, God is."[13] This is

---

12. Hölderlin, too, speaks of the Godhead, and from both Eckhart and Hölderlin Heidegger adopts this term to refer to the divinity of God. Because divinity as the being of God precedes God or the gods, Heidegger will most often demand that we think about the divine or the holy rather than God to avoid confusing God with a being and thus lose the divine or godly nature of God.

13. Meister Eckhart, *Deutsche Predigten und Traktate,* ed. and trans. Josef Quint

the *unio mystico,* a term Eckhart almost never used, but which is certainly there in all but the name. In the unity of God and soul, humans are being; they are both nothing and freedom and the plenitude of being the whole. The soul reflects this being and is free from particular beings and free for receiving the grace of God.

The connection between these two moments is what Eckhart called the "birth of the Son" in the soul.[14] In accordance with the Christian understanding of the Son of God as *logos,* for the soul to give birth to the Son is to receive grace from God as divine reason. The soul is the Son by grace; through grace the soul is transformed into the image of God. Since Eckhart understood the divine spark to be intellect, grace is the receiving of the divine *logos,* which means the comprehension of the Son by nature, or nature itself. In the birth of the Son in the soul, God speaks and the soul receives and understands. In simple terms, God bestows on us an understanding of what is. This bestowing of understanding is the birth of the Son in the soul.

This divine revelation which transforms the soul allows us to truly understand beings as they are, and through this revelation the other faculties of the soul first receive their essential grounding, that is to say, only by understanding the meaning of the whole in divine revelation do things in the world receive their proper places. To use a Platonic metaphor, divine reason orders and balances the other faculties. Eckhart wrote, "The man to whom God is ever present, and who controls and uses his mind to the highest degree—that man alone knows what peace is and he has the Kingdom of Heaven within him."[15] This is important for considering the proper bearing to beings that humans need to adopt. Eckhart maintained that good works alone are not sufficient; it is necessary to first transform one's own being. One's being must be holy in order to properly perform holy works. This is similar in turn to the classical understanding of the relation between virtue and action; only the truly virtuous person can act virtuously, although it is possible for a unvirtuous person to accidentally perform a good act.[16] Truly good acts are an effect of good being, and for

(Munich: Carl Hanser, 1955), 207; *Meister Eckhart: German Sermons and Treatises,* trans. and ed. M. O'C. Walshe (London: Watkins, 1979), 2:145.

14. Eckhart, *Deutsche Predigten und Traktate,* 415; *Meister Eckhart: German Sermons and Treatises,* 1:1–6.

15. Eckhart, "The Talks of Instruction," in *German Sermons and Treatises,* 3:20–21.

16. Also similar to Luther: "Good works do not make a good man, but a good man does good works." Luther, "Freedom of a Christian," 69.

Eckhart that meant having one's being or soul transformed so that it mirrored divine reason and thus understood the whole. This is the only path available to humans to act justly in the world, for there are only two choices available to us: to learn to hold fast to God in our work or to give up work altogether. Since humans cannot live without working, however, that means that the only path is to "first commit himself strongly to God and establish God firmly in his own heart, uniting his senses and thought, his will and powers with God, so that nothing else can enter his mind."[17] Only through holding onto God—or being—can humans properly engage and work in the world.[18]

The soul is transformed by God's grace, but this transformation is possible only because the hidden ground of the soul is capable of being united with God. Thus the essence of the soul is capability or possibility; there is always the possibility that the soul will not actualize itself as the birthplace of the Son. "But God cannot work His will in all hearts, for, although God is almighty, He can only work where He finds readiness or creates it."[19] The conditions for realizing this capability are first the grace of God and second the preparation of the soul so that it is free to receive God. Because God is love, the first condition is always given. The second condition, however, lies within the power of humans, for humans are capable of either turning toward God and so receiving divine wisdom or turning away from God and being absorbed in worldly pursuits. Thus in order to receive God's grace, one must properly prepare the soul so that God can effect his will within the soul. The practice of properly preparing the soul is detachment (*Abgeschiedenheit*) and releasement (*Gelassenheit*).

Both detachment and releasement denote the same stance one takes toward beings and consequently toward God. Detachment means detachment from worldly attachments or sensual pursuits. People who pursue sensual goods are more properly called animals because they neglect their intellects.[20] Animals are ruled by their appetites and thus their self-will. To

17. Eckhart, "Talks of Instruction," 3:21.

18. This is a more general Christian sentiment. Luther says something similar in "Freedom of a Christian," 67–69. Chapter 3 of this essay will go in more detail how Heidegger tried to realize this sentiment in the modern world.

19. Eckhart, "On Detachment," in *Meister Eckhart: German Sermons and Treatises*, 3:125. The second case refers, as far as I can tell, exclusively to St. Paul, who was decidedly not, as Eckhart points out, prepared for God.

20. Ibid., 3:124. This means divine intellect, since the soul has another type of reasoning capacity which is really deliberation in the service of the will to satisfy desires. Despite

act according to self-will can be extended to include heavenly goods as well, so that the person who acts because of the threat of divine punishment or reward of heavenly bliss is still acting out of self-will. To act out of self-will and therefore as an animal means to be charmed by creatures; it means always to pursue this or that particular goal. In this state the soul has an inverted relationship to beings because it takes them to have being in and of themselves and not by virtue of being.[21] Detachment separates the soul from its dispersal among things. This detachment is a gradual emptying of the soul until it is only a void or nothing; the soul is free from every this and that.[22] Since God is also nothing, and thus detached from particularity, in the state of detachment the soul is in some sense God. "Here God's ground is my ground, and my ground is God's ground."[23] Detachment prepares the soul as a vessel or receptacle, closed at the bottom to creatures and open at the top to God. By emptying oneself of things and detaching oneself from one's self-will to this or that, the soul can be filled with God's will: "Similarly, if God is to write the highest on my heart, then everything called 'this and that' must be expunged from my heart, and then my heart stands in detachment. Then God can work the highest according to His supreme will."[24] The soul in its highest and most divine moment is a vessel into which God pours his being and will. This pouring is performed by God's "agent," the holy spirit. The detached soul is infused with the holy spirit; as the spirit moves, so the soul and thus the self move. In detachment, one's will becomes identical with the divine will or holy spirit.

Gelassenheit works according to the same principle as detachment. *Gelassenheit* draws its principle from two meanings of its root word *lassen*: it means both "let" in the sense of "to let go, let be, or relinquish," and "let" in the sense of "permit or allow." In this manner *Gelassenheit* signifies the letting go of beings in order to allow God entrance into the soul. As such, *Gelassenheit* signifies the same as detachment; it is the calm state of being nothing by which God, through the holy spirit, can effect His will in the soul.

---

the contemporary overtones of sexuality to "sensual," Eckhart (while meaning that as well) means by "sensual" anything having to do with the senses: desires could mean anything from hunger to sexual appetite to ambition to curiosity.

21. Eckhart, "Talks of Instruction," 3:13–14.

22. Eckhart, "On Detachment," 3:125–26.

23. Eckhart, *Deutsche Predigten und Traktate*, 180; *Meister Eckhart: German Sermons and Treatises*, 1:117.

24. Eckhart, "On Detachment," 3:126.

To sum up the formal structure of Eckhart's mystical path to the divine: in the soul is the hidden ground of God. This hidden ground, however, must be conceived as potential; it can either lie dormant or it can be realized as the birth of the Son, the transformation of the soul into the image of God, which is simultaneously a divine wisdom and the reception of the holy spirit as the will of the self. The active condition for the realization of this potential lies in the self preparing the soul through the practice of detachment and *Gelassenheit* to free the soul from its absorption in the pursuit of worldly goods and from its self-will, so that it can be an empty vessel free for receiving God.

Anxiety as Detachment

For Eckhart, the soul has an "inverted" relationship to beings because it takes them as having being in and of themselves and through God. Detachment returns the soul to its proper ground and in so doing frees the soul for its receptive transformation. Exactly the same inversion-reversion structure is found in Heidegger. Humans are alienated from their proper being because they have been absorbed into beings. Absorption into beings can occur in two different ways, which correspond to the two different "methods" by which Heidegger tried to overcome metaphysics. First, we are absorbed into beings when we pursue this or that thing in our everyday lives; the way we recover from this dispersal is anxiety (*Angst*). Second, we are absorbed into beings by metaphysics itself and the principle of reason, which establishes a being as the being of beings. Even when humans try to think metaphysically, that is to say, when thinking transcends beings to being, they think of this being that lies "beyond" beings as a being. In this manner metaphysics is the "forgetting of being," and the concealing of the essence of humans, which is Dasein.[25] The way that this is overcome is the deconstructive thinking that thinks on the unthought that lies concealed behind metaphysics. Heidegger referred to this thinking as a prepara-

---

25. Heidegger has caused considerable confusion by completely altering the meaning of "metaphysics" between his early work and his later work. One can easily notice the difference when one compares the "Introduction to 'What is Metaphysics'" added in 1949 to the 1928 essay "What is Metaphysics." In the original address, "metaphysics" referred to the "science" which transcends beings and so can respond to the question of being as the nameless; in the "Introduction," "metaphysics" refers to the epoch delineated by the question, "What is the being of beings?" a question which is always answered by a what-being, i.e., a being. What Heidegger originally called metaphysics, he later called thinking (*Denken*), which leaves metaphysics behind.

tory thinking which prepares the way so that humans may again experience the question of being.[26] The preparatory quality of this thinking echoes Eckhart's idea that we must prepare the soul through detachment so that it can receive God.

Although both of these ways are intended to free Dasein from its absorption and free it for its calling, they are marked by at least a superficial difference. The difference is that anxiety is a mood or attuning (*Stimmung*) and thus passive—moods come over us—while thinking is an action and thus willed.[27] The difference is not so strong in Heidegger as one might expect, for thinking for Heidegger is a response to that which calls for thinking or what gives food for thought (*das Zu-denkende*). Thinking is always attuned and determined (*gestimmt*) by what calls for thinking and is drawn out toward it. In this way, thinking, too, is a *Stimmung*.[28] However, since Heidegger's understanding of thinking is quite complex and intentionally mysterious, I will focus on his presentation of anxiety, which is not only more readily comprehensible, but also demonstrates more clearly its relation to its mystical roots and furthermore includes both the moment of clearing away our absorption in beings and the second moment of ecstatic thrownness upon our factical possibilities. Both moments are also present in the thinking on being, but it is easier to see them in the moment of anxiety.

Anxiety provides us with a concrete experience of the nothing (WM, 111). What is this nothing? Heidegger has broached the subject of anxiety because he is attempting to show how philosophy must think what the sciences cannot in order to root the sciences in their proper ground. Sciences are concerned with particular regions of being, which equate to the subject matter appropriate to each individual science: physics studies being as motion, biology studies being as life, history studies being as historical, etc. (WM, 104). The sciences study this or that being, and thus always remain at the level of this or that being. A concern for the this or that, particularity, is not limited to the sciences; in our everyday concerns we deal with

---

26. Cf. ZS, 423; SR, 182.

27. *Stimmung*, from the verb *stimmen*, ordinarily means "mood," and so is translated in Macquarrie and Robinson's translation of *Being and Time*, but it also can mean "attuning" or "being in accord." In "What is Metaphysics" Heidegger relates *Stimmung* to *gestimmtsein*, or being attuned. It is also related to the word *Stimme*, which means "voice." In his later philosophy Heidegger often plays on various forms of *stimmen*.

28. Heidegger calls attention to this in the postscript to "What is Metaphysics," where he says that thinking is "thanking," and the "echo of the grace of being" (WMn, 309–10).

this or that affair; getting up, taking a shower, fixing breakfast, driving to work, working at our tasks, etc. Every human, not just the scientist, is absorbed by beings in their work. However, each particular region of being, each particular being of our daily concern, must be related to beings as a whole, "if only in a shadowy way," as Heidegger cautions (WM, 110). In order to get a sense of beings as a whole, Heidegger distinguishes between an absolute knowledge of beings as a whole, which he holds, following Kant's antinomy, to be an impossibility on principle, and finding oneself amidst beings that are somehow revealed as a whole (WM, 110). This second understanding is what was discussed earlier as the being of beings, or primary being, which is how beings show themselves as what they are. From the point of view of beings, this being of beings is nothing. Since it is not a being, the sciences have no way of thinking on it, and so dismiss it as a nullity, something that does not exist and has no relevance for thinking, since it cannot be thought (WM, 106).

Heidegger, however, claims that the nothing which is the wholly other than beings can be experienced and is experienced precisely in anxiety. Anxiety brings us face to face with the nothing (WM, 112). Anxiety can provide us with this experience because of what it is. Anxiety is distinguished from ordinary fear because fear is always fear of something determinate whereas anxiety is fear of . . . nothing in particular. "Anxiety is indeed anxiety in the face of . . . , but not in the face of this or that thing" (WM, 111). Lacking a particular this or that, anxiety lets indeterminateness come to the fore such that nothing is there. The indeterminateness is not a lack of determination, but the impossibility of determining it (WM, 111). For this reason all utterance of "is" falls silent, for we say "is" only of particular beings, or to put it another way, finite beings demand a declination of the infinitive into a conjugated form, e.g., I *am*, it *is*, etc. (WM, 112). This description of the indeterminateness of anxiety is very reminiscent of Eckhart's description of detachment, which is detachment from this or that, detachment from particularity, and so making oneself a nothing that is identical with the pure being of God. "Now I ask: 'What is the object of pure detachment?' My answer is that the object of detachment is neither *this* nor *that*."[29] This "object" is not particular being, but rather pure being, or the godhead. It is what is wholly other than beings.

When the "is" falls silent, it means that the meaning of what is collapses

---

29. Eckhart, "On Detachment," 3:125.

to nothing, for meaning comes about only in language. Meaning needs to be taken in two different ways. First, as the meaning of individual propositions, e.g., the chalk is white, and second as the meaning of all that is, in other words, that by which we make sense of the world. This second sense is the answer to the question "Why?" the reason why things are the way they are. We use this second sense to indicate, for instance, the meaning of actions; the meaning is the reason for the action or our intention. Intention points toward movement and direction, for the intention of our action is the aim of the action; it is the aim or goal toward which we intend and thus are directed. Sense in this sense is sense as in having a sense of direction.[30] In meaningful action, humans are directed out toward something which is the reason or meaning of the action. That toward which we intend are the matters (*pragma, Sache*) of action. Considered individually these matters are the things we deal with in our everyday work, but these individual things are connected in a web of meanings that form the world, or the whole of what is, which is present in each action in some shadowy way. Heidegger says in *Being and Time,* "Here the totality of involvements of the ready-to-hand and the present-at-hand discovered within-the-world, is, as such, of no consequence; it collapses into itself; the world has the character of completely lacking significance" (*BT,* 231).

When the meaning in which we are involved collapses, we lose our sense of direction. We "hover" in anxiety; it leaves us hanging (WM, 112). The hovering image is significant. We hover because we are not moving in any particular direction. In hovering, we are not on any ground; we "stand" on an abyss that does not give us any hold. Both of these meanings signify pure possibility. In anxiety, humans experience the nothing as the moment of possibility, the freedom from any particular determination, pure indifference. The image of hovering, however, includes a moment of anticipation, an expectancy that at any moment the hovering being will cease hovering and move in some direction, like the bee that hovers for a moment before flying toward a flower. Hovering accurately captures the image of possibility as that which can be; in this moment Dasein is pure potentiality-for-being.

As potentiality-for-being, possibility necessarily includes the second moment associated with hovering, the anticipation of direction. Although

---

30. Cf. SR, 180. The question of being raised in *Being and Time* is "What is the meaning [*Sinn*] of being?" It is not accidental that the book is devoted to explaining the structure of intentionality. I will explain this in more detail in Chapter 3.

Heidegger tended to emphasize the dependence of what is on this prior moment of freedom, the sense-giving direction is part of the total "action" of the encounter with the nothing; it is for this reason that the nothing is conceived as possibility and not pure nothingness. When Heidegger says that Dasein means being held out into the nothing, he means that Dasein is constituted by lack of a hold (*Haltlosigkeit*) that is a holding oneself in possibilities, in which it should be able to take a particular, factical hold (WM, 115; *GA27, 342*). The ground of this second moment is that Dasein is being-in-the-world. World, as the totality of significations, is the equivalent of the being of beings; world is the wholly other to beings. This odd equivalence is clear when one compares the presentation of anxiety in *Being and Time* with that in "What is Metaphysics?" In the former, anxiety brings us face to face with the world as such, whereas in the latter, obeying exactly the same logic of negating particularity, anxiety brings us face to face with the nothing (*BT*, 232; WM, 112). Because Dasein is being-in-the-world, Heidegger can claim in the "clear night of the nothing of anxiety," the original openness to beings arises, what he later in the "Postscript" called the "wonder of all wonders: *that* beings *are*" (WM, 114; WMn, 307). Anxiety attunes us to our bare naked being-in-the-world. It opens up the twofold conditions of possibility of experience: first, that Dasein is in its essence possibility, and second, that these possibilities are situated in the naked being-in-the-world from which any factical decision takes its determination. That beings are, that "there is" being, poses to us the question of being: why are there beings and not precisely nothing? The question Why? attunes us to inquiring into the meaning-sense of the whole. The experience of the nothing in anxiety propels us toward an answer to the question of being, an answer that makes sense of beings. This answer is the world. Thus Heidegger calls the structure of transcendence "transcendence to world," by which he means the transcending of things to the condition that allows us to experience them, that is, being, which is understood now as the openness in which beings can appear.

Truth as Letting-be

The structure of anxiety is *freedom from* absorption in beings so that Dasein may be *free for* one's particular possibilities as revealed in the clear night of the nothing. In becoming nothing, Dasein is properly attuned to receive beings as they are, that is, as they show themselves. This second part of the movement of anxiety is spelled out in another key essay written around this time, "On the Essence of Truth."[31] As is the case with almost all of his treatments of the topic of truth, Heidegger begins with the traditional determination of truth as the correspondence of things and speech, and then demonstrates that this determination never considers the nature of this correspondence—how does a statement correspond to a thing about which it speaks?—or what one might call the condition that makes it possible for speech and thing to correspond (ET, 119–23). The condition for this accord is what Heidegger here calls *das Offene* (the "open"). In this openness, beings show forth as what they are and we comport to beings as they show themselves and so correspond and respond to them. "But all comportment is distinguished by the fact that, standing in the open, it adheres to something open *as such*" (ET, 124). Speech is true insofar as in conforms to the directive given in and by the openness.

The directive is sense-giving; it is how we take something *as* something so that it becomes meaningful. Again in this essay, Heidegger understands meaning as direction; the directive of *das Offene* is the twofold director (actor) and direction (end). The end, that is to say, the reason, moves us. Heidegger's understanding of this relationship is taken almost straight from Aristotle, for whom motion is caused by a mover, in the final analysis a prime mover, which is understood according to its teleological cause as the end. Cause in this sense means reason. The efficient cause of our action is the final cause or end toward which we intend; in each case it is possible to substitute reason for cause in order to come to our understanding of what we mean when we say that we acted for a reason. The directive of the open space is what Heidegger elsewhere calls *Entwurf*, "sketch" or "project," or in its full expression, *Seinsentwurf*, "the project or sketch of being." Like most of Heidegger's genitive expressions, this one must be understood in two ways, as a sketch of beings, the blueprint for their being taken and understood according to their way of being, and second as a sketch *by* being. The first sense of the genitive responds to the second. The first sense, the objective genitive, is the assigning of what Heidegger names the standard or measure by which we take our bearings in the world (ET, 124–25; LH, 238–39). Heidegger takes this directive to be binding for us;

31. The essay was first presented as an address in 1930, but was not published until 1943. There is considerable evidence that it underwent heavy revisions in the meantime. However, much of what I want to bring out can be found in lectures held around the same time, the 1928/29 *Introduction to Philosophie* (in GA27), and the 1930 *On the Essence of Human Freedom* (in GA31).

it determines our comportment to beings, that is to say, how we relate to and engage with them. As I will show later, this understanding of binding oneself to the project of being is exactly how Heidegger understood the German nation's responsibility to the task assigned it.

To bind oneself to the directive given in *das Offene* is the essence of freedom, which is the essence of truth. "*The essence of truth is freedom*" (ET, 125). Freedom is understood to mean, "To free oneself for a binding directedness is possible only by being free for what is opened up in an open" (ET, 125). Freedom is freedom for. Thus it is distinguished from merely negative freedom, understood as freedom from constraint (ET, 128). Freedom for is further taken to be letting beings be, which is being exposed to beings as they show themselves in their being. In being exposed to being, humans are ek-sistent; they stand out into the openness of being. "Letting-be, that is, freedom, is intrinsically exposing, ek-sistent" (ET, 128). The neologism "ek-sistent" is an attempt to connect existence to ecstasy. To exist, to be Dasein, is to be ecstatic, to stand out.[32] To stand out into being is to be Dasein, that is, to be the disclosing opening in which things show themselves; in standing out and being exposed to beings, humans are Dasein and that is to be the opening itself, the "Da" (ET, 128). The "there" of being is the opening in which beings show themselves; it is the *Seinsentwurf*. The "Dasein in man" is more accurately expressed as the "Da-sein in man," the "there" or open region of being. Humans can be ecstatic only because being itself is ecstatic. Being's ecstasy is Da-sein, which we are in our ek-sistence (LH, 205, 217). Our familiarity with the term Dasein conceals from us that it means being there, not here; it is projected out there as the project of being. This is the second, subjective sense of the genitive. Humans are carried away by the ecstasy of being. This is the ground for the taking of *Stimmung* as an attuning mood; like a mood, "it" comes over us and attunes us to the world; this attuning is the comporting to the openness and what it opens as the sketch of being. Therefore

---

32. To a certain extent this language of ecstasy was Heidegger's way of overcoming the inside/outside distinction that plagued neo-Kantianism and Husserlian phenomenology that arose in the problem of proving the reality of the outside world or demonstrating the connection between the interior consciousness and outside world of sense impressions. For the most part, Heidegger shrugged off these problems as non-problems that arose only because of the tradition's insistence on the priority of consciousness. It is to the credit of post-Husserlian French phenomenology, which was very taken by the language of ek-sistence, that it tried to show from within the Husserlian legacy how every inside must be exposed to an outside; Heidegger simply dismissed the issue with a wave of the hand.

Heidegger says, "Man does not 'possess' freedom as a property. At best, the converse holds: freedom, ek-sistent, disclosive Da-sein, possesses man— so originally that only it secures for humanity that distinctive relatedness to beings as a whole as such which first founds all history" (ET, 129). Man is the site of freedom. "Human freedom is freedom, insofar as it breaks through in man and takes him up and thereby makes him possible" (*GA31,* 135). Freedom, that is to say, being, breaks through man and so enables humans to irrupt into the whole of beings (WM, 105). As such, "With 'Dasein' is rather named what should be experienced and correspondingly thought in the first instance as site, namely as the location [*Ortschaft*] of the truth of being" (WMe, 373). Truth is *alētheia,* the unconcealing revelation of Dasein. Dasein is the site for being's ecstatic revelation.[33]

Being's ecstatic revelation in humans is how we are exposed to beings. In this exposure, humans are "thrown" into the world of beings. This is why the sketch of being is more properly and fully the thrown sketch (*geworfene Entwurf*) (*BT,* 331). Thrownness is clearly related to the "passive" nature of being attuned that is the true essence of freedom as freedom for the binding directive. In *Being and Time,* Heidegger says that we are thrown upon our possibilities (*BT,* 434). Where do these possibilities come from? The possibilities come from the "Es gibt." They come from the primal disclosure of the world in anxiety: *that* beings are (WM, 114). This "that" is the ground of our that-being, or what Heidegger calls facticity. Facticity signifies fact, that which there is no going behind. Facticity indicates that the world is, and there is no getting around it; we are thrown into a world that is arranged in a particular manner, what Heidegger in one place called the "facts of the situation" (*GA19,* 158–60). These facts preclude certain possibilities while leaving others open; for instance, it is

---

33. Heidegger developed this understanding of freedom while working through Kant's understanding of freedom. It is for this reason that the illustration Kant gives for freedom— I stand up from my chair and create a new chain of subsequent effects—is probably the clearest illustration of what Heidegger means by freedom. Immanuel Kant, *Critique of Pure Reason,* trans. Norman Kemp Smith (New York: St. Martin's Press, 1965), 414 (A451/B479). This understanding of freedom is almost identical to Arendt's Augustinian notion of freedom as inception, the possibility of a new beginning in action. Hannah Arendt, "What Is Freedom?" in *Between Past and Future: Eight Exercises in Political Thought* (New York: Penguin Books, 1968), 167. Kant's illustration is raised in the context of the antinomy of freedom and necessity, but Heidegger was sufficiently conditioned by the Christian emphasis on revelation and divine omnipotence to pass over the antinomic nature of the illustration and affirm it in isolation from its context. Where Heidegger differs from Kant and Arendt is in who the I is that wills the action; Heidegger, I believe, is much more in line with Nietzsche's notion that the true will is really the will to power or life.

not possible for me to become the emperor of the Roman empire; my being in the twenty-first century precludes that particular possibility. To be thrown into our possibilities means to be thrown into the world and that means into a particular situation; thrownness refers to each of these different expressions.

Being thrown into the world means being exposed to beings as a whole. In this exposure we receive our directive; this receptivity is a submission and acceptance (*hinnehmen*) (*GA27*, 74–75). In another essay Heidegger understands this submission through the verb *loswerfen*, to cast off; "For *die Einsamkeit* has the originary power, that it does not individuate us, but rather casts [*loswirft*] the entire existence [Dasein] off into the broad nearness of the essence of all things" (WBW, 11). I left *Einsamkeit* untranslated because Heidegger is using the term in a special way. Normally, *Einsamkeit* means "solitude," and indeed that connotation is present in the sentence above, but it literally means the condition of being one. Heidegger explicitly says that it does not mean to be alone; nor does it mean to be individuated (WBW, 11). To be individuated means to be separate from the rest of being; it expresses the alienation of the individuated thing from being. *Einsamkeit* is being at one with existence and the world as a whole, because it throws us off into the essence of all things; it unites us with being by dispersing us in being.[34] *Hinnehmen* means to be united or rather in an originary oneness with beings. The ecstatic standing out into being is the union, even if only for a moment, of human being and being, a union expressed in the word "Da-sein."

Historically this experience has been expressed in many ways by many people. There is the ecstasy of the mystical *unio mystico*, the Romantic submission into nature or life, Nietzsche's description of the Dionysian ecstasy in *The Birth of Tragedy*. Shelley, for instance, writes: "Those who are subject to the state called reverie, feel as if their nature were dissolved into the surrounding universe, or as if the surrounding universe were absorbed into their being. They are conscious of no distinctions. And these are states which precede, or accompany, or follow an unusually intense and vivid apprehension of life."[35]

---

34. In the next chapter I will go into the difference between this authentic dispersal in beings and the inauthentic absorption into beings, for Heidegger describes authenticity as a gathering of the self from out of its absorption into the world.

35. Percy Bysshe Shelley, "On Life," in *Prose*, vol. 6 of *The Complete Works of Percy Bysshe Shelley*, ed. Roger Ingpen and Walter E. Peck (New York: Charles Scribner's Sons, 1929), 195–96.

Nietzsche describes the Dionysian in a like manner, "Under the charm of the Dionysian not only is the union between man and man reaffirmed, but nature which has become alienated, hostile, or subjugated, celebrates once more her reconciliation with her lost son, man." This union is the collapse of the "*principium individuationis.*"[36]

What Nietzsche describes as the Dionysian is far older than the Greek god Dionysus; it is a constant element of Eastern religions which survived in the West in the contact between Neoplatonism and cultic mysteries and was transmitted to the Christian-ascetic union with the divine nothing, in which one experienced the beatific vision, the unmediated vision of divine reason. In each of these cases the mystical union with the one is hindered by some alien force from which humans must free themselves: body for the ascetics, or for the Romantics reason, particularly mechanical reason.

Heidegger names this "one" from which we are alienated and with which we are reconciled in the ecstatic epiphany in a variety of ways; the earliest comes in his *Habilitationschrift*, when he names it the "living spirit" (*GA1*, 407). The soul is the point of contact between life and humans, for the soul in Greek is *psychē*, which means "life" or "the living principle," the animating force to use the Latin term. The reason the soul is the point of contact is because it is identical—at least as a possibility—with the one-ness of life. As Heidegger explains in his first lecture after the First World War, phenomenology peels away the layers of theoretical life in order to find the "primal intention" of true life in general so that it can be experienced, especially "in moments of particularly intense living" (*GA56/57*, 109–10, 115). In these moments of particularly intense living, humans are united with the living spirit of life, a union compatible with the experience of the total manifold richness of life. In fact, far from being disorienting, a night in which all cows are black, this union with the living spirit is the ground of meaning, or meaningful engagement with beings (*GA1*, 409–10; ET, 127).[37] The union with the living spirit provides the meaningful sense to our everyday living with beings; the spirit is the directive or standard which is revealed in the open space; it is the project of being; it is Da-sein.

By virtue of the total structure of anxiety, "nothing less transpires than the irruption by one being called 'man' into the whole of beings, indeed in

---

36. Friedrich Nietzsche, *The Birth of Tragedy and The Case of Wagner*, trans. Walter Kaufmann (New York: Vintage Books, 1967), 36–37.

37. "The night in which all the cows are black" is Hegel's description of Schelling's *Identitätsphilosophie*, the moment of absolute indifference.

such a way that in and through this breaking open irruption [*aufbrechende Einbruch*] beings break open and show what and how they are" (WM, 105).[38] This total structure obviously parallels Eckhart's understanding of the union with God. The identity of the ground of the soul and God is the condition for any possible union. However, our absorption in beings and particularity deflects us from opening ourselves toward the nothing; the more we turn toward beings, the less we turn to the nothing which is the Godhead (WM, 116). Thus we need to detach and free ourselves from our absorption in the world, either through the practice of detachment or through thoughtful anxiety; in this moment, we become ourselves nothing, an empty vessel. Being empty, however, is the precondition for being filled by the revelation of what is, either as the birth of the Son in Eckhart or the disclosive unconcealing of being—*das Ereignis,* the event of being—in Heidegger. In both, there is something "in" humans—the interiority in the expression "Dasein in man" should be taken no more literally than saying that the soul lies in us—that serves as the site for this revelation. In this union, the identity of the soul and God or being the "there" of being, humans receive an understanding of being as the directive which grounds and roots all of our everyday human practices.

Despite the formal parallels between Eckhart and Heidegger, I should again recall the one important, vital difference that opens up an abyss between the two: for Eckhart, God is eternal and unchanging, whereas for Heidegger, the living spirit is the "historical spirit" (*GA1,* 407). Being for Heidegger is indeed the eternal, but eternity is not thought of as the unchanging, but as that which is not in measured time. This is the *kairos,* the coming to presence (*parousia*) of the spirit which breaks into ordinary time and creates the new measures of time that are the epochs of history. The "breaking in" (*Einbruch*) of humans into beings, which is identical with the ecstatic breaking forth (*Aufbruch*) of being into its there, and thus as the disclosure of beings as a whole, founds time. "The primordial disclosure of beings as a whole, the questioning concerning beings as such, and the beginning of Western history are the same; they occur together in a 'time' which, itself immeasurable, first opens up the open for every measure" (ET, 129). This understanding of time is founded upon Augustine's

38. Both *einbrechen* and *aufbrechen* signify violence; they are quite vivid and powerful words. The nominative form of *aufbrechen, Aufbruch,* has the meaning of revolution; it was common to describe the Nazi revolution as an *Aufbruch,* the bursting forth of primordial energy through the rotted crust of bourgeois society.

conception of the creation of time with the birth of Christ. Heidegger has in effect adopted another Christian motif to his own project; the birth of the Son in the soul, or the bringing into time of the eternal, is the ground of history. Unlike Eckhart, for whom the Son is always the same because God is eternal and unchanging, Heidegger makes it plain that each birth of the Son, the event of being, is a new beginning. What is decisive in the case of Western history is that such a new beginning has not occurred in over two millennia, as a line Heidegger took from Nietzsche's *The Antichrist* to serve as the motto to his book on Nietzsche states: "Well-nigh two thousand years and not a single new god!" (*N1*, 1).

Thus despite the Christian roots in Heidegger's understanding of kairological time, his conception of historical time leads him away from the Neoplatonic understanding of eternity that has dominated the Western tradition since at least Plotinus and Augustine.[39] However, the Christian and mystical understanding of the free occurrence of being which carries humans along with it also distances Heidegger from both Aristotle and the modern notions of action. Whatever Aristotle's separation of action from technical practice may signify, action was something controlled by deliberation; it is something for which we may be held accountable, except in certain exceptional cases. In this respect, it closely resembles the modern notion of action as governed by free will which can be conjoined with science to make a technique of action. Heidegger radically distinguishes action from technique for the purpose of separating action proper from the will, or at least from the free will of the individual. Heidegger's "mystical" understanding of freedom quite clearly distinguishes him from either Aristotelian or modern thought.

Heidegger's difference from both the classical and modern traditions of free action is based upon his understanding of the relation between humans and being. If in both of these traditions freedom and reason are properties of humans, Heidegger decisively rejects that path: "Human freedom no longer means: freedom as a property of humans, but rather the reverse: *man as a possibility of freedom*. Human freedom is freedom insofar as it breaks through in man and takes him up itself, thereby making him possible" (*GA31*, 135). Humans are free only insofar as they respond to the

---

39. Heidegger's 1922 lecture course, "Augustine and Neo-Platonism," connects Augustine to Plotinus while simultaneously seeking to recover the more authentically religious notion of care (*cura*) to hold up against what Heidegger considered to be the unfortunate neo-Platonic influence in Augustine's thought. See also Kisiel, *Genesis*, 192–217.

ecstasy of being as it breaks through them; in this way, humans share in the free revelation of being. Action for Heidegger thus must be understood as freeing oneself for the revelation of being in the resolution; the act is nothing other than the resolution itself. In letting the action of being occur in and through them, humans become authentic Dasein, which overcomes their everyday alienated existence.

Heidegger's own radical politics grew out of his understanding of freedom. Rather than understanding politics as a mediation between free and rational individuals, Heidegger takes the issue to be a turning toward being and thus allowing the event of being (*Ereignis*) to occur through humans as the ground of their existence. "The liberation is only genuine if he himself becomes free, i.e., comes to himself and stands in the ground of his essence" (*GA34, 37*). This event of being, and not the mediation between individuals, is the ground of authentic politics, for it is only by sharing in the ground which is the revelation of being that humans overcome their alienation. On the basis of this understanding of freedom, which he takes as being free *for,* Heidegger consistently rejected liberal notions of individual freedom, which he understood as negative freedom or being free *from* something (*GA34, 58*).[40] Freedom for means to stand in the light or clearing of being which provides the measure which is "from the first and in advance" binding on the free self (*GA34, 59*). To be an authentic self means to be free for and so share in the binding revelation of being. This ideal of authenticity leads to a politics far removed from our everyday understanding of politics.[41]

This religious understanding of human freedom does contain an ambiguity, for it is possible to understand the overcoming of our alienation in the public realm as an inward turning toward God that is in fact merely a withdrawal into inwardness. Authenticity understood correctly as the religious life can be taken to mean that in becoming free for the divine, the authentic individual withdraws from public, profane life. Thus authenticity becomes a withdrawal from politics and a retreat to solitary dwelling with the divine. This understanding of authenticity's relationship to politics is fairly widespread, and is a common interpretation of authenticity in *Being and Time.*

---

40. Thus Heidegger strikingly parallels the two concepts of freedom made famous by Isaiah Berlin. Isaiah Berlin, "Two Concepts of Liberty," in *Four Essays on Liberty* (Oxford: Oxford University Press, 1969).

41. I will discuss this topic in more detail in Chapter 5.

Such an interpretation, however, does not fully comprehend all of the moments of authenticity. Authenticity fully understood encompasses the centrality accorded to the notion of being-with (*Mitsein*), which is Heidegger's way of talking about Dasein's social being. Because being-with is an essential category of human existence, there can be no withdrawal from social life; authentic existence must be understood as a "modification" of our social life (*BT*, 168). In accordance with the centrality of being-with, authentic action is the action of a group; being always reveals itself for a group. This accords with Heidegger's understanding of freedom. Since being is revealed to humans as their language, the rejection of freedom understood as a property of an individual subject is not merely a rejection of the notion of freedom as will, but also of individualism as such, at least as commonly understood. Being-with is properly understood as a sharing of the openness in which beings are manifest; this sharing is authentic community (*Gemeinschaft*). In this way, overcoming our alienation from being not only restores our genuine living relationship with beings, but also with other humans.

Being-in-Common

Authenticity Interpreted as Inwardness

Even when the ethical dimensions inherent in authenticity are seen, its full public character remains concealed to most readers. There are several reasons for this, some specific to Heidegger's own formulations, some specific to our intellectual heritage. In the first case, the oversight is caused by the way Heidegger seems to set up his oppositions. *Das Man* is equated with the public sphere such that I lose myself in being for others, which constitutes the basis for my "subjugation" to others (*BT*, 164). Even more broadly, I am dispersed into the "concernful absorption in the world we encounter as closest to us" (*BT*, 167). Heidegger appears to make being-in-the-world itself inauthentic. "In so doing, it is driven about by its 'affairs'" (*BT*, 441). Being "driven about," it is alienated, heteronomous. When *das Man* rules, I am ruled by others. Heidegger, however, holds out the hope of authenticity, that Dasein can "*pull itself together* from the *dispersion and disconnectedness* of the very things that have 'come to pass'" (*BT*, 441–42). In pulling myself together, I throw off the disguises which *das Man* puts forth to tranquilize me. The primary way in which Heidegger says Dasein sees through *das Man* to what is most its own is death. Death is "nonrelational"; it cannot be shared. As nonrelational, it individualizes. Only in being free for my death can I be authentically resolute, and authentically for the sake of my own individual self. In short, it appears that authentic Dasein means to free oneself from the falseness of being in the world of concern for others which constitutes the public sphere. Heidegger seems to say this clearly enough: "As something that understands, Dasein can understand itself in terms of the 'world' and others or in terms of its ownmost potentiality-for-being" (*BT,* 264). The latter disclosure is *"authentic* disclosedness" which is *the "truth of existence"* (*BT,* 264). Authenticity is opposed to being in the world with others.

Many have come to this conclusion, even some of Heidegger's close friends, students, and lifelong Heidegger scholars. I want to suggest, however, that they came to this conclusion, particularly his students from the 1920s, not just on the basis of *Being and Time,* but also and perhaps primarily on account of their intellectual milieu.[42] There are two facets of this that are relevant. The first is a traditional differentiation between religious/ethical life and temporal/political life; the second is the influence of Kierkegaard.

The first has a long history in Western thinking, perhaps going as far back as the first Greek philosophers, who realized that their individual well-being was not identical with communal well-being, that there was a split between being a human and being a citizen. Taken to an extreme, it could even mean that to be the highest and most virtuous human required withdrawing entirely from the public realm because the public realm could seduce and corrupt one's virtue and lead one away from one's own authentic self. This possibility found its way via Stoicism into the bedrock of Christian experience, whose asceticism renewed itself periodically in the face of increasingly lax morality, most dramatically in the rise of monastic orders in the Middle Ages and the later rise of radical Puritan sects. The Christian emphasis on personal moral purity in the face of corrupt society was adopted and secularized in Rousseau's brilliant condemnations of his contemporary society and the concomitant approbation of sincerity,

42. Dreyfus goes so far as to call this interpretation "German," although one could probably extend it to the French as well, particularly by way of Sartre. Hubert L. Dreyfus, "Mixing Interpretation, Religion, and Politics: Heidegger's High-Risk Thinking," in *The Break: Habermas, Heidegger, and the Nazis,* ed. Christopher Ocker (Berkeley, Calif.: The Center for Hermeneutical Studies, 1992), 17.

integrity, and the honest soul. This split between the moral self and corrupt public life was taken up in a decidedly anti-Christian spirit by Machiavelli and much subsequent modern political theory, which reverses the traditional hierarchy in favor of insincere public existence, but whose reversal maintains the split itself. Moral sincerity and political hypocrisy, for all their obvious differences, uphold the split between ethics and religion on one side and the political sphere on the other.

Not everyone has been content to let that opposition stand. There have been many attempts to reform politics to accord with higher ethical standards. In the Christian tradition these reformers have sought to unite Augustine's two cities by bringing divine justice down to earth. This attempt to unite the City of Man with the City of God has fueled many revolutionary movements from mendicant sects in medieval times, to the radical Anabaptists and their revolutionary Puritan successors, to their terrorist conclusion in Rousseau's most incorruptible follower, Robespierre. These idealistic revolutionaries oppose both individual sincerity and political hypocrisy because they stand against that split itself; society itself must become sincere. This demand necessitates that their revolution be political.

If I may be permitted a gross generalization, political revolution in the modern sense occurs only where the idealists believe they can successfully actualize their ideals. When they cannot imagine winning the necessary power to change society, they have a tendency to retreat to individual moral sanctity; if society cannot be saved, at least one's soul can be. The preeminent importance of religion and ethics in bourgeois Germany stems in no small part from the bourgeoisie's lack of real political power. Lacking political power, sincerity remained a matter for individuals; authentic religiosity was in this sense their way of coping with a corrupt society they could not—or would not—reform.[43]

Kierkegaard's extraordinary influence on German intellectuals in the first decades of the twentieth century cannot be explained apart from this social fact. His call for authentic religious feeling, the necessary personal and individual nature of authentic religiosity, and not the least his denunciation of contemporary religion because it was compromised by its association with a shallow and corrupt society spoke to the young, alienated,

---

43. I follow Herf's suggestion that the German bourgeoisie's lack of political power (or experience of a successful revolution) indelibly colored the way in which political alternatives were set up. Jeffrey Herf, *Reactionary Modernism: Technology, Culture, and Politics in Weimar and the Third Republic* (New York: Cambridge University Press, 1984).

politically ineffectual bourgeoisie in Germany at this time. Heidegger himself was vulnerable to Kierkegaardian enthusiasm—we have already seen that he credited the introduction of the moment of vision to Kierkegaard—and some of his students, notably Löwith, drew a direct connection between the two. Arendt likewise ascribed Kierkegaardian motives to Heidegger's notion of authenticity. In so doing, she was arguing that Heidegger was motivated primarily by religious purity, in opposition to the *vita activa,* the life of the public sphere. Her entire reading of the ethics of authenticity consciously or unconsciously echoed the long-standing split outlined above between religious sincerity and political hypocrisy, placing Heidegger solidly on the side of sincerity.[44]

Following this link to Kierkegaard brings out the fundamentally religious nature of Heidegger's work. In this general sense, Löwith, Arendt, and Strauss are correct. This attempt to link Heidegger to Kierkegaard under the increasingly popular rubric "existentialism" as varieties of ethical doctrines of radically individual sincerity, however, rest on the premise that Heidegger's religious authenticity demanded withdrawal from the public sphere; that is to say, it assumes the dichotomy between authenticity and the world, ethics and politics. This is wrong. Heidegger was one of those idealists and revolutionaries who sought to unite ethics and politics. These revolutionaries are necessarily political revolutionaries. Heidegger's desire to transform the everyday world is part and parcel of this necessity. His political activism flowed from his religious motives. Many of his students were shocked not only that he joined with National Socialism, but that he exhibited any political inclinations at all, but their shock is misplaced. Their error was to ascribe to him a conception of reli-

---

44. Whatever the state of affairs of her personal relationship to Heidegger at various times, she maintained this reading until the very end. It accounts for the silly picture she gives in her address "Heidegger at Eighty" of Heidegger coming down from his cabin to briefly meddle in politics before returning chastised to his proper abode. Or one could turn to the earlier "What Is Existential Philosophy?" for a scathing indictment that essentially presents the same facts of the case. More generally, because Heidegger stands in her thought as the contemporary exemplar of great thinking, her understanding of the Heidegger's relationship to politics comes to be identical with the relationship between politics and philosophy as a whole; as her view of Heidegger mellowed, she mellowed the hard distinction she drew between philosophy and politics in order to make room for the life of the mind. However, it must be noted that the relationship between specific case and general rule worked both ways: her reading of Heidegger followed her prior belief that philosophy was a solitary activity, the dialogue of the soul with itself. Since this is not Heidegger's self-understanding, it is not surprising that she goes astray in understanding Heidegger's philosophical politics.

gion foreign to his endeavors. The Kierkegaardian revival in Germany fed on the disenchantment with a compromised liberal Protestantism in favor of an intense personal relationship to God that rejected churches and society. Although Heidegger's motives were similar, they differed in one decisive respect: he did not reject society in general, only bourgeois society. As I showed earlier in this chapter, the description of *das Man* contains an implicit historical locale, that of late modern capitalist society. It would be a mistake to generalize from Heidegger's rejection of this specific society to a rejection of sociality altogether. Indeed, authenticity fully understood is being in and with an authentic community. Heidegger's religion was thus social from the start.[45]

It is necessary to see this in order to correct a persistent error in understanding Heidegger's path of thinking between *Being and Time* and 1933. This interpretation holds that Heidegger's thinking changed within its religious framework from the individual authenticity of *Being and Time* to the Hölderlin-inspired *Volksreligion* during the Nazi period. According to Löwith, the most important propagator of this interpretation and not coincidentally the leading proponent of a Heideggerian debt to Kierkegaard, Heidegger translated the former into the latter political concretion:

> Whoever looks ahead from this standpoint to Heidegger's support of Hitler's movement, will find already in this earliest formulation of historical existence an intimation of his later link with political decision. It requires only one step beyond the still half-religious notion of individuation, and one step beyond the application of one's own Dasein and its Having-To to the proper "German Dasein" and its historical fate, in order to carry over the energetic idling of the existential categories . . . into the universal movement of German existence and then to destruct these categories upon political ground.[46]

45. A distinction Walzer makes in *The Revolution of the Saints* is apropos here. Calvin's Protestantism led to a religious commonwealth and revolutionary politics, but Luther's mystical religiosity did not. Michael Walzer, *The Revolution of the Saints: The Origins of Radical Politics* (Cambridge: Harvard University Press, 1965). Heidegger expounded a third path of Protestant politics: a revolution of mystical saints.

46. Karl Löwith, "European Nihilism: Reflections on the Spiritual and Historical Background of the European War," in *Martin Heidegger and European Nihilism*, ed. Richard Wolin (New York: Columbia University Press, 1995), 215.

Although the categories remain the same, the "step" from *Being and Time* to 1933 was to replace individual Dasein with German Dasein.[47] This step completely eliminates religion from Dasein, beyond "the still half-religious notion of individuation." By this Löwith means Kierkegaard. Although indebted to Kierkegaard, Löwith argued Heidegger's own work slowly shed the specific Christian content found in Kierkegaard's writings.[48] One can see that Löwith's interpretation is oriented by the distinctions between religion and politics, individual and society. Curiously enough, he alludes to the very place in *Being and Time* where Heidegger renders this distinction moot, section 74.[49] It is the notion of "co-historicizing" which is predicated upon Dasein's essential constitution of being-with (*BT*, 436). Correctly understanding the place and importance of co-historicizing and therewith being-with fills out what it means to be authentic, which is to be in a community with others. There is no "step beyond" *Being and Time* to the political decision of 1933; Dasein is always resolute as a community.[50] Only on this basis is it possible to make sense of that enigmatic claim that authenticity is an "existentielle modification" of *das Man*.

Dasein is constituted by being-in-the-world. Heidegger emphasized this in order to ward off an interpretation of authenticity as a religious stance that counseled withdrawal from the world. We saw already at the end of his early interpretation of Paul's Letters to the Thessalonians that he wanted to emphasize quiet work in the world as opposed to the otherworldly directed aspirations in Christianity. Designating authentic Dasein as authentic action again points to Dasein's being-in-the-world in a particular situation at a particular time. Dasein is not, however, a bare being-in-the-world, but rather more fully being-in-the-world-with-others: "By reason of this "with" character of being-in-the-world, the world is always one that I share

---

47. Wolin follows Löwith in this belief. Richard Wolin, "Karl Löwith and Martin Heidegger—Contexts and Controversies: An Introduction." in *Martin Heidegger and European Nihilism*, ed. Richard Wolin (New York: Columbia University Press, 1995), 17. Also Habermas, *Philosophical Discourse of Modernity*, 157.

48. Löwith, "European Nihilism," 212–13.

49. Ibid., 217.

50. Pöggeler described the invocation of community and generation in section 74 as *handstreichartig*, a reference to painting which translates loosely as, "dabbed on after the bulk has been applied." Pöggeler means this in two senses: first, that there is no real path from nonrelational Dasein to community, and second, that it is added with no real connection to the rest of the book. For the opposite viewpoint, see Johannes Fritsche, *Historical Destiny and National Socialism in Heidegger's "Being and Time"* (Berkeley and Los Angeles: University of California Press, 1999).

with others" (*BT*, 155; translation modified). Being-with means more than being present at hand with several other beings like Dasein, but must be understood existentially, that is to say, as part of the essential constitution of Dasein. It is part of Dasein even when no others are present at hand, that is to say, even solitude is being-with (*BT*, 155–56). The point therefore is that being-with is not an accidental characteristic of Dasein—whether someone else is present "beside" me, a feature which can change depending on the location of others in relation to me—but rather that my own being is constituted by being with others. Any time I say, "I am," I must say, "I am with others." Dasein can never be individual quite in the way that Löwith, Arendt and others believe because Dasein is at its roots a social being.[51]

Being-in-Common and Authentic Community

This point becomes clearer in lectures given in 1928 after the publication of *Being and Time*, where Heidegger develops the notion of being-with in more detail than he did in *Being and Time* with the express intent of dispelling the individualistic interpretation of Dasein that had quickly taken hold. In particular, the lecture held in the 1928/29 Winter Semester, *Einleitung in die Philosophie,* contains the richest and most detailed analysis of being-with, and carefully explores how disclosure is always a disclosure-with-others. Dasein is there always by having a share of the open disclosure.

In this lecture, Heidegger enters into the discussion by his normal routine of laying out the basis for our experience. As in the 1919 War Emergency Semester course, we experience things only through their connectedness with all other things, a connectedness that makes up the world or the meaning of the whole against which things appear as what they are (*GA27*, 75–76). A new emphasis in this lecture is the centrality given to the notion of openness or manifestness (*Offenbarkeit*), which directly ties this lecture to the 1930 essay "On the Essence of Truth."[52] The world is

---

51. Thiele sees this character of Dasein, even if he does not investigate the grounds for it or the difficulties with it. Leslie Paul Thiele, *Timely Meditations: Martin Heidegger and Postmodern Politics* (Princeton: Princeton University Press, 1995).

52. *Offenbarkeit* is related to the German word for Christian revelation *Offenbarung*. Heidegger rarely uses *Offenbarung* to refer to the revelation of being—I have found only one instance, in *GA39*, where he speaks of the "Offenbarung des Seyns"—but he does make use of a preponderance of "revealing" words, e.g., *Entschließen, Entbergen, Unverborgene* (*GA39*, 6). The use of *Offenbarkeit* still has manifest religious significance; as per his usual

the opening (*das Offene*), the disclosing "there" in which things appear. Heidegger here makes it explicit that this open space, this totality of connections of significations, is a medium, which makes clearer the idea that *what* things are is mediated by this medium which is being as its specific there (*GA27*, 76). The medium is the middle ground that stands between the thing and the perceiver and mediates the thing for the perceiver. The danger inherent in the terminology is that it makes it appear that there are three distinct things—subject, object, and medium—whereas Heidegger understands these "things" rather as three moments of the categorial act, which is precisely the medium itself. The medium precedes objects and perceiving subjects: "This connection however is earlier for the things, that which already lies at the basis of them [*das ihnen schon Zugrundliegende*]" (*GA27*, 76). *Das Zugrundliegende* is a literal German translation of *hypokeimenon* or *subiectum*. Thus one can see that the medium is the a priori subject that constitutes things.[53] Unlike other things, humans have a special relationship to the open because they are the open; to be Dasein means to be the disclosive "there," to be the medium or between itself (*BT*, 170). Because Heidegger, at least at this point in his career, thinks of the medium as the subject, one can clearly see the grounds for the charge of subjectivism that Heidegger himself leveled at his earlier thinking.

To say, however, that Dasein is the subject does not mean that the subject is each individual human being, although that is our normal understanding of subjectivity. Thinking subjectivity as the medium which encompasses both perceiver and what is perceived alters this common conception; since the medium is prior, it is more accurate to say each person participates in the medium or the open "there" of being. As such, Dasein is "in the middle of beings" (*inmitten des Seienden*) (*GA27*, 328).[54] This

---

method, Heidegger uses *Offenbarkeit* to designate the essence of *Offenbaren* and *Offenbarung*. By *Offenbarkeit*, Heidegger wants to talk about the condition of possibility for any revelation. His criticism of Christianity can be expressed as follows: by attending wholly to the actual revelation of God, it misses what made it possible at all, which is the capability of revealing in general.

53. This constitutes Heidegger's dual appropriation and alteration of his Kantian legacy. By making the categorial act the real subject that is prior to individual subjects and objects, Heidegger comes closer to Fichte. It must be kept in mind, however, that Heidegger's "subject" is not the equivalent of the Cartesian subject, the *res cogitans*, at least not as we ordinarily think of it.

54. Usually the phrase, "inmitten des Seienden," a common locution of Heidegger's during this period, is translated as "amidst beings." I altered it to make clearer the being in the middle quality of this experience.

accords with the description of how the truth of being permeates each human as the Dasein in man. The Dasein in man can now be fully understood as the medium in which each person has a share (*Teilhaben*) (*GA27*, 101–7). From this understanding of the open space as a medium (*Mittel*) it is but a short step to the next theme Heidegger takes up, being-with (*Mit-sein*).

It is important to make clear the connection between the medium and the with-character of Dasein because the very term "being-with" confuses Heidegger's intentions. Being with someone makes it seem as if there were two independent beings who are physically present with each other. Heidegger spends considerable effort dispelling this misconception, but the misconception is rooted in the terminology itself. Humans are indeed physically present to each other and other things in the world, but this is not what Heidegger means by the with-character of human existence. The central clue is that Dasein can only be with other Daseins; otherwise Dasein is "next to" other beings (*GA27*, 85). The with-character is something other than physical presence of two independent beings.

Heidegger lays out the structure of the with-character by analyzing how humans can relate their intentional acts to each other. He discusses how the students in the lecture perceive the piece of chalk in his hand. Each person perceives the same thing; their intentional act is directed toward the same object. In being directed toward the same object, each person relates to the same thing in the same way. The common comportment toward the intentional object is how we are with one another: "Being-with-one-another means to comport oneself in the same way towards . . ." (*GA27*, 89). Dasein is with others insofar as it has the same comportment toward the same object, that is, insofar as it shares the experience. From this comes the two meanings Heidegger gives for "with": " 'With' is to be grasped as participation [*Teilnahme*]" and "the 'with' indicates commonality [*Gemeinsamkeit*]" (*GA27*, 85, 88). We participate in the same experience insofar as we have the same experience in common. Being-with thus means sharing something. Being-with really means being-in-common.[55]

---

55. I adopted the phrase "being-in-common" from an essay of the same name by Nancy. The terminology in this section of *Einleitung in die Philosophie* remarkably foreshadows Nancy's language of sharing. I fully endorse Nancy's rendering of being-with as being-in-common, which Nancy understands as a radicalization of being-with, but which with this new volume has been shown to be Heidegger's own understanding of being-with all along. I differ from Nancy, however, in my reading of what is shared; the being which Dasein has in common is far more "substantial" in Heidegger's view than Nancy allows. Jean-Luc Nancy, "Of Being-in-Common," in *Community at Loose Ends*, ed. Miami Theory Collective (Albany: SUNY Press, 1990).

Since we experience things through the medium which is the open space in which things appear, we are with other Daseins insofar as we all participate in the unconcealment of beings: "Being-with-one-another by beings is sharing in the unconcealment (truth) of the beings concerned" (*GA27*, 106). What Dasein has in common is the truth of beings, that is, the specific "there" of being, the specific meaning of being. Dasein participates in common in the medium.

To put this together with the experience of truth as the Dasein in man developed earlier, humans are ecstatically exposed to beings in the ecstatic attunement toward beings of being; this is the mystical birth of the meaning of being for humans. For Heidegger, however, this ecstatic experience is something we have in common with other Daseins. The commonality is grounded in being carried away by the attuning mood of being in the same way. "The communal [*Gemeinschaftliche*] is situated in that the one is equally carried away [*hingerissen*] as the other, that the same is commonly valid for both" (*GA27*, 88). This idea of being equally carried away gives rise to Heidegger's extraordinary example of genuine community: two travelers round the bend in a mountain road and are enraptured by the spectacular view of the mountain. In this experience, Heidegger claims, is genuine being-with (*GA27*, 88). The mystical experience of rapture is something we share with others.

What is striking about this example is that it does not involve communication, although it is a type of communion. In fact, Heidegger stressed that being-with is not to be understood as reciprocal communication (*GA27*, 88).[56] It is the basis for communication, but cannot be grounded in mutual communication (*GA27*, 87). This seemingly differs from what Heidegger had indicated to be the basis of being-with in the years before *Being and Time*, where all disclosive letting-appear occurs in *logos*, speech. The various ways of letting-appear, the dianoetic virtues, are in fact various ways of speech; they are dia-noetic precisely because pure *noesis* is not possible for humans, since humans are always constituted by speech (*GA19*, 17–19; *BT*, 208). "It is predominantly in speaking that man's being-in-the-world takes place" (*CT*, 8). Speech is never a private language, to use Wittgenstein's famous expression, but rather "fully considered, speaking is expressing oneself *with* another *about* something" (*CT*, 8).

---

56. Heidegger echoes this sentiment later in a famous passage of "Schöpferische Landschaft: Warum bleiben wir in der Provinz?" where he says that genuine community can be seen when farmers gather at the local inn and smoke their pipes in silence (*WBW*, 10).

In actuality, the two discourses are not all that different. As the way of disclosing language is the medium itself, in speaking about something, we are participating in the medium with others. What seems counterintuitive here is that language is seen as prior to the individual speakers; in speaking we are participating in the disclosure that occurs as the particular *logos* or the meaning of being. This notion of language as the a priori disclosure of being is one that Heidegger makes central in his later philosophy. Humans do not so much speak as are spoken by language; humans do not have language, but rather language has them (*GA39*, 67). From the point of view of the participating humans, there is a certain passivity with regard to language. This passivity toward language is what makes the disclosive *logos* a mood or attunement (*Stimmung*). Insofar as a group shares a language, it shares the attuning medium which is the meaning of being.

With this notion of language Heidegger wants to repudiate a certain understanding of being-with that is based in the subjectivity of the individual ego. The two specific targets are Buber's I-Thou relationship and the neo-Kantian emphasis on empathy. Both of these are based upon the idea of an independent individual who must then somehow relate to others who are also independent. For Heidegger, these notions rest on "the basic mistake of solipsism," that the I can be genuinely alone (*GA27*, 119; also WBW, 11). For Heidegger, since Dasein is constituted as being-with, which means to share in the openness, there can be no *sole ipse*, no genuinely alone, self-subsistent being. Dasein is never a capsule that must find a way outside itself; as existent, it is already outside itself by being the openness toward beings (*GA27*, 122, 138). Since it is already outside itself with others insofar as it dwells within speech, Heidegger finds the whole problematic of the I-Thou a non-problem, since it presumes a manner of human beings foreign to their actuality (*GA27*, 141–42). "Unconcealment of things present is essentially something communal, it never belongs to an individual Dasein as an individual" (*GA27*, 133). Since Dasein is communal, there is no point in trying to locate community on the basis of individuals associating with one another as something subsequent to the individual self-subsistence. As being-in-common, each Dasein is never an individual, but rather a part of the whole.

The essential character of being-with indicates why Heidegger repudiates individual freedom. Not because he rejects freedom, but rather because he rejects individuality, or at least what he called subjectivity "in the bad sense" (*GA27*, 122). Humans participate in the freedom of being as it opens itself. Insofar as they participate, they are free and thus free with each other as a free community.

It is thus necessary to see the central importance the chapter on being-with understood as community has for the whole of *Being and Time*. If all of the ways of Dasein are in fact ways of speaking, and all speaking is necessarily being-with, all of the various formal indications of existence in *Being and Time* must be thought about in terms of being-with. In all honesty, however, it is virtually impossible to integrate death into this structure, precisely because in his analysis Heidegger wants to make it clear that death is "nonrelational," that it is something that can never be shared with others. When I die, it is my death, and no one else's. For this reason, death individuates Dasein such that in its ownmost being it is something that cannot be shared with others. Heidegger goes so far as to say that death makes being-with irrelevant (*HCT*, 318). Thus this chapter more than any other is the solid foundation of the individualist interpretation of *Being and Time*. The anticipation of death, however, like the other individuating constituents of Dasein, namely anxiety and conscience, both individuates and thrusts Dasein back into the world. Death, anxiety, and conscience are all described by Heidegger as encounters with the nullity that lies at the basis of Dasein. He understands this nullity as thrownness; the nullity is the fact that Dasein is not master and creator of the world into which it is thrown (*BT*, 329–30). This is the understanding of individuation Heidegger draws upon in his subsequent lectures. "This individuation does not mean, however, something like isolation, but rather it brings in each case Dasein in the whole of its relations in the middle of beings" (*GA27*, 334). What is individuated is the situation, which is something we share with others (*GA27*, 334). By invoking situation, Heidegger brings the matter back to the chapters on *phronēsis* culminating in the resolute moment of vision which discloses the "there," which is the specific historical situation into which we are thrown (*BT*, 346). Because the situation is shared, the possibilities contained in a situation can be grasped in common by a generation or people.

If Dasein is to be understood as essentially constituted as being-in-common, there is no "step beyond" individual fate to communal destiny. Close attention to §74 in *Being and Time* makes this clear. Having shown how authentic historicizing culminates in one's grasping of one's own fate, Heidegger then adds:

> But if fateful Dasein, as being-in-the-world, exists essentially in being-with others, its historicizing is a co-historicizing and is

determinative for it as destiny. This is how we designate the historicizing of the community, of a people. Destiny is not something
that puts itself together out of individual fates, any more than
being-with-one-another can be conceived as the occurring together
of several subjects. Our fates have already been guided in advance,
in our being with one another in the same world and in our
resolvedness for definite possibilities. (*BT,* 436)

It is unfortunate that Heidegger put this key thought so casually as
if to make it an afterthought to the central point, for it is in fact perhaps
the central point in this chapter. Our fate is always bound up in the destiny of the community to which we belong. This is because our fate is something we already share with others insofar as Dasein participates in the
medium which is the specific meaning of being. My fate or self is bound
to the destiny or self of the community. Co-historicizing "goes to make up
the full authentic historicizing of Dasein" (*BT,* 436). *Phronēsis* is political
action with others in the world. Politics belongs necessarily to the full
enactment of authenticity.

One must bear in mind, however, the Christian deflection of action that
occurs in Heidegger's thought. *Phronēsis* is understood mystically as the
ecstatic flash of being that exposes humans to their there; in this manner,
humans are attuned toward beings by being thrown into the middle of
beings. Because being-with or being-in-common is essential to human existence, it is now possible to see that humans are carried away together by
the attuning flash; in participating in the medium that is the openness of
being, humans participate with each other in common. This participation
in the medium is how humans recover, not only from their alienation from
being, but also from each other. In being integrated with beings in the clearing of being, humans are also integrated with each other; communal being
belongs to the authentic self. "For only in its being-there-with others can
Dasein surrender its individuality [*Ichheit*] in order to win itself as an
authentic self" (WG, 175). Thus humans exist authentically as a community of the "living spirit," to use one of the expressions Heidegger adopts
for being (*GA1,* 407). The living spirit, the Dasein in man, actualizes itself
as a living community in which each individual loses his separated and thus

57. Nancy traces this motif, "the nostalgia for a more archaic community," back to
Christianity, which understands community as communion, the common partaking of divine
life, the desire for pure immanence. Nancy, *Inoperative Community,* 10–11. Nancy wants to
take a certain understanding of Heidegger in order to establish genuine community as the

alienated existence (*GA60*, 322).[57]

The connection between spirit and community in the full actualization of Dasein points to some interesting comparisons. Spirit, for Heidegger, is the "there" of being, the specific historical open space or medium in which things appear as what they are; spirit is the particular world, the totality of the connections between things, how things hang together as a totality. This medium assigns the standard or directive by which beings are ordered (ET, 124). Spirit thus stands for the unity of the directive in each particular there of being. This directive unity of being is in Greek, the *archē*, the guiding origin and principle of being (WBP, 247). This understanding of spirit as the principle of being is remarkably similar to the conception that Montesquieu offers in *The Spirit of the Laws,* where spirit stands for the relations of laws to the manifold of objects, the principle which governs the relations between things and humans under different types of government. I would not suggest that Heidegger was familiar with Montesquieu, but Montesquieu's idea had a powerful influence on someone Heidegger did know, Hegel.[58] In Hegel's thought, spirit becomes actualized as concrete spirit, the historical shape of spirit in the laws and institutions of peoples. Concrete spirit is *Sittlichkeit,* Hegel's translation of *ethos,* which stands for the substratum that governs the feelings and intuitions that guide how people comport toward the world and each other.[59] In his *Philosophy of Right,* Hegel wrote: "But if it is simply identical with the actuality of individuals, the ethical [*das Sittliche*], as their general mode of behavior, appears as custom [*Sitte*]; and the habit of the ethical appears as a second nature which takes the place of the original and purely natural will and is the all-pervading soul, significance, and actuality of individual existence [*Dasein*]. It is *spirit* living and present as a world, and only thus does the substance of spirit begin to exist as spirit."[60]

---

community of death which is the impossibility of immanence. Nancy, *Inoperative Community,* 14–15. Heidegger's own understanding of community is precisely this Christian communal partaking in the divine life that Nancy criticizes.

58. I also would not suggest that Heidegger was directly influenced by Hegel's political philosophy. Between Montesquieu (via Herder and the romantic notion of a "genius" of a people) and Hegel, this understanding of spirit as actualized in a historical people had a dominant influence on nineteenth-century historiography, which is the probable source of Heidegger's own thinking on the subject. I do not speak here of influences, though, but rather of affinity of thought patterns.

59. A similar connection between spirit and *ethos* is found in the title of Max Weber's *The Protestant Ethic and the Spirit of Capitalism,* trans. Talcott Parsons (New York: Charles Scribner's Sons, 1958).

60. Georg Wilhelm Friedrich Hegel, *Elements of the Philosophy of Right,* trans. H. B. Nisbet. (New York: Cambridge University Press, 1991), §151, p. 195.

In Heidegger's thought, this same concept appears in his discussion of the *polis*, although Hegel's distinction between first and second nature, based upon an understanding of nature foreign to Heidegger's interpretation of *physis*, is dropped. The *polis* appears as "the site of the human historical abode of man in the middle of beings" (*GA53*, 101). The *polis* is the open site that is the medium for human life; it is the unity of all of the relations (*Bezüge*) of human life (*GA53*, 101–2). The *polis*, in other words, is the historical "there" of being, which "prevails in permeating all essential activity and every stance adopted by human beings" (*GA53*, 101). As such, it is identical with the binding directive of the there of being which is the determination of the being of beings. The connection between this thought and Hegel's lies in the priority of spirit, or the concrete being, and the permeating or all-pervading character of the *polis*; the *polis* is a simple immediacy with the medium, where individuality is annulled and virtue is fitting into one's station.[61] On the priority of spirit, Hegel wrote: "The spirit has actuality, and the individuals are its accidents. Thus, there are always only two possible viewpoints in the ethical realm: either one starts from substantiality, or one proceeds atomistically and moves upward from the basis of individuality. This latter viewpoint excludes spirit, because it leads only to aggregation, whereas spirit is not something individual but the unity of the individual and the universal."[62]

Heidegger expressed an identical understanding in his 1934 lecture course on Hölderlin: "If each individual comes from there [the ground of its Dasein], then the true gathering of individuals in an primordial community [*Gemeinschaft*] has already occurred in advance" (*GA39*, 8). Later in the same lecture he wrote, "This primordial community arises in the first instance not through the taking up of reciprocal relation—so arises only society [*Gesellschaft*]—but rather community is through the prior connection of each individual to that which commandingly binds and determines each individual" (*GA39*, 72).[63] The true community of humans arises when each individual comes to the ground of its being, which it shares "already in advance" with others. The priority of community, what is shared in advance, is the priority of being-in-common over any reciprocal

---

61. Ibid., §150, p. 193.
62. Ibid. §156, p. 197.
63. Nancy takes issue with this distinction, which he believes is rooted in the (Christian) nostalgia for a lost community. He says, "No *Gesellschaft* has come along to help the State, industry, and capital dissolve a prior *Gemeinschaft*." Nancy, *Inoperative Community*, 11.

relations between the I and Thou; this is the reason that being-in-common is the condition of possibility for the latter (*MFL,* 187). True community is formed when the meaning of being that is given birth in the soul is shared with others.

This community provides the circumstances in which an individual's responsibility means taking up one's station in life. Heidegger wrote: "Knowledge means: in our decisions and actions *to be up to* the task that is assigned us" (NSE, 58; *GA16,* 239). This knowledge is knowledge of the situation in which Dasein finds itself, knowledge which governs our action in the world; it is *phronēsis.* This knowledge is something we share with others; for the particular Dasein, *phronēsis* gives the directive for action which is in service to the *Volk,* the "organic unity" of the whole to which the particular belongs (NSE, 59–60; *GA16,* 236–37).

Heidegger's depiction of the authentic community of spirit, the immediate unity of feeling and intuition which was his goal for the recovery of the authentic religious life, it should be pointed out, bears great similarity to Hegel's description of the Greek *polis,* not to Hegel's own full description of the modern state which must mediate individuals with reality through a complex structure of institutions. Heidegger's community owes more to Romanticism and the Augustinian notion of community as the community of saints.[64] The religious and mystical path to being leads us out of our alienated existence and unites us with the meaning (*logos*) of being and with other human beings who share in an equally immediate manner this being-there.

The centrality of being-with or being-in-common forces a change in the conception of religion in Heidegger's thinking. Religiosity is not to be construed as the individual existence against secular being, but rather as a religious community of the living spirit versus a society riven by alienation that mistakes freedom to be something belonging to the individual. Thus the opposition in *Being and Time* cannot be between the individual and society as many construe it, but rather between various types of being-with. Heidegger said as much in an earlier lecture: "This is the basis upon which this being-with-one-another, which can be indifferent and unconscious to the individual, can develop the various possibilities of community as well

---

64. Also to Luther, whose description of the communion of saints suffused by the Holy Spirit is inspired by Augustine. Martin Luther, "Sermons on the Catechism," in *Martin Luther: Selections from His Writings,* ed. John Dillenberger (New York: Anchor Books, 1962), 212–13.

as society. Naturally these higher structures and how they are founded cannot be pursued in greater detail here" (*HCT*, 241). Or in any detail, one might have wished to interject. That blithe "naturally" indicates quite clearly that Heidegger thought little of the details of political and sociological questions concerning types of regimes and social structures. Such details I will flesh out in a later chapter. At a general level, though, these differences correspond to the different types of speech and ways of disclosing the world that Heidegger outlines. Heidegger's political philosophy returns to and bases itself on his understanding of authenticity as he developed it in his work on *phronēsis;* community is the political structure which corresponds to authentic disclosure. *Phronēsis* co-historicizes as a community or *Volk*. Heidegger did not have to take a "step beyond" *Being and Time* to arrive at his *Volksreligion in* the 1930s; it was always there, from the very start.

Conclusion

Authenticity is the religious way of life which cares for the self. Care of the self, despite the many structural parallels with traditionally religious modes of being, should be construed neither as simple self-interest nor as protecting the purity of the inward self from its entanglements in the world, but rather as finding the true basis of the self within the question of being. By posing the question of being, Dasein clears away the obscurities of its alienated self-understanding, not so that it withdraws into an inner sanctuary, but so that it is exposed to the event of the meaning of being, the medium in which Dasein participates. In authentically participating amidst beings, Dasein is healed from its alienation, and integrated into the whole. The integrity of the self is the unity of feeling and intuition that is the goal of Heidegger's ethical project. To this integrity of the self belongs our being-with others as sharing in the medium; insofar as Dasein is authentically in the world, it is authentically with others in a community. Heidegger's religious ethic of authenticity is not individualistic, but communal from the ground up.

However, there is an ambiguity at the heart of authenticity in *Being and Time,* an ambiguity Heidegger was soon to address. The ambiguity concerns the very notion of being-in-the-world. Heidegger had made this the central constituent of Dasein, and certainly emphasized that authentic Dasein was action in the world with others. When he concretely analyzed being-in-the-world, he turned to work, for in the work-environment we relate most holistically with the meaningfulness of things, but it was not lost on him or subsequent commentators that work or *technē* was often included with the inauthentic enactment of our being. This ambiguity left the status of action vs. work unresolved. What separates meaningful, careful involvement with things from inauthentic absorption in them? This question gave birth to the quintessential problematic of the late Heidegger, the question concerning technology. The next chapter will show how this question attempts to think past the ambiguity raised in *Being and Time* concerning the essence of work.

One may justly distinguish modernity from antiquity in that modernity characterizes the human being as *homo rationales et laborans*—the rational and working animal. The difference can be seen most clearly in Aristotle's depiction of the natural slave, whose lack of sufficient reason condemns him by nature to labor, whereas for moderns one's highest and freest being is found in creative labor to transform the world through science and technology. These differing characterizations of human being reflect a profound theological difference. If for Aristotle humanity's divine potential lay in its ability to contemplate the eternal truths of nature, the moderns found the divinity of human beings in their infinite will. Like his creator god, the modern human's highest potential lies in the conjunction of will and reason brought together in the immense technological project to re-create nature.

Although Heidegger's theologically inspired critique of modern science forms the centerpiece of his early philosophy, it was not until he turned this critique on this technological project that one can genuinely characterize his thought as antimodern. This expansion of his earlier project created some massive difficulties for Heidegger. Unlike Arendt, who rejected the modern technological project in favor of a reappropriation of the Aristotelian elevation of the political over the economic, Heidegger could not simply dismiss labor, because he believed that Dasein's primary mode of being was work.[1] In this respect, Heidegger is closer to Marx than to Aristotle. On the other hand, Marx's wholly modern understanding of human freedom through labor is completely at odds with Heidegger's theological project to locate authenticity in *phronēsis*. Heidegger cannot equate work with action, as Marx does, nor does he wish to radically separate action from labor, as Aristotle and Arendt do. Labor must be integrated into and yet subservient to the revelation of being of *phronēsis*. Heidegger wants to take a position almost identical to a sentiment expressed by Eckhart: "To be right, a person must do one of two things: either he must learn to have God in his work and hold him fast there, or he must give up work altogether. Since, however, man cannot live without activities that are both human and various, we must learn to keep God in everything we do, and whatever the job or place, keep on with Him, letting nothing stand in our way."[2] Heidegger's later philosophical project centered on the attempt to ground our everyday working existence into the totality revealed in the moment of vision.

This project provided the underpinning for Heidegger's noteworthy critique of modernity. The modern technological project, which aimed to free humans through labor, instead perverted work and enslaved humans to a system beyond their control. Not only has the economic and technical sphere steadily grown to incorporate much of the political, religious, and cultural spheres, but modern technology has developed into an autonomous power that no longer serves as a tool for the human good, but indeed turns humans into raw material. In a profound analysis of modern life, Heidegger showed how a unique historical interplay between metaphysics, science, and work developed into a system governed solely by the principle of maximum efficiency, a system that forces even its purported masters to obey.

---

1. Hannah Arendt, *The Human Condition* (Chicago: University of Chicago Press, 1958).
2. Eckhart, "Talks of Instruction," 3:21.

Against this enormous force, the capacity for genuine human reason and action shrinks; modern technology has the capability of swallowing all of human existence into its measure.

In an age dominated by modern technology, the hopes Heidegger had earlier placed on action weakened. The problem, then, became how to overcome the devastation caused by modern technology while still accepting the centrality of labor for human being. The only possible solution in Heidegger's view lay in the hope of transformation of the essence of technology so that humans would be able to open up the question of being and experience being as presencing through work.

If for the earlier Heidegger *phronēsis* experienced being in this manner, the later Heidegger found this possibility in *technē*, but it had to be a possibility of *technē* that avoided its enactment as modern technology. Surprisingly enough, Heidegger's understanding of the ambiguity of *technē* predated his explicit concern with technology. In the 1924/5 lecture on Plato's *Sophist*, Heidegger briefly analyzed *technē*, since it was one of the dianoetic virtues under discussion in book 6 of the *Nicomachean Ethics*. Although he spent little time on it as he hurried to his more pressing opposition between *sophia* and *phronēsis*, he noted that *technē* had two excellences, *sophia* and *phronē sis*. That is to say, although it is classified as that which concerns beings which can be otherwise, it has a tendency to reveal beings in terms of that which is eternal and unchanging. These few pages broach what later turned into his full-blown interpretation of metaphysics as Platonism, which is productionist metaphysics. These pages are the root of the connection between *technē* and metaphysics, such that metaphysics is coterminous with the "technical," that is, modern, interpretation of technology.

In order to recover the phronetic possibility of technology, Heidegger had to rethink the meaning of *poiēsis*. Ordinarily, *poiēsis* means making; *technē* is the knowledge that guides the making. Heidegger transformed *poiēsis* so that it meant bringing something forth in its being. While this could be a verbose way of saying making, Heidegger wanted this translation to emphasize the connection between "bringing forth" and "being." A thing is what it is by being brought forth, namely, through presencing. This points to the experience of being as presencing. *Poiēsis* makes being come to presence as the twofold measure of being. In this way, rethinking the essence of *poiēsis* effects a transformation in the experience of being and in the essence of work such that in and through work human beings can experience being as presencing.

In the first instance Heidegger rethought the essence of *poiēsis* through its immediate cognate, poetry or art. The revelatory nature of great art echoes the revelation that defines the instantaneous moment of vision that is the enactment of *phronēsis*. Art thus becomes equivalent to authentic action. This equation has long concerned commentators troubled by Heidegger's reduction of action to aesthetics in a sort of grand Romantic gesture. Action, however, is not reduced to art; rather, it is thought through art, that is to say, through *poiēsis*. However, art is also thought in terms of action, that is to say, work. The two halves of the equation meet in poetic dwelling. Poetic dwelling, whose contours turn out to be based in Heidegger's earlier turn to Luther's theology of the cross, establishes an authentic link with the divine and therewith allows humans to regain their authentic relationship to being and thereby recover their authentic being-in-the-world as the shepherd of being. The shepherd of being is Heidegger's counterpoint to the nihilistic world of modern technology; it is his Eckhartian-inspired ideal of the postmodern human being who dwells and works authentically on earth.

The Ambiguity of *Technē*

The null point for Heidegger's understanding of technology lies in his 1924 interpretation of book 6 of the *Nicomachean Ethics*. In "The Question Concerning Technology," Heidegger directs our attention back to the Greek understanding, particularly Aristotle's, of technology: "Aristotle, in a discussion of special importance (*Nicomachean Ethics,* Bk. VI, chaps. 3 and 4), distinguishes between *epistēmē* and *technē* and indeed with respect to what and how they reveal. *Technē* is a mode of *alētheuein*" (QCT, 13). What was seen at the time as a peculiar way of thinking about technology should be by this time familiar to the reader. What is even more significant is that the opposition Heidegger sets up between the instrumental and anthropological understandings of technology and the other possibility hidden in its essence was broached in the earlier lecture. Here Heidegger lays out the ambiguous nature of technology in terms of its essential possibilities.

In the broadest sense, *technē* is a type of knowledge that guides *poiēsis,* making; it is knowing one's way around, being familiar with (in German "das Sich Auskennen") that guides concern, busying oneself, and making (*GA19,* 22). Since all making concerns bringing something forth that is not yet there, making a finished product out of raw material, *technē* concerns knowing things that can be otherwise (*GA19*, 28–29). As such *technē* is a *logistikon*, a member of that category of knowing which deliberates (*GA19*, 28). *Technē* belongs in the same category as *phronēsis* and is thereby distinguished from *sophia*, because *technē*, like *phronēsis*, concerns that which can be otherwise and *sophia* is directed to that which is always there, that which one cannot produce (*GA19*, 28). There seems to be a clear division between *technē* and *sophia*, a division that in *Being and Time*, is expressed as being between concernful being-in-the-world (*Besorgen*) and scientific knowledge (*epistēmē*).

Technē, however, points in two different directions. The mutual point of contact lies in the principle of production, which is the *eidos*, the idea. *Technē* is a way of knowing about making. In all making, the producer must have a clear picture how the thing to be produced must look before production can begin. This "look" of a thing is its *eidos*. "Thus the *eidos* of the producer, what might be called the blueprints, is determined before the producing itself. On the basis of these plans the producer, what might be called the master-builder, begins the carrying out of the work itself" (*GA19*, 41). This is fairly obvious. When one wishes to construct a house, one must know what a house looks like in order to construct it. What determines how a house should look can incorporate many different levels: beauty, utility, the climate against which it must provide shelter, the number of people it must house, the availability and scarcity of material, and so forth. This is why concern is "circumspection" (*Umsicht*), a looking around, an environmental seeing. The further this circumspection is carried out, the more it comes to resemble *phronēsis*, which is also a circumspection (*GA19*, 22). When it makes the entire situation of action accessible, it is *phronēsis* (*GA19*, 29). It is on this basis that the later Heidegger will appropriate Plato's theory of Ideas as a "looking" (verbal) that "sketches" being in "creative thinking" (*GA34*, 71–73). It is possible to appropriate *eidos* to the moment of vision that sketches or "reveals" being.[3] At this earlier stage, however, Heidegger remains content to follow Aristotle's separation of *technē* and *phronēsis*. What separates them is that

---

3. "Reveals" translates *ent-bergen*, the same word Heidegger uses in "The Question Concerning Technology" to relate the "bringing forth" that is *poiēsis* to truth, *alētheia*, which *entbergen* translates. In this 1931 lecture, Heidegger is deliberately appropriating Plato to his new ideal of poetic thinking. It should be pointed out that this appears to be one of the few places where Heidegger gives such a "poetic" interpretation of Plato.

for *technē*, the *telos* of the action lies outside the action itself, and as such, is inauthentic (*GA19*, 41). Put more concretely, the *telos* of production, the work to be produced, stands before the producer only so long as the production is under way; when the product is finished, the producer is no longer guided by the *telos* (*GA19*, 41–42).

It is the nature of being-finished that begins to lead *technē* astray toward *sophia*. *Technē* regards being as being-made, being-finished. The look of a product when it is finished corresponds to its *eidos;* the *eidos* or being of a thing is thus equated with its finished appearance (*GA19*, 46–47). This again is obvious. The look or blueprint of a house that guides the house-builder in producing is the appearance of how it will look when completed. As Heidegger pointed out, this is the sense of Plato's theory of ideas, where the idea is the being of an object. This theory of being is grounded in *technē*, where it becomes most immediately visible (*GA19*, 47). The theory of ideas is in a straightforward and nonjudgmental sense the technical under-standing of being. So long as *eidos* remains indifferent to the question of time, however, it can tend toward *phronēsis* or *sophia*. Despite its concern with things that can be otherwise, the *eidos* that *technē* brings forth tends toward *sophia*. This is because the being-finished quality that makes out the being of a work remains outside the producing itself; the *eidos* remains separated from the process that sets it into a being. A work has its being in being-finished only when the action ceases, only when, in other words, it lies outside change or becoming. As being-finished, the *eidos* can be taken as that which is always and unchanging. Rather than guiding action, the *eidos* can simply uncover something as it is. "In the tendency to the merely uncovering observation as regards the *archē* lies the *sophoteron*. Thus the indication for sophia is given in *technē*" (*GA19*, 77). Because it lies in the nature of *technē* itself to shake itself free from occupying oneself with some-thing, it can understand the look of something "without regard to any use" (*GA19*, 93; Heidegger is quoting Aristotle). In this way, *technē* becomes an everyday synonym for *epistēmē*, the knowledge of that which does not change. This lies within the possibility of *technē* because that which it uncovers, the *eidos*, is understood as being-finished and outside action proper. The ideas become understood as eternal. Being comes to be (mis-) understood in terms of the ideas and thus in terms of "being-always."

This sketch forms the basis of the sections in *Being and Time* where Heidegger lays out how the "readiness-to-hand" of equipment is the pos-sibility of the "presence-at-hand" of objects of pure observation. As is the case with most of his earlier writings, Heidegger was concerned with the

dominance that theory and mathematical sciences exercise over our understanding of being, and also concerned to undercut this dominance by showing that our primary access to meaning and the being of things occurs in
working or handling things in our everyday traffic with them. Part of this
demonstration seeks to show that the being of objects accessible to theory
is derivative from this primary world of meaning. As Heidegger relates in
Being and Time, equipment is known by its function in accomplishing a
task; when we wish to drive a nail, we use a hammer, and we know what
a hammer is by virtue of knowing what kind of thing is needed to drive
the nail. This sort of tool-using knowledge, what we call "technical"
knowledge, is what Heidegger called "readiness-to-hand." It is only when
a piece of equipment fails to be ready to hand through its absence or failure to function properly, that it suddenly stands on its own, as if for the
first time we notice the hammer as a hammer, with a wooden shaft and
iron head (*BT,* 105). This latter "presence-at-hand" is however, merely a
deficient mode of concern, that is, of "readiness-to-hand" (*BT,* 103). The
theoretical world of pure observation is derivative, in both the neutral and
negative sense of the word, from concern, work, and *technē.* For this reason, sections 15–17 have become the locus classicus of the pragmatic interpretation of *Being and Time.* According to these interpretations, meaning
is primordially accessible through involvement in an environment. What
the pragmatic interpretation fails to consider is the full implication of the
derivative status of theory. If theory is indeed derived from concern or
technē, it means that it is a possibility of the same. The deflection of work
into theory is in fact one possibility of work, one in which work is understood in terms of theory. This is the important point. One cannot merely
oppose work to theory (or pragmatism to positivism), but one type of work
to another, whose point of distinction is whether it is authentic or not.

One cannot fully understand Heidegger's writings on technology without grasping this last point. When he points to the ill effects on human
being caused by the technical understanding of being, he always calls it
modern technology; the modernity of the technology is the problem, not
technology itself. This has caused commentators, such as Pöggeler and
Habermas, to criticize Heidegger's hand-craft orientation to technology as
hopelessly backward.[4] This is not quite correct, as I shall explain later, but
it does capture something important. Modern technology, as Heidegger

4. Otto Pöggeler, *Schritte zu einer Hermeneutische Philosophie* (Munich: Karl Alber,
1994), 252–53.

saw it, operates under the demand of maximum efficiency, which in turn necessitates exacting planning, careful allocation of resources, and the standardization of parts. Such planning and standardization depend upon scientific management, both of labor power and natural resources. This scientific management is nothing other than applied science. In short, this account describes how work gets deflected into theory, or to put it another way, how a whole system developed out of a unique interplay between work and theory, the scientific management of work and the application of science in work. This unique configuration of work and science is what Heidegger called modern technology.

There is little that is novel in this explanation at this level. The whole of this system of science and manufacturing was termed "rationalization" by Weber, and to a large extent Heidegger's social analyses are Weberian in character. We are accustomed to acknowledging the great shifts in society caused by the changes in manufacturing that made up the Industrial Revolution, and make up its continuation in the present-day Information Revolution. Heidegger's analyses are unique and important because of how his explanation of rationalization dovetails with his constant questioning of being and the meaning of being. His analysis of technology grew out of his early concern with the dominance of theory in understanding being. Because he understood modern technology essentially as applied theory, Heidegger could apply his own earlier interpretations of Aristotle's texts with their essential differentiations of the dianoetic virtues to the problems and possibilities inherent in modern civilization.

The first great innovation of Heidegger's later thinking lies in the realization that the question of being is closely tied up with the question of work; in the end, everything comes down to *technē*. To say that it all comes down to *technē* does not mean that we are abandoned to nihilistic technology.[5] Because *technē* is capable of different possibilities, one which coincides with the rise of theory and another that coincides with working

5. Heidegger says as much in the *Spiegel* interview: "It seems to me that you take technology too absolutely. I do not think the situation of human beings in the world of planetary technology is an inextricable and inescapable disastrous fate; rather I think that the task of thinking is precisely to help, within its bounds, human beings to attain an adequate relationship to the essence of technology at all" (Sp, 111; *GA16*, 677). Nonetheless, some have thought that Heidegger himself took technology too absolutely, Dreyfus and Harries for example. See Hubert Dreyfus, "Heidegger's History of the Being of Equipment," in *Heidegger: A Critical Reader*, ed. Hubert Dreyfus and Harrison Hall (Cambridge, Mass.: Basil Blackwell, 1992), and Karsten Harries, "Heidegger as Political Thinker," in *Heidegger and Modern Philosophy*, ed. Michael Murray (New Haven: Yale University Press, 1978).

revelation, the later thinking still retains much of the inauthentic-authentic division even if these terms have disappeared. If one possibility of *technē* develops into what Heidegger characterized as "cybernetics," the other possibility is still open, but only if we "step back" from the dominance of modern technology to see the other way hidden in technology itself.

The second great innovation lies in the historical dimension of the analysis of modern technology. The distinctions among the intellectual virtues or the various layers uncovered in the analytic of Dasein in *Being and Time* are functional distinctions, timeless in their being, even if it is possible to note, as Pöggeler does, the historical character of Heidegger's hand-craft model of work in *Being and Time*. Later Heidegger confronts the modern character of modern technology head-on by attempting to explain the origin and principle of modernity as a whole. Thus the unique system of interplay between work and science becomes the principle that guides modern life; it becomes, in essence, the unique connection of significations and meanings that make up the modern world. World, or the connection of meanings, is also Da-sein, the peculiar constellation of being at any time. The modern world means the meaning of being peculiar to it. The explanation of the origin and principle of the modern world takes the form of a history of being.

The History of Being—The History of *Technē*

Heidegger's history of being obeys the way in which history is known and studied that he laid out in *Being and Time:* in the moment of vision being is "there" as it projects toward the future and reflects back out of this future and into the past, the whole of which makes up the particular "there" of being, or its world. A concrete example of this logic relevant to this chapter is how neolithic anthropology studies its subject. Since we understand the distinctive feature of our humanity to be its progressive tool-using capability, anthropologists study the quality of tools they find to judge the stage at which those tool-bearing humans were and how they were developing toward us and our technological future. The past is understood out of the insight into the meaning of being or the direction that this meaning carries us. "Insight" thus crops up often in Heidegger's analyses of modernity, particularly when Heidegger wishes to emphasize Nietzsche's fundamental insight into the reality of modernity. Heidegger himself does not often appropriate "insight" for his own vision, but it is significant that the addresses later published as "The Question Concerning Technology" were originally called "Insight into That Which Is," or to make it obvious, an insight into the being characteristic of the present age.

I point this out so that the reader is properly apprised of the status of Heidegger's history of being, and thus his explanation of the origin and principles of modernity. The history of being in the sense of Heidegger's presentation of the working-out of metaphysics in the texts of great philosophers depends upon his insight into being, or how being revealed itself to him. His characterization of modernity and its thoroughly problematic quality depends upon how he thought being should be properly understood. For Heidegger, this meant that one had to understand the ontological difference, the difference between being and beings, and how this difference is the source of possibility and freedom. Thus his analysis of modernity is primarily how this proper understanding of being becomes forgotten or covered over by the understanding of being inherent in modernity; it analyzes how being understood as possibility becomes understood as either constant presence or standing presence, that is, scientifically and mathematically. In the first instance for Heidegger, modernity is a philosophical and scientific revolution; in the second instance this revolution in metaphysics extends itself to all spheres of human existence via modern technology, but one must understand that the two instances are parts of the same principle at work in modernity, what I called the unique interplay between work and science that makes up the technical understanding of the essence of technology. One must bear in mind the astonishing audacity of Heidegger's attempt to explain everything modern as a result of one unifying principle, the "oblivion of being." For clarity's sake and because that one unifying principle is quite obscure at first glance, I will break up the presentation into more familiar categories: first, the metaphysical revolution Heidegger saw in the birth of modern science, and then the technological changes that occurred with modern science, before finally turning to the significance for human being Heidegger sees resulting from modern Da-sein.

The general outlines of Heidegger's history of being are well known. Taking the narrative of the Fall as its model, it begins sometime in the past when primordial meaning occurred. This primordial moment fell into self-evidence and eventually became our modern technological society.[6]

---

6. When this occurred changed depending on when Heidegger wrote this history and

Despite the controversies that his interpretations of individual philosophers have ignited, the general outlines of the history of philosophy fits the standard textbook model: a basic division between ancient and modern, with Descartes as the central figure in the birth of modern philosophy; it shares with the textbook the aim of explaining the origins of modern scientific thinking. Heidegger, of course, treated these subjects more complexly and in a far harsher light than the textbook version does, but its similarity to standard ways of viewing the history of philosophy made Heidegger's presentation fit comfortably into contemporary philosophical discussions. That very strength is also a weakness, for Heidegger's history shares with the textbooks an obliviousness to other important facets of the thinkers under consideration; for instance, his desire to make Descartes into the founder of human-centered subjectivity overlooks the specter of an infinite god in Descartes mature philosophy.[7] That said, textbooks become such by virtue of their apparent justness to their subject matter, and Heidegger's surpasses these in depth of analysis and coherence of presentation.

Heidegger wanted to explain the principles of modernity, but the rise of what is distinctively modern has its origins in earlier thinking. As Heidegger developed it, the technical deflection of technology had its origins in the tendency of *technē* to be taken in terms of *sophia* and *epistēmē*. Heidegger wanted to look at the metaphysical significance of this way of thinking, which appeared in Aristotle, how beings (and thus being) were known scientifically. Central to the technical deflection of knowledge is the proposition that the *eidos* or idea becomes separated from the production itself so that it achieves a sort of self-sufficiency, standing on its own without regard to its actualization. In this way the "what" of a being, its essence, becomes separated from the "that" of a being, its existence (MHB, 11). This sepa-

---

also on what facet of the constellation he was considering. Thus Heidegger initially posited the model of primordial connectedness in the medieval mystics, and in subsequent texts worked his way backwards in the history of philosophy to Aristotle, to Heraclitus, and to Parmenides, and in the end Heidegger decided what he wanted to find could not be found in Parmenides either. The "Fall" has no one single origin because the various facets worked themselves out differently. Almost every narrative, however, is united by the fact that Descartes figures as the chief villain.

7. See for instance, Jean-Luc Marion's excellent "The Essential Incoherence of Descartes' Definition of Divinity," in *Essays on Descartes' Meditations,* ed. Amélie Oksenberg Rorty (Berkeley and Los Angeles: University of California Press, 1986). See also Michael Gillespie, *Nihilism Before Nietzsche* (Chicago: University of Chicago Press, 1996).

ration has a profound effect on how being is thought, as can be seen by the equation of the "what" of a thing with its essence. "Essence" comes from the Latin *esse,* or "to be." The being of a thing is what it is, its essence, and this essence can be thought about without regard to its existence, that is to say, without regard to its temporality. The essence or idea of a thing is what is constant in the face of change; for this reason being is understood as constant. Being is what is constant, and thus appropriately grasped by *sophia.* The love of *sophia* is philosophy, so that the philosopher is the one who desires to know being in its constancy. This is only to say that philosophy is an inquiry into what things are; the classic Socratic question is "What is *X*?" This Socratic question leads to further metaphysical or epistemological questions as to how we know what *X* is, for instance, Plato's theories on the Ideas, or Aristotle's analysis of categories, or to jump ahead many centuries, Kant's critical idealism. Heidegger's basic claim is that this whole philosophical enterprise rests on the separation of the "what" of a thing from its "that," its essence from its existence, and most generally, being from time.

Modern science belongs to this enterprise, but it works this separation in a new direction. To take the rise of modern science as an example, modern science is distinct from ancient and medieval science in that it is mathematical. As Heidegger insists, however, ancient science was also mathematical, but in a different sense. *Mathēmata* in the most general sense is what can be taught and likewise learned (*WiT,* 69).[8] All learning is through practice, but practice assumes a vague background of prior knowledge; to use Heidegger's example, learning to use a rifle already presumes we know what a weapon is and what it is used for (*WiT,* 71–72). *Mathēsis* is "taking cognizance" of this prior knowledge. Learning is knowing what we already know (*WiT,* 72–73). At its broadest, "the mathematical is the fundamental presupposition of the knowledge of things" (*WiT,* 75). It is taking cognizance of being. Ancient science is mathematical in that it is metaphysics, the study of being.

This depiction of the essence of mathematics is, oddly enough, very similar to Heidegger's own hermeneutic phenomenology. Since Heidegger's point is to distinguish his way of philosophizing from modern ways, the

---

8. This is also one of the characteristics of *technē. Technē* and *mathēsis* belong essentially together. A central point of contention between Socrates/Plato and Aristotle is whether virtue can be taught and would thus be a technique.

rise of modern science must occur as a narrowing of mathematics. This narrowing occurs as a result of the separation between essence and existence which understands being fundamentally as constancy or invariability. Mathematics in the narrow sense (geometry, arithmetic) is the most familiar instance of knowledge that does not vary. The sum of the internal angles of triangles always adds up to 180; 1 and 1 always equal 2. Mathematics in the narrow sense can thus stand as the exemplary type of propositional knowledge, where the constant truth of the proposition can be adequate to the thing, because only where the thing is constant is it possible for a proposition to be true in the absolute sense. Taking cognizance of things, mathematical knowledge in the broadest sense would only be truly knowledge where the being that it cognizes is constant. There is thus an internal consistency between truth claims, mathematics (in the narrow sense), and the being of beings. The science of beings would thus become tied to mathematics.

This realization exercised a profound influence on the Greeks and subsequent thinkers. For the Greeks it led in the first instance to a division of ways of apprehending truths appropriate to the character of the thing, namely, whether it changes or not. This separation already points to one essential character of ancient thought: that there is a knowledge of things in time which cannot be the same as eternal things which are known mathematically. There might be some debate about which type of truth is higher, but there is no attempt to understand things of one nature in terms of another. It might have occurred to Aristotle that we could understand nature, that which grows, in terms of mathematics, but he would in any case have rejected it as a confusion of categories.[9] Modern science arose in a contrary attempt to understand nature in terms of the highest possible knowledge, mathematical constancy.[10] It is precisely this rejection of the ancients' presumption of a category error in the mathematical science of nature that makes modernity distinctive.

This project required changing the understanding of nature so that mathematics in the narrow sense could come into play. Physics had to become

9. See Amos Funkenstein, *Theology and the Scientific Imagination from the Middle Ages to the Seventeenth Century* (Princeton: Princeton University Press, 1986), 303–5.

10. This means primarily modern physics, the science of motion, which was for many centuries after Galileo and Newton the leading scientific field. Biology has always resided uncomfortably with physics because it retains, even today, some of the older teleological underpinnings.

a geometrical science of motion. It could develop mathematical relationships that explained the change in position of things. In metaphysical terms, being came to be understood as matter in motion within an infinite universe, motion governed by unchanging laws of motion expressed in mathematical relationships.

For Heidegger, the true significance of this development in science lay in the change in the relation between humans and being. No one has ever directly observed any matter in motion obeying these pure mathematical laws; no one has ever seen an object obey the law of inertia, that a being continues indefinitely in a straight line. We can explain this fact by including other factors such as drag, but it remains the case that laws of motion are unobservable limit cases. They are "observable" only in the human mind. That was the true significance Heidegger saw in the change in the modern understanding of nature and being. In one of Heidegger's presentations, this change crystallized in Galileo's and Newton's new laws of motion, the primary one being the law of inertia. As Galileo developed it, the law applies to "corpus quod a viribus impressis no cogitur," a body left to itself (*WiT*, 89). It is not possible to find such a body. The law speaks of a thing that does not exist except in thought. Heidegger quoted Galileo: "Mobile mente concipio omni secluso impedimento" [I think in my mind of something moveable that is entirely left to itself] (*WiT*, 91). Heidegger fastened onto this "I think in my mind." This is a taking cognizance that is a determination of a thing. Thus it belongs to the essence of *mathēsis* (*WiT*, 91). It is a taking cognizance out of oneself that skips over the thing itself, as it were, by determining "what" a thing is in advance. This anticipatory determination is the sketch (*Entwurf*) of being. It opens the space (*Spielraum*) within which something shows itself: "How they show themselves is prefigured in the sketch" (*WiT*, 93). This is general to Dasein. As Heidegger outlines in *Being and Time*, all understanding is a sketch by which we take something as something. The distinctively modern, however, cannot lie in this anticipatory sketching. The distinctively modern lies rather in the determination of being as constant and the ground or subject of this being as the *cogito sum*, "I think." This determination allows mathematics in the narrow sense to come into play as the science of being.

The *cogito sum* points directly to Descartes's attempts to ground being in what can be absolutely certain. Descartes's metaphysics are the deepest thinking-out of the modern mathematical project. Newton's laws of motion are founded upon axioms, the fundamental anticipatory determinations of thingness, the "blueprints" (*Grundrisse*) of the structure of beings as a whole (*WiT*, 92). This blueprint in Heidegger's terminology is Da-sein, world, the openness within which things appear as what they are. As part of Heidegger's hermeneutic deconstruction of Western metaphysics, he is digging behind the objects of science to determine how they are what they are, that is, in what way they are determined as knowable objects. One corollary to this project is that it is possible to find this fundamental metaphysical determination of being in the fundamental texts of metaphysics, for it is in these texts that the fundamental determination of being takes place. I deliberately used the locution "takes place" because according the Heidegger being reveals itself in language; the author does not effect the determination of being through an act of will. Descartes is central to the modern project, not because he is an innovator, but because in his metaphysics one finds the deepest expression of the fundamental grounds of this modern project. These fundamental grounds are the axioms of science, those principles out of which it knows both how it should know and what types of objects fall within its knowable domain. The fundamental axioms of the modern project to know nature through mathematics are found in the character of the *cogito*. Descartes was led to this conclusion because he wanted to make truth certain. This move was both based upon Christian theology and a reaction against it. It was based on Christian motives because Christian theology understands the highest being to be that being which is fully actualized, that is, constant. Thus one of God's determinations was omnipresence (MHB, 16). Only that which is ever present is "real." Thus the transformation of truth into certainty is determined by being as *actus purus* (MHB, 24). This transformation, however, reacted against Christian theology in pushing away revelation as the ground of knowledge. According to Heidegger, medieval science held that knowledge of nature that was not grounded in Scripture had no intelligible basis (*WiT*, 96). That is to say, for medieval science, nature was the effect of a free act of creation by God, the meaning of which was revealed in Scripture, and more important, could change as a result of another act of will by God. Descartes and modern science had to find a way around this contingency of nature because this contingency was incompatible with the constancy of mathematical truths. Thus part of the modern project involved a rejection of the revealed truth of Scripture. Heidegger wanted to push beyond this local rejection of Christian revelation to a rejection of revelation in general. The axioms that ground knowledge must be self-grounding (*WiT*,

97). This need for self-grounding axioms led to Descartes's famous experiments in doubting. Descartes did not doubt because he was a skeptic, but because he needed to show the true self-grounding axiom which could be the basis, the *subiectum,* because it could not be doubted (*WiT,* 103).[11] This basis is, of course, the *cogito,* the "I think." Only on this basis is it possible to find the axiom which is absolutely first and as absolute, absolutely certain.

One can clearly see the connection Heidegger was attempting to draw between Descartes's philosophy and Galileo's physics. The laws of motion that make possible a mathematical description of nature exist "in the mind," as Heidegger quoted Galileo; the pure geometric motions of bodies in Galileo's and Newton's formulas have existence and being only in the mind. Galileo, however, accepted the self-evident truth of geometry and the truth of the reason that apprehended it. Descartes, on the other hand, began by doubting even these truths, but could not doubt the truth of "I think therefore I am." In this way he showed the absolute self-certainty of grounding being in Galileo's "I think in my mind."

All subsequent knowledge must be founded on this absolute axiom of the self-certainty of the *cogito.* This is to say that all knowledge must conform to the certainty of the positing which posits itself. Other propositions are certain when they are presented before the thinking I clearly and distinctly, namely, when they are represented. These clear and distinct representations are the ideas. Descartes's "ideas" borrow from the Greek *idea* in that ideas in representation are certain and thus constant and continuous: "What is thus represented has also already presented what is constant, that is, what is real, to representational thinking" (MHB, 25). The ideas, that which is represented, for Descartes are mathematical truths, which are now the most real beings. "Reality" must be construed "ideally," which is

---

11. In other places Heidegger indicates that the importance of certainty relates to the Christian preoccupation with personal salvation. Although he never discusses it so far as I know, there is another Christian basis for Descartes's profound worry about certainty. The nominalist philosophy arose out of the fundamental conviction of God's absolute freedom of the will. One of the great debates in Scholastic philosophy was whether God could invalidate laws of reasoning, particularly the law of noncontradiction. Pushed to maintain God's absolute freedom, the nominalists maintained He could, even if out of His goodness He chose not to. All one has to do is take freedom more seriously to realize that goodness is only a stopgap measure which cannot contain the ultimate contingency of knowledge. In the barest of shifts, Ockham's free God became Descartes's evil genius. Descartes turned to the certainty of the *cogito* because the freedom of God's will upset any grounding of knowledge in God, even God's own revelation. Cf. Gillespie, *Nihilism Before Nietzsche.*

to say, it must be represented in terms of representing, or to put it in more familiar terms, reality is constructed: "Accordingly, the reality of what is represented and added in all representing is characterized by *being represented*" (MHB, 29).[12] The object thus has a passive character, since what it is is dependent on the positing, representing subject, the ego cogito. Kant's "Copernican" revolution is prefigured in Descartes and the modern project itself.

This reference to Kant points to something important in Heidegger's presentation. There is a fundamental ambiguity in the laws of nature that modern science discovers: are they descriptive or prescriptive? This ambiguity also appears in the meaning of representation: are they re-presentations of something already present or are they representations made present by a positing mind? It is not clear in Descartes whether laws of nature are discovered by or willed by humans. This ambiguity led to a disjunction between reason and nature that increased in the post-Cartesian period and came to a head in Hume's absolute split between analytic truths and knowledge of nature. Kant attempted to reunite reason and nature while simultaneously obeying Hume's injunctions against uncritical metaphysics. His means of reuniting reason and nature or reason and being was his "Copernican revolution," which made being synthetically posited by a thinking or transcendental I. There could be no knowledge of things in themselves, but only of those objects synthesized by the transcendental I. The posited nature of being becomes quite clear in post-Kantian philosophy, such as that of Reinhold or even more explicit in the thought of Fichte, who combined Kant's pure and practical reason into one absolute self-positing I that wills being itself.

For Heidegger, this willed character of being is the key to modernity. Thus his reading of Descartes is derived from this key; he interpreted Descartes through the prism of Kant and Nietzsche. Heidegger really wanted to show that the willing that posits being wills according to the determination of being as what can be absolutely certain. It is never the case for Heidegger that there is an I that posits reality, as some crude constructivism holds; being always reveals itself. In modernity, being reveals itself as self-certainty, which is to say, as that which is posited by a self-certain I. All willing must conform to this self-certain character of being,

---

12. The connections are clearer in German, where the common word for reality is *Wirklichkeit*, or literally, that whose character is being effected (*wirken*). This has an obvious etymological connection with *werken*, "work," and *Werke*, "a work."

or to put it clearly, the will constructs in accordance with mathematics and calculation. Reason and will, thinking and acting, shape themselves into a mutually dependent system that constructs the world according to this systematic rationalization.

The constructed nature of modern reality is the central fact of modern technology. It connects production and science in a way that goes beyond saying that production is applied science. According to Heidegger, science is already in itself technical. The common ground of science and modern production lies in the metaphysical determination of being as that which is posited by an absolute and self-certain subject. That which the subject effects (*wirkt*) is being thought of as reality (*Wirklichkeit*); the real is what is brought about through the work (*Werken*) of the subject. I began with Heidegger's account of the metaphysics of modern science and have now come to the point where this same metaphysics of the self-certain subject constructs the world, that is to say, both nature and society, in accordance with itself. Science is technical because it too obeys the technical determination of being, that is to say, the rationally willed construction of reality, that comes to light in Descartes's and Kant's metaphysics. For this determination, all reality is effected and its reality lies in its being effected by a subject. The subject works. The subject works in accordance with the determination of being in modernity as what can be known through representation of the will. Because the will as representation demands certainty of itself, it must will itself because only this self-grounding or self-willing can be certain. All willing is thus what Heidegger calls the will-to-will.[13] The will-to-will, according to Heidegger, is the essence of modern technology. The will-to-will means to effect effectiveness. Modern technology as the will-to-will is thus the construction of reality that obeys the fundamental stricture to construe everything in terms of what can be most effectively effected. Modern technology operates under the demand of maximum efficiency. Thus in the metaphysics of science Heidegger also finds the metaphysics of modern society. Modern social organization as well as modern science lies under the domination of the technical determination of being.

---

13. It is via this circuitous route that Heidegger designated Nietzsche's true teaching to be the equation of the will-to-power and the will-to-will and thus as the completion of metaphysics. This is quite a controversial interpretation, the consideration of which will not be undertaken here.

Technology and the Death of God

In depicting how the demands of the modern technological and scientific project develop into the demand for maximum efficiency, Heidegger has presented a sort of "dialectic of enlightenment." It was the belief of the early moderns such as Descartes that the new science being developed would enable human beings to become the masters and possessors of nature. We become masters of nature by subjecting it to our will; our knowledge of how things function enables us to manipulate nature to attain our desired outcomes. Through science, we will be able to construct a new Eden here on earth. This seemingly imminent prospect inspired (and inspires still today) great and sometimes fantastic hopes for the future; as science and technology progresses, all sorts of heretofore "natural" limitations disappear, exciting speculations of further progress, of a kinder, gentler human race that has overcome all material need and want and lives in peace and comfort. This vision stands in direct linear descent from the dreams of early moderns such as Bacon or Descartes.

Unfortunately, this "instrumental" understanding of technology fails to capture the true dynamic of modern technology. We are no longer (if we ever were) capable of mastering technology. Heidegger suggests that "the distinctiveness of modern technology lies in the fact that overall it is no longer a mere 'means' and no longer stands in the 'service' for others, but itself enfolds its own character of domination. Technology itself commands out of itself and for itself and develops in itself its own type of discipline and its own type of consciousness of victory" (GA53, 53–54).

The "type of discipline" modern technology develops and subjects itself to is the demand for maximum efficiency. As a principle of being, it stands outside all human willing, which is to say, it achieves an objective reality beyond the consciousness of human beings. As the principle of the modern will, it rules in all willing, even to the detriment of the individual who "wills." Individuals do not freely will; the real will is the will-to-will, which Heidegger sees as absolute subjectivity. In contrast to our usual conception of humans as actors effecting their will on the world, Heidegger believed that human beings can only accord themselves with this absolute willing subject and become themselves the effected rather than the effectors. The obvious modern example is capitalism, which operates explicitly under the demand for maximum efficiency. To achieve this goal demands that humans fit themselves to function within the demands of production. This fitting to function is what Heidegger calls cybernetics (*FBSD, 7–9*). Humans become cogs in the machine, mere raw material in the "total mobilization" of all resources. Modern technology, which initially aimed at the betterment of the human condition and the realization of human freedom, ends in the absolute slavery of humans to efficiency.

This dialectical transformation of modern technology found a strong resonance in social theory for several reasons. In no small part this was because of its congruence with a large body of existing theories that analyze modern society, such as Marx's critique of capitalism, Weber's sociology of rationalization, and the work of the Frankfurt school. Moreover, it anticipated newer theories such as radical environmentalism, even as it echoed older Luddite worries about the nature of machine technology that cropped up in response to the Industrial Revolution. Thus Heidegger could be taken as another, perhaps more radical, voice in the chorus that held modern technology in suspicion.[14] By "suspicion," however, I do not mean "rejection," although in the case of radical environmentalism or neo-Luddism that might hold true, but a view of technology that refuses to see it as the advocates of technology like to see it, as a constantly progressive savior of humankind that will make life easier, more comfortable, freer, and more secure.

Whatever the manifest parallels in motifs or general outline that exist between other social theorists, particularly Weber, and Heidegger's critique of technology, one cannot easily assimilate Heidegger to these other theories because of the distinctive theological context that shapes his analysis of modernity. What is innovative in Heidegger's approach is that he combines his analysis of technology with his analysis of nihilism, and nihilism for Heidegger means above all that God is dead and the divine no longer

---

14. Among those who have worked to appropriate Heidegger to these theories are Fred Dallmayr, Steven K. White, Wolfgang Schirmacher, Albert Borgmann, and Michael Zimmerman (particularly where he puts together Heidegger and Marcuse). See Dallmayr, *Between Freiburg and Frankfurt*; Steven K. White, *Political Theory and Postmodernism* (New York: Cambridge University Press, 1991); Wolfgang Schirmacher, *Ereignis Technik* (Vienna: Passagen, 1990); Albert Borgmann, *Technology and the Character of the Life-World*; and Michael Zimmerman, "Heidegger and Marcuse: Technology as Ideology," *Research in Philosophy and Technology* 2 (1979). Zimmerman has since distanced himself from his earlier attempts to appropriate Heidegger. Michael Zimmerman, *Heidegger's Confrontation with Modernity: Technology, Politics, and Art* (Bloomington: Indiana University Press, 1990), and idem, *Contesting Earth's Future*, 4–5. In their own way, Derrida, Lacoue-Labarthe, and Nancy also point to some common ground between Heidegger and Marxist critiques of contemporary society.

comes into presence in the modern world. God has died because the question of being no longer poses itself to humans; we suffer under the twin fates of *Seinsverlassenheit* and *Seinsvergessenheit,* the abandonment of being and the forgetting of being. To say that modern technology is nihilistic means that through it we have been cut off from the ground of our own being, a ground that is opened only by questioning being. Without understanding the connection of technology and nihilism, appropriations of the later Heidegger's approach to technology cannot focus the issue as he wanted, and thus cannot understand the political conclusions Heidegger drew from the confrontation of humanity and modern technology.

These connections are made in their most concise form in "Overcoming Metaphysics," written between 1936 and 1946. When Heidegger expanded upon the historicity of being to analyze specific historical constellations in terms of their being or their appropriations of being, he designated modernity as the age of completed metaphysics. The completion of metaphysics includes "the fact that metaphysics is now for the first time beginning its unconditional rule in beings themselves, and rules as beings in the form, devoid of truth, of what is real and of objects" (OM, 67). As we have seen in the previous chapter, things show themselves against the totality of significance that makes up a world. Heidegger was interested in gaining access to this pretheoretical worldhood of world, or how things are. The way in which things are is the how of beings, which Heidegger calls world or Dasein, the "there" of being. Things show themselves in their being according to the specific "there" of being. We understand a thing in its specific historical constellation when we understand the overall significance of a historical epoch of being. Heidegger therefore understands an era through its understanding of being or the determination of being that is authoritative for its time.[15]

15. The accusation sometimes leveled against Heidegger, in particular by Adorno and Habermas, that he loses the ability to analyze history in a concrete fashion because he turns to historicity, is untenable. Theodor W. Adorno, *Negative Dialectics*, trans. E. B. Ashton (New York: Continuum, 1990), 128–31; Jürgen Habermas, *The New Conservatism: Cultural Criticism and the Historians' Debate*, trans. and ed. Shierry Weber Nicholsen (Cambridge: MIT Press, 1989), 146. While it is true that Heidegger lumps together seemingly disparate phenomena under the rubric of "metaphysical," it does not mean that "metaphysics" lacks concrete specificity, only that Heidegger found an underlying connection among a broader range of phenomena than other analysts have. All theory is abstraction, and Heidegger's is neither more so or less so than a "Dialectic of Enlightenment" or a social process of rationalization.

According to Heidegger, the authoritative determination of being in contemporary times is metaphysics. Metaphysics constitutes the history of the
West as its destiny determined from its beginning in early Greek thinking
about being. This thinking of being was open to a peculiar deformation by
which being could appear in beings yet disappear behind the dominance
of beings. "Metaphysics is a fate in the strict sense, which is the only sense
intended here, that it lets mankind be suspended in the middle of beings
as a fundamental trait of Western European history, *without* the Being of
beings ever being able to be experienced and questioned and structured in
its truth as the twofoldness of both in terms of metaphysics and through
metaphysics" (OM, 72).

Heidegger calls this the "most extreme oblivion of being" (*Seinsvergessenheit*) (OM, 72). This oblivion of being is itself the being of beings,
which is to say, the being of beings, how things show themselves, is pecu-
liarly enough a type of being in which being itself does not come forward
and does not appear as a question. The failing to appear of being is itself
a way of being (N4, 214). We will return later to this vital and difficult
point. Metaphysics is the oblivion of being because in metaphysics, being
disappears behind beings. This requires a little explanation. The oblivion
of being occurs because of the type of question that has been asked about
being ever since the Greeks. The question of being which came about in
Aristotle's metaphysics is "What is being?" or "What is the being of beings?"
This question takes the form of the Socratic question, "What is X?" The
point Heidegger wishes to make is that this is the type of question one asks
about beings, e.g., "What is a tree?" Metaphysics questions being as if "it"
were a being. In this way, being disappears behind beings, or is released
into beings, as Heidegger sometimes puts it. In treating being as a being,
metaphysics forgets the ontological difference, the difference between being
and beings so central to Heidegger's thinking. Metaphysics forgets being
not because it does not ask about being, but rather because in asking the type
of question it does, it treats being as a being, and thus overlooks being itself.

As metaphysics works itself out in the history of being, being becomes
interpreted as the attempt to absolutely secure beings for the mathematically rational subject. The most extreme oblivion of being, that is to say,
the completion of metaphysics, is the will to will (OM, 72). Heidegger spec-
ifies the concrete forms the will to will takes as technology: "The basic
form of appearance in which the will to will arranges and calculates itself
in the unhistorical element of the world of completed metaphysics can be

stringently called 'technology.' This name includes all the areas of beings which equip the whole of beings: objectified nature, the business of culture, manufactured politics, and the gloss of ideals overlaying everything" (OM, 74).

Technology has a being-character, which is to say, it unifies the connection of significance that makes up the modern world. Technology signifies the being of the modern world. As such, it coincides with the term "completed metaphysics" (OM, 75).

By what path does Heidegger come to make this connection? Earlier I examined why Heidegger calls modern metaphysics "technological," but his equation of technology and metaphysics is a hallmark of his later philosophy. One should keep in mind that Heidegger early thought of his hermeneutical phenomenology as metaphysics; even as late as his 1935 *Introduction to Metaphysics* he retained the term "metaphysics" for the authentic questioning of being.[16] To practice metaphysics means to transcend the obviousness of the given understanding of being in order to let the openness in which beings appear come to presence. This underwent a subtle but decisive shift later, once Heidegger understood the metaphysical question of being which lets beings appear as what they are as a question concerning the "what" of being; that is to say, a question that takes being to be a being. This oblivion of the question of being itself in metaphysics is the advent of nihilism. Heidegger thus establishes a connection among metaphysics, technology, and nihilism.

Although Heidegger had broached the technical understanding of being before *Being and Time,* it was not until the early 1930s that he began concerning himself with the connection between technology and nihilism. The attempt to uncover the metaphysical substratum between technology and nihilism led through Nietzsche, but it was a twisting path that eventually led Heidegger to the opposite conclusion about Nietzsche than the one with which he began. The figure that stands behind and guides Heidegger's readings of Nietzsche as the last metaphysician is also the probable source of the connection Heidegger drew between technology and the modern being of beings: Ernst Jünger. Two works in particular have relevance in this regard: the essay "Total Mobilization" (1930) and the book-length

---

16. One can trace this shift in the meaning of the term "metaphysics" across the various editions and additions to "What is Metaphysics?" In the 1928 original, "metaphysics" meant the questioning of being; in the "Introduction" appended in 1949, "metaphysics" meant that calculating thinking which is the forgetting of being.

expansion of the same subject *Der Arbeiter* (1932). In an accounting of his political involvement written after the war, Heidegger wrote that at that time he viewed the historical situation through these two books. "Among a small circle at that time I discussed these writings with my assistant Brock and tried to show how an essential understanding of Nietzsche's metaphysics was expressed in them, insofar as in the horizon of this metaphysics the history and present of the West was seen and foreseen" (FT, 18; *GA16*, 375). What he had seen in 1932 held true for 1945, "In this reality everything stands today, may it be called communism or fascism or world democracy" (FT, 18; *GA16*, 375). This reality is stamped under the sign of the worker. In "Overcoming Metaphysics" Heidegger reiterates, "For labor (cf. Ernst Jünger, *Der Arbeiter*, 1932) is now reaching the metaphysical rank of the unconditional objectification of everything present which is active in the will to will" (OM, 68). If we are to understand Heidegger's appropriation of Nietzsche, we need to examine Jünger.

Jünger received his epiphany on the slaughterfields of World War I; the brutal war showed him that mechanization had completely overtaken warfare and we could find only aesthetic pleasure in this process. "Total Mobilization" seeks to find the metaphysical grounds for Germany's defeat and possible resurrection. Jünger found the source in the economic and social structure of the allies, particularly America. Because America did not have a traditional class structure which partitioned certain classes to warfare or the war economy, it could mobilize its entire economy and laboring power to the conflict, giving it a great advantage in the new "battles of material."[17] America would have been the inevitable winner of the war had it not ended when it did.[18] Germany's only path to power lay in imitating America (or Bolshevism; Jünger was actually more drawn toward the Soviet Union than to America). In *Der Arbeiter,* Jünger put a more metaphysical slant to the thesis, calling for a transformation of reality by stamping it in the shape (*Gestalt*) of the worker and soldier. *Gestalt* in Jünger's terminology functions similarly to Heidegger's being; both are

17. Ernst Jünger, "Total Mobilization," in *The Heidegger Controversy,* ed. Richard Wolin (Cambridge: MIT Press, 1993), 117.

18. Although Jünger is often derided in scholarly publications, it should be noted his prediction was accurate, particularly if one views the Second World War as a continuation of the First. America's resource mobilization for the Second World War is astonishing in hindsight. It is also worth noting that after the war, the only power who could compete with the United States was another "classless" system, the Soviet Union.

wholes that encompass more than the sum of their parts.[19] How reality is transformed and mobilized Jünger names "technology."[20] We must transform ourselves into workers so that we will be in accordance with underlying historical life processes, the will to power, which will thereby give workers a world-historical meaning. The will to power must be embraced wholeheartedly; the mobilization of workers and material under the stamp of labor must be total. In this queer mixture of history, metaphysics, and geopolitics, the will to power takes form as the worker who would transform reality into material for work. The worker and total mobilization became the principle of being or in Heidegger's language, the being of beings.

The effect on Heidegger was lasting. The connection of greatest significance for Heidegger's thinking on technology lies in the connection between *Gestalt,* easily convertible into Heidegger's being, and technology. Jünger showed Heidegger how technology could constitute the being that makes up the world. Beyond this overarching theme, individual formulations influenced by Jünger crop up in "Overcoming Metaphysics." "Since reality consists in the uniformity of calculable reckoning, man, too, must enter monotonous uniformity in order to keep up with what is real" (OM, 88). "This release [of being into machination] takes man into unconditional service. It is by no means a decline and something 'negative' in any kind of sense" (OM, 83). Since Heidegger views machination as the desolation of the earth, this sentence makes sense only by keeping in mind that machination was an escalation of power and a manifold increase in production and consumption. The whole notion of unlimited production and consumption principles, of nature and man understood as raw materials, takes its cue from Jünger (OM, 84). So too, although this is often overlooked, is Heidegger's prediction of the end of a distinction between war and peace (OM, 84).[21] The notion of reality completely transformed by human beings as the laboring animal owes its image directly to Jünger. Since Heidegger himself maintains this, it should not be a controversial point.[22]

19. Ernst Jünger, *Der Arbeiter: Herrschaft und Gestalt* (Stuttgart, Klett-Cotta, 1982), 33; *GA33*, 17–18. Heidegger's lecture course was held in 1932. The similarity in themes is probably not coincidental.

20. Jünger, *Der Arbeiter,* 311.

21. Heidegger is sometimes given praise for prescience in this regard; he is actually repeating a formula of Jünger's. Jünger, "Total Mobilization," 126–27.

22. What is more controversial is the claim, made by both Pöggeler and Zimmerman, that Heidegger was positively influenced by Jünger which led to a proximity with National Socialism. Pöggeler, *Schritte zu einer Hermeneutische Philosophie,* 254; Michael Zimmerman,

What has been more controversial is how close the result is to Nietzsche, for as Heidegger said, he was convinced that *Der Arbeiter* expressed at a different level the metaphysical truths enunciated earlier by Nietzsche, which meant that Heidegger had to interpret Nietzsche's thought so that it would be made consistent with Jünger's quasi-Nietzschean insight into reality.[23] *In nuce,* the will to power must become the will to will, whose basic form is technology and rationalization. This interpretation has been controversial since Heidegger published it, all the more so since Nietzsche had been considered beforehand (and is often considered today) a sort of irrationalist.[24] Heidegger, fully aware of Nietzsche's reputation, had to show that the ostensibly antirational will to power must in the end take the form of Jünger's worker society, that is to say, modern technological society. In the barest sketches, Heidegger begins with the last sentence of *The Will to Power: "This world is the will to power and nothing besides!* And you yourselves are also this will to power—and nothing besides!"[25] According to Heidegger, this proposition states that Nietzsche thought that the will to power constituted the whole of reality, that is to say, it was the being of

"Ontological Aestheticism: Heidegger, Jünger, and National Socialism," in *The Heidegger Case: On Philosophy and Politics,* ed. Tom Rockmore and Joseph Margolis (Philadelphia: Temple University Press, 1992). While it would admittedly make for a clear connection—the Nazis were after all a workers' party—I find it hard to fathom that Heidegger would advocate total mobilization as the solution to the death of God. In his postwar "Facts and Thoughts," Heidegger gives two key principles for reality, the worker and the death of god, technology and nihilism. If I am correct in my overall interpretation, these two belong to the same constellation of being. If so, it would be difficult to believe that for a time Heidegger would believe that total technology represented an adequate replacement for the dead god. A more likely hypothesis is that Heidegger interpreted Jünger similarly to the way in which he would later interpret Nietzsche: they provided an insight into the nature of modern reality, but their thinking, instead of overcoming modernity, only radicalized it. Heidegger appropriated Jünger's depiction of modern technology, but whereas Jünger's answer was to submit to it, Heidegger wanted to resist it.

23. This is consistent with Heidegger's reservations about Jünger's metaphysics, which is to say, its inadequacy for penetrating to the roots of nihilism. In the cases of both Jünger and Nietzsche, Heidegger felt that their way of posing the problem closed them off to the essence of the problem.

24. Many of the French postmodernists have taken particular umbrage at Heidegger's claim that Nietzsche was the last metaphysician, emphasizing instead an interpretation of the will to power as difference resistant to the principle of reason. See for instance, Deleuze's *Nietzsche and Philosophy* or Jacques Derrida's "Interpreting Signatures (Nietzsche/Heidegger): Two Questions," in *Dialogue and Deconstruction: The Gadamer-Derrida Encounter,* ed. Diane P. Michelfelder and Richard Palmer (Albany: SUNY Press, 1989).

25. Friedrich Nietzsche, *The Will to Power,* ed. Walter Kaufmann, trans. Walter Kaufmann and R. J. Hollingdale (New York: Vintage, 1968), 550.

beings (WN, 86). At this point, Heidegger stands on relatively stable ground. The interpretation becomes more questionable as Heidegger moves to think through the meaning of will to power. Ordinarily, one would think of having a will to power as meaning that one desires or wills to have power or to have the ability to exercise domination over things. As Heidegger points out, however, willing is in itself the exercise of power over things; one must already have power in order to will. This means that the power that is willed in the will to power is not one chosen goal among others, but the one that wills the essence of willing itself. The will to power must be the will to will (WN, 77–79). The will to will is still the will to power, but of a peculiar type. Because it wills its own self, the will to will is the will to power become self-conscious (WN, 88–89). This means that the will wills whatever is necessary to expand its power over things; it must become ever more efficient in order to become effective as will to power. The will to power that becomes self-conscious as will to will is thus equivalent to modern technology; the will to power must will itself to operate according to maximum efficiency. The name of the being who knowingly wills himself as will to power is the overman, whose task is "taking over dominion of the earth" (WN, 96–97). Nietzsche's overman for Heidegger is Jünger's worker, the new race of humans that will dominate the earth. While this deepens Jünger's account, whether this is actually what Nietzsche meant by the will to power is not at all clear. What is clear is that Heidegger's interpretation of the will to power as the will to will and the essence of modern technology as a principle of being is heavily influenced by Jünger's vision of modern society.

As a comprehensive principle of being, technology means more than just production and equipment, although it does encompass these phenomena; it includes all facets of modern life, including even ostensibly nontechnological areas such as faith or the human sciences. Historiography and its inherent historicism, for instance, both arise from and are dominated by the technological understanding of technology (OM, 74). Technology as the particular constellation of being determines and orders all things, including human beings, in accordance with the fundamental logic of its development. This development grows out of the abandonment of being which releases human beings into unconditional service to the will to will (OM, 83). In unraveling the meaning of this statement, Heidegger launches into one of his most concise indictments of modern society. Human being is understood out of the determination *animal rationale*. Heidegger takes the two parts of this term and shows how the two parts develop in conjunction with their extremes so that humans become both subhuman and superhuman simultaneously because these two extremes are in the end the same thing (OM, 83–84). This is to say, our "higher," rational side, reason and science, comes to serve our "lower," animal side, our bodily drives and desires. "The drive of animality and the *ratio of* humanity become identical" (OM, 86). This is another way of expressing the fact that the will to power is in essence the will to will; power enhances itself as it becomes technically rational. The expansion of reason in the guise of technologically progressive science and technology allows for greater satisfaction of our drives and passions. Science becomes the domination of nature whereby humanity becomes the "master and possessor of nature." "The consumption of beings is such and in its course determined by armament in the metaphysical sense, through which man makes himself the 'master' of what is 'elemental'" (OM, 84).[26] Heidegger understood the modern impulse out of its birth in early modern thought, such as that of Bacon, Descartes, and Hobbes. Each saw science as the means to mastering nature for the ends of the satisfaction of human desires. Because it is driven by the unconditionality of the will to will, the twofold escalation of drives and science is itself unconditional, which is to say, unlimited (OM, 84).[27] Because drives satisfy themselves through consumption, beings are conceived as raw materials that stand under the "principle of production" (OM, 88). The reverse side is the "circularity of consumption for the sake of consumption," which "is the sole procedure which distinctively characterizes the history of a world which has become an unworld" (OM, 87). This principle is in turn governed by the will to will. "Man" as the "rational animal" is equivalent to "economic man," or the human type that comes about in an instrumentally rational society devoted to production.

26. Heidegger is thinking primarily of atomic science, but he was also aware of the enormous possibilities offered by genetic research, which can manipulate another type of "element." He even hypothesized that eugenics would become a normal practice in modern society in order to engineer superior types of humans better able to match the efficiency of machines.

27. This unhealthy dialectic of passions and reason has been noted by several Heideggerian environmentalists. Wolfgang Schirmacher, *Technik und Gelassenheit: Zeitkritik nach Heidegger* (Munich: Alber, 1983); Zimmerman, *Contesting Earth's Future.*
A recent example of this unlimited drive of science is the recent furor over cloning. While even many scientists are spooked by this breakthrough, almost all say that the research will continue because, according to them, if it can be done, it will be done. This can be seen as evidence for Heidegger's claim that technology possesses a logic that overpowers and masters its human "masters."

In this technological world of "economic man" politics is swallowed up into economic thinking. Politics becomes subsumed into machination, and as a result political leaders become overseers of technological and economic expansion. The whole process of calculation and efficiency requires a central administrator who can direct everything in the most rational and efficient manner. "Herein the necessity of 'leadership,' that is, the planning escalation of the guarantee of the whole of beings, is required. For this purpose such men must be organized and equipped who serve leadership. The 'leaders' are the decisive suppliers who oversee all the sectors of consumption of beings because they understand the whole of all those sectors and thus master erring in its calculability" (OM, 85).

This "leader," by virtue of his superior intellect, transcends his immediate desires so that he can properly calculate for the whole. This little section on leaders hits three different targets. On the one hand, it understands the political necessity for a command economy in a system of ultimate efficiency, and of an administrative class, à la Weber, to oversee this system. Second, it twists Nietzsche's attempt to ennoble philosophical leadership into its opposite, the rule of small-souled technocrats. Heidegger manages an interpretation of Nietzsche which explains the existence of a human type Nietzsche held to be impossible. We will examine later how this is possible. Third, by using the term "leader" (*Führer*), Heidegger openly criticized the direction he believed Hitler had taken, for Hitler led in the service of machination. It should be noted Heidegger carefully put "leader" into quotation marks, indicating that there can be a leader who is not a so-called "leader" who preserves the essence of leadership and does not fall into the seeming leadership (the distinction between true and seeming "leadership" necessitates the use of quotation marks) which falls under the sway of the will to will and the abandonment of being. This type of "leadership" results from the subsumption of the genuinely political under economics and management techniques. While Heidegger's account here may be rightly construed as a criticism of Hitler, it does not represent a break with his advocacy of the *Führerprinzip* in his days as rector. Rather, I suggest it represents his belief that Hitler proved in the end to be a "leader" and not a leader.[28]

---

28. Both Pöggeler and Vietta cite this text as proof of a break with National Socialist tendencies at the philosophical level. Otto Pöggeler, *Heidegger in seiner Zeit* (Munich: Fink, 1999), 213; Silvio Vietta, *Heideggers Kritik am Nationalsozialismus und an der Technik* (Tübingen: Niemeyer, 1989). The careful use of quotation marks belies this hope, and indeed points to the underlying conclusion that genuine leaders, the "shepherds of being," are the

If thus far the summation of a society dominated by instrumental rationality fits comfortably with the left Heideggerianism I outlined earlier in this chapter, the account of unfettered technology does not exhaust the meaning of the will to will. If it did, the will to will would have no greater explanatory power than Adorno's dialectic of Enlightenment or Habermas's colonization of the lifeworld, being distinguished only by a greater obscurantism in the terminology.

Heidegger's focus, however, is primarily on the nihilistic consequences of modern technology; the baneful effect of technology is that it aims at nothing. The will to will is a willing, which is to say, a striving. This is the source of the escalation, the sheer motion toward, of the development of technology. At the barest level, willing is motion toward something to be brought about, an "out toward" motion that enables humans to transcend their given existence. Readers familiar with the early Heidegger will recognize the will's similarity to care, which is also characterized as a motion "out toward." The question is always in what direction does—or should— the will aim. Taking his lead from Kant's understanding of practical reason, Heidegger asserts that to willing belongs consciousness; the object striven after is posited and known beforehand. If the willing is not mere wishing, the means to the end are given along with it. When the object is obtained or consumed, this completes the movement of willing. We are familiar with this operation of the will even in our most trivial pursuits; I desire to scribble a note, and I pick up a pencil and write the words I conceived in my mind. This same operation can describe grander designs and plans, from conceiving and executing a business plan, to urban planning, to commanding an entire national economy. If we shift to Heidegger's understanding of the will metaphysically, the question is what it strives to effect. The will to will is a unique kind of will because in the will to will, the object and the striving are the same. The will to will, as the term indicates, moves toward nothing other than itself and its own perpetuation. If willing is usually represented as a segment, the will to will is an infinite spiral, but a spiral that circles in on itself until it is left only as a point. A point, geometrically considered, has no direction and no aim. Thus it is essentially aimless. "The aimlessness, indeed the essential aimlessness of the unconditional will to will, is the completion of the being of will which

---

answer to the problem of technology. The break is with Hitler, not with the political-philosophical underpinnings of National Socialism.

was incipient in Kant's concept of practical reason as pure will" (OM, 81). Put together, it means that modern technology is aimless or meaningless. It works toward no end but itself. This would be one understanding of the essential nihilism of modern technology.

What makes technology and machination aimless? If efficiency or functionalization is the aim, this produces aimlessness because it turns a criterion for measuring the means into a measure for ends. It means that the ends themselves are forgotten. The meaning of work is lost, for as I explained in the first chapter, meaning is sense in a directional sense; things have meaning insofar as they aim at an end. The individual labors for a wage in order to consume and the product is made in order to be consumed. The human being in the age of technology has become fixed as the laboring animal, which "is left to the giddy whirl of its products so that it may tear itself to pieces and annihilate itself in empty nothingness" (OM, 69). The change from understanding humans as working beings to laboring beings is important. Work refers to both the production of a work and the end product itself; labor refers only to the sheer process of production. Labor is pure power. In modern capitalism, laborers sell their labor power to the owners of capital. In the production process, labor power is on the same level as machine power; both are blind components of the production process. This leveling of work into labor is the root, according to Marx, of the dissociation between a laborer and the product of his labor; labor is the source of alienation. Heidegger has a quite similar view.[29] Labor is simply power in the service of the will to will, which in itself cannot posit any goals beyond itself. Labor signifies the alienation of work from the ultimate "in order to" that gives it meaning. Transformed into labor, work serves no purpose; it has lost its transcendental meaning.

There is a close connection among transcendence, purpose, and service that bears closer inspection. The will, as pointed out above, is a striving to overcome, a striving to go out toward some aim. This striving to overcome is the source of human transcendence; it is how we get beyond where we are now. The goal toward which we strive is the purpose of the striving. This purpose is the meaning of the striving; it answers the question of why we strive. The work we do in striving toward the goal is done in service of accomplishing this purpose. All meaningful work is in service of some transcendent goal. The will to will operating in modern technology upsets

---

29. So too did Arendt. See *The Human Condition,* 79–174.

these connections. Because it aims at nothing besides its own perpetuation and becomes both means and end, modern technology loses its transcendental purpose and its service-oriented character. "The distinction of modern technology is that it is above all no longer mere 'means' and no longer stands in the 'service' for others, but rather unfolds out of itself its own ruling character" (*GA53*, 53). As an end it itself, modern technology cannot serve anything. Without serving something else, it loses its transcendental and meaningful character.

All meaning, it should be remembered, comes from being, or to put it in terms of the earlier chapter on Heidegger's early phenomenology, the meaning of any individual thing exists only against a backdrop of the totality of meanings that make up the world or the "there" of being. The loss of meaning in modern technology means that being itself is lost. "The essence of the history of being of nihilism is the abandonment of being in that in it there occurs the self-release of being into machination" (OM, 83). While "machination" (*Machenschaft*) derives etymologically from "making" (*machen*), the term refers, via the connections Heidegger drew between metaphysics and modern technology, to the totality of the system of being of the modern world. It is this total system of modern science, modern technology, modern society, and modern metaphysics that causes the loss of being. Therein lies the peculiarity of the modern world. It is an "unworld," which means that "the 'world' has become an unworld as a consequence of the abandonment of beings by the truth of being" (OM, 84). Humans are abandoned by being and left merely with beings because metaphysics cannot experience being itself, that is to say, it no longer asks the proper question of being. Only by posing the authentic question of being can humans let being presence as the coming into being of the world as a meaningful whole. Only by passing beyond metaphysics to the question of being can humans let being come to presence as a world that would give authentic meaning to their work.

The use of "authentic" here is meant to underscore an essential connection between "Overcoming Metaphysics" and *Being and Time*. The meaning of being for Heidegger is both the meaning of any particular system of meanings, that is to say, a particular world or culture (as we would put it today), and also the historicity of any particular world. Authenticity means a moment of vision in which both meanings of being became visible, both the specific historical situation in which one finds oneself and the nullity that lies at the heart of being, which is the root of the historicity of being, or the truth that things can be and will be otherwise. Authentic knowledge knows being as the coming into being of the temporary "there" which constitutes its history. "For 'world' in the sense of the history of being [*Seyn*] (cf. *Being and Time*) means the nonobjective presencing of the truth of being [*Seyn*] for man in that man is essentially delivered over to being [*Seyn*]" (OM, 84).[30] Knowledge of the world is only authentic when it acknowledges the historicity of this world, that is to say, that this world in which I live comes into being not as the effect of human willing and planning but rather as an effect of the coming to presence of being. The technological world does not have authentic knowledge of the truth of being, which is to say, its character of coming-to-presence. It does not have this truth because technical thinking is representational thinking, which fixes its object in advance and understands truth as correspondence of the thought with the object, or conversely put, admits as the object only what the subject can represent. The thinking subject is driven by the need for certitude and thus stability. It stabilizes the being of the object as constant presence or the unchanging.[31] To think being as the unchanging means the absolute subject cannot think being as presencing, that is to say, as coming to be. The will to will, or the will to absolute certitude and stability, cannot think of the belonging together of being and nothingness, and thus cannot be authentic knowledge. In essence, the later Heidegger developed and enriched the fundamental impulse of his earlier thinking, which contrasted *phronēsis* with *technē*. Modern technical thinking assumes that it grasps being, which is to say, reality, but in actuality it fixes reality as a constancy and objectivity that can be ordered, and so misses being itself. Yet this missing of being is of a peculiar kind, because metaphysics believes it has indeed grasped being or the reality of the world; reality for it lies in its objectivity. Believing it has being in its grasp, modern thinking no longer questions being, and the questioning of being is the first step to enabling the opening of being whereby it can come to presence. That is why the highest need is to recognize the distress caused by our abandonment by being (OM, 83). It is the peculiarity of our distress concerning being, however, that we do not experience this distress, at least not directly. We do experience the effects of nihilism, that is to say, we experience some of the

---

30. "*dem Seyn wesenhaft übereignet ist*" (VA, 88). "*Seyn*" is the archaic spelling for "*Sein*."
31. This extremely bare sketch cannot do justice to Heidegger's complicated theory of truth developed in many writings after 1930. The outline is essentially correct, though.

emptiness of modern society, the lack of a meaning for our lives, but we do not experience its root cause. Indeed, our attempts to redress this lack of meaning results in a search for values. Heidegger has Nietzsche in mind, for Nietzsche saw the distress of the modern world in the death of God, and even experienced the abandonment of being, but for Heidegger, Nietzsche's solution was the ultimate completion of modern metaphysics, the substitution of man for God by making man the ultimate subject and cause of what is. Nietzsche may have experienced the loss of being, but rather than experiencing it as distress, he rejoiced in it as the noonday of man who was free to again project his virtues into the heavens as gods. His poetic project was reevaluate all values is the grandest of all Cartesian schemes to create the world through our will. Nietzsche takes us into the heart of nihilism, but cannot uncover the real source of our distress. He is for his sometimes-disciple Heidegger the last and greatest metaphysician that we must overcome in order to move beyond our technological desolation amidst the abandonment by being.

By taking us into the heart of modern nihilism, however, Nietzsche pointed to the essential point of distress. As Heidegger put it after the war, "This reality of the will to power can be expressed in Nietzsche's sense by the proposition: 'God is dead'" (FT, 18). The death of God is for Heidegger the essential feature of nihilism. How does it come about that God has died? Heidegger dismisses the conservative explanation that God died because moderns became secularized and less religious. God did not die from a lack of faith; rather, a lack of faith is a consequence of the death of God (*WN*, 65). Because being (or God) revealed itself in Nietzsche's thought to be nothing, there was nothing to believe in. Heidegger believed that with this thought Nietzsche had expressed the fundamental insight into the being of the modern world, and he felt that if nothing fundamental were to change regarding being, eventually whatever resistance to the truth of Nietzsche's dictum there still remained would die out; eventually, everyone would come to agree with Nietzsche that being was entirely dispensable. Although God did not die from lack of faith, humans did play a role in the death of God. Following a passage from Nietzsche's *Gay Science*, Heidegger proclaims that we killed God (WN, 105). How did we kill God? The answer lies in the previous three centuries of European history (WN, 106). Modernity is the time of a subjectivity that has taken its final form as the will to will or modern technology. "The doing away with what is in itself, i.e., the killing of God, is accomplished in the making secure for himself material, bodily, psychic, and spiritual resources, and this for the sake of his own security, which wills dominion over whatever is—as the potentially objective—in order to correspond to the being of whatever is, to the will to power" (WN, 107). This making secure of all resources is the hallmark of technical thinking. It is thus modern technology that killed God.

Heidegger's interpretation of Nietzsche's pronouncement on the death of God flows into his own understanding of our present situation in which being has abandoned us. That is to say, what Nietzsche calls God Heidegger calls Being. Those very factors which have killed God—the securing of material, bodily, psychic, and spiritual resources—coincide exactly with Heidegger's description of modern metaphysics. While Heidegger cautions us against any straightforward equation of being with God, there is a harmony, even mutual dependence between the two that cannot be overlooked. Modern technical thinking and metaphysics prevent being from appearing as what it is; it stops up our ears and prevents us from hearing the voice of being so that we can let being come to presence. When being fails to come to presence, it closes off the holy and therewith God. "The failing to appear of the unconcealment of being as such releases the evanescence of all that is hale in beings. The evanescence of the hale takes the openness of the holy with it and closes it off. The closure of the holy eclipses every illumination of the divine. The deepening dark entrenches and conceals the lack of God" (N4, 248).[32] Despite differences in tone, this passage harks back to the basic impulses of *Being and Time*. There the concealed purpose was to examine how to find an authentic meaning to things in the world; Heidegger worked from the worldly meaning of all things back to the types of possible ways of the world or worldhood in order to find the authentic way of existence for humans vis-à-vis their own being as temporal beings. The path led through the acceptance of the freedom of being, which allowed being to come to presence as a particular world dependent on this freedom of being. Beings are restored as what they authentically are only in this dependence upon the freedom of being. The same intent is

32. White fastens upon a supposed change in Heidegger's thinking on gods which comes through in a change in terminology from "godliness" to the "holy," which supposedly supports his contention that gods are strangely unnecessary in Heidegger's later thought. White, *Political Theory and Postmodernism*, 66. In truth, concrete God or the gods are secondary things which arise out of thinking on the holy or the divine, which are, to use earlier terminology, formal indicators for gods. It was Heidegger's intention that thinking on the divine would open up space for concrete gods to appear. To substitute the "holy" for "gods" does not render gods unnecessary.

at work in the later passage. Technical thinking, like theory with which it shares a close affinity, cannot think of being as freedom; thinking about beings through the principle of reason, it understands all things as static and ordered by human reason, that is to say, as raw material to be shaped by the will. The rational will substitutes itself for God and thereby strips things of any sort of holiness. The unspoken premise in the later passage is that God or being is freedom. The point is the same in the 1940s and in the 1920s: to think of being as freedom and thus restore the divine to its proper place.

Thus the central problem of modern technology, technical thinking, or metaphysics is that it cuts humans off from the divine. To restore the divine in human affairs, and in so doing find a home for humans, it is necessary to overcome metaphysics.

With the end of metaphysics, the possibility arises for a postmodern age of shepherds who will watch over being.[33] The task of moving humanity beyond the modern age requires an "anticipatory escort" who will transform existence and bring "mortals to the path of thinking, poeticizing building" (OM, 90). This transitional task of the deconstruction of metaphysics was one Heidegger explicitly took upon himself in his later years. It was not, however, the postmodern age itself. Like many prophets, Heidegger gives us a glimpse of the coming age. The postmodern age of the shepherds will be the age of poeticized building. In this simple description lie important clues. "Shepherds" points to the religious context, but also to the specific role that humans will play: they are shepherds of God, caring for their flocks in service of God. They serve through building. This points directly to the role that work—*technē*—will play, for it is one of the strange turns in the later Heidegger that technology is both curse and salvation; it is only through a transformation of technology that human existence is altered. This transformation is brought about by the poeticization of work. Poeticized work cares for and serves the properly divine and restores humans to their proper home and place in the order of things.

33. Heidegger has a complex understanding of what the "end" of metaphysics means; it means both coming to a close and fulfilling its destiny. In its completion, though, the absolute abandonment of being that is expressed in the phrase "Being is nothing," lies its overcoming. All that is necessary is to understand that the nothing in that phrase should not be taken as a vapor or nullity, but rather as the "wholly-other-than-beings" no-thing, and a new thinking of being will begin. For these issues, see "What is Metaphysics?" "The Question of Being," and "The End of Philosophy and the Task of Thinking."

Reappropriating Technology

Despite the ills caused by modern technology, Heidegger's path to over-coming nihilism leads through technology. Only by coming to an adequate relationship with the essence of technology can human beings relate them-selves to being as freedom. Heidegger quotes Hölderlin: "Where danger is, grows / The saving power also" (QCT, 28). The source of the danger, tech-nology, is also where our salvation lies. While this phrase sounds inspir-ing, we must ask whether it is truly profound or simply bad dialectic. In the *Spiegel* interview Heidegger says that the task of that thinking which is to overcome modern technology "is to help, within its bounds, human beings to attain an adequate relationship to the essence of technology at all" (Sp, 61). If we can attain this adequate relationship, we can restore humans to their proper essence, which is poetic dwelling. Despite his polemic against modern technology, Heidegger thus did not counsel reject-ing technology out of hand: "For all of us, the arrangements, devices, and machinery of technology are to a greater or lesser extent indispensable. It would be foolish to attack technology blindly. it would be shortsighted to condemn it as the work of the devil" (G, 22). Humans are by life's neces-sities dependent upon technology and labor. Until manna falls from heaven and the elements withhold their violence from our bodies, nature demands that we cultivate and build. Heidegger thus considered a blanket condem-nation of technology ridiculous.

As I pointed out in the beginning of this chapter, Heidegger's thinking on this matter echoes Eckhart. The problem is not technology *per se*, but our relationship to technology. In the modern world we have an inverted relationship to technology and beings.[34] This point is important in deter-mining what it is that Heidegger wished to change. By condemning mod-ern technology, he wanted to condemn modern metaphysics and its relationship to being, not necessarily modern machine technology. The con-dition and size of modern society demands a high degree of technical sophistication; there is no going back to premodern production techniques without a drastic reduction in population. Heidegger, I believe, recognized this fact (G, 22).[35] The distinctive character of modern technology is not

---

34. Cf. Eckhart, *Deutsche Predigten und Traktate*, 55; idem, "Talks of Instruction," 3:13.

35. This point is not without controversy. Pöggeler accuses him of an untenable Romantic nostalgia on precisely these grounds. Otto Pöggeler, *Neue Wege mit Heidegger* (Munich: Alber, 1992), 173. It does not help matters that Heidegger usually chose premodern exam-

its mechanistic quality, but rather that it no longer serves the human good understood as being at home in the world; modern metaphysics has perverted our relationship to being (*GA53*, 53–54).

Our present relationship is determined by what Heidegger called alternately the will to will, technology, or *Gestell*. *Gestell*, often translated as "enframing," is a neologism Heidegger coined to express the totality of ways in which subjectivity imprints itself. *Gestell* expresses how things are ordered for our manipulation; as so ordered, things are what Heidegger called *Bestand*, or "standing-reserve."[36] In line with what I claimed above, the danger of *Gestell* "does not come in the first instance from the potentially lethal machines and apparatus of technology" (although that is a consequence), but from "the possibility that it could be denied to [human beings] to enter into a more original revealing and hence to experience the call of a more primal truth" (QCT, 28). This "more original revealing" is being experienced as a coming to presence, an experience that metaphysics forgets. We have seen that this is the essence of nihilism. According to Heidegger, if we can overcome nihilism and thereby take up an adequate relationship to technology, "we can affirm the unavoidable use of technical devices, and also deny them the right to dominate us, and so to warp, confuse, and lay waste our nature" (G, 22–23). This is a "yes and no" to technology that Heidegger called *Gelassenheit* (G, 23). To bring about this delightful state of affairs requires that "a new ground and foundation be

---

ples to make his contrasts starker. A close reading of his examples, however, supports my case: the point is almost always the relationship to things or nature inherent in using modern technology. The question thus is not, Can we do away with modern technology? but rather, Is it possible to use modern machinery in Heidegger's postmodern poetic world? One could also put it, Is modern metaphysics a necessary conjunction to modern machinery? Heidegger wants to deny this, but it is not entirely clear if this is tenable.

This point also impacts how we read Heidegger's environmentalism. He is, I would assert, far closer to modernity than deep ecology, yet far more premodern than what I would call "technical environmentalism" (finding better technical means of overcoming environmental problems, e.g., cleaner-burning engines). Heidegger finds himself in this position because he is not really an environmentalist; the central thrust of his thought is concerned with the divine, not the natural.

36. The German indicates a little better than the English the connections Heidegger is trying to make with his terminology. *Stellen* is a transitive verb; a thing which has been place (*gestellt*) is now standing (*stehen*, from which the noun *Stand* is derived). This motion of putting things in their position is related to subjectivity; although the word generally used for "positing" is *setzen*; *stellen* is almost synonymous with *setzen*, but *stellen* is also related to *vorstellen* and *darstellen* (both mean "representing"), the key terms in Kant's epistemology. Since Heidegger claimed that representing is the hallmark of modern metaphysics, *Gestell* is meant to tie modern technology to modern metaphysics.

granted again to man, a foundation and ground out of which man's nature and all his works can flourish in a new way even in the atomic age" (G, 21). To find a ground and foundation means to find a reason why work is done in order to give work meaning, that is to say, to put it in service of the divine and thus ultimately of being. The meaninglessness of work (the abandonment by being) and the inability to discover its meaning (the forgetting of being) is precisely the problem of modern technology. It will not be possible to restore work to its proper place as service to something higher unless being is reestablished in its authenticity.

In order to restore work to its proper place, authentic being must be opened up through work itself. In order to serve the whole, work itself must be part of the whole. Heidegger had to find a way to think about working and making that escapes the problems of modern technical thinking. This means that we have to return to the original possibilities of *technē*. Heidegger, one must bear in mind, always thought in terms of the possibilities of human existence, and the ways that these possibilities can enact themselves as being in the world. The history of Western metaphysics has been the progressive enacting of one possibility of work and thus one way of being human: "Thus the history of being is primarily revealed in the history of *energeia* which is later called *actualitas* and existential actuality and existence" (MHB, 11–12). At work in this history is a change in the concept and nature of work, and thus a transposition to another way of being human (MHB, 12). *Energeia* connects the two parts of metaphysics and work. *Energeia* is derived from *ergon,* the work produced. *Energeia* refers to the producing, the bringing of the work to presence in the truth. According to Heidegger's interpretation of Aristotle, *energeia* is a fundamental meaning of being, that is to say, it is the being of being according to the Greek way of thinking. As such, it has a fundamental connection with *physis,* nature, another fundamental word for being. In Heidegger's understanding, both are essentially the same because both refer to the being of beings as the act of coming to presence of the beings. Both work and nature let beings come to presence as what they are.[37] The Latin transla-

---

37. Whether this is what Aristotle really meant is quite another point, one which would take too long to go into here. It is generally held that Aristotle divides being into that which comes to be on its own (*physis*, nature) and what requires human art (*technē*) to come into being. Heidegger is attempting to explode this distinction by setting everything back into what is common to both: that they come to be. Thus for Heidegger, coming to presence names the being of beings. This coming to presence can be called either *energeia* or *physis*.

tion of *energeia, actualitas,* the reality of work, would seem to preserve this connection between work and being, but Heidegger insisted that *ergon* and *actus,* in Roman thinking the effect of an act, have decidedly different connotations. This leads to the metaphysical understanding of being as what is effected by action, understood by Christianity as being created by God, and further radicalized in modernity as what is effected by a representing, willing subject. "The *ergon* is no longer what is freed in the openness of presencing, but rather what is effected in working, what is accomplished in action. The essence of 'work' is no longer 'workedness' in the sense of distinctive presencing in the open, but rather the 'reality' of a real thing which rules in working and is fitted into the procedure of working" (MHB, 12).[38] Or as he later wrote: "But never can it be sufficiently stressed: the fundamental characteristic of working and work does not lie in *efficere and effectus, but* lies rather in this: that something comes to stand and to lie in unconcealment" (SR, 160). These confusions belong to the technical interpretation of technology, which derives in turn from the abandonment of being, which culminates in the absolute dominion of the will to will. Heidegger wants to return to the earlier understanding, where work is understood as a letting presence. Letting presence means the revealing of something as it is. Earlier Heidegger called this *alētheuein.* Later he called it *poiēsis.*

The changed understanding resulted from a change in what Heidegger meant by *poiēsis.* In 1924, *poiēsis* meant the way of enacting corresponding to *technē (GA19,* 38–39). In more prosaic terms, *poiēsis* meant making or producing. This is the normal translation of *poiēsis,* but one can see from Heidegger's own history of being that making is in fact only the metaphysical translation of *poiēsis;* the poietic act is the effecting of a work by a producing subject. Thus technically seen, the being of a work is its "being-made" (*Gemachtsein*), which is derived from the making (*machen*), which becomes crystallized in modernity as "machination" (*GA19,* 46; for "machination," see *GA65*). The later Heidegger wanted to get behind the metaphysical interpretation of *poiēsis* as making, which even he had unthoughtfully followed earlier, in order to free up another possibility, *poiē sis* as revealing, by which he meant not just one type of revealing, however, but revealing per se.

---

38. The connection between reality (*Wirklichkeit*), effecting (*wirken*), and working (*werken*) is easier to see in German.

If we understand his reading of the history of metaphysics, another motive for this rethinking of *poiēsis* becomes clear: Heidegger needed to rethink *poiēsis* because he needed to find a way around Nietzsche's own appropriation of poetic revaluation of values. Nietzsche took the position that all values were poetically created by humans, even if they have forgotten this fact and treat their creations as real in themselves.[39] In taking this position Nietzsche was following a common Romantic path to overcoming a technically rationalized world by elevating aesthetics and art above science and rationality. This position, and the way it dominates modern thinking about possible alternatives to modern society, posed a danger to Heidegger, all the more so because of how close his path is to the path of Romanticism. Although Heidegger opposed art to scientific rationality, he could not simply take over the German Romantic position, because according to his interpretation this alternative was simply a more extreme version of Cartesian metaphysics. Art for moderns was creation, often thought on the same par as God's creation of the universe. For Heidegger, as we have seen, this view of artistic creation represents the metaphysical misunderstanding of *energeia*, or the bringing to presence of things through work. If Heidegger was to truly find a way past metaphysics in either its rationalist or poetic guise, he had to reinterpret the meaning of *poiēsis*, and thus of art.

If *technē* can be regarded in normal discourse as instrumental rationality, it is because technology as a means belongs within the domain of bringing something forth (QCT, 12). Making means bringing forth. Bringing forth is generally synonymous with creating, but this equation is a result of metaphysical thinking that has forgotten the original Greek insight into being as presencing. "Aristotle's fundamental word for presencing, *energeia*, is properly translated by our word *Wirklichkeit* only if we, for our part, think the verb *wirken* as the Greeks thought it, in the sense of bringing hither-into-unconcealment, forth into presencing" (SR, 161). *Poiēsis* is now thought of as *energeia*, that is to say, as bringing forth, as bringing to presence.

Heidegger thus thought of technology through this rethinking of making as a bringing forth into presence. In essence, he reversed his earlier metaphysical understanding of *poiēsis* as the way of enacting *technē;* instead, *technē* is to be something poetic. "*Technē* belongs to bringing-forth, to *poiēsis;* it is something poietic" (QCT, 13). As a bringing forth

39. Friedrich Nietzsche, *Thus Spoke Zarathustra*, trans. Walter Kaufmann (New York: Viking Press, 1966), 58–59.

into presence, *poiēsis* is equated with *alētheuein*, which Heidegger translated as "revealing." All human life is poetic; even modern technology is a revealing, albeit a particularly uncanny one which reveals everything as ordering and regulating and no longer permits the revealing of its own fundamental characteristic as poetic (QCT, 27).

If the goal of the 1924 lecture was to find a mode of *alētheuein* that was the most proper way of being human, the goal of the later essay was similar, yet subtly transformed. The key is finding in *poiēsis*, now understood as synonymous with *alētheuein*, a possibility that eludes its deflection by metaphysics into machination. This possibility is *poiēsis* thought of as revealing. This means that *technē* thought through *poiēsis* is a revealing. This insight allows us to think of technology as bringing to presence; it puts human being in relation to the authentic meaning of being. If we compare this idea to Heidegger's earlier work, we can see what he is doing. If the earlier Heidegger believed that *phronēsis* was the mode of *alētheuein* that allowed human existence to be authentic, the later Heidegger found a mode of technology that had the same effect. In essence, he found a phronetic mode of work. This mode of work can be called phronetic because both are poietic, which is to say, both are revelatory.

Phronetic or authentic work played a role in the later Heidegger that is equivalent to the one played by *phronēsis* in *Being and Time*. To recall, the central moments of *phronēsis* are mortality, temporality (historicity), and revelation of being as the situation for action together in the world; its possibility was established by a deconstruction of the tradition, which opened the space for a possible repetition of the originary event that opened up our primordial connection with meaning and the divine.

Poetic dwelling encompasses all these moments. Heidegger approaches the issue of poetic dwelling on two different scales: the poetic moments of great art and the equally poetic moments of craftsmanship. It is vital that the inner connection between the two discourses, so often opposed in tone, becomes visible: both are concerned with regaining a sense of being as presencing, which is the ground that enables humans to come to a proper relationship to technology. It is vital because Heidegger has been seen by some commentators as offering two different pictures of art, a Romantic vision broached particularly in the middle 1930s in such works as *The Origin of the Work of Art,* and a later, non-Romantic view developed in his later writings on language. According to these commentators the later Heidegger overcame the Romanticism and Nietzscheanism of his first works concerning art, and thus came to a more thorough break with the dangerous tendencies of Romanticism.⁴⁰ If, however, one understands the unity of the questioning of being that takes place in both the early and later writings despite their differences in tone and style, one comes to a firmer understanding of the role that art was meant to play in Heidegger's thought; poetic dwelling recasts Luther's *theologia crusis* into a postmodern setting.

Poiēsis is a revealing. Revealing is *alētheia* or truth (QCT, 11–12). *Poiēsis* is a revelation of truth. Truth, however, must be thought in terms of *poiēsis*, which is to say, in terms of bringing forth into presence. Truth is enduring presencing; truth as the there of being comes into being and is held there in the openness as the truth or meaning of the world. As enduring presence, truth has a definite time and site. *Poiēsis* is, however, (also) a making. This making is how the presencing endures; the work that is made is the enduring of the presence of being or truth. Thus *poiēsis*, and that is to say, authentic *technē*, is the setting-to-work of truth (OWA, 74). This setting-to-work endures as a world, or the "there" of being. A work of art reveals truth in the sense of opening up a world. Just as authenticity in *Being and Time* contained two moments, the essence of being and the specific being of a world opened by the questioning of the essence of being, so too does a work of art. One moment is that a work reveals a specific concrete possibility for a people, a specific historical Da-sein. The other is that it reveals the condition of this possibility as presencing, that is to say, as historical. Works must be thought about in terms of both these moments.⁴¹ Put together, a work of art is the enduring presencing of historical truth, one that keeps ever in mind the presencing character of what it brings to presence.

A work of art is brought into being by *technē*. *Technē*, as one mode of *alētheuein*, is thus one type of knowledge. This is to say that working is one way of knowing beings in their being. "The word [*technē*] names a type of knowing. It does not mean making and producing. Knowing, however, means having in sight beforehand that which appears in the bringing

40. Pöggeler, *Neue Wege;* Philippe Lacoue-Labarthe, *Heidegger, Art, and Politics,* trans. Chris Turner (Cambridge, Mass.: Basil Blackwell, 1990); idem, "The Spirit of National Socialism and Its Destiny," in *Retreating the Political,* ed. Simon Sparks (New York: Routledge, 1997).

41. Heidegger plays these two moments against each other in varying degrees. In the case of Hölderlin, he makes them one: the substance of what Hölderlin reveals and gives to the German people is that we have forgotten the essence of the poetic, its historical presencing, which has caused the flight of the gods. In Hölderlin, form and substance are identical.

forth of a picture or work" (HKBD, 137). *Technē* as a way of knowing glances ahead into the as-yet-invisible yet authoritative (literally in German, measure-giving, a meaning Heidegger emphasizes by splitting "*Maß-gebende*") which become visible first in the work itself (HKBD, 137). Essential poetry is a measuring (PMD, 221). It looks to the boundary wherein something is gathered into one (HKBD, 138). The anticipatory gathering that determines beings in their "original coordination" is *legein, logos,* the lightning-flash of being that steers all (*EGT,* 62–64, 70, 76). *Technē* is the sketch of being (*Seinsentwurf*), the disclosure of the world. This means that here *technē* holds a position equivalent to the one that *phronēsis* holds in *Being and Time;* both disclose a world in a revelatory vision. This world disclosure occurs in the setting-to-work of truth in the work of art, which is the historical coming to presence of truth for a people in their sayings which determine the manner in which they dwell.

One can see how Heidegger's analysis of art is meant to hold together the two moments of the truth of being. On the one hand, a work of art discloses a world, that is to say, a particular measure of being, or Da-sein. On the other hand, work draws attention to the presencing character of that which is brought into being, for in a more immediate sense than *phronēsis, technē* points to the act of bringing forth, to change itself. Put together, the two levels indicate that a particular measure is authentic only when this presencing, historical character is part of the measure. The measure of being is both a particular measure that maps out being (objective genitive) and a measuring by being that bears the trace of being as possibility and freedom (subjective genitive).

As a measure of being, that is to say, of freedom, art can initiate new possibilities of human being. Already in 1925 Heidegger hinted that "discourse, especially *poetry,* can even bring about the release of new possibilities of the being of Dasein" (*HCT,* 272). Because this line concludes a section on idle talk, Heidegger means that poetry has the possibility of releasing possibilities of speech not already held by *das Man.* In Heidegger's early philosophy this role was generally taken on by *phronēsis* and its resolution in the moment of vision, but here (along with the example concerning Sophocles in the 1919 lecture) Heidegger implicitly equates poetry with *phronēsis,* as the exemplary way of releasing new possibilities of the being of Dasein (*GA56/57,* 74–75).

It is necessary to consider these "new possibilities" in both the objective genitive and subjective genitive moments of the measure of being.

Objectively, that is to say, in the specific form in which a work of art takes shape, the work of art opens up a new world which delivers the originary "sayings" or myths to a people, in which their gods become present. Considered in this way, poets are the founders of peoples. They found by "instituting," that is to say, sketching or giving the measure for, being as a saying (*GA39*, 214). Because "giving measure" is authoritative (*Maß-gebend*), poets are the architects of the order of a world. Poetry is the architectonic "science." This authoritative measurement of being is the authentic meaning of *polis* (*GA39*, 30, 214, 216; PMD, 227; *GA53*, 100–101). For Heidegger, poets are, to use a famous phrase of Shelley's, the legislators of mankind. Politics in this way has been turned into art.

This conception of art as political measure-giving has strong Romantic overtones.[42] It would be possible to agree with Heidegger's critics on this point if they did not miss what is most important for Heidegger in the work of art, the subjective genitive dimension of the measuring of being that art offers: that it allows the authentic being of Dasein to come to presence. Art enables us to rethink the being of Dasein in a manner other than that

---

42. Several commentators have taken up this theme, most notably, Schwan, Pöggeler, and Lacoue-Labarthe. Alexander Schwan, *Politische Philosophie im Denken Heideggers*, 2d ed. (Opladen: Westdeutscher Verlag, 1989); Pöggeler, *Neue Wege*; Lacoue-Labarthe, *Heidegger, Art, and Politics*; and idem, "The Spirit of National Socialism." All three believe that Heidegger's thought developed out of this Romantic infatuation, although they draw different political conclusions from this change. Pöggeler's first book on Heidegger and politics responded to Schwan's contention that Heidegger's authentic political teaching was found in the "Origin of the Work of Art," to which Pöggeler half-countered by conceding that there was some truth to this, while arguing that Heidegger had grown past this early Romantic enthusiasm into his mature conception of art in the technical age. Otto Pöggeler, *Philosophie und Politik bei Heidegger*, 2d ed. (Munich: Alber, 1974). Pöggeler has retained the essential parameters of this argument through the years, although in more recent years his criticism of Heidegger's politics has grown harsh and he no longer sees Heidegger's critique of technology in quite so unambiguously positive a light. In Schwan's view, Heidegger grew out of his Romantic phase, but also thereby grew out of any political philosophy at all. Alexander Schwan, "Zeitkritik und Politik in Heideggers Spätphilosophie," in *Heidegger und die praktische Philosophie*, ed. Annemarie Gethmann-Siefert and Otto Pöggeler (Frankfurt a. M.: Suhrkamp, 1989). Like the other two, Lacoue-Labarthe finds essential continuities between Heidegger's attempts to refound metaphysics in 1933 and the desires of the German Romantics to create peoples as works of art, a desire that found its worst form in Nazism's national aestheticism, whereby "the political (the City) belongs to a form of the *plastic art*, formation and information, *fiction* in the strict sense." Lacoue-Labarthe, *Heidegger, Art, and Politics*, 66. He believes, unlike the other two, however, that Heidegger's slow disentangling from Romanticism, completed by his 1955 letter to Jünger, published as *Zur Seinsfrage*, offers a path beyond metaphysico-fictive politics. Lacoue-Labarthe, "The Spirit of National Socialism," 151.

given by *das Man* or modern metaphysics. To recall, both *das Man* and metaphysics understand being in terms of theory, which is to say, they understand being as the unchanging. *Phronēsis* is another possibility of being because it understands being as something that can be otherwise, as possibility. This thinking is grounded in authentically grasping one's mortality, as what cannot be mastered or represented, and as the juncture of being and nothingness.

Phronetic art represents this in a variety of ways. In the first instance, art points to that which cannot be ordered and steered (HKBD, 148). This can be seen particularly in poetry, which derives its richness from ambiguity of meaning. This puts it in opposition to ordering and steering because all ordering and steering is grounded in the univocity of terms; only on the basis of univocity can knowledge predict, and prediction is the root of steering.[43] The second way of representing limitedness is the "strife" at play in the work of art between world and earth. World is the opening of the "there" within which things show themselves. A work sets up a world (OWA, 45). Into this world juts forth the earth. A world lets the earth be earth (OWA, 46). Earth is the self-secluding, by which Heidegger means that which conceals itself, that which withstands manipulation. In this way the materiality of things shows itself differently in works of art than in equipment. In equipment, the material disappears into the use of a thing; it is only as material for use (OWA, 46). To technical thinking, material appears as raw material which exists only for use in human constructions. In a work of art, however, the material comes into the open on its own; as such it is no longer material in the sense of material for use, but rather material as earth, the limit of the possible (OM, 88–89). For earth to be earth, it must escape every scientific determination of its being. "The earth appears openly cleared as itself only when it is perceived and preserved as that which is by nature undisclosable, that which shrinks from every disclosure and constantly keeps itself closed up" (OWA, 47). Earth and world belong to each other; neither would be possible without the other. The world disclosed in the work of art is set back on the earth; by this Heidegger means that the "content" of the work of art includes the earth as earth, that is to say, as what cannot be mastered. The previous

---

43. This connection between unequivocation and a "steering" science can be found in exemplary form in Hobbes's *Leviathan*, particularly chap. 5, pt. 1. Thomas Hobbes, *Leviathan: or the Matter, Forme and Power of a Commonwealth Ecclesiasticall and Civil*, ed. Michael Oakeshott (New York: Collier Books, 1962).

and perhaps most important way the work of art is authentic is that it preserves the mystery of being. This point goes to the heart of Pöggeler's contention that Heidegger abandoned the Romantic understanding of art in favor of a modern poetry of the "trace."[44] Trace is a mark left behind by something that does not itself appear, like footprints left in the snow. According to this understanding of Heidegger's post-Romantic stage, modern poetry must learn "renunciation," the impossibility of making present that which grants all presence except in its trace; it makes the self-concealing come to presence as what is self-concealing and thus as mystery (PMD, 225; W, 151–56). However, this reflexive gesture also appears in 1934 in the middle of Heidegger's "Romantic" stage. Saying never makes anything immediately manifest, nor does it conceal it absolutely, but is both at once and thus a "hint" (*Winke*) (*GA39*, 127). "Poetry is: to place the Dasein of the people in the realm of this hint, i.e., a showing, a pointing, in whose pointing the gods become manifest, not as something somehow meant and observable, but rather in their hinting" (*GA39*, 32, 214). Since poetry is the "institution" of being as its "there," this means that the being is instituted as a mystery which must be preserved (*GA39*, 214). The people who preserve the truth instituted in the sayings thus know being, and that means in the highest instance their own being, as the invisible origin that cannot be mastered. Poetry and art always institute and preserve this ontological dimension which points to the unmasterable fate to which humans are always delivered. To put it concretely, poetry institutes being as a mystery worth questioning.[45] Thus despite its often overt Romantic bearings, Heidegger's early understanding of art escapes the attempts to classify it as Romantic. Poetry in Heidegger's presentation is always the twofold measuring of being.

This second side to Heidegger's understanding of poetry is brought out in his celebration of one of his favorite lines from Hölderlin: "Full of merit, yet poetically dwells / man on this earth."[46] In his 1934 interpretation, Heidegger connects the first phrase, "full of merit," to what is made by

44. Pöggeler, *Neue Wege*, 307–8; 317–29.

45. Thus Heidegger's great love for Hölderlin's poetry, which he thought raised the question of its own being; Heidegger's reading of Hölderlin makes the poet into almost a twin of the later thinker. In a later chapter I will deal with the difficulties caused by Heidegger's desire to institutionalize the question of being.

46. "Voll Verdienst, doch dichterisch wohnet / Der Mensch auf dieser Erde." Friedrich Hölderlin, "In Lieblicher Bläue," in *Sämtliche Werke*, vol. 2/1, ed. Friedrich Beissner (Stuttgart: W. Kohlhammer, 1951), 372.

man (*die Gemächte des Menschen*) (*GA39, 36*). He then draws particular attention to the "yet" that sets the second phrase in "sharp opposition" to the first (*GA39, 36*). No human artifacts, although full of merit, touch the essence of human existence. Poetic dwelling has nothing to do with human accomplishments (*GA39, 36*). This interpretation of poetry stands in direct opposition to the Romantic interpretation, which ultimately rests on taking the work of art as something made by a human subject. For Heidegger, art understood as a "cultural accomplishment" belongs to the technical world that is full of merit, yet not poetic (*GA39, 36*). Genuine poetry falls under a different relation between humans and being; rather than making being, in genuine poetic dwelling humans are exposed to being by virtue of their relation to language, which is not something humans have at their disposal, but rather is something that has human being (*GA39, 67*). Being gives itself to humans through language; poetry steers this gift into a work of art.

The relationship between humans and being points to the source of Heidegger's interpretation of poetic dwelling: Luther's theology of the cross. In the years of his first crisis of faith, Heidegger approvingly cited Luther's opposition to the Catholic theology of God's glory in favor of a theology of the cross which related to God as the mysterious source of grace. For Luther, the distinction rested upon the role of the human being in attaining salvation: he could hold no truck with any theology that asserted that salvation could be attained through human accomplishment, no matter how meritorious. From this distinction comes his famous opposition between faith and works. Heidegger's opposition between technology and poetry rests on the same basis. This comes through quite clearly in his interpretation of Hölderlin's "Full of merit, yet poetically . . ." The "yet" highlights the "full of merit" in such a way as to draw attention to the Lutheran background, which explains why Heidegger counterintuitively opposes human works to poetry; in Luther's theology, works may be meritorious, but in the end have nothing to do with salvation. Heidegger is interested neither in personal salvation nor in faith, but like Luther he does believe that humans must renounce the sufficiency of their accomplishment in order to establish an authentic relationship to being and hence the divine. For Heidegger, like Luther, the stance humans take toward God determines how they receive God. Poetic dwelling brings humans into an authentic relationship to being by opening them to revelation as the gift of being.

Heidegger reinterprets technology and work in light of this understanding of poetry as a twofold revealing measure of being. Poetry sketches out and institutes being as a whole, but in terms of being as that which cannot be mastered. In so doing, it escapes the technical understanding of technology which concludes in cybernetics, and it lays the ground for authentic dwelling. "Poetry first of all admits man's dwelling into its very nature, its presencing being" (PMD, 227). Insofar as man dwells, man builds. Authentic building is also rooted in poetry. "Authentic building occurs so far as there are poets, such poets as take the measure for architecture, the structure of dwelling" (PMD, 227). This means that we must think about dwelling and building in terms of poetry; the dimensions Heidegger sketches out for poetry reflect back onto how to think about dwelling and making, that is to say, our earthly existence in relation to the divine.

In "Building, Dwelling, Thinking," Heidegger relates this new understanding of dwelling specifically to themes raised in the first part of *Being and Time*. To be authentically human, that is, mortal, means to dwell on this earth. "Dwelling" recalls Heidegger's interpretation of the "in" of "being-in" as "'to reside,' '*habitare*,' 'to dwell,'" all in the sense of "to be familiar with" (*BT*, 80).[47] To dwell means in the first instance to work with something, to take it into one's care and concern. In the later essay, Heidegger follows this up by equating dwelling with building and finding the meaning of building in caring and cultivation (BDT, 147). Building signifies more than just construction; it is the category of all concernful activity in the world, of which construction of edifices is one type (BDT, 147). Heidegger specifically calls building *technē*, to let something appear (BDT, 159). To let something appear in its presence is also the quality of work (SR, 160). Dwelling, building, working, and *technē* are all related to the poetic dwelling of human beings. In *Being and Time*, dwelling (work, *technē*) occupied an ambiguous place because it was the primary way of being meaningful and yet also could not be authentic knowledge because it could not make Dasein itself present, that is to say, its own being. By rethinking dwelling through poetry in the new sense, "Building, Dwelling, Thinking" permits Dasein to come to presence authentically. In this way, poetry lets the world "world," that is to say, come to presence as a world

---

47. The German words are *Wohnen* and *sich auf halten*. In the later essay, "dwelling" renders *Wohnen*, but the other word should be kept in mind, particularly since it has the connotation of temporary residence. Time is never far from being in Heidegger's thought.

(OWA, 44).[48] In *Being and Time* "world" stands for the totality of connections of meanings; here in the later essay "world" is the fourfold of earth and sky, divinities and mortals. The fourfold is Heidegger's shorthand poetic description of this totality, since it spans the total sphere of being; that is to say, everything that is can fit into one of these categories. The fourfold gives the poetic measure for all building and dwelling (BDT, 158). Dwelling and building preserve the fourfold by letting it come to presence in things (BDT, 151). Things make up a location which gives being to spaces; space is a clearing within a boundary or horizon into which the fourfold is admitted (BDT, 154–55). Authentic, that is to say poetic, building lets the world unfold as a whole in the work; it permits the primal dwelling with the revelation of being through work in a work.

There is an ambiguity in Heidegger's presentation of the relation between building and the fourfold that needs to be clarified: the presentation refers both to a general description of how being comes to presence and to an authentic relation between the two. As a general description, Heidegger says that all human existence is poetic, that is to say., technical or work-oriented. Since work lets the fourfold come to presence in the work, all work is a location of the fourfold. The fourfold—being—is always present in some form or another. The fourfold, however, like being, is essentially possibility or play, as the later Heidegger will say; the elements of the fourfold can take up different positions in regard to each other. The shifting positions make up the play space (*Spielraum*), or openness, in which things appear as what they are; as such, the fourfold is the "there" of being, for as Heidegger says in *Being and Time*, the "there" is the openness in which things appear. To keep within the language of *Being and Time* for the moment, this description of the fourfold is worldhood, the index of possibility that makes up human existence (Dasein) that enacts itself in various configurations which make up a specific historical world. This means that the fourfold is gathered together in things in all types of building, even in modern technology. Modern technology is a specific way of letting the fourfold come to presence; the fourfold is thus present even in the modern

48. Heidegger's use of the word "world" as a verb dates from his work in the early 1920s; Gadamer mentioned its use in one of his recollections on the early Heidegger. Gadamer, "Die Religiöse Dimension," 309. He used it in the phrase "es weltet" (it worlds); it is meant to draw attention to the presencing character of the world. Since it is related to another well-known phrase Heidegger used for the presencing of being, "es ereignet" ("it occurs," or sometimes "it events"), it also indicates that the event of being comes to presence as a world.

superhighway. It is present, as we have learned in this chapter, in a very peculiar way, such that being is absent, or as Heidegger makes it plain in this essay, the gods are present in their absence (BDT, 152–53). The absence of god is one way in which the gods "enact" themselves. This absence of the gods upsets the balance of the fourfold such that their counterparts, mortals, usurp the position of the gods. Feuerbach and Marx make this explicit.[49] This usurpation, however, changes the nature of the other elements; without the gods, mortals are no longer considered as mortals, and both the sky (form, ideas, the unconcealed) and earth (material, the concealed) come under modern human sway, that is to say, the sky becomes mathematical representations and the earth raw material for exploitation (GA39 104–5). This puts the analysis of modern technology presented earlier into the language of the fourfold. The uncanny aspect of modern technology, however, is that we do not even notice that the gods are absent; modernity is marked by this twofold absence of the gods. Modern technology may be poetic, but it is poetic like no other kind of poetry. Authentic building, on the contrary, admits the fourfold, but admits it so that the fourfold is made present to the builders.[50] Authentic building is making a location that grants a space in which the fourfold is admitted and instituted (BDT, 158). Heidegger's concrete example: a farmhouse in the Black Forest. "Here the self-sufficiency of the power to let earth and heaven, divinities and mortals enter *in simple oneness* into things, ordered the house" (BDT, 160). It took into account the weather (earth and heavens combined); it made room for a childbed and a "Totenbaum" to honor the dead (mortals); it did not forget the alter corner (divinities). The authentic building which is a dwelling maintains the presence and balance of the fourfold that is necessary for authentic human existence. Thus the kind of building that Heidegger connects to dwelling is one possibility of the general index of possible kinds of building. Since it lets being be as it is, it is

49. Medieval philosophers, even Aquinas, maintained that human reasoning was inherently flawed and thus could not reach the full level of being of God's knowledge. Descartes rid himself of this compunction. He used the term "ideas" for that which we can know clearly and distinctly because that was the term reserved for the forms that God perceived. In exercising our freedom of will by use of our clear and distinct ideas (mathematics), humans could truly be the image of God.

50. This could mean that the gods are present only as absence, or as the flight of the gods or the death of God. Both Nietzsche and even more Hölderlin occupy an elevated position in Heidegger's thinking because for him they alone among moderns made our present situation present as the absence of the gods; they are therefore the only genuine poets of modernity.

authentic building, and thus the ground for authentic human existence.

Authentic human existence is dependent upon maintaining a proper relation to the divine. Without this proper relation, the fourfold, and therewith human being, is thrown out of joint; we develop an inverted relationship to beings. Building establishes human relations to the divine. All setting-up and instituting is a "consecrating, in the sense that in setting up the work the holy is opened up as holy and the god is invoked into the openness of his presence" (OWA, 44). Again, this is often taken as evidence of Heidegger's Romanticism, in line with the Jena Romantics' vision of uniting religion and politics in a new mythology. As such, he seems to fall within the scope of Greek aesthetics as Hegel described it; unable to think abstractly, the Greeks could only conceive their gods in art, which gave a specific shape to that to which they paid homage. This reading of Heidegger is not wholly correct, for while Heidegger desired some sort of concretion of the gods in works of art, like that of the statue of Athena which gave meaning to Athenian life, his interest is more formal (HKBD, 136–39). The concrete shape of the god is an indicator of the divine against which and in relation to which human being is measured. It is the divine and not particular gods that are Heidegger's concern. The condition of possibility of any particular god coming to presence for a people lies in awakening a sense of the divine (LH, 218).

A close look at the fourfold sheds light on this difficulty. Humans stand in a relationship not only to each element of the fourfold, but also to the fourfold as a whole. This whole is being. As Heidegger puts it, human being *is* the relationship to world, earth, and gods (GA53, 52). This twofold relation indicates the nature of the elision in Heidegger's thinking. Within the fourfold, humans are paired off with the gods; in such a pairing humans are the mortals. What makes humans mortals, that is to say, what makes them think their being as primarily mortal, is that the gods are immortal; death takes its central place as the limit that divides humans from gods (GA39, 173–74). Humans come to their proper being only in relationship to gods. Because of the twofold nature of humanity's relation, though, this means that humanity's relation to the whole is also characterized as a relation to godhood or the divine; being itself is the divine.

This twofold relationship of humans to gods and hence the divine matches the twofold measuring of poetry. In the first sense, poetry establishes a relationship between a people and the gods which they serve; for instance, the Greeks with their gods or Christians with Christ. In the second sense, poetry measures out the being of humans as mortals in this institution of the gods for a people. Thus Heidegger's call to the gods or divine is not a call to establish a universal and eternal system of rule for all humans, but rather an attempt to call us back to our proper historical being.

The connection between the divine and history points to a curious, yet vital point Heidegger makes about the divine. The pairing of gods and mortals is supposed to be the opposition between immortal and mortal, eternal and changeable; this is what marks off humans as mortals. Yet while Heidegger means for us to establish a relationship to the eternal, he does not mean by this the unchanging. The divine, the whole to which we stand in relation, is the condition of possibility of mortality, that is to say, of change; it is temporality itself. Being is time, or to put it slightly differently, being is the spacing of time, its extension into a determinate historical era. As such, the divine is not within time and is thus eternal (without time, outside time). It appears as time, not within time. The divine is thus temporality itself. In establishing a relation to the divine, poetry makes possible history; to use the language of *Being and Time,* the poetic vision, just as the phronetic moment of vision, historicizes itself as the history of a people. The ecstasy of being as Da-sein, which once took place in the moment of vision, now occurs in essential poetry. "Poetry as institution effects the ground of possibility for humans in general to settle on earth between it and the gods, i.e., become historical, and thus able to be a people" (*GA39* 216; *BT,* 436). A people is the community that shares this history, a history constituted by a shared understanding of the particular gods whom they serve and to whom they pray.

The service character of work is an essential element in authentic human existence. In a properly balanced fourfold, humans stand in relation to the divine and therewith to their gods. This relationship is one of service (if not quite dependence) because humans recognize these gods as the independent source of meaning for human existence. Heidegger's intent is clearer if the reverse state of affairs is seen. In modernity, humans usurp the position of the gods, that is to say, they make themselves the condition of all that is, including the gods, whether rationalist (Leibniz) or value-oriented (Nietzsche), that alone can be admitted as the divine in the will to will. God serves humans, rather than the reverse. The god of onto-theological metaphysics, however, is not authentically divine (*ID,* 72). This opposition again is clearly tied to a Lutheran distinction between reason and faith; God as the highest mystery cannot be known through reason.

The gods to whom we can bend the knee and make sacrifices are the gods brought to presence in poetry, that is to say, as "hints" which preserve the mystery. This sacrificial character of the relationship between humans and the divine is vital. For Heidegger, we cannot bow down to our own creation, for bowing down is a sign of giving thanks, and giving thanks to ourselves is silly. We give thanks only to one we do not control. Thus authentic dwelling is giving thanks and serving those who stand outside our control and are the possibility of our existence. Our proper existence is dwelling in a meaningful world. "As long as man is godless, he must also be worldless" (*GA50*, 115). It is only in the proper relation to the divine that we authentically dwell and build in the world.

Poetry establishes an authentic relationship to the divine—and that means likewise to ourselves—that grounds authentic building and dwelling in the world. Through his rethinking of *poiēsis*, and thereby *technē*, building, and work, Heidegger hoped to reestablish a sense of the authentically divine in human existence as that which we serve, thus restoring meaning to our working and dwelling on earth.

Conclusion

Humans are technological beings. Unlike the gods, humans are not self-sufficient; they require labor and tools in order to provide for the necessities of their existence. The central importance of work for human being forced Heidegger into a reworking of his earlier philosophy. If there he had followed Aristotle in elevating practical wisdom and action above technical knowledge and work for the sake of restoring a sense of the divine in human affairs, he had done it at the expense of relegating the bulk of human life to godlessness. If he was to make the divine more fully constitutive of human existence, it was necessary to integrate work and technology into the whole of authentic existence.

In rethinking the possibilities inherent in work, Heidegger thought through an ambiguity of *technē* he had found in his earlier 1924 lecture on Aristotle. There he showed that *technē* could present the being of beings either as changing or unchanging, either as coming to presence (*energeia*) or as constant presence (*idea*). The latter possibility being the ground of metaphysics, Heidegger developed a profound and comprehensive understanding of the mutual interplay between metaphysics and work that developed into the system of modern technological society.

Despite similarities with other contemporary critiques of modern society, particularly with Weber's, Heidegger's differed from these in naming the central problem to be nihilism understood as the death of God. Modern technology was inhuman not because it could be physically or morally harmful, but rather because it was godless. Modern technology and modern metaphysics could not think of the truly divine and so denied to humans a relation to the divine necessary for their meaningful working existence.

Heidegger's attempt to overcome modern society involves a thorough and complicated rethinking of *poiēsis* and thereby of *technē*. Because *poiēsis* is revelatory, it preserves the sense of being as *energeia,* as presencing. Human being must stand in essential relationship to this sense of being in order to make work meaningful. Human existence is poetic dwelling. As such, it stands in a twofold relationship to the divine: humans exist in a particular world with its particular gods and also to the divine itself, the mysterious origin which is the source of meaning of the whole. The poetic possibility of work enables humans to dwell in the world, that is, to be authentically in a historical community in which the individual labor is directed toward the divine whole which gives it meaning.

Is this postmodern transformation of the essence of work a real possibility in the modern world? Can there be a practical theological-political revolution that can transform modern society? For at least a time, Heidegger believed there could, and his choice of the politics meant to transform work according to his ideal goal is striking: National Socialism. For at least a moment—and perhaps more than a moment—Heidegger fervently believed that National Socialism was the politics that matched his goal of transforming work so that it stood in service to the divine. I turn in the next chapter to the connection between his philosophical and religious goals and his commitment to National Socialism; at the heart of it lies his rethinking of technology and work.

There is no doubt Heidegger was a National Socialist. There is, however, a highly contentious debate concerning the implications of that fact, particularly regarding the status of his philosophical legacy. Was his Nazism the expression of personal idiosyncracies or ideological biases wholly distinct from the central thrust of his most profound thought, or is there an essential connection between Heidegger's philosophy and his politics? The stakes in this incident are high because at issue is the question of whether and in what way a great thinker is implicated in the greatest horror of our age. It is not just a question of one man's guilt, but of the dignity and greatness of philosophy itself.[1] Thus

1. Robert Bernasconi, *Heidegger in Question: The Art of Existing* (Atlantic Highlands, N.J.: Humanities Press International, 1993), 56.

Heidegger's political misadventures have ignited a passionate battle over the nature of his politics that began the day he stepped forth as Nazi rector in Freiburg and continues unabated today, the slings and arrows of outrageous polemic sometimes spilling beyond the ivory towers of academia to become the stuff of mass journalism.

In stepping into the battleground surrounding this troubling episode in his life, one enters onto a field torn by such strong passions, biting polemics, and bitter accusations that one may despair of ever peaceably offering one's own considered opinion in the midst of warring bands. One is expected to be either prosecutor or defender. To be a judge, however, one must be impartial; one must extract from the partial cases a whole case that will stand as the truth.

In my judgment, Heidegger's national socialism arises out of the "factical ideal" that dominated his thinking from his early philosophy until his death. Thus there is no absolute separation between his thinking and his concrete politics. There was no "turn" against the ideal of National Socialism. *Being and Time* is not an apolitical text. The same commitment to an authentic religiosity that underlies his early phenomenology and his later considerations on the essence of technology also underlies his political engagement in 1933. This means that Heidegger's attachment to National Socialism is the concrete political expression of his factical ideal of authentic religiosity.

This said, some clarification of this complex matter is required. To say that Heidegger was a National Socialist is not as cut and dried as one would imagine. Heidegger was a National Socialist and even defended it, albeit obliquely, as late as his 1966 *Spiegel* interview. But on the other hand, he hurled invectives at and cast aspersions on Hitler and the Nazi regime that rivaled any he directed against modernity.[2] To say that Heidegger was a National Socialist does not sufficiently explain the nature of his engagement with the Nazi party.

---

2. To demonstrate the complexity of the entire debate over Heidegger's politics, Heidegger's criticism of Nazism has itself come under criticism because he denounces Nazism in the same terms as the rest of modern society, causing critics to charge Heidegger with possessing a defective moral compass. Habermas, *Philosophical Discourse of Modernity*, 133–34, 158–60; idem, "Work and *Weltanschauung*: The Heidegger Controversy from a German Perspective," in *The New Conservatism: Cultural Criticism and the Historians' Debate*, ed. Shierry Weber Nicholsen (Cambridge: MIT Press, 1989), 163; Ferry and Renault, *Heidegger and Modernity*, 61–65; and Richard Wolin, *The Politics of Being* (New York: Columbia University Press, 1990), 168.

In coming to terms with his engagement, one must consider three biographical facts of the case: he joined the Party, he left it, and he kept the faith after leaving it. Any interpretation that does not consider all three facts will be necessarily one-sided and partial. The first two facts have received much attention; the third, very little. Even when the question of his continued faith in National Socialism is raised, it is usually limited to his passion for Hölderlin-inspired *Volksreligion* in the middle 1930s, which he subsequently outgrew. It is the third fact, however, that lends the others, the second one in particular, their peculiar color. He joined (enthusiasm for the revolution); he left (dissatisfaction with its course); he kept the faith (enthusiasm for its potential despite his dissatisfactions with the limited thinking of its leaders). In this shorthand form, the nature of his political ideals is really not so strange. It is not uncommon for someone to be enamored of an ideal, to be subsequently disappointed in the failure of its standard-bearers to uphold the ideal, yet still cling to an unattained ideal that was perverted in practice. So much attention has been directed to proving the extent of his complicity in Nazi practice that too little focus has been directed to the peculiarity of his defense: standing before a denazification committee, Heidegger vigorously upheld his reasons for becoming a National Socialist while simultaneously distinguishing his hopes and ideals from the subsequent reality of the Nazi regime. This points directly to the problematic: what is the ideal of National Socialism that inspired Heidegger's entrance into the Party such that he could think for a time that Hitler was its realization and also on the basis of the same ideal subsequently criticize the Party for failing to fulfill its promise? In what way could one think the real existing Party "went in that direction?" (Sp, 111; *GA16*, 677). What did "national socialism" mean to Heidegger?

The task of reconstructing Heidegger's political ideal requires that one attend to both the philosophical and political elements in his thinking during this period, as well as his *post hoc* apologies, for contrary to what many believe, he was actually quite forthcoming about the philosophical motivations in his engagement. He claimed he wanted above all to reform the universities, to restore the community of learning in the face of their increasing technical organization. For the moment, let us accept this claim, and inquire into what he thought was necessary to accomplish this. Heidegger argued that a reform of the universities required a change in the essence of science, which in turn was possible only on the basis of a new basic experience of being, which included a change in the essence of truth and a change in the essence of work. His political goal, in other words, dovetails exactly with his philosophical project outlined in the previous two chapters. In his political texts, we see that National Socialism in his view represented the appropriate politics for bringing about his desired philosophical revolution of overthrowing modern metaphysics and modern society.

Why National Socialism? The unifying principle of the National Socialist Worker's Party of Germany was that it was a worker's party, a party dedicated to reshaping German Dasein in accordance with work, and as the previous chapter showed, a new understanding of the meaning and purpose of work is central to Heidegger's political ideal. Yet this only pushes the question aside, for liberal capitalism and communism are also labor politics. Why specifically National Socialism? Again, the name provides us with the essential clue. Labor for Heidegger is essentially national (against communism's internationalism) and social (against capitalism's individualism). National socialism fills out the skeletal presentation of being-with in *Being and Time*.[3] Of the two elements, however, nation is the more important, for nation as Heidegger explicates it is the ground and principle of our earthly existence. As the world in which we are, the nation is fatherland and homeland; it is Da-sein, the site of our poetic dwelling. National Socialism is thus the authentic political manifestation of Heidegger's vision of a postmodern world.

Heidegger and National Socialism

Figuring the Issue

It is inevitable that a study of the political in Heidegger's thinking will intersect in some fashion with his commitment to Nazism. Whether one believes that his philosophy had nothing to do with the engagement or that his

---

3. In *History of the Concept of Time*, Heidegger stated that being-with-one-another-in-the-world is the basis for developing the various possibilities of community and society, but adds that he cannot pursue this in greater detail (*HCT*, 241). We can consider the political texts from the 1930s Heidegger's attempts to fill in the details. In a like vein, Pöggeler hints that under the influence of Max Scheler and Nietzsche, Heidegger became concerned with the real-worldly practical implications of his philosophy after 1928. Otto Pöggeler, *Heidegger in seiner Zeit* (Munich: Fink, 1999). 203, 223–25; idem, "Heidegger, Nietzsche, and Politics," in *The Heidegger Case*, ed. Tom Rockmore and Joseph Margolis (Philadelphia: Temple University Press, 1992), 128–30.

thought was "fascist to its innermost cell" to cite Adorno's verdict, to take up the political here means to address the question of his politics. The question of Heidegger's commitment to National Socialism has exercised and vexed three generations of scholars. The appeal of this issue is obvious. What made it possible for the philosopher many believe to be the greatest of our century to join and support its most horrific tyranny?

The question, simple as it may seem, conceals a tangle of issues and regions of inquiry incompatible with a simple explanation. To explain how a philosopher is related to concrete politics, one must address the difference between philosophy and political activity, the difference between one individual's political activity and the overall course of the politics for which he is engaged, the difference between the philosopher as a concrete individual with the normal range of passions, needs, and character and his texts, and, finally, the differences and unity of the texts themselves. These categories are further complicated by either mixture, such as the difference between political philosophy and philosophy, or the ambiguity of these categories that allow different interpreters to bring their own understandings of the categories to bear on the explanation. For instance, Arendt's explanation of Heidegger's fall from his proper sphere of philosophy into concrete politics is predicated upon her insistence that philosophy is necessarily apolitical, an understanding that would make no sense to a Marxist philosopher. Since neither the categories themselves nor their use is consistent from account to account, it allows for great variation in their depth and viability.[4]

In Heidegger's case, one can examine his concrete political activities while he was rector of Freiburg and an active participant in the *Gleichschaltung* or synchronization of the universities with the National

---

4. Take Reiner Schürmann as an example of the interaction of these categories: his theory credits Heidegger with a new thinking of action as an-archic. To reach this conclusion, he separates the man from his text: "Heidegger" names the authorship of the texts. He further winnows "Heidegger" via an ingenious backward reading which finds in the late "Heidegger" the true "Heidegger," which had progressively developed and pruned the occasionally misleading notions broached in the early works; he accepts, in other words, the truth of a "Turn" in "Heidegger" away from the subjectivity of *Being and Time*. This cleaned up "Heidegger" provides a basis for an-archic action, which is fairly close to Arendt's distinction in type between philosophy and politics. In response to Heidegger's Nazism, Schürmann would say: on philosophical grounds "Heidegger" is definitely no Nazi, and even provides a thorough critique of the theoretical and subjective humanism at the basis of Nazism. Schürmann, *Heidegger on Being and Acting: From Principles to Anarchy*, trans. Christine-Marie Gros (Bloomington: Indiana University Press, 1987).

Socialist revolution to see how these activities fit in with the overall course of the movement, how Heidegger understood his role in the revolution, whether his goals were consistent with those of the Party, what his motivations were for his actions and in what way, if any, that these motivations were or could be plausibly grounded in his philosophical texts, which in turn requires an understanding of Heidegger's philosophical texts, which may necessitate differentiating between philosophical texts and political tracts or at least between the genuinely philosophical content of the texts from any incidental social commentary they may contain.[5]

As complicated as this already is, Heidegger himself further muddied the waters by his own subsequent accounts of his motivations and the practical import of his time as rector. After the collapse of the Nazi regime, Heidegger was forced to appear before a denazification committee to determine how much responsibility he bore for the synchronization of Freiburg University and ultimately what penalties, if any, he should incur for his guilt.[6] During these proceedings he put forth his defense, the details of which remained surprisingly consistent whenever Heidegger would in subsequent years answer questions concerning his engagement. In his defense he made two major points: the motivations that led him to support the Nazi movement, and an account of what he did when and to whom while in office. Since it constituted a very real legal defense in which his very livelihood was at stake, Heidegger naturally painted his motivations and activities in the best possible light.

The nature of the defense thus raises questions as to its veracity. Although afterwards skeptics would step forth from time to time, the issue more or less slumbered after the committee presented its recommendations.[7] With the publication in 1983 of Heidegger's defense (entitled "Facts and Thoughts," published together with the Rectoral Address, along with a brief defense written by his son), the Heidegger controversy received a

5. Habermas and Young recommend distinguishing Heidegger's philosophy from his ideology. Habermas, "Work and Weltanschauung," 140, 148–49; Young, *Heidegger, Philosophy, Nazism*, 13.

6. For a detailed account of these proceedings, see Ott, *Martin Heidegger*, 291–327.

7. There have been several "Heidegger controversies": the first occurred when he took over as rector of Freiburg and publicly aligned himself with the Nazi revolution; the second when Löwith raised the issue for the French existentialists immediately after the war; the third occurred when the *Introduction to Metaphysics* was published in 1953; the fourth in 1969 when Schwan's book elicited a response from Pöggeler; then finally, 1983 through the present.

decisive boost.[8] The first to make a public splash was Victor Farias's polemic *Heidegger and Nazism,* which sparked an enormous, heated debate over Heidegger's Nazism, particularly in France, where through the fame of postmodernist philosophers Heideggerianism had more standing than in other countries. Although Farias hunted through archives to uncover sources that shed new light on Heidegger's conservative background, his own slipshod methods and tendentious argumentation gradually overshadowed the value of his significant findings. Far harder to dismiss was the work of historian Hugo Ott, who, like Farias, diligently scoured archives, letters, proclamations, to build a more complete picture of Heidegger's time in office than the one he left behind. Unlike Farias's polemic, however, Ott's work is careful, balanced, and exemplary. Ott discovered that Heidegger was more eager to assume office than he let on after the war, that Heidegger collaborated in denouncing colleagues, that he was a poor administrator (something Heidegger admitted), that he was naive, that he was petty and mean-spirited, and that he was capable of denouncing his opponents on political or racial grounds.[9]

If Ott helped set the facts aright, he still had to account for the motives. Ott locates the kernel of Heidegger's motivation in his outright hostility to Catholicism. Earlier it was shown how Heidegger's crisis of faith led in no small part to his phenomenology of life, but this consideration of Heidegger's philosophy is entirely missing in Ott's account. Ott the historian deliberately excluded this field of concern from his study, citing his incompetence in understanding metaphysics. It is good that he is aware of his limitations, but to exclude an account of Heidegger's philosophy is to exclude the animating force behind his life. To an astonishing extent, Heidegger's thinking was his life. Ott has no way of incorporating this

---

8. The occasion was the fiftieth anniversary of Heidegger's Rectoral Address and entrance into the Party. The purpose, as the editor Hermann Heidegger explained in his foreword, was to set straight the "many falsehoods and untruths" that had been spread both about the Rectoral Address and the nature of Heidegger's commitment to National Socialism. Hermann Heidegger, "Vorwort," in *Der Selbstbehauptung der deutschen Universität* (Frankfurt a. M.: Klostermann, 1990), 5–6.

9. This side of Heidegger comes through in some detail in an interview with one of his assistants whom Heidegger subsequently denounced, Eduard Baumgarten. Baumgarten, although equanimous about the affair, makes it plain that Heidegger's actions were motivated by petty vindictiveness and wounded vanity. Baumgarten does omit one significant motivating factor: he was an admirer of American pragmatism, something Heidegger abhorred. See the appendix to Berel Lang's *Heidegger's Silence* (Ithaca: Cornell University Press, 1996), 101–11.

great overriding passion into his biography. On narrowly factual grounds, Ott's work is dependable and valuable. It eliminates the distraction caused by Heidegger's self-serving defense concerning the facts of his actual behavior while rector and Farias's obviously prejudiced account. Because it does not address the philosophical motivations that animated the man, however, it is not *the* answer to the question.

The entwining of Heidegger's motives with his philosophy points to the issue of how one relates his concrete actions to his philosophy. This fact alone eliminates the accounts put forth by Arendt and Rorty as insufficient, since they completely separate the man from the thinker.[10] In Arendt's words, "Heidegger, too, once gave in to the temptation to change his 'abode' and to involve himself in the world of human affairs."[11] In this way, she sought to save Heidegger from his own conception of practicing philosophy, which is nothing other than confronting the worldly situation in which one finds oneself, although one's understanding of the situation may be not compatible with the character of everyday politics. Rorty considers linking Heidegger's philosophy to his politics merely an ad hominen argument. Although far less charitable toward Heidegger's thought, Habermas also faults those who want to see a seamless continuity between a thinker and his thought.[12]

Habermas, like several others, instead tries to distinguish Heidegger's philosophy from his extraphilosophical, ideological worldview. This distinction in effect seeks to duplicate the distinction between the man and his thought, but at entirely at the level of his thought. Like those who distinguish the man from his thought, those who distinguish Heidegger's ideology from his philosophy seek to isolate a core of genuine philosophy that is still powerfully valid from politically and socially relevant beliefs that stem from Heidegger's own personal take on the world.[13] The advantage

10. Hannah Arendt, "For Martin Heidegger's Eightieth Birthday," in *Martin Heidegger and National Socialism: Questions and Answers*, ed. Günther Neske and Emil Kettering (New York: Paragon, 1990); Richard Rorty, "Taking Philosophy Seriously," *The New Republic*, 11 April 1988, 31–34. For an examination of this issue, see also Bernasconi, *Heidegger in Question*, 56–73.

11. Arendt, "For Martin Heidegger's Eightieth Birthday," 216.

12. Habermas, "Work and *Weltanschauung*," 142.

13. Besides Habermas, this approach is taken up most notably by Young, Dallmayr, and Schürmann, even if Schürmann does not use the term "ideology." Habermas, "Work and *Weltanschauung*," 148–49; Young, *Heidegger, Philosophy, Nazism*; Schürmann, *Heidegger on Being and Acting*; Fred Dallmayr, *The Other Heidegger* (Ithaca: Cornell University Press, 1993), 51. Bourdieu similarly emphasizes the role of ideology, but he entirely reduces

making the distinction between ideology and philosophy has over making the distinction between the man and his thought is that the former better appreciates the enormous power ideas exercised in Heidegger's life; thus rather than highlight deficiencies in Heidegger's character, one can address politically motivating beliefs. The chief and great difficulty besetting this approach is how one distinguishes ideology from philosophy. Heidegger's philosophy is both personal and political: his philosophical activity is motivated by the crises of our contemporary situation; moreover, he thought his philosophy offered the best solution to these crises.[14] This intertwining of thought and political situation within Heidegger's philosophy makes any attempt to distinguish an ideology from an authentic philosophy tendentious and suspect.[15]

Even as she tried to separate the man from the thought, Arendt pointed toward this intertwining of philosophy and politics that motivated Heidegger's change in abode by calling attention to his "déformation professionelle," the desire to realize a theoretical ideal in practical affairs.[16] The question becomes: what is the source of this ideal? A related question would be whether he had a positive ideal at all, or whether he just wanted to overthrow existing structures. This is a pertinent question because in many respects it is easier to see what Heidegger was against than what he stood for: he rejected modern science, modern technology, modern religion, the Enlightenment, bourgeois society—in short, modernity. A slew of interpreters take this wholesale rejection of modernity as the key to explaining why Heidegger allied himself with Nazism, the sole deliberately antimodern political movement of his time.[17] Standing opposite this group

---

Heidegger's philosophy to ideology. Pierre Bourdieu, *The Political Ontology of Martin Heidegger*, trans. Peter Collier (Stanford: Stanford University Press, 1991).

14. Habermas, for instance, following Pöggeler's lead, distinguishes Heidegger's academic philosophizing up to 1929 from his subsequent attempts to conduct an ideological critique of the present age. Habermas, "Work and *Weltanschauung*," 147–48, 153–54, 165. Heidegger's early philosophy, however, is not nearly so academic as Habermas believes.

15. In general, the interpreter identifies as the core of genuine philosophy that aspect of Heidegger's thought most congenial to the interpreter's own political views. This method of reading tends to result in tendentious and deficient interpretations of Heidegger's philosophy. One exception to this rule is Schürmann; although I disagree with both his method and conclusion, his reading is quite ingenious.

16. Arendt, "For Martin Heidegger's Eightieth Birthday," 216–17.

17. Bourdieu, *Political Ontology*; Herf, *Reactionary Modernism*; Ferry and Renault, *Heidegger and Modernity*; Pippin, *Modernism as a Philosophical Problem*; Habermas, *Philosophical Discourse of Modernity*; Zimmerman, *Heidegger's Confrontation with Modernity*, among others.

is a group that maintains contrarily that Heidegger fell in with the Nazis precisely because of his modern/metaphysical impulses.[18] The actual object of this debate concerns the nature of Nazism and thus by way of contrast the nature of healthy politics; the attempts to find Heidegger's link to Nazism is a proxy to examining what in the intellectual tradition made Nazism possible: so, on the one hand, Heidegger's critique of rationalism or mysticism fits with Nazism's irrationalism, and on the other hand, Heidegger's Romantic conception of the state as a work of art fits Nazism's totalitarian aestheticization of politics, to use Lacoue-Labarthe's term.[19]

Pöggeler and Schwan also see in Heidegger's Romantic ideal of the state as a work of art the ground for his engagement, but unlike the postmoderns, they do not thereby denounce all of modernity, only the Romantic anti-Enlightenment part of it. Both view the aestheticization of politics as a dangerously insufficient understanding of politics. Both also agree that Heidegger overcame his Romantic tendencies in his later thinking on technology, although Schwan believes that his later thinking, which began as early as 1936 in the *Beiträge,* constitutes a total withdrawal from politics altogether, whereas Pöggeler finds in these same writings a beginning point to a decisive and necessary political confrontation with the technical domination characteristic of the contemporary world.[20]

18. Jacques Derrida, *Of Spirit: Heidegger and the Question,* trans. Geoffrey Bennington and Rachel Bowlby (Chicago: University Of Chicago Press, 1989); Gianni Vattimo, *The End of Modernity* (Cambridge: Polity Press, 1988); Philippe Lacoue-Labarthe, "Transcendence Ends in Politics," in *Typography: Mimesis, Philosophy, Politics,* ed. Christopher Fynsk (Cambridge: Harvard University Press, 1988); idem, *Heidegger, Art, and Politics;* Schürmann, *Heidegger on Being and Acting.* In a slightly different, more explicitly Arendtian form, this thesis is represented by Jacques Taminaux, "Heidegger and Praxis," in *The Heidegger Case: On Philosophy and Politics,* ed. Tom Rockmore and Joseph Margolis (Philadelphia: Temple University Press, 1992); Richard J. Bernstein, *The New Constellation: The Ethical-Political Horizons of Modernity* (Cambridge: MIT Press, 1992); and Dana Villa, *Arendt and Heidegger: The Fate of the Political* (Princeton: Princeton University Press, 1996). They see the problem as a confusion of *poiēsis* and *praxis,* i.e., of art and politics. Villa explicitly connects Taminaux and Lacoue-Labarthe on this issue. Villa, *Arendt and Heidegger,* 228, 248–53.
19. Lacoue-Labarthe, *Heidegger, Art, and Politics,* 61–76.
20. See Schwan, *Politische Philosophie im Denken Heideggers;* also see Alexander Schwan, "Heideggers 'Beiträge zur Philosophie' und die Politik," in *Kunst, Politik, Technik,* ed. Christoph Jamme and Karsten Harries (Munich: Fink, 1992); and idem, "Zeitkritik und Politik"; Pöggeler, *Philosophie und Politik bei Heidegger;* idem, *Neue Wege;* idem, "Heideggers politisches Selbstverständnis," in *Heidegger und die praktische Philosophie,* ed. Annemarie Gethmann-Siefert and Otto Pöggeler (Frankfurt a. M.: Suhrkamp, 1989); idem, *Heidegger in seiner Zeit;* idem, *Philosophie und Nationalsozialismus am Beispiel Heideggers;* and idem, "Heidegger und die praktische Philosophie." *Philosophie und Politik bei Heidegger* is a direct response to Schwan's book. In more recent years, Pöggeler has come closer to

The possibility of a philosophical overcoming of the philosophical motives that led Heidegger to affirm National Socialism points to the matter of textual history and what part of the totality of his writings most closely aligns itself with National Socialism. This raises the problem of understanding the whole trajectory of Heidegger's path of thinking, which in turn depends on an understanding of each text that makes up the whole. Here again there are grave complications. Concerning the issue of the whole of the path of thinking, there is a general belief, stamped with Heidegger's approval, that his thinking underwent a "turn." The approximate date of this turn is fixed at 1930 with his address, "On the Essence of Truth."[21] This, however, cannot coincide with any rejection of Nazism, since both the joining and rejecting still lay in the future, although as the 1928 *Einleitung in die Philosophie* makes abundantly clear, Heidegger first raises the issue of the essence of the truth in the context of grounding a possible spiritual renewal of the universities, a goal that forms the core of the Rectoral Address. Since this lecture equates the essence of truth with the essence of freedom as *Gelassenheit,* a theme taken up two years later in another lecture course of the essence of human freedom, and most famously in Heidegger's "Towards a Discussion of *Gelassenheit,*" several thinkers have viewed this "turn" toward a passivity in the face of worldly events as the ground for his affirming the awakening of the German nation under Nazism.[22] This theme, however, is related to another understanding of *Gelassenheit* or "destinal historicism," which sees these concepts as a total rejection of action and politics through a renunciation of the human will.[23]

Schwan's position, that is to say, he wavers on whether Heidegger's thinking of technology is sufficiently differentiated to provide a good point of departure for confronting the dangers of modern science and technology. See, for example, *Heidegger in seiner Zeit,* 243. Pöggeler also agrees with Schwan that Heidegger's political thinking is opposed to liberal democracy. Pöggeler, "Heideggers politisches Selbstverständnis," 55–56.

21. With the recent publication of the 1928/29 lecture *Einleitung in die Philosophie* one can push that date back even further, since he broaches the issue of the "essence of truth" in a manner very similar to how he would pursue the matter for the next several decades.

22. Alexander Schwan, "Heidegger über das 'Wesen der Freiheit,'" in *Philosophie und Poesie: Otto Pöggeler zum 60. Geburtstag,* ed. Annemarie Gethmann-Siefert (Stuttgart: Friedrich Frommann, 1988), 26–31; Harries, "Heidegger as Political Thinker," 312.

23. This is quite a widespread belief; to give some examples: Schwan, "Zeitkritik und Politik"; Karsten Harries, "Philosophy, Politics, Technology," in *Martin Heidegger: Politics, Art, and Technology,* ed. Karsten Harries and Christoph Jamme (New York: Holmes & Meier, 1994); Bernstein, *New Constellation;* Villa, *Arendt and Heidegger;* and Stanley Rosen, *Nihilism: A Philosophical Essay* (New Haven: Yale University Press, 1969), 129–31. "Destinal historicism" is Janicaud's term for being delivered over to technology. Dominique Janicaud,

Although again some see this elevation above politics as itself deficient, most see it as a rejection of Nazism insofar as it rejects all human projects. Some of these interpreters thus find a ground for a better politics in Heidegger's earlier writings.[24]

Since *Gelassenheit* is a rejection of the will and particularly the will to will or modern technology, many interpreters see the later philosophy as a rejection of voluntarism and the closely related subjectivity. They thus interpret the turn to mean a critique of voluntarism that makes it easier to see the later philosophy as a rejection of National Socialism because it forms a critique of technology and can be used to criticize the very voluntarist language of willing Heidegger constantly used in his Nazi period. In this scheme, the turn is held to have occurred sometime around 1936 or 1937 in Heidegger's Nietzsche lectures.[25] This makes any text before 1937 fair game for a connection to National Socialism. One way of understanding Heidegger's voluntarism is the decisionist reading of *Being and Time,* which finds the cause of Heidegger's political engagement in a groundless resolute decision; the what of decision does not matter, only the how.[26] Another

The Shadow of That Thought: Heidegger and the Question of Politics, trans. Michael Gendre (Evanston: Northwestern University Press, 1996).

24. Habermas, "Work and *Weltanschauung.*" Van Buren returns to the pre-*Being and Time* writings to find a congenial ethics; he has found some support from Caputo. Van Buren, "Ethics of *Formale Anzeige,*" 168–69; John D. Caputo, *Demythologizing Heidegger* (Bloomington: Indiana University Press, 1993), 41–42, 57–59.
The presumed deficiency in Heidegger's later thought has sparked a debate over the significance of Heidegger's postwar silence regarding the Holocaust. See Maurice Blanchot, "Thinking the Apocalypse," *Critical Inquiry* 15, no. 2 (1989): 475–80; Emmanuel Levinas, "As if Consenting to Horror," *Critical Inquiry* 15, no. 2 (1989): 485–88; Lang, *Heidegger's Silence;* Alan Milchman and Alan Rosenberg, eds., *Martin Heidegger and the Holocaust* (Atlantic Highlands, N.J.: Humanities Press, 1996); and Jacques Derrida, "Heidegger's Silence," in *Martin Heidegger and National Socialism: Questions and Answers,* ed. Günther Neske and Emil Kettering (New York: Paragon, 1990). There is an ambiguity in the charge that Heidegger's silence is damning: he was not completely silent, but the very few times he brings it up are all the more shocking for stunning equanimity, his now infamous equation of the Holocaust with the "motorized food industry" being the central example (*GA79*, 27).

25. Both Arendt and Pöggeler cite this date. Otto Pöggeler, " 'Praktische Philosophie' als Antwort an Heidegger," in *Martin Heidegger und das "Dritte Reich,"* ed. Bernd Martin (Darmstadt: Wissenschaftliche Buchgesellschaft, 1989), 71; Hannah Arendt, *The Life of the Mind,* vol. 2 (New York: Harcourt Brace Jovanovich, 1978), 172. In various configurations this basic scheme also underlies the bulk of postmodern readings of the whole, for instance, Lacoue-Labarthe, *Heidegger, Art, and Politics;* Schürmann, *Heidegger on Being and Acting;* and Vattimo, *The End of Modernity.*

26. Karl Löwith, "The Political Implications of Heidegger's Existentialism," in Wolin, *Heidegger Controversy,* 173–75; Wolin, *Politics of Being,* 35–40; Harries, "Heidegger as

more common way to interpret his subjectivist voluntarism is to understand the will either as the ground of modern technology or as the ground to thinking of the state as a work of art. Within this group there is a further distinction between those who find this technological grounding in Heidegger's fundamental ontology as far back as *Being and Time,* or alternatively those who see a decisive change after *Being and Time* in the direction of a Romantic metaphysics of a great creator understood as the founder of states and peoples.[27] Either way these interpreters see a decisive break from this earlier metaphysics in Heidegger's later thinking on modern technology, a break which gives the philosophical basis for a critique of Nazism and a self-critique of his metaphysical beliefs during the Nazi engagement.

I see little reason to doubt his postwar defense that Heidegger's critique of modern technology constituted a spiritual rejection of the party. First, he despised the party and in particular the "party hacks" from the beginning, and believed that Hitler would transcend the party doctrine and its metaphysical basis in the biological-racist weltanschauung.[28] By perhaps 1938, and certainly after the war, Heidegger regarded fascism as a political arrangement equivalent to communism and world democracy, all advancing blindly under the sway of the will to will; in this sense his analysis of "leaders" in "Overcoming Metaphysics" most certainly included Hitler. Thus Heidegger's critique of modern technology is a profound philosophical rejection of National Socialism. Second and more interestingly, he claimed that party members accused him of holding to a "private National

Political Thinker," 308–9; Hans Jonas, "Heidegger's Resoluteness and Resolve," in *Martin Heidegger and National Socialism: Questions and Answers,* ed. Günther Neske and Emil Kettering (New York: Paragon, 1990).

27. In effect, the first alternative sees one break that divides the corpus into a Heidegger I and Heidegger II, whereas the second distinguishes between two turns, one after *Being and Time,* and then another during the Nietzsche lectures. The first alternative is represented by Lacoue-Labarthe, *Heidegger, Art, and Politics;* Schürmann, *Heidegger on Being and Acting;* Vietta, *Heideggers Kritik am Nationalsozialismus;* and Friedrich-Wilhelm von Herrmann, "Das Ereignis und die Fragen nach dem Wesen der Technik, Politik und Kunst," in *Kunst, Politik, Technik,* ed. Christoph Jamme and Karsten Harries (Munich: Fink, 1992). The second, two-turn hypothesis, by Pöggeler, *Neue Wege,* and Janicaud, *Shadow of That Thought.*

28. On "party hacks," see *BwHB,* p. 62; for Hitler transcending party doctrine, see Martin Heidegger, "Schreiben Heideggers an den Vorsitzenden des politischen Bereinigungsausschusses Prof. v. Dietze (15. Dez. 1945)," in *Martin Heidegger und das "Dritte Reich,"* ed. Bernd Martin (Darmstadt: Wissenschaftliche Buchgesellschaft, 1989), 210 (*GA16,* 414). Pöggeler makes reference to this latter letter to explain Heidegger's preference for a Führer figure. Pöggeler, "Heideggers politisches Selbstverständnis," 31–32.

Socialism" (FT, 23; *GA16*, 381).[29] This "private National Socialism" creates the greatest complication in determining the connection of Heidegger to Nazism because the private version obviously differed from the public, concrete Nazism. A fair and rigorous examination of the question at hand will not only have to understand Heidegger's political metaphysics, but also explain how this could be compatible with a private National Socialism that presumably reflects its "inner truth and greatness," while rejecting that real concrete version that was in the process of transforming Germany for the great war to come. In effect, to adequately come to terms with the relationship between Heidegger and the Nazis, one must find the connection between the private and public National Socialism such that the private can still be legitimately called a National Socialism that nonetheless differs from and ultimately rejects the public version. It is necessary to determine why Heidegger rejected concrete National Socialism, that is to say, the party, in favor of "true" National Socialism and what makes the latter more "true" than the orthodox party doctrine.

In a letter to the Denazification Committee, Heidegger explicitly indicates that we should pursue this angle: "He [Hitler] had brought me in 1933/34 to a no man's land where I affirmed the social and national (not in the national-socialist manner) and denied the intellectual and metaphysical foundation in the biologism of the party doctrine, because the social and national, as I saw it, was not essentially tied to the biological-racist Weltanschauung theory."[30]

Although he was opposed to their weltanschauung, Heidegger hoped to steer the party onto the path laid out by his own thinking of the national and social, a path he held to be "consistent with the social and general political tendencies of the movement."[31]

This complication suggests that the same factor underlies both Heidegger's joining the Nazis *and* his rejection of them. This suggestion has seldom been followed up in the secondary literature, particularly by those interpreters who see a decisive break from National Socialism in Heidegger's

29. Carl Friedrich von Weizsäcker confirmed having heard students report of a "Freiburg National Socialism" in reference to Heidegger. Carl Friedrich von Weizsäcker, "Begegnungen in vier Jahrzehnten," in *Erinnerung an Martin Heidegger*, ed. Günther Neske (Pfullingen: Neske, 1977), 245–46.

30. Heidegger, "Schreiben Heideggers an den Vorsitzender des politischen Bereinigungsausschusses Prof. v. Dietze (15. Dez. 1945)," 210 (*GA16*, 414).

31. Ibid.

new understanding of technology. The critique of modern technology is indeed a criticism of real, concrete Nazism—the total mobilization of German society for war, the imperialism, the jingoistic nationalism, and not the least, the racism—but as his letter to the Denazification Committee suggests, that does not mean a rejection of national socialism. Against the proposition that he broke definitively from National Socialism, however, a passage from the *Spiegel* interview is important:

> I do not think the situation of human beings in the world of planetary technology is an inextricable and inescapable disastrous fate; rather I think that the task of thinking is precisely to help, within its bounds, human beings to attain an adequate relationship to the essence of technology at all. Although National Socialism went in that direction, those people were much too limited in their thinking to gain a really explicit relationship to what is happening today and what has been under way for three centuries. (Sp, 111; *GA16, 677*)

That last line is a rather extraordinary claim to make twenty years after the end of the war and thirty years after Heidegger left the party, but it offers valuable clues to the character of Heidegger's national socialism. First, Heidegger directly connects National Socialism to the central goal of his later thought, to help humans attain an adequate relationship to the essence of technology. For proponents of the view of the later Heidegger as critic of Nazism, this is a crushing blow. It is hard to escape the conclusion that Heidegger's interest in the question of technology, rather than causing his break with Nazism, instead actually pushed him toward it, and that thirty years later, he still considered it a viable alternative to modern technology. His postwar explanations point us toward that conclusion because in attempting to justify his joining the Nazis, he points to his (and by implication their) confrontation with the technical and nihilist character of modern civilization. To take the example closest to Heidegger's heart, let us examine the situation of science and the universities. In 1919, 1928, 1933, and again in 1966, Heidegger called for the renewal of the German university in the face of its degeneration into mere technical organization.[32]

---

32. In a letter written to Elizabeth Blochmann in 1919, Heidegger remarkably anticipates the same set of concerns regarding a *Volkshochschule* that he would bring to his plans in 1933 to set up a *Dozentenhochschule* (*BwHB*, 15, 73–74).

This degeneration results from the hegemony of metaphysics which takes the form of modern technology and modern science and culminates in nihilism. Heidegger himself directs our attention to the sentence "God is dead" in the Rectoral Address, which he ties back to his understanding of Jünger and the will to will (FT, 18; *GA16*, 375–76). He wants us to understand that his political engagement was part of his ongoing philosophical attempt to find a way past modern metaphysics and modern society.

We need to reflect particularly on the other implication of that last line quoted from the *Spiegel* interview. "Although National Socialism went in that direction, those people were much too limited in their thinking to gain a really explicit relationship to what is happening today and what has been under way for three centuries." National Socialism was a step in the right direction, but those who led it were too limited to really understand how to keep going in that direction. Since it is clear that Heidegger believed that he had a much more profound understanding of "what is happening today," one can infer that Heidegger believed that if he had been the leader rather than Hitler, or if Hitler had been the leader Heidegger thought he was, National Socialism could have fulfilled its potential or at least come closer to this goal. The important conclusion to draw is not that Heidegger, like many intellectuals, thought the world would be better if he were in charge, but that he understood the true potential of National Socialism even if its leaders did not. If Heidegger had been the leader of the National Socialist movement, then it could have come closer to fulfilling its promise: helping humans attain an adequate relationship to the essence of technology. This is the content of Heidegger's "private National Socialism," the one he also characterized as the "inner truth and greatness of this movement (namely, the encounter between global technology and modern man)" (*IM*, 199).[33] For Heidegger, a national socialism led by himself or a gen-

---

33. My theory helps put to rest one of those academic battles which has taken on far more importance than warrants. When it was finally published in 1953, one line from the 1935 lecture became the center of a firestorm of controversy that persists even today. The line reads, "The works that are being peddled about nowadays as the philosophy of National Socialism but have nothing to do with the inner truth and greatness of this movement (namely the encounter between global technology and modern man)—have all been written by men fishing in the troubled waters of 'values' and 'totalities'" (*IM*, 199). The textual controversy revolves around the parenthetical insertion, which Heidegger said was in the original lecture, even if he did not say it aloud, while most observers believe it was added in 1953 before publication (see, for example, Petra Jaeger's editorial note to the Gesamtausgabe edition). While I agree that the parenthetical remark was added at a later date, I do not think it changes the overall meaning of the original statement. In the "Age of the World Picture," written

uine leader is still one, perhaps the only, viable alternative to the domination of modern technology and metaphysics.

Everything in the modern world can be traced back to the sway of metaphysics: industrialization, technology, modern science, bureaucratic states,
and the universities. Heidegger's lifelong task was to uncover the hegemony
of metaphysics in all its guises and to find a path beyond it. In essence, this
means to renew the question of being. If we are to change anything, we
must alter metaphysics, which means to undergo "a new basic experience
of being. This includes: first, a change in the essence of truth, second, a
change in the essence of work" (*GA39*, 195–96).[34] The question is in what
way National Socialism "went in that direction." In answering this question, we gain an insight into the connection between Heidegger's deepest
philosophical commitments and his political engagement.

The Meaning of a National Socialism

Heidegger's philosophical aim is quite clear: to pose anew the question of
being in order to make possible a new revelation of being, a new beginning. The burning question has been: what does this have to do with politics, and specifically, why National Socialism among other political
alternatives? I have shown in the previous three chapters that Heidegger
hoped that responding to the question of being would make possible

---

almost at the same time as the original lecture, Heidegger makes the same connection between
value thinking and the frenzy of modern technology, and offers it as a criticism of actual
National Socialism, presumably different than its "inner truth and greatness." In any case,
one should concede the kernel of Habermas's objection: that Heidegger did not need to
include the line, with or without its parenthetical qualification, at all. Jürgen Habermas,
"Martin Heidegger: On the Publication of the Lectures of 1935," in Wolin, *Heidegger
Controversy*, 196–97. By including it, and adding a remark totally apposite for the postwar
period, it makes National Socialism appear as attractive in 1953 as in 1935. I believe that
that is the reason Heidegger added the parenthetical remark.

34. Heidegger says in this text that we need "an other metaphysics." This might be puz-
zling to those who enlist Heidegger as an antimetaphysical thinker; or it might be dismissed
by one (like Lacoue-Labarthe) who see this as the motives of the "bad" Heidegger. What
causes the confusion is that Heidegger changed the meaning he ascribed to the word "metaphysics" around 1938 or so; it went from the highest type of philosophizing to that form of
thinking he called the "end of philosophy." This change can be clearly seen in comparing
the original address "What is Metaphysics?" written in 1929, to the "Introduction to 'What
is Metaphysics?'" first published with the original in 1949. This is a change in connotation,
not in the direction of Heidegger's thinking. The "other" metaphysics is clearly not the one
that dominates modernity, and whether we call it an "other metaphysics" or "poetic thinking" seems to me to be mere nit-picking and hardly worth the effort some have invested in
the wording; in either case there must be a new experience of the question of being.

authentic human political action, a possibility he believed the two-thousand-year domination by metaphysics and science had gradually extinguished. But why National Socialism?

The name the movement gave itself, the National Socialist Workers Party of Germany, gives some clues. If one analyzes the meaning of the name the Nazis gave themselves, most of the clues are evident for projecting its principles. The National Socialist Party was a workers' party; metaphysically seen, reality and being were revealed through work. National Socialism was a form of socialism, which means it made the social whole primary to individuals; individuals acquire their meaning only within the social whole. Lastly, it was based upon a nation or *Volk*; it was not internationalist, like the Communist party, or universalistic like liberal regimes that based themselves in theories of human rights. In this particular case, the nation was Germany. I want to suggest that these principles constitute an essential part of the potential of National Socialism that attracted Heidegger.

Without a doubt the reader will notice that I left out two other central principles of Hitler's party, for it is on these crucial points that Heidegger's national socialism differed from actual Nazism. These principles are its racial doctrine and its quest for world domination. It is not possible to understand Hitler's National Socialism without accepting the central role these two principles, the quest for world domination being in fact an extension of the racial doctrine, yet Heidegger's national socialism included neither principle. If the reader suspects that like a good defense attorney I have conveniently left out from my case the doctrines that made National Socialism the truly horrific force that it was for the sole purpose of exonerating Heidegger, I would respond that convenience has nothing to do with it; Heidegger claimed that these doctrines were manifestations of the very metaphysics he thought the movement should overcome.[35] The Nazi

35. My position thus puts me at odds with Arendt's reading of Nazism as presented in *The Origins of Totalitarianism*, and those who follow her equation of national and racial, notably, Lacoue-Labarthe. Hannah Arendt, *The Origins of Totalitarianism*, new ed. (New York: Harcourt, Brace & World, 1966). My contention is not that the Nazis did not make this equation and understand the "German" in terms of the Aryan race, but rather that one can think of nationalism without linking it inextricably with racism, unless one follows Lacoue-Labarthe in equating the expulsion of difference necessary to constitute national identity as racist. Lacoue-Labarthe, *Heidegger, Art, and Politics*, 75–76. While I can go partway with Lacoue-Labarthe, it does not help us to understand Heidegger's thinking in the context of the "Jewish Problem" in Germany, because Heidegger was perfectly willing to incorporate Jews (of "noble character") into the new German Reich; in other words, in the context of Nazism's racial program, Heidegger was not racist. There are degrees of racism; Heidegger's racism was not as central and virulent as Hitler's.

racial doctrine constituted a betrayal, as Heidegger saw it, of the essential promise of National Socialism.

That said, it is significant that in his defense Heidegger relies on Nazism's biological principle in order to distinguish his philosophy from Nazism. On this ground Heidegger is clearly within his rights, but it does not address the entirety of Heidegger's racism. He had an antipathy toward Jews—not necessarily individual Jews, nor even the whole of German Jewry— due in part to the general social climate in Germany and more importantly due in part to an implicit equation of Jew with liberal cosmopolitanism. This latter equation is the basis for his remark about the "Jewification" of the German spirit, prompted in part by prominence of Jews in the neo-Kantian movement, which Heidegger wrote was "tailor-made for liberalism," and served as the vanguard of "an indifferent, general world-culture" which turned its back on "man in his historical rootedness and his national belonging to his origin in earth and blood" (*GA16*, 132). His noticeable hostility to Ernst Cassirer at the famous debate at Davros undoubtedly originated from this concern.[36] Even here, however, the bulk of the animosity is directed toward the rootless cosmopolitan aspect; there is nothing specifically Jewish about cosmopolitanism, and Heidegger was willing to except Jews who were of noble, that is to say, German, character. His antipathy toward cosmopolitanism led Heidegger to overlook Nazi discrimination and brutality toward Jews; in the context of the university, he probably saw the Nazi racial laws as ways of eliminating the liberal neo-Kantian spirit that "has already deceived many young people and led them astray" (*GA16*, 132). Heidegger may not have been a biological racist nor opposed to Jews as such, but willingness to go along with Nazi racial policies does stem from a principled opposition to what he took to be a Jewish-cosmopolitan danger to the German spirit.

The essential promise of National Socialism lies in its revolutionary potential to overturn the existing experience of being, that of modern metaphysics, along with the institutions and modes of thinking that are founded upon modern metaphysics, such as liberalism, cosmopolitanism, and a science that "is thinned down to a general, logical world-reason" (*GA16*, 132). One central institution of this modern edifice is the university.

---

36. Knowing this background lends the debate a rather sinister hue; what could be taken as philosophical rigor on Heidegger's part instead resembles a political and cultural battle for the heart and spirit of Germany. It is hard to believe that Heidegger did not see the debate in these terms.

Universities are central for Heidegger because they are the home of science; the university is the institution most directly related to the investigation of beings and thus to the question of being itself. Under the sway of metaphysics, however, the question of being is forgotten, pushed aside in the business of the scientific comprehension of beings. This means that the universities become the home of the individual sciences, separated from one another because they have lost the ground of their unity, which is found in the question of being in the search for the meaning of the whole. This forgetting of the question of the whole is exacerbated in modernity by the liberal concept of the university, which has as its essential principle freedom to pursue individual research; such freedom is a negative freedom from religious and dogmatic constraints, which Heidegger understood as a freedom from the necessity to raise the question of the meaning of the whole.

Heidegger took over the office of rector with the express desire to carry out a project near to his heart: the reformation of Germany's liberal universities. This desire to transform and renew the university system was not a new desire for Heidegger; he had long advocated this renewal, first in a short lecture he gave in 1919, again publicly in his inaugural address in 1928, and then again in 1933. Heidegger shared this desire with many of his colleagues and returning war veterans, for there was a widespread sense that the disaster of the German collapse was due in some part to the failure of the universities, and that the ensuing social crisis required their radical restructuring. For the most part, however, Heidegger despised these reform programs. "The much-discussed reform of the universities is entirely misled and a total misunderstanding of all genuine revolutionizing of the spirit, when it extends itself presently in appeals, protest gatherings, programs, orders and federations: unimaginative means in the service of ephemeral ends" (GA56/57, 4). Heidegger contrasted these superficial reforms with a genuine "rebirth of the authentic scientific consciousness and connections to life" (GA56/57, 4–5). This must be accomplished through making the essence of science, which means the essence of truth, manifest, for it is only through a genuine awareness of the essence of truth that Dasein wins itself back and finds itself genuinely rooted in its existence.[37] For Heidegger, this means responding to the crisis in the question of being, for

---

37. The steps which Heidegger followed in drawing this conclusion can be seen clearly in a lecture course from 1928/29: first, he presents the crisis of the sciences; second, he states that this crisis can only be addressed by a deconstruction and transformation of the dominant understanding of truth, which leads him into his discussion of the essence of truth as the essence of Dasein as being-in-the-world, so enabling Dasein to hold on to itself and so

the failure to take this question seriously as a question is the source of the distress of metaphysics and thus of science and the universities.

The liberal university, the brainchild of Wilhelm von Humboldt, shared the general distress of the time of metaphysics, which is to say, the essential meaninglessness of the work carried out there. This is not to say that scientific knowledge had not advanced or that the university's organization was not suited to the advance of science; indeed, like any other productive enterprise, specialization and division of labor brought about an acceleration in the growth of knowledge. Specialization is a symptom of modern technology, and thus of the forgetting of being. A system of specialized labor, as Adam Smith well knew, causes the laborer to become a stunted individual; in the end, the pinhead maker becomes a pinhead. Academic researchers are not immune to the effects of specialization. In the case of the university, the departments attain autonomy over their areas of research, which means that nothing coordinates the whole; physicist do not study philology and philologists do not carry out physical research. The departments do not work together out of a common ground, and therefore the university becomes nothing more than its merely technical organization, the accumulation and disbursement of funding so that individual research may take place.

If specialization of labor is modern in character, it is not necessarily liberal. Specialization, as Smith pointed out, both promotes and undermines liberal well-being. Smith's solution to the real possibility that the system of productive capital would produce stunted, and that is to say inhuman, laborers was publicly funded liberal education. Liberal education would educate and cultivate the rational and moral qualities necessary for human well-being and citizenship. One must question, however, whether the solution can stand up to the problem. The animus of Smith's attack on the aristocracy is directed at its unproductive use of capital, but to be consistent, liberal education must be counted as unproductive use of capital; the fact that Smith assigned the obligation to provide this education to the state indicates that capitalism left to itself will not fulfill this obligation because it is at odds with its underlying principle. Since in modern liberal democracies the state is a sometime tool of capitalism, Smith's solution is at constant risk from the need to make capital investment productive. We can see this in the justifications made for the need for universities. The fore-

---

recover itself from its being "lost" in the "busy-ness" that dominates modern being (*GA27*, 26–62; 149–220; 365).

most is that the universities serve as a home for research which will provide the inventions and advances in knowledge that will make capital more productive. This conception of a university as the advanced technical wing of the capitalist enterprise is most prevalent in state universities. Capitalism, however, has a powerful influence even on those private universities which take upon themselves the obligation to educate students liberally and not just for technical skills. However, in today's world, the foremost justification of liberal, as opposed to purely technical, education is that it makes the student more adaptable to changing economic needs; liberal education teaches skills that can be applied in many settings and in many sorts of labor. In this perverse way, a liberal education is thus actually a more effective means of making the labor force ripe for total mobilization.

If forces external to the ideal of liberal education push it toward technical training, there are problems internal to the ideal of a liberal university which make it open to the domination of technical thinking. Liberal education is humanist; it is supposed to cultivate the human virtues. Historically, this meant to free education from its subservience to religious dogmatism, and cultivate in its stead independent reason and an ethos of tolerance. These principles and goals animated Humboldt's organization of the liberal university in Germany. Following in the path laid out by earlier humanist thinkers, he separated religion from the university and established science in its place as the unifying principle of the university. His intention was to keep confessional wars outside academia by emphasizing instead each individual's freedom to pursue his or her own scholarly projects. Emphasizing private research interests, he believed, was the best means of accomplishing this end. It is true, though, that German universities retained much of their religious heritage for years afterward. Indeed, the faculty at the Protestant university at Marburg was persuaded to take on the "Catholic" docent Heidegger (who was more Protestant than Catholic at the time, but that was not widely known, particularly if one knew him only through his vitae) only when Husserl persuaded the suspicious philosophers that Heidegger was no longer Catholic. This legacy notwithstanding, Humboldtian reforms did in fact eliminate religion as an essential element in the university. The point is not that science debunks religious claims, or that individual members of the university no longer believe in God, but that religion loses its effective force in university life, and its place is taken by the pursuit of scientific knowledge.

That means, however, that the nature of science must also change. To maintain its liberal ethos of toleration, the university as a unity cannot be grounded in a single, overarching positive value. If science is to be a unifying force in the weak sense of a liberal university, it must be of such a sort that leaves values free for choosing. Thus one arrives at "value-free" science, or science freed from responsibility to ask about the meaning of the whole. Tolerant science contents itself with investigating beings and no longer raises the question of being, the question of the meaning of the whole. The weak unifying principle the technical university provides matches the almost nonexistent unifying force of the sciences themselves. The human and natural sciences broke apart under the strain of uniting facts and values, and afterwards science concentrated on facts and shoved values to the realm of nonscience, nonsense. "Value-free" science was the only sort of science that could survive in a liberal university because the minute values are put back into the mix, academic fights become pure power struggles over undecidables.[38] Value-free science that rigorously investigated only universally valid facts is the legacy of neo-Kantianism. Liberalism is not merely an accidental value for neo-Kantianism, but is necessarily tied to its practice of science. The only unity left to the university lies in its administration.

So in fact on principle the liberal university collapses into a technical university. The above gloss on the liberal university correlates with Heidegger's own description: "The scientific fields are quite diverse. The ways they treat their objects of inquiry differ fundamentally. Today only the technical organization of universities and faculties consolidate this burgeoning multiplicity of disciplines; the practical establishment of goals by each discipline provides the only meaningful source of unity. Nonetheless, the rootedness of the sciences in their essential ground has atrophied" (WM, 104).

---

38. Weber, one of the last great neo-Kantians whose science was to be value-free, well understood the lesson he had absorbed from Nietzsche: the great wars of the future would be fought over values and gods. The liberal in him thus wanted to insulate science from the seduction of values so that science would not be a tool in this fight. This of course assumes that Nietzsche is (half-) right and that values are ultimately undecidable (it denies the other half of Nietzsche's thought, that facts are only values in disguise). Both Weber and Nietzsche take for granted that values are irrational, and we who live in the age of the "cultural wars" in the university, in essence of Weber vs. Nietzsche, would do well to understand the essential similarity in their positions, for if value-free science is in fact a chimera, nothing can save the liberal university from its destruction. It is not an accident that some thinkers, Strauss and Voegelin for instance, have been accused of antiliberalism, because they believed that Weber culminates against his will in Nietzsche, which is to say, liberalism will become some variant of fascism in the end.

When after the war Heidegger formulated his defense, he quoted this passage and added that the university's most urgent concern was "to renew itself starting from its essential ground, which is precisely the essential ground of the sciences, that is to say from the essence of truth itself" (FT, 16; *GA16*, 373). To reform the universities requires a change in the essence of truth. To change the essence of truth is, however, profoundly political, and Heidegger understood it to be, for he opposed neo-Kantianism's technical understanding of science to a science that investigates man "in his historical rootedness and his national belonging to his origin in earth and blood" (*GA16*, 132). Humboldt's ideal university is thus political in nature, not in a narrow sense of being the tool of one party or another, but political in the sense of being a response to a political problem. Heidegger wanted to counter the ill effects Humboldt's liberal-cosmopolitan solution inflicted upon the German spirit. He wanted to find a new place for the university in the whole of the political realm, which is, as we have already seen, the order of beings as a whole. Heidegger's reformation of science was necessarily political because Heidegger saw the world as a unified order of being; institutions correspond to the ways of thinking about being. If the liberal conception of the university and the virtues it champions is in fact deeply rooted in modern technical thinking, then overcoming modern metaphysics means overthrowing the political regime and ethical virtues that are part of the modern world. Thus Heidegger was quite consistent in his desire to overthrow the cornerstone of the modern liberal university, its purely negative academic freedom, for in fact this freedom is bound to modern technology and thus reveals itself to be a form of slavery (SA, 10; *GA16*, 113).

It is possible to go even further than this negative claim. If academic "freedom" is bound to a conception of science that cannot inquire into the meaning of the whole and thus belongs to an alienated existence, then the positive solution lies in a conception of science that inquires into the meaning of the whole and understands this whole as the source of meaning in whose service it stands. True academic freedom is being free for the essential question concerning the whole, and so free for the meaning of the whole revealed through the questioning. This whole which science serves is the nation. As Heidegger understood the essence of truth, at least during this period, it correlates politically to the very "private National Socialism" to which Heidegger gave his allegiance.

The essence of truth, according to Heidegger's play on the Greek word for truth *alētheia,* is that truth means unconcealment or revealing. The verbal quality of "revealing" means that truth occurs. Truth happens as the truth of being. This truth of being is the meaning of being that gives meaning to existence. For some groups of people, it comes to light through work. We have already covered this in the previous chapters. At different times during his life, Heidegger defined the shape and definition of this group of people for whom the truth occurs. In the 1930s and 1940s, this group corresponds to a *Volk,* a people or nation. A *Volk* is instituted by its language, which is does not mean German or English or French, but its sayings, its sagas and myths. These poetic sayings give the nation its goal, its world, its Da-sein. A nation in this sense is the basic political unit of authentic community. It is the basic unit because it is prior to the individuals which make up the community. Heidegger thus explicitly rejects the cornerstone of liberal theory, that the individual is prior to the community. "This original community does not arise first of all through the establishing of reciprocal relations—thus arises only society—rather community is by the prior binding of each individual to that which each individual commandingly binds and determines" (*GA39,* 72). Heidegger takes up a distinction made in the nineteenth century between community (*Gemeinschaft*) and society (*Gesellschaft*); and, it should be noted in passing, he adopts the moral connotations that each term carried, as indicated by the sneering "only." *Gesell* means "companion" or "associate"; *gesellen* means "to associate." It carries the connotation of an associate in trade or in a trade. According to the distinction, a *Gesellschaft* is primarily an economic association, however broadly one wishes to construe "economic." As such, it was used to refer to a society constituted by a social contract, or at least one purported to be founded on a social contract, that is to say, a liberal society. A contract signifies that the wishes of the contracting parties, in the case of liberal theory individuals, have precedence. The association binds only so far as that to which the contracting parties have agreed. It is exactly this point that distinguishes a *Gemeinschaft* from a *Gesellschaft.* A *Gemeinschaft* has an overarching binding and determining principle. The community is thus prior to the individuals and any contracting they do. This principle is not supposed to be alien to the individuals and thus oppressive; *gemein* means common, and particularly relevant for Heidegger, is derived from *mein,* mine, my own.[39] In *Being and Time,* Dasein was characterized by *Jemeinigkeit,*

---

39. Charles Taylor relies on much the same logic in his communitarianism. He even

in each case my own; *Gemeinschaft* is the being-with expression of *Jemeinigkeit*. It is not accidental that Heidegger uses *Gemeinschaft* to characterize the group which co-historicizes.[40] A community is a nation. The nation's co-historicizing is the historical event of being, the coming into being of the world. Heidegger's political theory in 1934 corresponds directly to that of *Being and Time*. The *Volk* is the historical "there" of being, the principle or *ethos* which guides and gives meaning to each individual's labor.

Volk adds something to the bare community. The historical community of *Being and Time* (the generation) indicates its connection with time quite clearly, but not its place, its where. It has a time, but no place. *Volk* adds the place. What is the place of a generation? It can be very broad, as the events of 1968 show. A nation has a place: its world is rooted in its earth, the land it works, the fields that provide food and shelter, the holy mountain where its gods live. The early Heidegger gave a phenomenological description of world without reference to earth. The later Heidegger set the world against the earth; a world was a world only so far as it was on this earth. Earth took its place in the fourfold as a necessary element of being. This essential element of Heidegger's later thinking in fact was introduced as early as 1933, even before his Hölderlin lectures or his lecture on the origin of art.

Understood as a community of people and not merely as an association, *Volk* points toward socialism or populism. Although there can be socialism without nations, there can be no nationalism without socialism. Because humans are essentially laboring creatures, Heidegger, like most

---

approvingly cites Heidegger for this thought. Charles Taylor, "Engaged Agency and Background in Heidegger," in *The Cambridge Companion to Heidegger*, ed. Charles Guignon (New York: Cambridge University Press, 1993). He considers Rawls's thin self tyrannical because it excludes what he considers legitimate expressions of what an individual considers valuable in his or her self. For Taylor, the self is not an isolated individual behind a veil of ignorance, but is part of a larger community with whom he or she shares certain conceptions of goods and values that go beyond distributive justice. His basic unit is a culture; one could easily call it a nation. Taylor is not by any means a fascist, and the comparison with Heidegger is not meant to imply that his theory eventually elides with that of the latter. Taylor wishes to preserve rights and the individual. Heidegger has no such concerns. For more, see Charles Taylor, *The Ethics of Authenticity* (Cambridge: Harvard University Press, 1992), and idem, *Sources of the Self: The Making of the Modern Identity* (Cambridge: Harvard University Press, 1989).

40. No one that I have read has picked up on the relationship of *Jemeinigkeit* and *Gemeinschaft*. My analysis in this paragraph indicates that Heidegger's political theory is more closely related to his analysis of Dasein than is generally thought.

modern socialists, understood socialism as a particular social arrangement of work in which the social group has ontological and moral precedence over individual laborers. For Heidegger, though, socialism must be understood in the context of nationalism; the basic social unit is not a class, but rather a nation. Since in German, one word for nation is *Volk,* which also means "people," Heidegger's socialism is really a type of populism. National socialism for Heidegger is a people is bound together into the one single estate, the (German) working class.[41] Work, as the previous chapter showed, assumed a central place in Heidegger's politics. In this regard, however, he is at one with the modern alternatives, for both capitalism and Marxism are also political philosophies of labor. Thus it is incumbent upon Heidegger to show that national socialism is the political regime that best embodies the transformed nature of work that he envisioned in his writings on technology. To put it another way, Heidegger had to show that work and nation belong essentially together. Work is the unifying principle of being, nation, and socialism. But this requires further consideration.

Work

In the previous chapter I showed that work understood poetically is authentic knowledge or *phronēsis,* which is to say, that it aligns with the essence of truth as unconcealing. In a speech delivered to unemployed workers in early 1934, Heidegger broached this staple of his later philosophy. "Knowledge means: to *know one's way around* in the world into which we are placed, as a community and as individuals" (NSE, 58; *GA16,* 234). To know one's way around is *phronēsis,* the practical knowledge, which for Heidegger is authentic knowledge. If we substitute "thrown" for "placed," the line could have been lifted straight from *Being and Time.* In this speech, though, as in the later philosophy, work is equated to authentic knowledge. *"For us, 'work' is the title of every well-ordered action that*

41. In a letter Heidegger wrote to Marcuse after the war, he said he expected the from Nazis "a reconciliation of social antagonisms and a deliverance of Western Dasein from the dangers of communism." "Letter from Heidegger to Marcuse of January 20, 1948," in Wolin, *Heidegger Controversy,* 162 (*GA16,* 430). The conjunction of those two factors is not accidental; the social antagonism Heidegger refers to is the class warfare advocated by the internationalist Communist Party. Communism advocates a universal workers' class that cuts across national boundaries; Heidegger instead wanted a national populism that cut across class boundaries.

is borne by the responsibility of the individual, the group, and the state and which is thus of service to the Volk" (NSE, 59; GA16, 236). Unlike Aristotle, who separates work from action proper, Heidegger combines them: work is well-ordered action. What makes work well ordered is that it is responsible to and thus in service to the nation. The nation is the "there" of being; it is the definite revelation of being, the principle that gives meaning to labor. In nuce, this is the change in the essence of work which he called for in the 1934 Hölderlin lecture, and which lasted throughout the rest of his life. Work is responsible ultimately to the *Volk*, which means that the workers derive the meaning of their work from the revelation of being which occurs as the truth of a nation. "Every one of our people who is employed must *know for what reason* and *to what purpose* he is where he is. It is only through this living and ever-present *knowledge* that his life will be rooted in the people as a whole, and its destiny" (NSE, 56; GA16, 233). This is the metaphysical significance of work.

The socialist character of work, in Heidegger's view, would correct the social imbalances and deprivations that existed in the liberal-capitalist world that preceded the Nazi revolution. He hoped first of all to heal social divisions and eliminate class warfare (*GA16*, 430). The social division he was most concerned about—undoubtedly because it lay closest to his personal experience—was the social distinction brought about between manual and intellectual labor. Like any modern industrial nation, Germany required a class of intellectuals to help manage the technical, economic, and political sectors of society: engineers, scientists, managers, and bureaucrats of all sorts. These positions require extensive schooling, and as is usual in modern societies, the German universities supplied the bulk of this class. As is also inevitable, distinctions in schooling produce inequalities: prestige, wealth, and power gravitate to those with much sought and difficult to replace skills and knowledge; and as is also usual, this class can perpetuate itself because its wealth and power give its children a better opportunity to gain admittance to the exclusive schooling which is the source of wealth and power. It is the exceptional student who comes to the universities from poverty.[42] This situation poses a problem for democracies, as present education debates in the United States concerning equal

---

42. Heidegger, incidentally, was one of those students, having advanced due to the good graces of a stipend from the Catholic Church. Ott and Safranski detail these early years of dependency and its possible effects on his view of the Church and his resentment against the bourgeoisie. Ott, *Martin Heidegger*; Safranski, *Ein Meister aus Deutschland*.

access and opportunity make clear. Heidegger was not so much concerned with equal access as he was with closing the rift in the social status between intellectuals and laborers.[43] In this respect, he was more radical than liberal reformers, for equal access addresses the problem of perpetuation but not that of the social division itself. To overcome a social distinction means to make separate and distinct individuals equal in the most important respect; it means to find a common ground that trumps individual differences. Liberalism addresses itself to the problem of political inequality by making everyone politically equal by nature. Other natural differences are left free by the political sphere and they thus generate multiple forms of inequality in liberal civil society. Socialists responded to these civil inequalities because they felt that these inequalities undermined political equality. Heidegger finds a common ground in the nation or the being-with of Dasein.[44] If all types of work, both intellectual and manual, gain significance by reference to the same source of meaning, they are all equal in some sense. Work in service to the nation unites all into one class: "There is only one single German 'estate.' That is the *estate of work* which is rooted in and borne by the *Volk* and which has freely submitted to the historical will of the state. The character of this estate is being pre-formed in the National Socialist *Worker's Party* movement" (CLS, 54; GA16, 239).[45]

One should not lose sight of the character of this one-class society. Specialization and division of labor remain; there is hardly a society that

43. Someone who has read both Heidegger's political texts and his philosophical texts from the 1930s might be hard-pressed to reconcile them, since the former are very anti-elitist, while the latter are held to be elitist and Mandarin (the great creators vs. the stinking masses). I think the error lies in our natural equation of masses with manual workers, an equation foreign to Heidegger's scheme. If anything, Heidegger held workers and peasants in higher regard than intellectuals. The opposition in Heidegger's thinking is really between cosmopolitanism and rootedness, and he expressed a definite preference for the latter.

44. I find it ironic that it is sometimes held that had Heidegger attended more thoroughly to *Mitsein* he would not have fallen in with the Nazis. Nancy, *Inoperative Community*, 14. On the contrary, it is precisely his conception of *Mitsein* which grounds the possibility of the folkish community he thought National Socialism would bring about. In this respect, I am in partial agreement with Lacoue-Labarthe, who writes, "One will always be able to say, in effect, that Heidegger's political choice begins (at least) when being-in-the-world and the being-with (or the advent-with) of *Dasein* is thought as a people." Lacoue-Labarthe, "Transcendence Ends in Politics," 286. My reservation lies in Lacoue-Labarthe's implication that there is another way that Heidegger thought of being-with.

45. Translation altered slightly; emphasis in the original. Heidegger's own emphasis on work and workers lends credence to my thesis in this chapter, that Heidegger was led to his Nazi engagement primarily through his revision of the concept of work.

does not divide its work. Heidegger's estate of work includes the normal divisions of labor, including those between intellectual and manual labor. These necessary divisions remain, but the class distinction are overcome by referring each task to the same source of meaning. There is a strong corporatist implication behind this theory, deriving in all probability from Heidegger's excursions into Platonic political philosophy, especially the *Republic*. Different people, different soul types, are assigned places in the ordered whole that best address the needs of their soul. The responsibility of the individual is do his or her best at the task to which they have been assigned. Heidegger writes, "Knowledge means: in our decisions and actions *to be up to* the task that is assigned us, whether this task be to till the soil or to fell a tree or to dig a ditch or to inquire into the laws of nature or to illuminate the fateful force of history" (NSE, 58; *GA16*, 235). From the "lowest" manual laborer to scientific research to prophet, each has the responsibility to work with utmost commitment for the whole. The examples clearly show how the tasks of the most varied sort could be equal in a national socialist regime. Each is equally in service to the meaning of the whole to which each belongs.

For labor to be redeemed, each must labor within a shared community that is as a whole devoted to some higher, genuinely binding principle dispensed by being. Heidegger's socialism grows from Dasein's necessary social character; Dasein's fundamental character of being-with makes all varieties of individualism, economic and political, an anathema to Heidegger. His socialism becomes a nationalism, because an authentic community is founded upon a clearing of being that is opened up and shared in and through language. Germany exists as such because Germans have access to being through the German language. Because language is the locus of being, the national community has precedence over other social organizations.[46] The gods humans serve "are always the gods of a people" (*GA39*, 170). Although it is a type of socialism, world communism must belong to metaphysics because it seeks to eliminate the natural divisions of the

---

46. See Catherine Zuckert, "Martin Heidegger: His Philosophy and His Politics," *Political Theory* 18, no. 1 (1990): 51–79. Zuckert bases her thesis largely on Heidegger's writings in the 1930s when the *Volk* loomed large in his thought, but one can also find this connection between language and community in Heidegger's earlier work on Aristotle. See Martin Heidegger, *Grundbegriffe der aristotelischen Philosophie*, SS 1924 (MS in Marcuse Archive), pp. 16, 23; see also Gillespie, "Martin Heidegger's Aristotelian National Socialism," 145.

world, that is to say, those originating in being, in favor of a universal class constructed by a leveling instrumental reason. Heidegger's path to redeeming labor in the technical age necessitates nationalism.

Heidegger did not rely only upon a vague sense of shared nationhood to unite the people. Relying on a very concrete psychological insight, Heidegger believed that the communal and service orientation to work was brought about through institutions designed to bring people to labor together. The most vital service to bringing about this goal was the labor service. Labor service was one of the three services Heidegger mentioned in his Rectoral Address, along with military and knowledge; of the three, military service played little or no role in Heidegger's thought, whereas labor service played a vital role in conjunction with knowledge service. The labor service was an institution set up to assign people to common tasks: in essence, they were work camps in which everyone was expected to participate. Through their organized routine, the camps would teach that work received its meaning from the task at hand, and that work meant working together in mutual dependence; everyone needed to do their part so that the task would be accomplished.[47] The labor service reinforces "the responsibility that derives for the individual from the fact that all belong together in an ethnic [volkhaft] unity" (CLS, 53; GA16, 238). Working together would foster social cohesion: "For what counts in the camp is exemplary acting and working together, but not standing by and supervising" (LSU, 42; GA16, 125). Heidegger wanted to strengthen the feelings of comradeship which signified the social bond of a community, which overcomes the proximal "indifferent modes" of being-with characteristic particularly of bourgeois society (BT, 161).

The labor service institutionalized authentic solicitous concern (Fürsorge). In Dasein's being-in-the-world, it encounters that which is environmentally ready-to-hand, "and it does so in such a way that together with it we encounter the Dasein-with of others" (BT, 160). In this way, we discover that our own being is essentially being-with:

---

47. This sort of training thrives today in various sorts of business executive camps designed to foster teamwork and trust among company executives. I believe that Heidegger viewed the function of the labor service, particularly as it applied to academicians, quite similarly. I am not certain if he was aware of the real function of the labor service: a covert military training facility to impart military skills and discipline to a much larger group than allowed under the Versailles Treaty.

> Knowing oneself is grounded in being-with, which understands primordially. It operates proximally in accordance with the kind of being which is closest to us—being-in-the-world as being-with; and it does so by an acquaintance with that which Dasein, along with the others, comes across in its environmental circumspection and concerns itself with—an acquaintance in which Dasein understands. Solicitous concern is understood in terms of what we are concerned with, and along with our understanding of it. Thus in concernful solicitude the other is proximally disclosed. (*BT*, 161)

Dasein understands its being-in-the-world for the most part environmentally, that is to say, in its everyday work world. In this work world we encounter others in their positions in this world: suppliers, buyers, and coworkers. In essence, solicitous concern means our economic relations to others. Being constitutive of Dasein's being-in-the-world, however, solicitous concern is a formal indication and can thus enact itself in any of several different possibilities. These possibilities belong to larger systems of enactment we have already examined, for instance, modern technology. In the system of modern technology, we encounter other humans as raw material, instruments of an aimless system of production. In such a system, one's coworkers are faceless and interchangeable, and because of this one is "indifferent" to them. Thus "indifference" is the mode of solicitous concern peculiar to modern technical production.[48] Heidegger envisaged a different mode of solicitude in the world of transformed labor. This mode is comradeship. Comradeship is an authentic enactment of Dasein because in this enactment one grasps one's situation while sharing the revelation of being with others. Comradeship means sharing the ground and goal of labor with one's coworkers; in other words, working together allows Dasein to know itself authentically, not as any bare working together, but when the task is one performed in common, when the "for-the-sake-of-which" is revealed to each in common. Heidegger presents two situations

48. Although I think Heidegger intends his analysis to apply to all modern social economies, the characterization works best for capitalist societies. It is similar to Marx's theory that capitalism not only alienates workers from the products of their labor, but also from each other. Like Marx, Heidegger is concerned also with the reflexive moment of understanding; we understand ourselves as alienated from one another, that is to say, as individuals, and thus lose connection to our essential being as social beings. Thus Heidegger's implied criticism of indifferent modes can function as a critique of contract theories of labor characteristic of capitalism.

that breed comradeship: "under pressure of a great common danger or from the ever-growing commitment to a clearly perceived task" (CLS, 53; *GA16*, 238). The first arises most particularly in war; the second in work. Without comradeship, no true community is possible; "at most it comes to an altered form of society [*Gesellschaft*]" (*GA39*, 73). The labor camps foster comradeship, which is part of authentic existence.

Labor and the labor camps fostered a nationalist socialism. A nation is characterized by being rooted in a particular place on this earth. Labor makes possible an experience of the soil. "Such service provides the basic experience of hardness, of closeness to the soil and implements of labor, of the rigorous law that governs the simplest physical—and thus essential—labor in a group" (CLS, 53; *GA16*, 238). Soil does not mean just any bit of dirt emptied of meaning or useful only as raw material; it means one's own soil, the soil of a nation which as soil has a history; in it we recognize the past labor of those who preceded us, out of which our own present and destiny arises. Because it is being infused with this history, the soil is the homeland of a people (*GA39*, 104–5). Working in the soil is supposed to be the type of dwelling which is the unity of past, present and future, in other words, authentic temporality. Authentic work arises out of this laboring dwelling; it is given meaning by being rooted in the soil of the nation. When we labor authentically, we gain an authentic experience of our environment; it ceases to be either raw material for industrial production or a beautiful sight for excursioners from the city. "And that once again not in the desired moment of a hedonistic submersion and artificial empathy, but rather only when one's own Dasein stands in his *work*. *Work alone opens* the space for this reality of the mountain. The movement of work remains planted in the happening of the landscape" (WBW, 10). The "movement of work" to which Heidegger refers in this passage is not manual labor alone; his own philosophizing arose out of his experience of his rootedness in the landscape of his home. Labor instills this rootedness, this essential nationalism.

For Heidegger, labor was particularly necessary to intellectuals, since manual labor for them was something done by the hired help. Heidegger hoped that working in these camps and experiencing manual labor would open academics to work as "a new and decisive educating force" (LSU, 42; *GA16*, 125). The labor service would institutionalize the new essence of truth, that work and knowledge were one and the same. Academics would experience firsthand the truth of being inherent in work. In this way,

Heidegger hoped that academic research itself would be affected by this new essence of truth. The essence of truth and work referred back ultimately to the nation. Through the labor service, Heidegger wanted to root scientific labor, the university, in the nation as a whole. In other words, to root scientific research means not just to root science in a new essence of truth which can be separated from the concerns of the nation as a whole, but to root it in service to the nation. "It is through such teaching that true research emerges, interlocked with the whole through its rootedness in the *Volk* and its bond to the state" (UNR, 45; *GA16, 763*). This is specifically why Heidegger was so enthusiastic about the labor service. Laboring in these camps would instill a sense of common destiny; it is out of this common destiny that all labor, including scientific research, finds its meaning. The labor service was a necessary component in the reformation of the university and of the nature of scientific research itself.

Work was the principle of unity of the National Socialist Worker's Party. It bound in an essential manner nationalism and socialism. Each of the three—work, nationalism, and socialism—implies the other. The mutual belonging together of these three elements is the essence of work and the essence of truth, which together made up Heidegger's new metaphysics. A National Socialist Workers' movement was necessary to bring about the revolution in metaphysics that was the highest political revolution possible.

Nationalism and *das Volk*

National Socialism was but one of the philosophies of labor available to Heidegger. His socialism clearly excluded any choice in favor of an individualistic and contract-centered liberal capitalism. There is, however, the matter of communism and its more virulent revolutionary branch, Bolshevism, another labor-centered politics that Heidegger could have chosen. The decisive difference in favor of National Socialism lies in its national character. Unlike the internationalist and universalistic Marxist party doctrines, the Nazis were specifically the National Socialist party of *Germany*.

Heidegger decided for National Socialism because he was foremost a nationalist. The word he used to signal his nationalism was *Volk*, a word which means nation, people, folk, or ethnic group.[49] The notion of *Volk*

---

49. The following presentation fits in tolerably well with the analysis of nation, culture, and state developed in Friedrich Meinecke's *Cosmopolitanism and the National State*, trans.

carried connotations more potent in Germany than in most other Western nations because of the historical precariousness of the German state. Nowadays we speak matter-of-factly of the rise in early modernity of the nation-state. In contrast either to the Greek city-states, which are often characterized as many political states in one nation, or an empire, which is often characterized as a multinational state, a nation-state is an entity in which the nation and the state are coterminous. The German nation-state had existed in name since the crowning of the Holy Roman Emperor, but a long history of delegating power to local cities, duchies, etc., combined with the enormous dislocations caused by the Reformation and the Thirty Years' War, gradually made a mockery of any pretense to a real German polity.[50] By the eighteenth century, Germany was split into hundreds of individual kingdoms, dukedoms, baronies, free states, and one greatly reduced Austro-Hungarian empire, all open to political domination by powerful neighbors, particularly, France.

In the eighteenth century, a desire to reassert the German spirit in the face of political and cultural domination surfaced, but so too did the realization that the fractured nature of the political situation made such a German nation-state at best a distant dream. In the face of these political realities nationalistic desires turned toward the suprapolitical sphere, the sphere of culture.[51] Folk, nation, spirit, people, and culture were all notions developed to discover, create, or build Germanness. "Politics" became culture, and culture rested on the *Volk*. The confluence of these terms was given a decisive and very influential direction through the efforts of Herder.[52] One notion that had a lasting impact was his belief that the spirit

---

Robert B. Kimber (Princeton: Princeton University Press, 1970). Particularly important is the distinction he develops between "cultural nation" and "political nation." Meinecke, *Cosmopolitanism*, 10. He makes a distinction between *Volk* and *Nation* which I do not follow because Heidegger did not. Meinecke, *Cosmopolitanism*, 24–25.

50. This legacy leaves its mark even today on German politics. The Federal Republic of Germany is very federal in nature, delegating extensive latitude and powers to the individual states.

51. Meinecke, *Cosmopolitanism*, 27–28.

52. Wulf Koepke presents a useful examination of Herder's use of the word *Volk*. Koepke, "Das Wort 'Volk' im Sprachgebrauch Johann Gottfried Herders," *Lessing Yearbook* 19 (1987): 209–21. Many of the senses in which Herder uses it—its spiritual-intellectual character, its opposition to a machine-like state built upon abstract reason, its status as a unifying way of thinking—are also valid for Heidegger's thought. Herder is quite obviously inspired by Rousseau's account of popular sovereignty; in what sense this could be true for Heidegger will be examined in the next chapter.

of a people is found in its legends and folk songs. The Grimm brothers' famous book of fairy tales takes its inspiration from this idea. For the Grimms, collecting the stories was an act of retrieving and preserving the spirit of the Germans in the face of the cultural dominance by outside forces; it was part of the cultural-political ambitions of the German intellectuals. Thus in the nineteenth century and especially after the failure of the revolution of 1848 it became standard fare among German intellectuals to find the essential ground of politics in the spirit or culture of the people. The state was imagined to be merely a superstructure built upon the real foundations of the national spirit.

This cultural-political ideal had a peculiar relationship to the actual ongoing political unification of Germany. On the one hand, since it had been developed in explicit contradistinction to the existing political situation, the nation or spirit of the people might be destroyed by the political necessities of asserting German power in the political sphere. This fear accounts for Nietzsche's rejection of the Bismarckian path to German unification. In the section of *Thus Spoke Zarathustra* titled "On the New Idol," Nietzsche wrote, "Somewhere there are still peoples and herds, but not where we live, my brothers: here there are states. State? What is that? Well, then, open your ears to me, for now I shall speak to you about the death of peoples."[53] By "state" Nietzsche meant the modern state. In order for it to assert its power politically, it had to acquire enormous economic power. So Nietzsche says, "They want power and first the lever of power, much money—the impotent paupers!"[54] The state is developed in order to rationally harness the resources of the nation for growth and domination. For Nietzsche, this technical monstrosity annihilates and devours the creative element that makes a people capable of being a people, of being the source of the esteeming which gives them their virtues and their gods.[55] If forced to choose between nation and state, Nietzsche chose the *Volk*, even if that meant the "nation" of Europe.

On the other hand, one can see how culture and state could seem to fit together. Cultural nationalism and political nationalism are both nationalisms, creating a natural alliance between the two groups. It is difficult to separate cultural assertion from political assertion, particularly if the polit-

---

53. Nietzsche, *Thus Spoke Zarathustra*, 48.
54. Ibid., 50.
55. Ibid., 59.

ical self-assertion is seen as a product of the peculiar virtues brought forth in the cultural renewal that make the political success possible.[56] Since the original program was a response to the political and cultural subservience to foreign powers, the original program to help build the political self-assertion of Germany from out of its basis in the spirit of the people is implicated in cultural nationalism. In his usual blunt fashion, this connection becomes apparent in Fichte's *Addresses to the German Nation,* which sought to incite German political nationalism during the occupation by Napoleon by calling on the German intellectual class to begin a program of proper German education.

Heidegger is caught up in this mishmash of German nationalism. Although he is far closer to the cultural-nationalist element, he is not immune to the connection between cultural self-determination and political self-determination. Indeed, political self-determination played a key role in Heidegger's stance toward the Nazis. One must see the Nazis' call for German self-assertion in the context of Germany's position under the Versailles Treaty. German nationalists hated the document because it rendered Germany subservient to foreign powers, either through the high level of reparations or physical occupation of German soil. Although the Weimar constitution is not mandated under the Versailles Treaty, since the Weimar regime upheld the treaty, it was seen as party to German subservience toward the Allies. In addition, there was always an underlying sense among conservatives that the Weimar Republic, with its parliamentary democratic form, was part of the Western ideological domination and thus un-German. Hitler appealed to nationalists because he wanted to reassert Germany's sovereignty. This appealed to Heidegger. It comes through in his mythologizing memorial to Albert Schlageter. Schlageter had been arrested and executed by occupying French forces for various acts of sabotage, including exploding a bomb on a French military installation. Heidegger portrayed him not as a terrorist but rather as a martyred freedom fighter. According to Heidegger, Germans should honor Schlageter because "alone, drawing on his inner strength, he had to place before his soul an image of the future awakening of the *Volk* to honor and greatness so that he could die believ-

---

56. This sort of thinking is not limited to nations or nationalism, but extends to how the European powers regarded their colonial conquests. Thus the European conquest of Africa and Asia led to attempts to discover the uniquely European virtues that made these conquests possible. This is the origin of the modern notion and use of race and racial superiority as justification of such conquests.

ing in this future" (Sl, 40–41; *GA16, 759*). Schlageter was great, from Heidegger's point of view, because he fought and died for Germany's independence from French domination. This will to German independence Heidegger elsewhere called the will to Germany's self-responsibility. Heidegger described this self-responsibility as why Germany should follow Hitler's lead and withdraw from the League of Nations.

> It is not ambition, nor desire for glory, nor blind obstinacy, and not hunger for power that demands from the Führer that Germany withdraw from the League of Nations. It is only the clear will to unconditional self-responsibility in suffering and mastering the fate of our people. That is *not* a turning away from the community of peoples. On the contrary: with this step, our people is submitting to that essential law of human being to which every people must first give allegiance if it is still to be a people. (DSAH, 50; *GA16, 191*)

Further on he glosses the essential law of human being to mean "the clear acknowledgment of each people's inviolable independence" (DSAH, 50; *GA16, 191*). Each nation has a right to self-determination. Just as in Heidegger's assertion in *Being and Time* that no one should "step in" for another Dasein and take away its own decision, thereby becoming dominant over the other, so too does this same authentic solicitude apply to nations (*BT, 158*). The invocation of *Being and Time* in this context is deliberate. For example, the issue at stake in the referendum to withdraw from the League of Nations is "whether the entire *Volk* wills its own [*eigenes*] Dasein, or whether it does not will it" (DSAH, 49; *GA16, 190*). For peoples to be authentically peoples, they must take responsibility for themselves, which means to take responsibility for their fate as meted out by being.[57]

---

57. Such passages are sometimes taken as proof, for instance by Löwith and Habermas, that Heidegger altered the individualist categories from *Being and Time* to put a philosophical sheen on his commitment to National Socialism. Since on my reading *Being and Time* is not so individualist as either Löwith or Habermas believe it to be, I do not think there is any noteworthy difference; the later passage makes clearer what is already evident in the passage in *Being and Time* where Heidegger says that our fates are bound up in the destiny of the community (*BT, 436*). Löwith, "Political Implications"; Habermas, *Philosophical Discourse of Modernity*, 157. I will discuss the connection between authentic self-responsibility and populism in the next chapter.

The philosophical arena is in Heidegger's mind never far from the concretely political one, as one would expect from any notion of nation as a culturally distinct unity. A culture is a distinct way of thinking, and philosophy is the highest realization of these ways of thinking. In this sense, one speaks of national philosophies—German, French, British, American—as one would speak of national movie cultures or national music cultures. A national philosophy could be polluted or infected by foreign ways of thinking.[58] There is at once some element of truth and something profoundly ridiculous about these notions. The element of truth is that national institutional pressures on universities mold philosophical training onto a model that through institutional reproduction becomes by default national. Thus today we speak of "Anglo-American philosophy" as opposed to "Continental philosophy," which describes the character of the bulk of the work carried on in departments in the respective areas. What is ridiculous is the reification of this de facto state of affairs as a supposedly indigenous way of thinking. There is, for instance, nothing indigenously German about Kant, nor would he have ever thought so: the three great spurs to his thought were Descartes, Hume, and Rousseau.[59] Nor is there, to take another case, anything indigenously Scot-English about Adam Smith; the principles of capitalism appeal to anyone interested in expanding the wealth of a nation.

Nonetheless, stereotypes persist, and Heidegger felt the influence of this way of thinking. Political occupation was only a symptom of a deeper danger posed for the German nation by foreign ideas. This had meant since the eighteenth century primarily French and British ideas, but was adapted after the First World War to include American and Russian/Soviet ways of thinking. Foreign ideas, whatever their national origin, primarily meant rationalism, materialism, utilitarianism, and later positivism: in short,

---

58. This worry reached a crescendo during and after both world wars. Particularly during the first, philosophers engaged in philosophical propaganda, praising one's philosophers for properly fulfilling the national virtues and denigrating the opponent's philosophers for exhibiting their nation's vices. This sort of behavior existed on both sides of the front lines, and could have lasting influences. For instance, the First World War almost completely destroyed British neo-Hegelianism because of Hegel's supposed influence on German absolutism, and the Nazis' use of Nietzsche blackened Nietzsche's work for many years afterward.

59. One could substitute Leibniz for this pantheon, as Heidegger does, but Leibniz, although German, wrote in French and Latin. For someone who placed so much weight on the specific natures of individual languages, it is curious that Heidegger overlooked this point.

exactly what Heidegger meant by modern technology.[60] Thus Heidegger spoke of Germany trapped between the pincers of America and the Soviet Union, which were metaphysically the same, since both represent the unleashing of "the same dreary technological frenzy" (*IM*, 37–38). In his wartime lectures he inveighed against the dangers of "Americanism," and the "Americanization" of the German language, by which he meant the "increasing wearing away of language into a technical-trafficking instrument" (*GA53*, 86; *GA52*, 10–11).

His lectures and essays on the origin of modern technology, however, point to the real cause, which lay not in America but in Rome. He was constantly at pains to point out how the Latin translation of Greek philosophical terms marked a transition point away from the Greeks, and that it is only by a return to the Greeks that we can overcome modern ways of thinking. For instance, he wrote:

> But with this Latin translation the original meaning of the Greek word is thrust aside, the actual philosophical force of the Greek word is destroyed. This is true not only of the Latin translation of this word but of all other Roman translations of the Greek philosophical language. What happened in this translation from the Greek into Latin is not accidental and harmless; it marks the first stage in the process by which we cut ourselves off and alienate ourselves from the original essence of Greek philosophy. (*IM*, 13)

Since philosophy thinks within language, that means in effect that every Romance language is infected by the Roman error. German alone retained an original connection to Greek. Thus only Germany is in a position to save Europe from the onslaught of the global technicization brought on by the latest scion of the Romans, the Americans and Bolsheviks.[61]

The necessity of a return to the Greeks that so animated Heidegger crops up frequently beginning in the early 1930s. In a letter to Elisabeth Bloch-

---

60. For an interesting account of the German academy's efforts to develop a specifically German culture opposed to foreign ways of thinking, see Fritz Ringer, *The Decline of the German Mandarins* (Hanover: University Press of New England, 1990), 81–90.

61. This position has drawn the sarcastic ire of many commentators, friend and foe, German and non-German alike. See Derrida, *Of Spirit;* Caputo, *Demythologizing Heidegger;* Rainer Marten, "Heidegger and the Greeks," in *The Heidegger Case: On Philosophy and Politics,* ed. Tom Rockmore and Joseph Margolis (Philadelphia: Temple University Press, 1992).

mann written in December 1931, he wrote: "It is becoming ever clearer to me, that and how the inception of our Western philosophy must again become present for us, so that we can again first learn from their model. . . . Contemporary philosophy is becoming ever more questionable to me, for it is so far away from the simple flourishing of the original questions of the Greeks, who fought in such questions for the essence *of* man, in which the breadth of the world and the depth of existence are one" (*BwHB*, 46).

In another letter dated from July of the next year, Heidegger clarified what he meant by Greek, "And what concerns antiquity, these men confuse —it is almost comical—the original antiquity with the later pre-Christian Roman world, which then later determined the 'world' of the German gymnasium" (*BwHB*, 55). Heidegger is intent on separating his return to the Greeks from the traditional humanist return to the Greeks that served as the foundation for generations of German humanist schooling through the influence of Winckelmann, Goethe, and Schiller. The humanist "Greek" was for Heidegger really the Roman adaptation of late Hellenic school philosophy, and so doubly removed from the original, that is to say, pre-Socratic Greek.[62] Heidegger invokes this genuine Greek antiquity in the Rectoral Address by insisting that the essence of the German university could only be renewed through grasping the essence of science, which itself could only be accomplished "when we submit to the power of the beginning of our spiritual-historical existence. This is the irruption of Greek philosophy," or alternatively the "original Greek essence of science" (SA, 6–7; GA16, 108). This original essence is the question of being, which arose in its essential form in the thinking of the Pre-Socratics before it was transformed in the thought of Plato and Aristotle into the metaphysical question of the being of beings which began the oblivion of being.

The essence of the German nation is determined by this repetition of the original Greek essence: it "means nothing less than to recapture, repeat, the beginning of our historical-spiritual existence, in order to transform it into a new beginning" (*IM*, 39). This repetition is not imitation, but a repeating of the original possibility found in the Greeks of authentically posing and thus living the question of being (*IM*, 39). In posing the question of being, humans open and hold open the openness of being that determines the meaning and measure of being as a whole; this is the "there" of

---

62. See in this regard the "Letter on Humanism," 200–201.

being, the truth of being, which is the foundation of a people. "The truth of the people is the momentary manifestness [*Offenbarkeit*] of being as a whole, according to which the sustaining and ordering and leading power receives its ranks and effects its accord. The truth of a people is that manifestness of being, out of which a people knows what it historically wills, while it wills *itself,* it wills to be itself" (*GA39,* 144).

In this standing in the openness of being the people experience the being of a nation as the fatherland and homeland. Fatherland indicates that the revelation of being is the source of each individual; it is experienced as the "authentic and sole being [*Seyn*], out of which the basic stance toward beings grows and earns its structural articulation" (*GA39,* 121–22).[63] The use of "authentic" means that each individual recognizes the fatherland as his or her own; one's own being and identity is bound up with one's nation. This recognition of one's place of origin as one's own is the profound feeling one has for one's homeland, the place where one feels at home and thus dwells. The word *Heimat* in the broadest sense means place of birth, but Heidegger is quick to emphasize he means something much more profound: "Homeland—not as mere place of birth, also not as mere familiar landscape, but rather *as the power of the earth,* upon which man momentarily, in each case according to his historical Dasein, 'poetically dwells'" (*GA39,* 88). The nation as fatherland and homeland is the origin, principle, and ground of our historical existence.

As fatherland, homeland, and site of the revelation of being, the *Volk* is the real site of politics. Heidegger makes this connection in a later text, where he says that the *polis* is the pole around which every being whirls; this pole is being. The *polis* is the site of the abode of human historical being in the midst of beings; it is "the open site of that fitting destining from out of which all human relations toward beings—and that always means in the first instance the relations of beings as such to humans—are determined" (*GA53,* 100–102). The *polis* is Da-sein, the openness of being in which things come to their presence. In this way, *Volk* and *polis* are the same.

The *Volk* is the ground and reason for each individual's existence. The term that Heidegger occasionally uses in this sense is *Bodenständigkeit,* sometimes translated as "rootedness," but which literally means "standing on the ground." It stands in contrast to Heidegger's characterization

---

63. During this period Heidegger adopted the archaic German *Seyn* to indicate the authentic, nonmetaphysical understanding of being.

of modern technical thinking as *bodenlos,* having no ground, a whirlwind with no moorings on which one can anchor.[64] To poetically dwell, to have a fatherland and homeland, is to be *bodenständig.* For the most part I have referred to the principles of the world in which we authentically dwell as goals or ends, something that stands before us in our future, but it should be noted that thought about in the Greek-Aristotelian manner, these goals or reasons also stand behind or under us in a certain sense. In Greek, "principle" is *archē,* which means both "principle" and "beginning." Since a principle can be an end, a *telos,* a principle is by nature both beginning and end. This survives in German in the word for "reason," *Grund,* which means "ground," and also in English, when we speak of a reason as the basis for something. Thus we say when we act for such and such reason that we act on the basis of this reason; we thus understand this connection between beginning or ground and end. To return to Heidegger's nationalism, to serve the *Volk* means to act on the basis of the *Volk; the Volk* is the ground on which each individual stands.

Although these texts I use date from after Heidegger's exit from any official role in the Nazi regime, the same sentiment flows through the more overtly political texts. For Heidegger, political self-determination is a necessary condition for national self-determination. One could say, though, that states serve merely to safeguard the borders and create institutions so that the people may discover and respond to their Dasein. It is no accident, then, that in the texts I used to indicate Heidegger's support for political self-determination he turns to the ground and source for historical action. In the memorial to Schlageter, after glorifying Schlageter's will to Germany's national awakening, Heidegger asks, "When this clarity of heart, which allowed him to envision what was greatest and most remote?" He answers his own question, "When on your hikes and outings you set foot in the mountains, forests, and valleys of this Black Forest, the home of this hero, experience this and know: the mountains among which the young farmer's son grew up are of primitive stone, of granite. They have long been at work hardening the will" (Sl, 41; *GA16,* 759). Then Heidegger demands, "Student of Freiburg, let the strength of this hero's native mountains flow into your will! Student of Freiburg, let the strength of the autumn sun of this hero's native valley shine into your heart! Preserve both within you and carry them, hardness of will and

---

64. For example, see *BT,* 212.

clarity of heart, to your comrades at the German universities" (Sl, 41; GA16, 760).

The most famous of Heidegger's odes to the power of the earth is the 1934 address: "Schöpferische Landschaft: Warum bleiben wir in der Provinz?" The occasion for this address was Heidegger's decision to turn down a chair in philosophy at the University of Berlin. He used the occasion, however, to expound on the opposition between city and country, bourgeoisie and peasant, always elevating the unremitting steadfastness of peasant thinking over against the superficiality of urban thinking. In Berlin Heidegger could see no *Boden* for his work; only in the country did his work have a ground (*BwHB*, 76). His labor was "planted into the occurrence of the land" (WBW, 10). "The inner belongingness of one's own labor to the Black Forest and its men comes out of a centuries-long, irreplaceable Alemannish-Schwabian *Bodenständigkeit*" (WBW, 10–11). "My entire labor, however," he continued, "is sustained and led by the world of these mountains and its peasants" (WBW, 11). The same turn of phrase occurs in the 1934 lecture course on Hölderlin; there he claimed the manifestness of being sustained and ordered and led (*GA39*, 144). But this openness of being is nothing other than the world which is set back on the earth, which only becomes earth, that is to say, a homeland, as it stands in the openness of a world (OWA, 46). To live in a world means to have a ground on which to stand, a ground that sustains and guides one's work. To this world of earth, soil, and homeland belong the gods (*GA39*, 140). The nation is thus the site of the fourfold. To work within the fourfold is how humans "poetically dwell."

Since poetic dwelling is Heidegger's vision of work in the postmodern age, the nation as ground and sustenance forms an integral part of authentic existence. As an authentic revelation of being, however, nationhood stands in a close relationship to being understood as historicity and coming to presence. This sets it on a collision course with the Nazi's racial understanding of *Volk*.

Although nation and race are not identical, there are similarities in the two concepts which make it possible to blend them. Both signify distinguishing characteristics which form an identity marked by its difference from other groups which have their own identity. The key distinction would seem to be that they stand for different categories of differences: "nation" refers to spiritual difference, whereas "race" refers to bodily or natural difference. The distinction is not, however, always so neat. Darwinism in particular broke down this barrier. A nation is a historical entity; the present generation inherits the national traits from its ancestors and passes them along to future generations, forming a historical unity. While for the most part we are accustomed to separating the spirit from the body, if one rejects this dualism as untenable, then one arrives at a holistic vision of the unity of blood and spirit, race and nation. We see this quite clearly in Nietzsche. Since Nietzsche is correctly identified as an opponent to dualism, his racist language and schemes for breeding a new humanity are actually quite consistent with his monism. It is to take seriously what Zarathustra announces in "On the Despisers of the Body," "But the awakened and knowing say: body I am entirely and nothing else; and soul is only a word for something about the body."[65]

Nietzsche's racism commended him to the Nazis, but his racism is historical; bodies change as different passions dominate and become the virtues of a people. His racism is really "spiritual," that is to say, free, founded upon possibility. Nazi racism was entirely different. Their racial doctrine was founded upon a biologism that held that by nature, the Jews were parasites and that non-Aryan races were capable of being creative or being educated to serve a role in the end state of natural history. Race was thought in terms of inherited blood. Blood was a natural element incapable of change, no more than one can hold that oxygen or carbon can change and remain what it is. Like any natural element, blood types can be blended with those of other races, which corrupts the purity of the race. The concept of nature underlying this theory is static, in accordance with the long history of metaphysics which defines nature or being in terms of constant presence.

Heidegger rejected this metaphysics in the name of an authentic understanding of being that recognizes that possibility is higher than actuality. The metaphysical underpinnings of the Nazi racial doctrine were thus at odds with Heidegger's own metaphysical hopes. From the earliest days of his political interest, Heidegger opposed the "biological" doctrine as propounded by Rosenberg or the "biological" reading of Nietzsche that had found favor with the Nazi hierarchy.[66] The particular edge to his polemic derives from the contest among intellectuals to direct or guide the move-

---

65. Nietzsche, *Thus Spoke Zarathustra*, 34.

66. See, for example, Heidegger, "Schreiben Heideggers an den Vorsitzender des politischen Bereinigungsausschusses Prof. v. Dietze (15. Dez. 1945)," *GA16*, 414.

ment; Rosenberg's or Kriek's biologism would ground the movement on the wrong metaphysics and must therefore be rejected or the movement would miscarry.[67] From our vantage, we can see the folly of Heidegger's reasoning; Rosenberg "triumphed" because the Nazi hierarchy had already embraced the racist doctrine. Heidegger could not or would not recognize the nature of the leadership of the party or the necessary and insuperable role that racism played at the heart of the party.

There is simply no point at which racism metaphysically conceived is compatible with Heidegger's philosophy of work and the grounds for his engagement in 1933.[68] The metaphysics Heidegger wanted to found in 1933 is not humanism in the sense Heidegger gives it in 1946, a doctrine that begins with a fixed human nature, nor does it obey the "mimetic" logic that Lacoue-Labarthe finds in all metaphysical politics since Plato.[69] The Nazi party was metaphysical in this sense, but this is the point at which Heidegger departed from them, which is to say, from the ground up.

Why did Heidegger not see this in 1933? Why did he not see Nazi ideology for what it was? There is no single, sufficient answer to this question (it is unlikely that Heidegger himself knew), but one important reason lies in the "folly" I identified above: believing that intellectuals could have a leading role in grounding and guiding the movement.[70] In a letter writ-

---

67. For this vain hope of certain German intellectuals, see Hans Sluga, *Heidegger's Crisis: Philosophy and Politics in Nazi Germany* (Cambridge: Harvard University Press, 1993).

68. As I discussed earlier, however, Heidegger was opposed on principle to liberal cosmopolitanism, which he identified to a certain extent with Jewish thinking.

69. Lacoue-Labarthe, "Transcendence Ends in Politics." Elsewhere Lacoue-Labarthe says, "Nazism is a humanism in so far as it rests upon a determination of *humanitas* which is, in its view, more powerful—i.e., more effective—than any other." Lacoue-Labarthe, *Heidegger, Art, and Politics*, 95. In this line, Lacoue-Labarthe shows clearly the way in which his argument uses Heidegger's critique of humanism in "Letter on Humanism." Heidegger also made use of this argument to critique National Socialism, but Lacoue-Labarthe overlooks the higher humanism invoked in that letter, a higher humanism that was Heidegger's ideal vision in 1933 as well as 1946.

The line "Nazism is a humanism" sparked an international volley of protests from defenders of humanism, led by Ferry and Renault in their book Heidegger and Modernity.

70. Thus I disagree with Lacoue-Labarthe's plausible suggestion that Heidegger's commitment to an explicitly racist regime was a compromise: "But one thought, or so we must assume, that it was worth putting up with a little bit of racism to see the movement victorious: anti-Semitism was simply regarded as an incidental cost." Lacoue-Labarthe, *Heidegger, Art, and Politics*, 33. As I see it, racism understood as biologism was definitely not one of the things worth putting up with in Heidegger's mind. On the other hand, I would believe that Heidegger was willing to tolerate what Habermas called common anti-Semitic bigotry as an incidental cost. Habermas, "Work and *Weltanschauung*," 154.

This passage from Lacoue-Labarthe is a clear illustration of the subtle double-game he

ten to the rector of Freiburg after the war's conclusion, Heidegger wrote: "However, I was nevertheless absolutely convinced that an autonomous alliance of intellectuals could deepen and transform a number of essential elements of the 'National Socialist movement' and thereby contribute in its own way to overcoming Europe's disarray and the crisis of the Western spirit" (GA16, 398). There was great potential in the essential elements of the "National Socialist movement," but these elements needed deepening by thinkers who had grasped the fundamental course of Western history. The political movement needed a philosophical leader. It needed Heidegger. Jaspers is not wrong when he says Heidegger wanted "to lead the leader."[71]

Heidegger was a socialist and nationalist. Both of these are intimately bound up with his philosophical thinking of being. He had hoped that Hitler's National Socialist Worker's Party would be the revolutionary vehicle for the "total transformation of German existence" in line with his own ideal vision of authentic laboring existence (GS, 46). His hopes, as he found out soon enough, were badly misplaced. National Socialism turned into the worst and most extreme form of modern metaphysics; everything about it perverted its inner truth and greatness. The failure of National Socialism to fulfill its potential lay in the limited thinking of its leaders. Only an authentic leader could let the German people face its own destiny and become an authentic nation. Nations need leaders to become nations. Thus the last common ground between Heidegger's "private Nazism" and the actual public Nazism is the *Führerprinzip,* the leadership principle. As we shall see in the next chapter, though, Heidegger's leadership principle points toward a vastly different type of politics than that which manifested itself under the Nazi regime.

---

plays. He knows that Heidegger personally was not strongly anti-Semitic, so he suggests he was willing to put up with "a little bit of racism" to further his own goals, that is to say, Heidegger was a shameless opportunist. The implication, however, is in joining the Nazis one is not putting up with merely a little bit of racism, but a movement founded upon racism. Thus "by becoming a member of the Nazi party . . . one was necessarily committing oneself to racism." Lacoue-Labarthe, *Heidegger, Art, and Politics,* 33. In this fashion, Lacoue-Labarthe conflates compromising with the "incidental costs" of racism and committing oneself to genocidal racism.

71. Karl Jaspers, *Notizen zu Heidegger;* quoted in Pöggeler, *Neue Wege,* 204.

If men were angels, no government

would be necessary.

—Publius, Federalist 51

The intimate relation between the question of being and what Heidegger holds to be the genuinely political put enormous pressure on Heidegger's attempts to find a politics that accords to his notion of authentic human being. This pressure inflected his basic consideration of politics such that key political concepts or institutions either became transformed or disappeared altogether, leaving in the end only an eviscerated hope for a coming reformation.

In this context, the tensions between the German nation and a German state tore at the fragile cohesion of Heidegger's commitment to practical political affairs. As we saw in the previous chapter, the concept of the German *Volk*, the nation or people, dominated Heidegger's political thinking. For Heidegger, the nation was the genuine bond of each person to the meaning of being; the nation, and not the state, was the passage of God on earth. In this scheme, the state played a decidedly secondary and supporting role; its primary purpose was to secure the national borders so that the nation could be free to develop its own relation to the question of being. Because the question of being is the center of Heidegger's thinking, it informs each particular aspect of his thinking, including the political. Even when he might have included the state as a legitimate arena for a relation to being, he did so by equating the state with the *polis,* whose essence "lies in its being the open site of that sending from out of which all human relations toward beings—and that always means in the first instance the relations of being as such to humans—are determined" (*GA53,* 101). The *polis* in this passage is identified with the clearing of being.

Heidegger made it clear that the essence of the *polis,* what he even called its "pre-political essence," has nothing to do with "modern state formations" (*GA53,* 101, 100). The *polis* thought of as the clearing of being has nothing to do with the modern state because they have their origins in two different understandings of being as a whole, which includes the relations of humans to beings and also of humans to each other. The modern state, understood as the locus of what is considered political in the contemporary world, belongs to the age of modern technology and metaphysics. The modern state belongs to metaphysics because it seeks to legitimate itself through the principle of reason in terms of a ground that can be technically secured through instrumental reason and the human will. According to Heidegger this goal eventuated in the modern, rationally bureaucratic state, which operates in accordance with the demand for maximum efficiency. As such, the state becomes colonized by nonpolitical factors; it ceases to be the site for genuine political action, and serves only as manager to the overall productive enterprise. Heidegger's depiction of the completion of the principle of reason in the political realm corresponds to the Weberian nightmare of a purely formalized bureaucracy.

Because the modern state is metaphysical, the disappearance of the political corresponds to the disappearance of being; *phronēsis* disappears behind the facade of technical effecting. In order to again make room for authentic political action, Heidegger turned to the question of being so that being can occur and transform human existence. Because the principle of reason that the metaphysical tradition used to solve the problem of politics leads ultimately to the oblivion of being which alone is the origin of authentic human dwelling, Heidegger had to frame the problem of politics differently than the tradition. The problem was no longer making the origin accountable to reason, but rather of letting the origin occur as the "there" of being and of bringing each individual to this ground in such a manner that is no longer ruling, but allows self-responsibility. Thus Heidegger's way of framing the question of politics flowed directly from his understanding of authenticity, which encompasses *phronēsis* and the integration of the self into being as a whole.

The attempt to find a politics that could escape the near-total grip technology exercises on modern life led Heidegger to embrace leaders as saviors of human being. Heidegger placed almost the entire weight of genuine politics upon leaders whom he called the "shepherd[s] of being." Such a leader bears this weight because he has two capabilities that distinguish him from traditional rulers. First, unlike technical managers, he is capable of *phronēsis*. Whatever superficial similarities there are to Aristotle's appeal to political rulers endowed with phronetic excellence dissolve, however, in light of Heidegger's startling transformation of *phronēsis* into the revelation of being as a whole.[1] Genuine leaders lead because they alone act in the genuinely political realm, that is to say, in the realm of being; through their action they open up the "there" of being for others. Opening the site of being is one function of a leader. The other is allowing the birth of an authentic community through self-responsibility. Leaders, in contrast to rulers, do not command. Rather they allow humans their genuine self-responsibility central to their authenticity and dignity by guiding them toward the ground of their being.

These two functions of a leader alone can bring about the type of community Heidegger thought belonged to authentic existence. Upon close examination, however, the authentic political community turns out to be modeled upon an Augustinian-inspired community of saints. The opposition between technical thinking and the authentic religious life carries through to the political structure; fearing the malevolence of technical thinking led Heidegger to deliver the whole of the political realm over to the question of being and the "piety of thinking." Heidegger's thought is apocalyptic; in politics, as in all other realms of human existence, "only a god can save us."

---

1. Although Gadamer, for instance, also wants to reintroduce *phronēsis* in order to save politics from technocratic rationality—a tack he freely admits was inspired by Heidegger— his more traditional understanding of *phronēsis* leads him down other paths than Heidegger.

Leaders, Not Rulers

In order to attain an adequate understanding of Heidegger's concept of leadership, we need to distinguish a leader from types of political actors with whom a leader can be confused, namely rulers and administrators. This confusion exists because rulers and administrators share some functions with leaders, and leaders lead in part by ruling and administrating. Heidegger, however, wanted to distinguish leaders from rulers and administrators by carefully distinguishing the functions; the genuine leader neither rules nor administrates at all. In this way, Heidegger wanted to establish the leader as a political actor that is an alternative to both classical and modern forms of rule, and thus as an alternative way of conceiving power relationships in a social setting.

It can be taken as axiomatic that political philosophy has always been concerned with the dilemma of finding the right answer to the question "Who rules?" This question assumes that politics is necessarily connected to rule; since politics is ruling, the investigation of politics is necessarily the question of good rule. Since rules originate from rulers, the problem is how to create a situation such that the origin of rule, the ruler, is in harmony with the end of politics, which is justice.

Political thought arises from responses to the problem that the actual ruler is almost never the best al ruler, that the origin of politics almost never coincides with the end of politics. The responses to this problem have varied widely throughout history, but all have aimed at the central task of curbing the self-interest of the ruler to ensure that he acts in the interests of the common good. In order to bridge the gap between the origin and the end, the particularity of the ruler with the common interest, reason has assumed a prominent position, for it has been generally assumed that because reason is common to all humans, the interests of reason will provide a check, *de jure* if not *de facto,* on the particular interests of the actual ruler. If the rule is in accordance with the common good, it should claim the legitimate obedience of the members of the body politic, for by virtue of its generality each subject recognizes the rule as an expression of his own will, in which he shares.[2]

2. Jean-Jacques Rousseau, *Social Contract,* vol. 4 of *The Collected Writings of Rousseau,* ed. Roger D. Masters and Christopher Kelly (Hanover: University Press of New England, 1994), 138–41. Gillian Rose points out the equivocation in Rousseau's formulation, one which he was aware of: the individual is both subject of the law, that is to say, its

The Modern State

There are many paths to securing the identity of the origin of law with the general will, which legitimates political rule. One can try to solve the problem of the formation of the general will by educating the rulers, by creating institutions and procedures that guarantee a just outcome, or by making the human rulers accountable to nonhuman rules, whether natural or divine. There is a fourth way that thinkers have sought to ensure the identity of the rulers with the general will, democracy, a regime type in which in some fashion or another the will of the rulers is necessarily identical with the will of the whole, but given the critical equivocation in how one can understand who the people are and thus the nature of the generality of their will, I will deal with this solution later. To briefly foreshadow the conclusion, Heidegger pursued a peculiar combination of the third and fourth ways: the people are identical with the clearing of being which gives the governing measure.

According to the first path, philosophic or religious education serves to moderate the selfish desires of the ruler so that the rational part is set free to rule according to its principle, which is the common interest. The aim was to ally *phronēsis,* or the ruling art, with temperance; the best ruler was one who could see what should be done with a discerning and disinterested eye. This solution was prevalent in classical and medieval times, in other words, during those undemocratic times when it was more practical to educate a small set of rulers than the whole of society. Thus according to their own fashion Plato, Aristotle, and Xenophon each tried to educate a ruler to be a good king; Xenophon's account, the *Education of Cyrus,* became the model for a genre of books popular in medieval and renaissance times on educating princes.

Modern politics arose in part out of opposition to this solution. To its way of thinking, the educational solution was too utopian to be practical; it was necessary to devise institutions that could safeguard the common interest even if a bad ruler should nonetheless come to power. This common understanding is, naturally, an exaggeration: Plato was in many ways more a "realist" about political power than Hobbes, and that is to say, all the more despairing about the likelihood of a just political order.

---

author, and subject to the law. Heidegger, like many other utopian socialists, wants to sidestep the equivocation by integrating each individual into the ground of his specific existence, which turns out to be held in common with others. Rose, *Broken Middle,* 241–43.

Modern politics also developed out of the breakdown in the medieval trust in natural law. The late medieval sense of the absence of God, or at least the politically unwholesome ambiguity of his revealed Word, made recourse to the third solution, divine or natural law, impossible or highly equivocal for moderns. Instead of a system of suprahuman positive laws, modern thinkers instead turned to a system of divinely sanctioned or naturally granted rights which more or less instituted procedures for arriving at just laws, but only specified the content of the laws in a very general fashion. Without the active presence of God in the world, ecclesiastical and temporal power were split; temporal power could only serve to check the inherent sinfulness of humans in the time before the apocalypse.[3] Given the impracticality of education in the face of sin and the corresponding absence of an unambiguous divine revelation, institutions or procedures of human origin that can check rulers from misusing their power, in sum the modern state, is the primary path in modernity to harmonizing the origins and ends of politics.

The intent of modern liberal political science is fairly clear: the separation as much as possible of the person of the ruler from the powers and privileges of the ruling office. Louis XIV's famous dictum, "L'état, c'ést moi," is the obvious foil to modern liberal theories of state. A clear example of the new theory of the state is Rousseau, who carefully distinguished the sovereign from the government: the former is the legislative power, which formulates the will that moves the body politic, whereas the latter is the executive power, which, as the name implies, executes the will of the sovereign.[4] Rousseau equated the government with the "supreme administration," which exercises power in the name of the sovereign who has entrusted it with executing its will.[5] The government is strictly a function in the service of the sovereign will. Kant, too, reiterated the reconstitution of government as the executor of the law. This conception appears in Weber's thought, somewhat ironically, as "the conception of the modern judge as an automaton into which legal documents and fees are stuffed at the top in order that it may spill forth the verdict at the bottom along with

3. Joshua Mitchell, *Not by Reason Alone: Religion, History, and Identity in Early Modern Political Thought* (Chicago: University of Chicago Press, 1993), 8–10. Also Martin Luther, "On Secular Authority," in *Luther and Calvin on Secular Authority*, ed. and trans. Harro Höpfl (New York: Cambridge University Press, 1991), 8–14.
4. Rousseau, *Social Contract*, 166–67.
5. Ibid., 167.

the reasons, read mechanically from codified paragraphs."[6] For Weber, the process of modernization is the ongoing routinization and rationalization of charismatic authority. While none of this directly attacks the separate problem of the generality of the will and law, one can see in these theories a disavowal of personal rule, with its constant possibilities of particularized abuse. Administration is seen as a necessary solution to the problem of tyranny.

Taken to an extreme, the modern theory of the state given above is an attempt to separate not only personal rule from power, but of the political process as a whole from public administration. The demand for pure administration of public affairs arises from the experience that obedient execution of the sovereign will does not solve the problem of the potential tyranny of that will; the proper execution of bad law is still bad rule, no matter how formally precise its execution may be. While the early moderns may have hoped that having the sovereign will originate in a parliament would better ensure its generality, in practice the legislative will is as open to partisanship as the executive. The partisanship of the legislative may take one of two forms. First, the members of the legislature are capable of being corrupted while in power. This may involve such matters as campaign contributions or outright kickbacks in return for providing services to clients. The multiplicity of the legislative body may make such corruption more difficult than if power rested in the hands of one or a few, but is hard to avoid. Nonetheless, institutional reforms are capable of restraining some or much of this behavior.

The greater problem is the other source of corruption, partisanship, for that lies in the very nature of a pluralist society. As long as the legislative body reflects the members of the whole, and that whole is heterogeneous, the legislative body will itself be heterogeneous on any particular issue. This situation holds whether the legislative body is representative or composed of the entirety of the people. Since in such a situation unanimity is impossible, as a practical matter if anything is to be done, it will require some number less than the whole, in the usual case a simple majority. As a practical matter, legislative politics requires the assertion of the will of the majority over the minority; the general will becomes identified with the majority will. As less than the whole, majorities (and minorities) are by definition parts of the whole. Partisanship is a necessary correlate of legisla-

6. Weber, *Economy and Society*, 979.

tive politics. This is particularly true to the extent that the legislature is open to pressure from social groups. The legislature reflects civil society, and the state becomes nothing other than an amplifier of the power struggles among various social groups. The administration of the sovereign will turns into the administration of one group's power over others.

This sort of corruption of the political process has long been an object of concern for those interested in the just rule of public affairs. The aim of those concerned has been to try to separate partisanship from state power. This gives rise to the attempt to turn the state into a purely administrative body. As such, the hope is to separate rule from the corruption of the partisan political process so that the state is no longer the tool of one party for the oppression of others, but instead a more fully rationalized decision-making body. This opposition between corrupt politics and administration appears among a group of thinkers as diverse as Marx's hope that the withering away of the state will usher in the rule of an administrative class that can rationally manage capital for the benefit of the proletariat to the Progressive reformers in the late nineteenth and early twentieth centuries who wished to replace the corrupt party patronage system with a professional political class that was freed from political pressures and thus free to rationally treat social problems.

The underlying assumption of this state reform is the belief that politics interferes with a rational and scientific approach to social matters. These reforming efforts make little sense if they intend only to turn the state into a more efficient tool of partisan rule; their moral weight is derived from the sense that theirs is an objectively rational means of dealing with social affairs. In this scheme, what matters is most efficiently finding solutions to public problems; public affairs are best served by technical rationality. From the point of view of pure technical rationality, the political process appears at best as a confirmation of its solution, more often, however, as a technical inefficiency. When problems arise, it is necessary to solve them in the best possible manner. The state becomes an efficient problem-solver. The end result is a technocracy: rule by a technically proficient class in the name of technical rationality. Technocracy and pure administration are extreme measures to solve the perennial problem of just rule.

The technical nature of the modern state, its pragmatic rationalism, makes it part of the total technical enterprise of modern life. In this way, the modern state comes under criticism from the heart of Heidegger's critique of modern technology. The state can no more resist technology's demands for maximum efficiency than any other part of human life, and becomes subsumed to economic rationality. In this respect, Heidegger's understanding of the modern state is Weberian.[7] Weber writes about monocratic bureaucracy:

> Experience tends universally to show that the purely bureaucratic type of administrative organization—that is, the monocratic variety of bureaucracy—is, from a purely technical point of view, capable of attaining the highest degree of efficiency and is in this sense formally the most rational known means of exercising authority over human beings. It is superior to any other form in precision, in stability, in the stringency of its discipline, and in its reliability. It thus makes possible a particularly high degree of calculability of results for the heads of the organization and for those acting in relation to it.[8]

Thus a rational bureaucracy develops as the most efficient means for attaining efficient production. Since for Heidegger modern society is dominated by the technical demand for maximum efficiency, which in turn demands stability, reliability, and above all, calculability, the state will inevitably become this formally rationalized bureaucracy that will serve the will to will. Politics is swallowed up by economics. Heidegger's picture of the modern state is an intensification of the Weberian nightmare.

Despite its continuing appeal, the technocratic solution has always found its detractors. As Bakunin admonished Marx, the administration of things is always the administration of people; Marx merely wants to exchange one ruling elite for another. No matter how rationally efficient the administration may be, a technocracy is a hierarchical power relation among social actors, a fact which offends democratic sensibilities and those who believe that political participation by all is necessary for good political regimes.

Another problem of technocracy is the question of where it takes its direction or the question of what should count as a problem. The secret assumption of those who advocate administration is that important social issues are objective and thus open to scientific management along the lines of private sector management, where the goal of production is given and

---

7. According to Pöggeler, in his conversations with Heidegger the latter evinced little understanding of or interest in Weber. Pöggeler, *Der Denkweg Martin Heideggers*, 372.
8. Weber, *Economy and Society*, 223.

the only choice is how best to achieve that goal. Only when social problems are analogous to a production model does this technical approach makes sense. The fear, given fuel by Weber's analysis of modern administration and capitalism, is that the merging of approaches will lead to a merging of the political and economic spheres as a whole; the state will turn into nothing other than the rational management of the national economy.[9] In this way, politics becomes completely monopolized by the demands of the economy and production. It makes no real difference if the economy is centrally planned or operates largely according to market dictates; in either case the state functions to facilitate production.

Heidegger understands modern society according to this technical model. Everything is being brought in line with the demand for maximum efficiency. His somewhat shocking assertion that there is no difference between the United States and the Soviet Union arose from this perspective; both are merely subspecies of "the same dreary technological frenzy, the same unrestricted organization of the average man" (*IM*, 37). This equation should be understood not as morally obtuse, but rather as extremely pessimistic; Heidegger thought that nothing could withstand (a delicious equivocation) the technological forces being unleashed in modernity, except a return to the question of being. One should therefore understand his advocacy of the leadership principle as a call for a rebirth of the genuinely political in the face of the colonization of the public sphere by nonpolitical forces.

The Leader as an Alternative to the Modern State

If administration can be considered the most extreme attempt to regulate ruling according to reason, then leadership constitutes an alternative, not merely to the faceless bureaucracy, but also to rule as a whole. Leadership can be thought of as an alternative to ruling in two different ways. First, there is the inevitable tension between rule and political freedom. Rulers rule by enacting rules; the traditional political problem of rulers has been to what extent their ruling is itself rule-bound. The long-standing equation of tyranny with arbitrary rule has led to a demand for increasingly formalized and systematic rules for delimiting legitimate rule. Whether arbitrary or rule-bound, ruling is in either case ruling: a ruler makes a rule for constraining those subject to the law. Even rulers with the best of intentions will run into resistance because no law governing a heterogeneous

9. See, for example, Arendt, *Human Condition*, 44–45.

population will meet with universal approbation; at a fundamental level, individuals believe that they are the best judges of what is best for them, and from time to time their individual wills conflict with the general will. Accordingly, many political philosophers have placed great weight upon the necessity of consent for legitimacy, but that still leaves the impossibility of reconciling the individual will with the general will in each instance.

Leadership addresses this problem at a very simple level: rulers rule and leaders lead. Leaders do not rule their subjects, but rather direct people toward a goal. They do this by means of persuasion and mobilizing public opinion. Leading respects political freedom because it requires the consent of those who are led: without the willing assent of followers, no one will be led anywhere. The opposition between general will and individual will inherent to ruling disappears in leading. In this way, leadership belongs with populism, for the leader articulates and represents the will of the people.

This last point also indicates the second way in which leadership represents an alternative to rule. The concern with tyranny leads to ways of controlling rulers through rules, eventually leading to a completely formalized system of rules in which officers of the law serve merely as functionaries; everyone becomes a blind servant of a system of reason cut off from genuinely political goals that can give meaning to social striving. These goals must come from outside the system and are articulated by leaders. Leaders, unlike rulers or administrators, are innovators and initiators; they serve as focal points for new articulations of the transcendent. This capacity for innovation and freedom is why Weber elevates the entrepreneur and the charismatic leader above the rational system of production.[10] If political leaders lead by articulating the will of the people, their articulations of the popular will would not be leading if this will were not in some sense merely latent or unvoiced in the will of the people. The leader articulates for the people a problem or goal in such a way that it comes to appear as the paramount problem that society faces. The true art of lead-

---

10. Weber's concern with the disenchantment of the world by rationalization should be understood also as a detranscendentalization of life; reason disenchants the world precisely by destroying transcendental and divine authority. This is the sort of world he described (in another person's voice) as "this nullity." Weber, *Protestant Ethic*, 182. His concern over the nihilistic direction of Western civilization led him to embrace plebiscitary democracy (*Führer-Demokratie*) with an emphasis on charismatic authority who introduced new values to a society. Similar fears led Heidegger upon the same path.

ership is innovation, in letting something be seen in a new light. Leaders have "vision." They are visionaries.[11] Leaders make their vision compelling for the whole such that they make the envisaged goal the object of their own will.

Leaders have an equivocal relation to democracy that in no small part depends upon how one understands the meaning of democracy. If one takes democracy in its usual liberal and pluralist sense, leaders are both a bane and a necessity. On the one hand, leaders are necessary to give direction to the body politic, whether in the form of strong political leaders or organizers of political groups who are necessary for pluralism to function properly. Such strong leaders, however, can abuse their power by acting contrary to the will of the people. There is another understanding of democracy, however, that justifies leaders not just on practical grounds, but also on principle. This other understanding of democracy holds that only a strong leader can unify a state otherwise colonized by pluralist groups; a strong leader can stand above the press of interest group politics and act in the interest of the whole of society, rather than its parts. Despite the common equation of pluralism and democracy, the equivocation of the term "people," which can refer to the whole as aggregate sum of each individual or the whole which is common beyond mere aggregation, allows thinkers to appropriate the mantle of democracy for this unifying leader who can speak for the whole which precedes the parts. The normative claim such a leader makes is that by speaking for the whole, the leader is the only nonpartisan and thus nontyrannical political actor. This is the basis for what Weber calls a "leader-democracy," or plebiscitary democracy. It is also the normative basis for the right-wing and fascist political ideologies advocated by Carl Schmitt and Mussolini.

The normative claim for the leadership principle is that only a leader can give a direction for the whole of the people that respects the political freedom of each individual. This claim assumes that there is a general will of the people that is something other than a mere aggregation of individual wills. Even if this last claim is granted, the theory is ambiguous as to the relation between the unvoiced general will in the heart of each individual and each individual's surface desires, that is to say, the degree to which coercive measures might be necessary to bring each individual in

---

11. Thus George Bush was held to be an ineffective leader because he lacked the "vision thing."

line with their own general interest. The promise of the leadership principle is that each will immediately grasp the heretofore hidden general interest as soon as the leader makes it appear, but practical experience shows that the line between leaders, however noble, and dictators is extremely fine. In practice, political leadership of a heterogeneous society necessitates an extensive police apparatus and state organization on a degree never thought in early times, destroying its promise in its very enactment.

Understanding the promise and dangers of the leadership principle goes a long way toward coming to an understanding of Heidegger's political engagement and his general political principles. The promise of leaders is their ability to give voice to the will of the people as a whole, a unity which precedes any mechanical creation of a popular will through the aggregation of individual wills. This understanding of the people as the unity which precedes any unity created through statecraft neatly parallels Heidegger's understanding of the being of beings as being as a whole, which differs from and precedes the aggregation of beings into a whole (*GA33,* 17–18; *WM,* 111). By identifying the clearing of being with a people, Heidegger can trumpet the virtues of a leader in terms of his understanding of the question of being. The leader allows authenticity to flourish in its two aspects: first, the leader excels in *phronēsis,* which allows him through questioning being to open it up to be a clearing for a people, and second, a leader, in contrast to rulers, allows each follower to come to the clearing as his own experience of being, that is to say, leadership alone allows self-responsibility of each to turn toward being and so be genuinely integrated into its clearing. Both of these aspects of leadership stand in direct opposition to modern state formations, which contain no space for *phronēsis* in Heidegger's sense, and do not allow genuine self-responsibility. In modern state formations, the unity of the people is created through law, that is to say, is a technical creation of the human will. Heidegger denigrates the unity created by human reason; genuine unity is given by the dispensation of being as the law or measure of being (LH, 238). The religious inspiration behind Heidegger's understanding of authenticity leads him to an attempt to conceive of a nonmetaphysical politics which reveals itself as a new ecclesiology; the *polis* is at heart a community of saints. Moreover, far from fundamentally altering his political principles, the failures of his political engagement actually strengthened the ecclesiological and apocalyptic tone of his principles, leading him not to moderate his views, but to radicalize them further.

The Shepherd of Being

In the course of his career Heidegger presented a wide variety of leadership figures: philosophers, poets, priests, statesmen, founders of states, and finally the "shepherd of being," a figure that encompasses each of the former. Behind this superficial variety, however, Heidegger maintains a unified ground that guides and directs the various permutations in his presentation of leaders. This ground is his religious vision of authentic human being. This religious background, however, divides into two parts, which correspond to the two ways of overcoming our alienation from being: first, raising the question of being anew so that a new particular meaning of being can occur, and second, integrating the self into the new particular meaning. The first corresponds to the visionary function of a leader, the second to his non-ruling, guiding function. Because raising the question of being is itself a two-step process, however—deconstructing existing understandings of being so that a revolutionary experience of being can occur historically—the first function can be further divided into a deconstructive, preparatory function and a creative, more explicitly visionary function. In Heidegger's presentations, leadership figures fill some or all of these functions, but because these functions both differ and are interrelated, Heidegger can combine different elements in various mixtures to form different pictures. Thus sometimes only one leader is depicted who fills the several function; at other times, Heidegger assigns types of leaders to each of the three functions. Sometimes Heidegger emphasizes one function over others; at other times he deliberately blurs the functions in order to create hybrid leaders. Furthermore, there is undoubtedly a correlation between Heidegger's treatment of leadership types and his practical political experience; his disenchantment with Nazism and Hitler led him to emphasize the preparatory function after the war as he took on his prophetic John the Baptist role. Even with this confusion, it is possible to reconstruct the functional and historical elements in terms of his unified goal of renewing the question of being. Both because of this underlying unity and because each function maintains its functional relationship to the totality of the question of being, it is possible to reconstruct these functional relationships so that one can understand the shifts in the way Heidegger depicts leaders.

The functional types of leaders—deconstructor, visionary, guide—correspond to the elements necessary to the question of being—making the question of being pertinent, setting the new experience of being into language, and letting the new experience be experienced authentically by each participant in the clearing of being. Because these elements of the question of being are more or less consistent throughout Heidegger's career, all of the types are likewise present, although Heidegger varies which functions are emphasized and which leadership figure fills the emphasized roles. One should not be led to conclude that Heidegger changed just because the presentations vary; because the functions correspond to the elements of the question of being, one can trace in the variety of emphases of functions the different means by which Heidegger pursued the need to raise the question of being for a new age.

When Heidegger takes his first stab at describing the appropriate character of a leader in the early 1930s, the parameters are heavily determined by the more personal element of authenticity taken from his work in the 1920s, particularly from *Being and Time* and the mystical vision of being turned toward being so that one can be filled by the new experience of being. Becoming authentic is presented as beginning with the twofold alienation of the self from its proper being: alienation from the meaning of being as historicity and as the particular epoch of meaning into which the self is integrated. Because of the identity between ways of (self-) understanding and ways of being a self, Heidegger conceives of the problem of alienation as primarily being directed toward the world inauthentically owing to an inauthentic understanding of being; being inauthentic means having a "false consciousness." Thus one role of the leader according to this way of setting up the problem is to clear away the obscurities and cobwebs fostered by the metaphysical tradition. A leader is the type proper to this exercise precisely because of the nature of belief, which must be accomplished by an inward persuasion of the mind. Rule and force have no power in this regard, for they only create that split in the self that Heidegger wishes to overcome. By clearing away the obscurities, a leader does not command, but rather lets the other accomplish its own enactment of the new experience of being. A leader, according to Heidegger's first formulation, allows a self to become authentic through self-responsibility. This idea of leading as letting the other come to its self-responsibility is what Heidegger in *Being and Time* calls *Fürsorge*, or caring-for. This idea becomes particularly prominent in Heidegger's thinking during his Nazi engagement, as can be seen in his political addresses.

From the perspective of a religiously conditioned concept of leadership, one can best understand how Heidegger developed a concept of a leader in the early 1930s through a thoughtful confrontation with Plato's philosopher-king. As his first stab at depicting a philosophical leader shows, it is a mistake to subsume Heidegger's leadership principle to kingly rule, for it is based upon the notion of turning the soul toward being.

The Philosopher-Leader: Turning Others Toward the Light

The connection between politics and a turn in the experience of being, always simmering in Heidegger's thought, began to percolate as Heidegger turned to a confrontation with Plato's *Republic* in the late 1920s and early 1930s. In a letter to Elizabeth Blochmann, Heidegger cites his intense interest and interrogation of the Platonic theory of the state, including, ironically enough in hindsight, Plato's Seventh Letter (*BwHB*, 54–55). Heidegger famously quotes from Plato's Republic to conclude the Rectoral Address: he translates it willfully as "Everything great stands in the storm." The line comes from the point in the dialogue where Socrates broaches the necessity of the philosopher-king. The three services allude to the three divisions of the ideal city in this same dialogue. Heidegger indicated he began his "turn" to rethinking the essence of truth through an interrogation of the Allegory of the Cave in the *Republic* (FT, 16; *GA16*, 373). The sheer number of allusions to Plato's ideal state and the rule of the philosopher-king are not accidental. It is through his interpretation of Plato in the early 1930s that Heidegger came to his political resolve.[12]

The first part of his 1931 lecture course, *On the Essence of Truth*, treats the Allegory of the Cave. This allegory formed the quintessence of almost all subsequent investigations into the relationship between philosophy and politics. Foremost, it allegorizes the discovery of a truth outside that of the city, both the historical discovery by sixth-century B.C. mystical thinkers of

---

12. It should be kept in mind that Heidegger had an amazing talent to find what he wanted to find in the texts he read, and thus the reading of the same authors can vary widely depending upon whether Heidegger wanted to appropriate them or consign them to Western metaphysics. His Nietzsche interpretations are the more famous example of this talent, but his readings of Plato vary even more. Thus the interpretation found in *GA34* is not necessarily consistent with his later understanding of Plato as the philosopher of eternal Ideas. It is dangerous, though, to read a break or an overcoming into this change; it is possible for appropriation to change to dispropriation without a change in the underlying intentions. My reading does not claim to have found the true Plato, or the true Heideggerian reading of Plato; it contents itself with presenting Heidegger's understanding of philosophical leadership as informed by his reading of Plato in 1931.

a universal logos and the change effected on the soul by this discovery, that is to say, the calling of the philosophical life. In the allegory, the philosopher sets himself free from the chains that bind him and his fellow citizens (although how this is accomplished remains a mystery) and ascends to the realm of the ideas and the blinding sun which he slowly learns to tolerate. This spatial metaphor describes the transformation of the soul as it opens to the universal logos. The tension between the mystic soul and the citizen is palpably evident in that there is no necessary harmony between universal *logos* and the *logos* and laws of a city. However, the immediate political effects of this can be muted owing to the godlike nature of the philosopher. If Aristotle is correct that a man outside the city is either an animal or a god, the mystic philosopher, whose soul has been transformed and opened to the universal god and thus become godlike, stands outside the city. In practical terms, philosophers were regarded as freaks and chose to live outside the city as hermits. According to legend, Heraclitus, the first mystic philosopher, forsook kingship to live in poverty in a disheveled hut apart from society. Aristophanes presents Socrates in *The Birds* as a dirty, ragged beggar. The calling of the philosopher's life set the philosopher outside the city, both spiritually and physically.

The true political problem that philosophy presents arises when the philosopher goes back into the cave to drag the others into the light of the sun. Why the philosopher does this is one of the great mysteries of Platonic philosophy, one with which we will not concern ourselves here. The political effect of bringing the truth of philosophy to the city is profound. The closed truth of the city is exposed to something beyond it which nonetheless has claims on each citizen. This dual claim opens up the distinction between truth and opinion; the truth of the city can suddenly fall to opinion and its legitimacy and rule become questionable. A new god is introduced which can conquer all of the old ones; the accusation that Socrates introduced new gods into Athens is essentially correct. That Socrates was accused, tried, and put to death by the city is the truest evidence of tensions brought on by philosophic truth. The Socratic gesture of bringing the truth of philosophy into the city remains a founding gesture for Western political philosophy to this day. The relation of truth to politics and the parallel relation of philosophers and rulers: these are the fundamental problems of political philosophy.

The Allegory of the Cave thus forms a point of departure for thinking of philosophers as leaders. In this project, Heidegger appropriates Plato's images to his own portrait of the human condition painted in *Being and Time* and other works. The cave is *das Man:* the realm of the everyday and tyranny of public opinion where those who are turned to the shadows exert no effort and take the easy road because they only want the "maintenance of the undisturbedness of the usual pressing about" (*GA34,* 28, 35). The prisoners remain shut off from the truth; the prisoners take what is present as the one and only possibility because they cannot see the shadows as shadows, and thus take semblance for the truth (*GA34,* 26). Foreshadowing his later thought of the forgetting of being, he says that the prisoners stand in the concealed in such a way that the unconcealed as such is not understood; they cannot question the question of what the unconcealed itself is (*GA34,* 27, 26). The initial liberation of the soul of the philosopher is a turning toward "original light," which is something other than beings; it is the being of beings (*GA34,* 41, 52). Light is not a thing, nor a property of things, but the "*condition of possibility* of sensing the visible in the narrower sense" (*GA34,* 53–54). This is the worldhood of the world, the clearing into which beings come to presence. This turning toward the light and recognizing the difference of being and beings is to exist (*Existieren*) (*GA34,* 37). To exist means to be "displaced into the truth" and to be "exposed to beings as a whole" (*GA34,* 75, 77). Existence is the "fundamental happening of Dasein," which happens as history; existing is a gaze that first of all builds the aspect of that at which the gaze gazes as the foregoing sketch of being. This sketch of being is the "there" of being, the clearing, the world, which makes a relationship to beings possible (*GA34,* 64). This depiction of authentic human being hews closely to Heidegger's other writings during this time, such as the 1928/29 lecture course "Introduction to Philosophy," and his essays "On the Essence of Truth" and "On the Essence of Reason." The philosopher frees himself from the cave (*das Man*) and envisions the world. The path of the liberation of the soul to the truth is the same path by which Dasein in *Being and Time* becomes authentic.

In this lecture, though, this sketch of the specific "there" of being occurs in the work of art and poetry (*GA34,* 62, 64). "That which is essential in the discovery of the real did not and does not happen by the sciences, but rather through original philosophy and through the great poetry and its sketches (Homer, Virgil, Dante, Shakespeare, Goethe). Poetry makes the beings beinger" (*GA34,* 64). As in his subsequent works in the middle 1930s, such as *Introduction to Metaphysics,* philosophy has an originary power; philosophizing is poetizing. At this point, however, great poets are merely invoked rather than given their own specific function; original philosophy or philosophy that works in the element of the origin which is the question of being bears the burden of all the elements of the question of being.

The suspicion, however, is that the equation of authentic existence and the philosophical life means that nonphilosophers are condemned to inauthentic existence. To be authentic requires removing oneself from the bustle of everyday life among nonphilosophers so that one can commune with being in lofty solitude. This is precisely how Arendt understood Heidegger's vocation. Heidegger's philosopher, however, like Plato's, comes down from the highest existence back into the cave. As we have examined previously, the move is in some way necessary to explain how historicizing is a co-historicizing or how the truth for the individual Dasein can be a truth for a community. The philosopher-leader (and I intentionally substitute leader for the usual king) is one of the few plausible attempts in Heidegger's oeuvre to explain this connection.

In Plato's allegory, the philosopher returns to the cave, breaks the bonds that chain the prisoners to the wall, and drags the resisting prisoners toward the sun. Taking the Platonic depiction of Socrates' life, the philosopher attempts to break the chains of opinion and dogma while turning Athenians toward philosophical truth through conversation, the unique dialogue between philosopher and layman which means to make questionable the layman's claim to truth and thereby open up a space within which the philosopher can play a "midwife" to the truth forgotten in the soul of the layman; knowledge is remembering, a return to what is one's own. The Socratic "gadfly" is the conscience of the layman, indeed of the city itself. This idealized portrait of the philosopher's political philosophizing has little to do with the usual image of the philosopher-king; it is not ruling, even by a wise man, but letting the truth rule in the consciences of each citizen.[13]

Heidegger's own depiction of the political effect of the philosopher is close to this idealized image. In the course of an interpretation of Plato this

---

13. In this scheme, rhetoric plays a large role. Although Heidegger does not discuss rhetoric in this interpretation of Plato, he does in a lecture from summer 1924 that takes up Aristotle's *Rhetoric* in detail. Heidegger does not, however, trouble himself over the ambiguity of rhetoric—Is rhetoric a technical art or a citizen virtue?—that so troubled Plato and Aristotle. For more on this ambiguity, see Eugene Garver, *Aristotle's "Rhetoric": An Art of Character* (Chicago: University of Chicago Press, 1994).

would be expected, but it goes deeper than just this interpretation. The philosopher turns into a sort of ideology critic; he seeks to show the apparent world in which the cave dwellers live is in fact mere appearance concealing the truth:

> However, he will attempt to show them that this unconcealing is such that just because it shows itself, thus is unconcealed, it does not show the being, but rather covers, conceals. He will attempt to make it comprehensible to them that something indeed shows on the wall that has an appearance, but that it only looks as if it were the being, not it itself; that here much rather a constant *concealing* of the being goes before them on the wall, that they themselves, the chained ones, are bedazzled and carried away by this constant concealing that goes before them. (*GA34*, 88–89)

What occurs in this attempt should not be misconstrued. This is not the usual attempt in ideology critique to replace appearance with a true determination of the world. The truth of being toward which Heidegger wants us to turn is not determinate; it is how a determination can come about. Precisely in showing that being includes appearance, which is to say, it is a mixture of concealing and unconcealing, such that our understanding about beings can change, the philosopher introduces the truth of being into the world. In effecting the transformation of the soul, the philosopher introduces the truth of the essence of being, that it is capable of transforming. That into which it transforms is beyond the power of the philosopher.

Heidegger's "ideology critique," being a critique of the appearance of being which holds us in its thrall, takes the form of the "destruction" of Western metaphysics. From his early calls for a destruction of the dominance of theory to his later deconstruction of the metaphysical heritage, Heidegger's political philosophizing—the writing, lecturing, hectoring—followed the same path. He meant to force us to consider the question of being in all its questionableness. Philosophy cannot create the order of being that will rule us, but can only prepare the ground through a destruction of metaphysics so that we can authentically appropriate an order.

This description of the peculiar maeutic effect of philosophy echoes two sections of *Being and Time*. The allusion above to the Socratic gadfly as the conscience points to Heidegger's interpretation of the conscience as that "voice of a friend" which says "Guilty!" and calls Dasein back to its own

(*BT*, 315–41). When Dasein becomes authentic, it can become the "conscience" of others (*BT*, 344). This becoming a conscience for others harks back to the section on caring-for (solicitude). Caring-for has two extreme possibilities: leaping in and leaping ahead. The first is welfare; one person "leaps in and takes away 'care,'" from the other, disburdening the other from the care of the self which is the task of authentic Dasein. The second does not take away care, "but to give it back to him authentically as such for the first time . . . it helps the other become transparent to himself *in* his care and to become *free for* it" (*BT*, 159). Care is always care of one's being; authentic caring-for, the leaping ahead for the other, is bringing the other to the way of caring for the self proper to Dasein. Because care is always care of one's own being, caring-for is a way of freeing the other so that he can authentically care for his own being. Caring-for is turning the other toward being so that he is free for it. In the later lecture on the Allegory of the Cave, Heidegger distinguishes freedom from and freedom for, in which the latter is authentic freedom (*GA34*, 59). The "for" in being free for means "out toward" (*hin zu*); to become free means to turn toward the light itself: "To become free to the light means: to let a light arise, to understand being and essence and so to first experience beings as such. The understanding of being gives freedom to the being as a such" (*GA34*, 58–60). This understanding of freedom is identical to what is portrayed in the essay "On the Essence of Truth," a portrait which draws heavily on mystical sources such as Meister Eckhart. Philosophizing is both the freeing of the self and the freeing of others to this source of freedom. This latter function of freeing others is the same as authentic caring-for. Authentic caring-for as freeing the others to their own being is the leadership function of the philosopher presented in this lecture course. Heidegger calls the philosophic leader a liberator, for he frees not only himself but others (*GA34*, 91). Unlike welfare, authentic caring-for does not leap in for the other, that is to say, it does not rule. It rather prepares the way so that the other can experience his own care authentically. By leaping ahead, the philosopher can serve as a guide for others, leading them to the meaning of being. The German word for "guide" is *führen*, nominative *Führer*, generally translated as "leader." Heidegger turns to the leadership principle on the basis of his mystically influenced understanding of how one becomes authentic. The genuine leader does not "leap in" for the other and rule or command, but indicates how the other can find in authentic care an authentic comportment to being.

Heidegger establishes a relationship between leadership and self-responsibility, for genuine leadership as caring-for is nothing other than freeing the other for his or her own possibility of becoming an authentic self. This relationship between leadership and self-responsibility or wanting to be a self forms the basis of Heidegger's political ideal of a leader-populism, to modify Weber's term, and thus of his engagement in the political arena in 1933.

Self-responsibility and Populism

Self-willing is a central part of Heidegger's political rhetoric, particularly in 1933 and 1934. Willing indicates movement, a directing oneself toward a goal. In the case of a people willing itself, it means that a people directs itself toward the goal that has come to appearance in the moment of vision; this goal it understands as its "historical mission" (SA, 13; *GA16,* 117). Self-willing is freely giving law to oneself; giving law to oneself means taking responsibility for obeying this law. Out of this free responsibility arise the "bonds and services of the German student body" (SA, 10; *GA16,* 113). This means that each member of the people comes to understand his or her position and task in the whole. In this vein, Heidegger wrote, "From this will to self-responsibility, every effort, be it humble or grand, of each social and occupational group assumes its necessary and predestined place in the social order" (DSAH, 50; *GA16,* 190). Although there is a Kantian ring to this rhetoric, the addition of "predestined" is not accidental. "Self-willing" must be distinguished from self-creation or self-positing understood subjectively. To will one's self means, to adopt a phrase of Pindar's that Heidegger liked, to become what one is, that is to say, to progress toward the end which has been posited for one's self. The end itself is not chosen, although one is still free to choose one's (authentic) end or to fall under the sway of *das Man.* According to this contrast, *das Man* means liberalism: it means an understanding of freedom that is purely negative, "lack of concern, arbitrariness in one's intentions and inclinations, lack of restraint in everything one does" (SA, 10; *GA16,* 113).[14] True freedom is taking responsibility for one's authentic self, that is to say, taking over one's historical possibility as it has been handed down to one in the moment of vision (*BT,* 435).

Through this connection between self-willing and self-responsibility

---

14. In this understanding of negative freedom Heidegger anticipates Berlin's identical use of the term. Berlin, "Two Concepts of Liberty."

Heidegger is attempting to overcome the problem of the opposition between the rulers and the ruled, the primary problem of which is the potential opposition between the will of the ruler and the will of the people. A leader, in a way neither a ruler nor administrator can do, permits and even requires the self-responsibility of a people. A leader's vision may inspire people, but their authenticity, and thus their political freedom, requires that they also will the end the vision proclaims. Thus when one looks at Heidegger's vision of political leadership, one finds almost a doctrine of consent. The opening paragraph of his "Declaration of Support for Adolf Hitler and the National Socialist State" reads: "The German people has been summoned by the Führer to vote; the Führer, however, is asking nothing from the people. Rather, he is giving the people the possibility of making, directly, the highest decision of all; whether the entire people wills its own Dasein or whether it does not will it" (DSAH, 49; *GA16*, 190). The occasion was a referendum on Germany's withdrawal from the League of Nations. In hindsight, we realize the vote was a foregone conclusion, and we also realize that Heidegger's rhetoric is more purple than the occasion warrants, but in terms of viewing Heidegger's idea of political leadership, the text is quite revealing. The German people have been summoned, but to a choice, not to their judgment in a court of law. Thus the leader is not demanding something from the people, but giving something to them. He is giving to the people the choice to will themselves as the German nation and take self-responsibility for their historical destiny (which is how Heidegger understood, or wanted to understand, the issue of withdrawing from the League of Nations; he also understood withdrawal as the surest guarantee of peace among nations, assuredly not how Hitler thought of it). Thus leadership, unlike rule or administration, lets people will themselves, that is to say, be authentically free.

The leader, however, has a necessary function that a purely democratic regime cannot perform. In a Hegelian spirit, "The Führer has awakened this will in the entire people and has welded it into *one* single resolve" (DSAH, 52; *GA16*, 193). This will of the people is somehow asleep, latent in the will. In fact, its sleep is normal for pluralism in democracy, which Heidegger understood as the contest of self-interested groups. It is difficult in pluralist democracies to speak of "the will of the people," or the "general will" simple because the people rarely, if ever, speak of one accord. We are one nation not because we have a common will, but because we live under a common law. The unity of society (*Gesellschaft*) is always a created unity, in distinction to a genuine community (*Gemeinschaft*) where the unity differs from a mere aggregation of individuated units by virtue of being the preceding union which each already shares in advance (*GA39*, 8). The people, whose will the leader awakens as "one single resolve," is this preceding union, which is the clearing of being. The leader anticipates this sleeping will, painting his vision of this will so that it appears vividly before the people, cutting through their normal day-to-day concerns. Heidegger makes this clear in an aphorism from the *Beiträge zur Philosophie*: "The essence of the people, however, is its 'voice.' This *voice* does *not* speak precisely in the so-called immediate effusion of the common, natural, unspoiled and uneducated 'one.' For this conjured characteristic is already very *spoiled* and has not for a time moved in the original relationship to beings. The *voice* of the people seldom speaks and then only in the few, and then only if it can *still* find its voice" (*GA65*, 319).

A leader is necessary for the articulation of the voice of a people. Against the normal operation of self-interest pluralism which divides a people, a leader is necessary for the will of the people; a leader is necessary for genuine populism. In this way Heidegger opposes his ideal of a leader-populism to pluralist and parliamentarian understandings of democracy.[15]

Viewed from the opposite perspective, genuine populism is the acclamation of the true leader: it is the sign by which he is known. This perspective played no little part in Heidegger's early evaluation of Hitler.[16] Although Hitler was elected with far less than an absolute majority, once in power the German people rallied around him to an extent that one can reasonably speak of a groundswell of popular support for his policies. This is in some respects understandable. Seen against the backdrop of the inef-

15. This opposition echoes the politically more sophisticated theory advocated by Carl Schmitt in *The Crisis of Parliamentary Democracy*, where he speaks of "the inescapable contradiction of liberal individualism and democratic homogeneity," that is to say, of parliamentarianism and Caesarism. Carl Schmitt, *The Crisis of Parliamentary Democracy*, trans. Ellen Kennedy (Cambridge: MIT Press, 1985), 16–17. The theory of democratic Caesarism Schmitt advocates is followed up in fascist political theory, for instance, by Mussolini. The extent of Heidegger's familiarity with Schmitt is not known; as far as I know he never cites Schmitt, but the two are known to have corresponded.

16. Although the Nazis perhaps permanently ruined the word *Volk* for the world (along with *Führer*), in ordinary German it expresses "people," and in compound words generally translates "populist;" for example, *Volkspartei* means populist party. The Nazi party was considered a *Volkspartei*, a term that has decidedly different overtones depending upon one's perspective: it can mean either party of the people or party of the rabble. The same overtones color the English term "populist party."

fectiveness of the Weimar parties to deal with the incredible social problems of the Depression, an ineffectiveness to a large degree caused by the fractured nature of the party system, Hitler must have seemed like a savior. He put people back to work, broke the chains of the hated Versailles Treaty, and restored German pride in their historical greatness. He seemed to pull Germany up by its bootstraps and put it back on track. He acted where others dithered and succeeded where others failed. Nowadays in public opinion surveys they often ask the question, "Do you think that the country is on the right track?" and not surprisingly answers to this question are strongly correlated with the public's opinion about its leaders. Because Hitler acted decisively to address the country's ills, it must have seemed to many of the German people that at last they had turned the corner and the country had gotten back on course. This would naturally create widespread support among the people for Hitler.

This public acclamation made a strong impact on Heidegger. The evidence for this is somewhat circumstantial. Although he had natural proclivities toward National Socialism and had as early as 1932 expressed his support for Hitler (although it seems until 1932 he voted for Hindenburg), he did not publicly enlist his support for the cause until after they took power and until the people, particularly the youth in the universities, rallied around the revolutionary leaders.[17] In essence, Heidegger waited until, as he famously put it in the Rectoral Address, the German youth had already decided the future course that Germany would take; he waited until the sign was given that Hitler had united the people behind him (*GA16,* 117).[18] Hitler appeared to Heidegger as a genuine populist leader who had awakened and united the will of the people.

Even the most infamous of Heidegger's enthusiastic effusions regarding the Führer can be explained along the lines we have been following. In what is often regarded as submission to absolute tyranny, Heidegger bluntly stated: "Let not propositions and 'ideas' be the rules of your being. The Führer alone is the present and future German reality and its law" (GS,

17. Hermann Mörchen joined Heidegger for an evening during a winter break in early 1932. In his journal, he noted that Heidegger expressed his support for National Socialism, commenting favorably on its renunciation of liberal half-heartedness, its whole-hearted opposition to communism, and the willingness of its dictator to take hard and necessary action. Like most of Heidegger's students, Mörchen was shocked at Heidegger's pronouncements. Mörchen's journal entry is quoted in Safranski, *Ein Meister aus Deutschland,* 267–68.

18. This did not, of course, play well with the older members of the Party, who could ask, So where were you during the hard years?

47; *GA16*, 184). The second sentence, the one that in hindsight really chills our blood, must be seen in its relation to the preceding line. Leadership is opposed to propositions and ideas because propositions and ideas seduce us away from our authentic being. Because *phronēsis* does not function according to universal rules, genuinely phronetic leaders can free us from ideas and platforms and so return us to our authentic connection with life. That is why the Führer can be the reality of the Germans. This also explains Heidegger's somewhat pathetic postwar excuse that he thought Hitler would rise above the party doctrine. He thought that an authentic leader was not determined by the propositions of a party doctrine, but rather acted through *phronēsis*.[19]

Leaders and Organization

This unity between leader and people in genuine populism is the ideal. In practice, however, this ideal incurs innumerable problems, most of which revolve around the problem opened up by this anticipatory awakening of the will. Most obviously, the leader in power may have drawn the wrong picture, the enforcing of which is the source of terrible tyranny. The picture need not be completely mistaken to cause problems: perhaps the people assented to some parts of the program without assenting to all. This fact causes resistance to parts from different segments of the people, whether they be conscientious objectors or just bad eggs, either of which necessitates punitive institutions to enforce the laws. There is the problem of moving the mass of society; even if the populace is captured by the end, it requires massive organization in order to coordinate the mobilization.

I want to call particular attention to this last problem because it is here that leadership finds its greatest danger. I deliberately used "organization," "coordination," and "mobilization" to indicate the connection this part of leadership has with technology in its administrative task. Heidegger uses all three terms as part of the metaphysical-technical constellation he wanted to do away with, but they seem to be a possibility of practical leadership. In "Overcoming Metaphysics" Heidegger says: "Herein the necessity of 'leadership,' that is, the planning calculation of the guarantee of the whole

---

19. See Pöggeler, "Heideggers politisches Selbstverständnis," 32. Ott somewhat tendentiously criticizes those who would "relativize" that infamous sentence, although he notes the connection between this sentence and Heidegger's philosophical opposition to ideas and doctrine. Ott, *Martin Heidegger*, 160–62.

of beings, is required. For this purpose such men must be organized and equipped who serve leadership. The 'leaders' are the decisive suppliers who oversee all the sectors of consumption of beings because they understand the whole of those sectors and thus master erring in its calculability" (OM, 85).

Although here Heidegger carefully uses "scare quotes" to distinguish "leaders" from genuine leaders who are the shepherds of being, even using "leaders" indicates that this scientific manager, this technical administrator, is nonetheless a type of leader. He is a leader because he understands the end toward which humanity is aiming and effects this goal by the coordinated mobilization of society. The similarity between the visionary planner of modern technology and the visionary leader that was Heidegger's ideal created profound problems for Heidegger's political ideals, but rather than deal with them, Heidegger increasingly separated the two spheres of leadership, the vision and the execution, such that the visionary part dominated almost completely. This manifested itself in the turn toward poetry and poets, particularly Hölderlin, as founders. In 1933, Hitler was the leader. In 1934, Hölderlin takes over this role, but an essential role is still played by the statesman, who brings the people to their truth that is instituted by the poet though the state; here poets, thinkers, and statesmen are cofounders of nations (GA39, 144). By 1942 at the latest, statesmen have been dropped out almost entirely and leadership is supplied by thinkers and poets, the shepherds of being. Common to all three stages, however, is the determination that "politics in the highest sense" means the institution of a particular historical world for a people; it is the opening of the truth of being as its "there" (GA39, 214; GA53, 100–101). What has changed is that human implementation of the measure of being has been removed from the sphere of politics and relegated to the administrative sphere. The great problem this causes Heidegger is that any implementation of the leader's vision becomes *ipso facto* technical administration and thus no longer an overcoming of the age of modern technology. The realization perverts the vision; politics becomes unrealizable prophecy.

Heidegger may have derived some measure of this truth from his own experience as "Rector-leader" of Freiburg. As rector, he instituted the two National Socialist goals of the *Führerprinzip* and *Gleichschaltung* (synchronization) of the universities into the goals of the movement. For Heidegger, the *Gleichschaltung* meant the transformation of the university in lines with his understanding of work; the *Führerprinzip* was the means to this end.[20] As a practical matter, it meant that Heidegger ceased to call together the academic Senate at Freiburg and instead ruled largely by decree.[21] This usurpation of power far exceeded the power granted the rector in the university constitution; therefore, Heidegger devoted considerable effort to a reformation of the university constitution, helping to draft a new constitution for regional universities in Karlsruhe.[22] His ultimate aim for university administration reform, however, was to create an integrated Conference of Rectors, which would rule the entire university system.[23] This body would put him in direct competition with other rectors and their conceptions for the role of universities in the new Reich. Heidegger's chief competitor and object of his especial animus was Kriek, an instructor of pedagogy who had been a committed Nazi longer than Heidegger and whose goals of a "politicized science" was more along the lines of the Nazi hierarchy's ideas for the transformation of the universities.[24]

Leading the universities does not in itself answer the question concerning the position of the universities in the whole. Rectors Kriek and Heidegger had entirely different ideas concerning this role. Kriek wanted to politicize the disciplines, shift research toward folk-oriented aims, and largely make the entire educational establishment a tool of the party. Heidegger, to the contrary, wanted to give the universities a "leading role" (*BwHB*, 61). Universities would become the training ground for the future "leaders and guardians of the fate of the German Volk" (SA, 11; *GA16*,

20. Although in another way, the *Gleichschaltung* meant a transformation of the university along the lines of the *Führerprinzip*; this is how Ott understands the relation of the two principles. Ott, *Martin Heidegger*, 188–89. They belong essentially together, so one does not really precede the other.

21. Ott illuminates in fine detail Heidegger's academic politics and the practical changes in university administration Heidegger instituted. Both Ott and Heidegger himself agree that Heidegger was a lousy administrator. Of course, it might have also meant he was an inept leader as well.

22. See Ott, *Martin Heidegger*, 191–92. It may help the American reader to keep in mind that German universities are state institutions; authority comes from state and national ministries of education, Heidegger participated in meeting to rewrite the Baden (the state in which Freiburg is located) university constitution. This naturally means that Heidegger would have to deal extensively with political rulers, in other words, the party.

23. Ibid., 188.

24. Sluga examines this competition in much detail. Sluga, *Heidegger's Crisis*. Heidegger vented some of his animus against Kriek in a letter to Elizabeth Blochmann (*BwHB*, 60–61). Because the letter dates from before he took office, it shows that Heidegger felt he could work with Kriek, but also demonstrates the grounds of the differences between him and the party that would later drive him from office.

114). Heidegger's pet project for this realization was an academy for university teachers (*Dozentenhochschule*) to be located in Berlin. Heidegger saw himself as head of this school to educate the educators, but the project never came to fruition.

His work in political committees gave him an insight into the dangers that his sort of leadership faced. While working he expressed concern that the whole could collapse into "mere organization" (*BwHB*, 69). Even more, his (losing) battle with Kriek and the Nazi hierarchy over the politicization of science taught him the true role of universities in the Nazi regime. Far from playing a leading role for the spiritual revolution they would become the training ground of those "leaders" who were educated to plan and coordinate the total mobilization of society (*BwHB*, 74). His own pretense to be a leader was stripped to reveal itself as an administrative position charged with bringing the universities in line with the Nazi ideology. The matter was not one of personal humiliation, but rather a realization that his hopes for the revitalization of the universities were not compatible with the National Socialist revolution, despite his earlier belief that they were.

Heidegger supported Hitler and the National Socialist revolution because he thought that the populist will was being brought to reality in the revolution. This results in a problem evident in Heidegger's political addresses. Although there is a lot of emphasis on self-responsibility and self-willing, there is almost no mention of what is willed beyond a vague invocation of German national destiny. This lack is not the result of an oversight, but rather that Heidegger believed the German national destiny to be self-evident. This lack is inherent in how he conceived of populism. Because the genuine will of the people precedes individual action, and Heidegger believed that the Nazi revolution indicated the Germans had already grasped the goal, the problem was not creating a party platform that could bind the nation but in getting everyone fully involved in the already ongoing national undertaking. The people were already present as the clearing of being; it was only a matter of getting them to turn toward the ground of their existence, which would prove to be this very clearing. That part of leadership which guides the people back to the ground of their existence is featured prominently in 1933 because Heidegger thought that the populist revolution indicated that the nation had already seized its historical destiny.

The lack of an account of politically achieved unity was not an oversight, but rather a necessary result of Heidegger's religious schema, with its opposition between authenticity and technology. Organization was denounced. It belonged to the old technical age which Heidegger hoped to overcome. Unfortunately, organization belonged to the function of a leader; it is how a leader moves a nation toward a goal. Heidegger recognized this ambiguity and the danger of leaders and organization. He hoped to limit organizations to a "makeshift provision," something that could be set aside once the nation had truly grasped its essence as a community (*GA39*, 8). However, if the nation failed in its task, or worse, if the leaders mistook technical organization for the essence of a community, all that was left was technical leadership in the service of the will to will. Here, "the 'leaders' are the decisive suppliers who oversee all the sectors of consumption of beings because they understand the whole of those sectors and thus master erring in its calculability" (OM, 85). These "leaders" were indeed types of leaders in that they served to mobilize the whole of society and they had a certain vision that allowed them to oversee and plan the whole. This denunciation of technical leaders in "Overcoming Metaphysics" can easily be seen as a denunciation of the path Hitler and the Nazis took, and as an expression of Heidegger's despair at the lost opportunity.[25] Because his fears concerning the dangers of mere organization date to his active participation in the Nazi regime, one should not see this denunciation of Hitler as a philosophical change, but rather as a recognition that Hitler's "limited thinking" could not achieve Heidegger's main goal.

The Leader as Phronetic Virtuoso

With the gradual recognition on Heidegger's part of the limitations of practical politics to achieve his metaphysical goals came a shift in emphasis on the leadership functions. The pervasive emphasis on self-responsibility in the early 1930s changed instead to an emphasis on pinpointing the origin of a new experience of being such that it appeared as a people. According to this new emphasis, the leader as poet took on a whole new significance. If earlier poets were invoked but not thematized, in Heidegger's works from the middle 1930s the poet takes center stage. The work of practical political leaders was shoved aside as the "business of the state," whereas in the work of poets politics occurred in the "genuine sense" (*IM*, 152; *GA39*, 214).

---

25. The despair worked its way into other ways that Heidegger understood his political engagement; just as he blamed Hitler for failing the cause, so too did he blame the people, particularly the students and faculty (*BwHB*, 70; FT, 22–26; *GA16*, 386–89).

The genuine sense of politics revolves around opening up a space for a new experience of being opposed to the mathematical ordering of modern technology. This revolutionary revelation of being occurs in the work of art; art is the setting to work of the truth of being, its clearing as world. This opening can occur in a variety of ways, including through the founding of states, the questioning of thinkers, and the "saying" of the poets. At heart, however, all are poetic in the sense they all establish the measure for what is. Consequently, when Heidegger takes up the theme of authentic philosophy in the *Introduction to Metaphysics,* he says that philosophy "imposes its measure upon its epoch" (*IM,* 8). This poetic philosophy is "a thinking that breaks the paths and opens the perspectives of the knowledge in which and by which a people fulfills itself historically and culturally, the knowledge that kindles and necessitates all inquiries and thereby threatens all values" (*IM,* 10).

The difference between the work in the middle 1930s and the earlier works is that Heidegger has in effect made an actor out of what was earlier presented as an action. The great historical epoch-creating action that is the revelation of being becomes localized in the struggle of the great poet, in the poet's confrontation with being. Thus what was presented in the Rectoral Address as the *Greek* passion for unconcealment becomes localized in the figure of Oedipus (*IM,* 107).[26] Rather than speak of the breaking open of the truth of being, Heidegger spoke of "violent men" becoming "pre-eminent in historical being as creators, as men of action," who are "without statute and limit, without structure and order, because they themselves *as* creators must first create all this" (*IM,* 152–53). These men of action create the structure and measure that is the truth of being, an act Heidegger calls the instituting (*Stiftung*) of being (*GA4,* 41). This instituting is identical to Heidegger's earlier "projecting" of being (*Seinsentwurf*), a sketching or bringing to form in advance that which is not yet (*GA39,* 214; HKBD, 137). This sketching, however, now bears a proper name: Nietzsche, Hölderlin, Sophocles.

One needs to be careful in understanding this personification of historical epochs into preeminent actors. Despite appearances, Heidegger never

26. This is the extent to which Pöggeler's thesis of Heidegger's Nietzscheanism during this period is correct. The Nietzschean element is to set the struggle over values only to the few or the solitary, a feature which begins to dominate Heidegger's thinking during the 1930s. However, Pöggeler goes astray in maintaining that this constitutes a decisive radicalization of Heidegger's politics. His politics were always radical.

makes the actor the author of what he creates. It is more accurate to say that the action takes place in and through the actor. Even in his most "Romantic" lecture, his first lecture on Hölderlin in 1934, Heidegger insists that humans do not have language, but rather that language has us, uses us as a tool (*GA39*, 23, 62). The poet stands exposed "bare-headed" to the overpowering might of being and directs the revelation into language (*GA39*, 30). As the one who excels in *phronēsis*, the poet is the vessel of the revelation of being.

As Heidegger makes abundantly clear in the *Introduction to Metaphysics*, however, the poet-leader is *deinon* or uncanny. This discussion recalls Aristotle's distinction in book 6 of the *Nicomachean Ethics* between genuine *phronēsis* and a related faculty he calls *deinotes* or cleverness.[27] The difference is that cleverness can be used for good or evil, whereas genuine *phronēsis*, Aristotle wants to insist, always discerns the noble and good end of action. The practically wise person is necessarily good, but the merely clever person is capable of anything. This unlimited capacity is precisely what commends the *deinos* to Heidegger, for it is only through this capacity that the poet-leader can initiate a new experience of being. Like Aristotle, Heidegger wants a leader who excels in practical wisdom, but because Heidegger wants a leader who is a revolutionary, he deliberately obliterates the distinction Aristotle wants to establish between practical wisdom and cleverness. For Heidegger, in order to institute a new order of being, practical wisdom must be capable of anything. The designation of a poetic leader in the *Introduction to Metaphysics* as *deinon* makes obvious what is present at all times in Heidegger's understanding of *phronēsis*: because *phronēsis* initiates a new revelation of being, it is beyond good and evil.[28]

By designating the poet as uncanny or terrible, Heidegger does not wish to establish tyranny as authentic politics, even if that may in fact be the result. A leader must be capable of anything because he must be open to the possibilities of being itself. To be capable of anything does not mean

27. Aristotle, *Ethics* 1144a23.

28. During this time period Heidegger frequently stresses the political goal of greatness, which requires *deinotes*. Greatness requires being beyond good and evil. While obviously indebted to Nietzsche, this theme recalls a famous passage from Pericles' funeral oration in Thucydides, where he says that the greatness and daring of Athens has left imperishable monuments to both good and evil. Thucydides, *The Peloponnesian War*, trans. Richard Crawley (New York: Modern Library, 1951), 106.

that a leader willfully tyrannizes his subjects, but rather that he is free for the measure of being as it reveals itself to him. His capacity for possibility is precisely what makes him capable of being a vessel or receptacle for being. As a vessel for being, the poet is a bridge between the original revelation of being and his nation. Because the revelation of being is the space for the appearance of the divine and the gods of a nation, Heidegger calls the poet a demigod, for as a vessel he stands halfway between the gods and the people. This demigod Heidegger calls a leader because as a vessel and bridge the poet stands out before the crowd; as leader he is struck first by the advent of the gods, and so can serve as a guide for his nation to follow (GA39, 166–75, 210, 100). Because of his new emphasis on preeminent actors, Heidegger has established a hierarchy in the order of being, with the poets on top leading the nation toward a new historical relationship to the divine.

Heidegger maintained the connection between leaders and the people characteristic of his political thought, but with a difference. If before the unity of the people was assumed in advance, now it is something that the poet institutes. A people is instituted in the saying of the poetic word, that is to say, the poet creates the myths of a people. These sayings (Sage) are the ground and meaning of being for a nation, and it is only on this basis that authentic human dwelling is possible. Heidegger said, "Poetry as instituting effects the ground of the possibility for the settling of humans on earth between it and the gods, that is, for becoming historical and so able to be a people" (GA39, 216). The poetic sayings institute what Heidegger later called the unity of the fourfold or being as a whole. This saying is the truth of a people: "The truth of a people is the specific openness of being as a whole, according to which the bearing and ordering and leading power receives its rank order and effects its harmony" (GA39, 144).

Heidegger explicitly adapted the categories of his earlier (and subsequent) understanding of the revelation of being to this notion of poetic institution. The difference in this 1934 lecture is the new status of the people. If before the harmony between the spirit of the nation and the body of the nation was presumed, after his parting from the Nazis Heidegger opened up a lacuna between the truth of a nation and its reality. This shift is evident already in the substitution of Hölderlin for Hitler, a substitution of a dead poet for a living ruler. For Heidegger, Hölderlin had instituted the German nation by instituting the "fundamental attuning" (Grundstimmung) that established Germany's historical mission; Hölderlin established the goal that Germans were obliged to take as their responsibility and task. Even as Heidegger established the identity of the poetic saying and the nation, however, he also created a gap between the poetic nation, the spiritual nation which is related to the revelation of being, and the actual nation, which since Hölderlin's time has been spiritually emasculated by the threatening powers of modern technology (IM, 45). As the founder of Germany's spirit, Hölderlin called to Germans in 1934 to become what they "already" were. Hölderlin instituted the clearing of being, but the Germans could come to it and thus be themselves only if they truly understood his sayings (GA39, 113).

This split allowed Heidegger to defend his own understanding of *phronēsis* while simultaneously denouncing the actual political course Germany was following under Hitler. If once Heidegger believed that Hitler excelled in *phronēsis*, he later concluded that Hitler and the Nazis had merely delivered Germany over to the domination of modern technology. Hitler was an uncanny leader only insofar as he participated in the uncanniness of modern technology, which, through the will to will, was capable of anything.[29] Heidegger turned instead to the shepherds of being, the poets and thinkers who through their scarcely heeded labor could found an authentic community.

The Polis as a Community of Saints

The removal of genuine politics to the realm of being and the instituting of a nation through the poetic word point to the unspoken model for Heidegger's new polis: the church. Despite Heidegger's manifest hostility toward organized religion at this time, this Hölderlin lecture is driven by an equally manifest religious goal: a new encounter with the divine (GA39, 97). A nation is founded upon a fundamental attuning toward being as a

---

29. Heidegger makes this connection in a rather extraordinary way. When he later (in 1942) again takes up the choral ode and the meaning of *deinon*, he interprets *deinon* to mean that humans are capable of anything, i.e., capable of taking being to be a being; we are uncanny because we have forgotten being (GA53, 107–13). Thus human beings are most uncanny or homeless (*un-heimlich*) in the age of metaphysics, modern technology, and the will to will. The will to will is *deinon* because it is limitlessly capable of anything. Under the dominion of the will to will, leaders, who are *deinon* insofar as they have a vision for the overall direction of the production process, "are the first employees within the course of business of the unconditional consumption of beings in the service of the guarantee of the vacuum of the abandonment of being" (OM, 87). Heidegger contrasts these leaders to the shepherds of being, who preserve the limits of the possible (OM, 88).

whole; the basic disposition Hölderlin instituted is the "holy lament," the lament that the gods have taken flight (*GA39*, 87). In order that a nation can be instituted toward a new relationship to its gods, it is necessary to take this flight seriously: "Not so cheaply can the gods of a people be created. First of all, the flight of the gods must become an experience, first of all this experience must thrust existence [*Dasein*] into a basic disposition, in which a historical people as a whole endures the need of its godlessness and inner disunion. This basic disposition is what the poet instituted in the historical existence of our people" (*GA39*, 80).

The flight of the gods is experienced as a holy lament because the flight of the gods leaves the readiness for an experience of the divine intact: "That the gods have taken flight does not mean that the divinity has also disappeared from the existence of man, but rather means here that it explicitly rules, but rules as no longer fulfilled, as a dimmed and dark, but still mighty" (*GA39*, 95). The experience of the flight of the gods, of the loss of the divine in modern life, in other words, the experience of nihilism, calls us to again fill that void in our existence so that we can rebuild our existence on earth.[30] "Insofar as the gods permeate the historical existence and being as a whole, the attuning pulls us out of the ensnarement while at the same time expressly inserting us in the mature connections to the earth, land, and home [*Heimat*]" (*GA39*, 140). Heidegger turned to Hölderlin because he properly grasped both the need for the divine in human existence and how this need is lacking in modern times. This needlessness is the real danger, for without the experience of neediness, we can never turn toward the coming of new gods; we simply will not be looking.[31] Hölderlin may not have created new gods, but by instituting the disposition of the holy lament, he at least allowed the Germans to be pointed in the correct direction to receive them.

The religious foundation went beyond the need to recapture the divine in human affairs; it also lay at the basis for his model of the *polis*. Because

30. Heidegger interprets Nietzsche's announcement of the death of god in this manner. For this reason, in an extraordinary statement he calls Nietzsche and Hölderlin the only believing men of the nineteenth century. See *GA39*, 95. See also his interpretation of the passage in *The Gay Science* where a madman announces the death of God (WN, 59–64).

31. Heidegger's emphasis on the danger of needlessness persists and indeed grows stronger over time; see, for instance, *GA65*, 125, and *GA79*, 55–56. This emphasis increases in no small part because Heidegger realized that others did not feel the need as strongly as he did, if they felt it at all. The path to "taking the long since begun flight of the gods seriously" was much longer and harder than Heidegger thought in 1933 or 1934 (*GA39*, 220).

our relationship to the divine is the center of human existence, it is perhaps not surprising that Heidegger's picture of social organization took its cues from churches. It is necessary, though, to take care in understanding what that means. There is an ambiguity in the Christian church that bears attention. A church is at once one type of social structure among others, such as the family or corporation, which distributes power in an organized manner; for instance, churches ordain ministers or priests in order to maintain the cohesion of teachings, and they may regulate and enforce certain forms of behavior among members. One may see this side of the church as its human side, a manner of rationally accounting for the vagaries of human insufficiencies and weaknesses in following the path to salvation. This human-organized church stands in some tension with the ideal of a church, which is all those who hearken to the Word of God, or what Augustine called the community of saints.[32]

This ambiguity in the notion of a church is analogous to the distinction made by Troeltsch and Weber in their sociologies of religion between a church and a sect. For Weber, the decisive characterization of a church is the separation of person from charisma and the transference of this charisma to the institution as such. The church is a bearer of an office charisma, and as such is characterized by the rise of a professional priesthood, the rationalization of dogma and rites, and compulsory organization and discipline.[33] For both Troeltsch and Weber, the church depersonalizes to a certain extent the attaining of salvation, for the sheer fact of belonging to the institution and its official dispensation of grace is what saves.[34] By virtue of its depersonalized, universal, and institutional character, a church encompasses a wide variety of religious types, from saints to heretics. The church is thus a type of bureaucratic organization. Both

32. Augustine, *City of God* (trans. Bettenson) 14.28. Luther writes, "I believe that there is a holy church which is a congregation [*Gemeinde*] in which there are nothing but saints." This holy church is the body of believers suffused by the Holy Spirit and the Word. Luther, "Sermons on the Catechism," 212–13. This is the sort of spiritual community I attributed to Heidegger in Chapter 2. See also Gillian Rose for a criticism of an agapic community similar to the one I am raising; in *The Broken Middle* she traces Arendt's political thought to her appropriation of Augustinian elements summed up by the "sociality of saints." Rose, *Broken Middle*, 228–35. In another book she refers to the same type of community as the "New Jerusalem." Gillian Rose, *Mourning Becomes Law: Philosophy and Representation* (New York: Cambridge University Press, 1996).

33. Weber, *Economy and Society*, 1164.

34. Ibid., 1166; Ernst Troeltsch, *Die Sozialphilosophie des Christentums* (Zurich: Verlag Seldwyla, 1922), 17.

Troeltsch and Weber distinguish a church from a sect. Unlike a church, a sect is a community of personally charismatic individuals, the "elite troops of religious *virtuosi.*"[35] The difference between church and sect lies in the personal excellence of members required to participate in salvation.[36] The sect adheres to the ideal of an *ecclesia pura,* the visible community of saints.[37]

Both Weber and Troeltsch note that sect types often serve as engines for reforming and revolutionary movements. Because of its universality, a church must compromise with the world, for it must dispense grace to each member despite varying degrees of religious virtue. Sects arise by rejecting this compromise. Sects demand a purity in behavior that churches cannot. The sect type leads to two social ends. One is a withdrawal from the world, either personally through mystical inwardness or communally through the formation of religious communities and monasteries. In either of these cases, the individual or community tries to establish a sphere of sanctity amidst the everyday world, a sphere in which piety can remain unsullied by contact with the impurities of the unvirtuous world. The second path is revolution. Rather than withdraw to a sphere of sanctity, the sect tries to extend this purified sphere to the whole of society by remaking society in accordance with its radical and thus revolutionary principles.

The difference between church and sect mirrors my distinction between the social church and the ideal church, for both a sect and an ideal church are understood as a community of saints.[38] Ideally, of course, these two sides of the church would coincide exactly, but both as a practical matter and a theoretical matter, these two churches create differently mediated bodies. As a practical matter, those who are members of the true church, the members of the elect, will be smaller and more dispersed than the whole of organized, social churches. Being called by God, the elect may be pulled out of their social church, severing social ties that are the heart of the social church. This sort of tension can exist because the two churches are based upon two different types of mediation. The social church is a human organ-

35. Weber, *Economy and Society,* 1170.

36. Ibid., 1205; Troeltsch, *Sozialphilosophie,* 17.

37. Weber, *Economy and Society,* 1204.

38. I am not adopting Weber's or Troeltsch's terminology because they are using ideal terms to designate types of organization, which puts them at odds with the self-understanding of churches; few churches consider themselves sects, even if they do consider themselves communities of saints.

ization in which the body of the church is such through human power, whereas the true church is divinely ordained based solely on the power of the Word to reach and transform the soul.[39]

These two understandings of church coincide with what in Heidegger's thought are the people and the state. The people are the divinely ordained community of saints, whereas the state is the humanly organized church. If in 1933 this division is blurred, by 1934 this division, while still blurry, comes into sharper focus. This can be seen in several places in the Hölderlin lecture. First, there is the distinction between the genuine sense of politics versus the despised "business of the state." Second, there is the distinction Heidegger drew between society and genuine community, paralleled by a distinction between organization and community. Society is based upon "the taking up of reciprocal relations," in other words, a social contract, whereas community is the "prior connection [*vorgängige Bindung*] of each individual to that which commandingly ties and determines each individual" (*GA39*, 72). Heidegger underlined the preceding nature of community by saying that the "truth gathering of individuals in a primordial community has already occurred in advance" (*GA39*, 8). Similarly, organization is the "rough depositing of the all-too-many," which may be a necessary preparation for, but is not the essence of community (*GA39*, 8). In both cases, community is something that precedes and eludes human power; human power is insufficient to bring it about.[40] Third, the original community arises when each individual comes to it from the ground of his existence, that is to say, only when each individual becomes authentic, which means to *be* the basis of his being-there (*GA39*, 8; *BT*, 330).

---

39. Compare Troeltsch's depiction of the Lutheran Church, which according to its ideal was the living incarnation of the miraculous power of the Word. As Troeltsch notes, however, it was not possible to rely solely upon the power of the Word; uniform interpretation had to be enforced, which required an ecclesiastical organization. Ernst Troeltsch, *The Social Teaching of the Christian Churches*, trans. Olive Wyon (New York: Macmillan, 1949), 2:518–20.

40. The difference between humanly created and divinely ordained is another reason I avoid Troeltsch's and Weber's terminology because for both a sect is a voluntary association. Unfortunately, calling a sect a voluntary association of charismatic individuals blurs the church-sect distinction they labor to draw, because through their association the individuals create an institution that rationalizes the path to salvation. In effect, Weber and Troeltsch distinguish between two types of social and law-enforcement organizations, the sect type merely being distinguished by making greater demands on its adherents; it is a difference in degree, not in kind. Unlike Heidegger, neither Weber nor Troeltsch take eschatology and apocalypse seriously.

Communities arise only when each individual undergoes the transformation of the soul so as to be a free receptacle for the there of being. In this lecture, the ground of existence (*Grund seines Dasein*) is the fundamental attuning (*Grundstimmung*) that is the truth of a people which is instituted in the poetic word, that primordial community that has already occurred in advance of any human deed. Furthermore, poetry is the revelation of the gods (as a hint and mystery, Heidegger makes clear) in the language of a people. Heidegger has thus translated the two elements of the Christian ideal of a church into the foundation of a people: the believer who has turned toward the ground of his existence which is nothing other than the instituted word of God. The people are a community of saints.

Having identified the nation with the ideal of a church, the state comes under increasing suspicion. At best, the state vaguely duplicates the national community, but the state is increasingly disparaged and discarded. This shift is buttressed by Heidegger's increasing concern with technology and metaphysics. Even if Heidegger was careful to say that modern technology is itself a certain revelation of being, modern technology is how humans dominate and transform the beings; in the age of modern technology humans acquire the illusion that they control nature, that it is theirs to command. The calculating and planning type of thinking characteristic of technical thinking carries through to all segments of human life, including human organization, which is planned as part of the production enterprise. Humans fill the void left by the flight of the gods. The problem is that this flight is not seen for what it is: it is either not seen at all or, as in Nietzsche's case, seen but wholly misunderstood so that his solution to nihilism was to create gods, as if they were as much a product of the human will as any artifact. The suspicion of the will and technical thinking leads to the suspicion of all willed organization; only that unity which comes from being can serve as the proper organization of human society.

Waiting for the Apocalypse

Thus Heidegger's famous statement, "Only a god can save us," should be taken at face value. Humans do not have the capacity for creating new gods or new experiences of being. "No mere action will change the world, because being as effectiveness and effecting closes all beings off in the face of appropriation" (OM, 89). At most, they can prepare themselves to be receptacles for the coming gods. The entire weight of the reformation of human life is delivered over to the divine element. In this respect, Heidegger's understanding of reformation was Lutheran, that is to say, apocalyptic.[41] All attention is directed toward the coming advent of the divine, for we stand in a time in which the gods are absent, the peculiar nihilism of the holy lament which can found a new relationship to the gods.

The apocalyptic motif dominates the leader figure that is featured in Heidegger's later thought, the "shepherd of being." All of the leadership figures in Heidegger's thinking are in one way or another shepherds of being, but by the end of the Second World War, when disaster was striking Germany, the religiosity implicit in the other figures becomes evident in the invocation of the shepherd. The two important passages where the shepherd is named, in "Overcoming Metaphysics" and the "Letter on Humanism," make clear the position Heidegger had taken in the aftermath of the Nazi disaster, one that he would maintain until the end of his life. In both passages the shepherd is brought forth as the savior to the technical world, opposed to those false "leaders" who would be masters and possessors of nature (OM, 88; LH, 221). In opposition to the futility of effecting action that is characteristic of those servants of the will to will, the position the shepherds hold in the apocalyptic scheme is now that of an "anticipatory escort" (OM, 90). The human element in the revolutionary transformation of existence is to anticipate the future coming of the gods, and in light of this anticipation to begin preparing for this advent. The leader has become a prophet.

The prophet is a leader, in many senses the leadership figure most true to Heidegger's powerless ideal of human political life. The prophet has no power and at best a borrowed authority; he leads by envisioning a future where the wrongs will be righted, hoping that here and there this vision will touch a heart and guide them on the path to the promised land.

By this point, Heidegger had forsaken any tangible connection with concrete politics. The concrete action of the political leader, or even the action of a poet who founds a people sinks into a vague mist in favor of a prophet who speaks of vague millenarian dreams. Toward the end of his life Heidegger quoted Kleist: "I step back before one who is not yet here, and

---

41. Oberman writes (paraphrasing Luther), "God himself must and will carry out the 'reformation.' Only he merits the title 'reformer,' because he will consummate the reformation at the end of time, on Judgment Day." Heiko Oberman, "Martin Luther: Forerunner of the Reformation," in *The Reformation: Roots and Ramifications,* trans. Andrew Colin Gow (Grand Rapids, Mich.: William B. Eerdmans, 1994), 27. Heidegger strips out the specifically Christian symbols in Luther's thought, but maintains the overall apocalyptic structure.

bow, a millennium before him, to his spirit" (TI, 87; *GA16*, 710). This millenarian resignation characteristic of his later thought is the result of the failure of Nazism to bring about his dreams. That heady mood of immanent revolution that gushes in all his writings from 1933 to 1935, that calling to "embark on the great and long venture of demolishing a world that has grown old and of rebuilding it authentically anew," to become the "builders of a new world structure," to "dare" to be with the gods, all that optimism had dissipated into a resignation of a millenarian hope that a god will save us (*IM*, 125–26; *GA39*, 221). A change in content or form cannot account for the difference between Heidegger in 1933 and Heidegger after the war in which "nothing decisive occurred," for the religious apocalypticism structures his political sense in both instances; the change rather is in mood and sense of his historical situation. The later resignation with its thousand-year hope is but the negative image of the optimism of the immanent revolution in human and German history present earlier. Rather than standing on the cusp of the apocalypse as he believed in 1933, Heidegger instead later glimpsed the apocalypse in the far distant future. His resignation should not be taken to mean that he had given up on his dream, but rather that the failure of the Nazis indicated that Germany was not ready for his dream; that Nazism served modern technology like the Americans and the Bolsheviks indicated to Heidegger that he had underestimated the dominance of modern technology. Not to underestimate the dominance of modern technology; this was the lesson he learned from Nazism. This lesson gave him his task and mission which he followed the rest of his life: to prepare the ground for a future advent by relentlessly and painstakingly deconstructing the Western metaphysical tradition so as to continue to hold open in the face of the tyranny of modern technology a possibility for the questioning of being. Heidegger takes on the role of prophet and shepherd of being because it is a type of leader uniquely in tune with an age bereft of the gods; no messiah himself, he could only play John the Baptist to that future thinker in whose service he stood.[42]

---

42. Compare this to Oberman's assessment of Luther's own assessment of his role in the divine play: Luther's mission is "the office of the 'pre-reformation' interpreter of Scripture, charged with the mission of giving voice once again . . . to the call of the prophet." Oberman, "Martin Luther," 31–33.

Conclusion

Heidegger's antimodern, antiliberal politics stem from his apocalyptic fanaticism. This fanaticism led him to found the whole of authentic human existence on an experience of the divine. The wholeness of the experience is what characterizes his thought as fanatical; Heidegger's ideal of authenticity cannot tolerate the differentiated spheres of life that make up modern civil society, particularly the separation of religion and politics, church and state. In this sense, Heidegger shared the error of all millenarian fanatics, the desire for a revolutionary transformation of society into a community of saints.

Heidegger's misguided enthusiasm for the Nazis is thus a symptom of a larger, more encompassing error that shaped his entire political philosophy. His postwar defense of his role in the National Socialist revolution underscores the framework of his political thought: the problem with the Nazis was not that they were too radical, but rather that they were not radical—not fanatical—enough. They proved to be as caught up in the web of metaphysics as the society Heidegger had hoped they would overturn.

Because Heidegger's political missteps are a symptom of a larger problem, and not a case all of their own, I have sought throughout to explicate how Heidegger's profound criticism of Western metaphysics is bound up with this issue of his religious-political fanaticism. Conversely, it is equally true that one can better understand the specific nature of his fanaticism by examining his criticism of metaphysics. Heidegger's critique of metaphysics impelled his fanaticism toward a distinctly radical end. Fanatical movements tend to become dogmatic and programmatic, what Weber called the rationalization of the charismatic. Even from early on, Heidegger's opposition to metaphysics was intended to counter the dogmatic tendencies of Catholicism. His turn to an antidogmatic Lutheranism represented by certain German Romantics such as Schleiermacher was part of his attempt to free religion and the divine from the effects of rationalization. Dogma, reason, and metaphysics are set opposite his new metaphysics of authenticity, which cannot compromise with rational law in any form.

Heidegger appropriated and extended Luther's distinction between law and spirit to create an all-encompassing theological-political philosophy founded upon a thoroughgoing rejection of rational law understood as metaphysics. His critique of metaphysics was at bottom a critique of law. This is the reason for calling Heidegger an antinomian thinker. Antinomianism is the most radical kind of fanaticism possible, for if fanaticism desires a holistic and undifferentiated community, the presence of law indicates the presence of differentiation, both between rulers and ruled and between individuals in their difference from each other. Antinomianism purifies the dogmatic tendencies inherent in fanatic movements. We saw, however, the effects of this solution in the previous chapter: equating dogma with institutionalization, Heidegger tried to maintain a sharp separation between political institutions and genuine politics, but was unable to conceive of a noninstitutional polity as anything but a community of saints.

Antinomianism is the key to understanding Heidegger's thinking. It underlay his attempts to find a nondogmatic religiosity, his attempts to overcome metaphysics, and his moral-political ideal of authenticity. The common thread shaping the antinomian cast of his theological-metaphysical politics was his transformation of *phronēsis* or practical wisdom into a kind of divine revelation. As I showed in the first chapter, Heidegger's appropriation of Aristotle's concept of *phronēsis* was central to his attempt to adapt ontology to a hermeneutical phenomenology that could establish an authentic connection to the whole of being in its historical specificity. This goal of hermeneutical phenomenology was central to the issues that precipitated his crisis of faith. For Heidegger, as earlier for Luther, the predominance of rational metaphysics in Catholic faith was alien to a genuinely religious way of life. Hermeneutical phenomenology was intended to free humans from the tyranny of theory and science and thus open the path to an authentic religiosity. Heidegger's return to ontology in the early 1920s was wholly shaped by this earlier crisis of faith and the desire for a nondogmatic religiosity. The wholeness of being must be sought in historicity; being is thought within the horizon of time. Heidegger's appropriation of Aristotle's notion of *phronēsis* as the basis of a new metaphysics makes sense only in this regard. *Phronēsis* apprehends the situation in its particularity, thus giving humans a knowledge of being that is not theoretical and atemporal. The theological background, however, gives Heidegger's appropriation a double oddity. First, *phronēsis* apprehends being as a whole; it is the architectonic knowledge, the knowledge of the *archē* or principles that shape the world. Second, Heidegger understood *phronēsis* as *Augenblick,* the moment of vision, the lightning-flash of the world come into presence. If perhaps one could read practical wisdom in Aristotle as architectonic, at least in the hands of a great statesman, the historical particularity that recommends *phronēsis* was not so radically new in Aristotle's thought as Heidegger implies. Aristotle's practical wisdom looked back to the tradition in which the actor is situated; Heidegger's practical wisdom looked to the future and what is possible. One is inherently conservative; the other, inherently revolutionary.

Because *phronēsis* reveals being as historicity, ontology is cast not as the propositional knowledge of beings, but properly as the *question* of being. Indeed, *phronēsis* is the question of being. The question of being becomes the path upon which the authentically divine element can give meaning and direction to human existence. This entrance contains two moments: the questionableness of being frees up possibility or sheer freedom, and the moment of vision provides a determinate path which we take up as our destiny. *Phronēsis* opens itself to the questionableness of being, and then provides an insight into the meaning of a particular whole over to which the questioning self is delivered as the fated space of its action. The question of being contains two equally necessary moments: possibility and actuality, freedom and necessity, abyss and ground, absence and presence. Being "is" both infinite and finite, both beyond definition and always definite. This paradoxical duality of being, what I call elsewhere the antinomy of being, creates many interpretative problems, but it is necessary to recognize both elements as moments of being.

This attempt to establish the priority of possibility over actuality, freedom over necessity, by means of the question of being has a clear theological-metaphysical predecessor in late medieval nominalism. In many ways, the question of being understood as the origin of beings resembles the nominalist god, the utterly free and thus utterly mysterious creator god. It is no accident that Heidegger saw Descartes above all others as the chief villain of modern metaphysics, for Descartes's philosophy is an attempt to limit and negate this nominalist god. In fact, Heidegger rejected *both* paths that stem from Descartes, the rationalist path which finds expression in Leibniz and the principle of reason, and the path of the will which is laid out by Fichte and later by Nietzsche. Heidegger's recasting of *phronēsis* attempted to steer between these paths in order to free up the nondogmatic divinity that belongs to the question of being; a god neither bound by the principle of reason nor fashioned by or identical with the will.

In the second chapter of the book, I examine *phronēsis* as an insight into a particular historical whole. This, I argue, is the ground of Heidegger's communitarianism. The moment of vision is an insight into the "there" of being, the open space in which all things, including humans, appear as what they are. The "there" of being is the particular meaning of the whole, and inasmuch as it is prior to each thing, each thing is referred to the meaning of the whole. In the moment of vision, we see ourselves as part of a whole which includes other humans. Dasein is properly understood as being-in-the-world-with-others. Part-whole logic is central to communitarianism, and Heidegger obeyed that logic, rejecting liberal individualism, which denies the appropriateness of part-whole logic to individual beings. This rejection of metaphysical individualism strongly differentiates Heidegger from earlier nominalist metaphysics. For Heidegger, individuals were not primary. Rather it is through a communal revelation of being that we become free. Like most communitarians, Heidegger thus saw alienation of the individual from the whole as the chief ethical and political problem. Also like most communitarians, to overcome alienation means to become (re)-integrated into the whole. Heidegger's term for this reunion is "authenticity." The idea of authenticity thus encapsulates Heidegger's religious communitarianism. Since it so closely parallels Eckhart's understanding of the mystical union with God, one could characterize Heidegger's politics as a mystical communitarianism.

In Heidegger's case, this mystical community is founded not by a prophet or theologian, but by a poetic leader. If one can see Heidegger's particularistic communalism as the philosophical source for his national socialism, this exaltation of leadership, which I examine in Chapter 5, ties him to fascism. If *phronēsis* reveals the meaning of the whole, the leader is the one endowed with phronetic excellence who reveals what should be done for his community, the one who brings each to the ground of his own meaning in the community. The leader is poetic because the revelation is an image, a definite shape of the whole. Heidegger recognized the strong similarity between this image of the leader and the older Romantic theories of great creators, and thus attempted to make authentic *poiēsis* akin to *phronēsis*. As I analyzed it in Chapter 3, Heidegger's understanding of *technē*—which subsumes poetry, technology, and work—as "revealing" rather than the usual "making" is consistent with his rejection of the Cartesian metaphysics of will, in which being is what is made. Instead, *technē* becomes the insight into the double nature of being as both presence and absence, that is to say, it becomes the same thing as *phronēsis*, and the question of being. His clear attempt to separate genuine poetry from anything willed is the clearest indication of the distance between his understanding of poetry and the Romantic theories with which it is often compared.

As I show in the final chapter, this persistent repudiation of the will makes his politics apocalyptic. Everything is delivered over to the noncoercive power of revelation, nothing is left to human device. Leaders bring members into a community through revelation and rhetoric, not force or law. Authenticity requires that each person come to the ground of his or her being, the particular meaning of the whole of which each is a part, on his or her own. This mysticism of community makes human artifice suspect. Heidegger thus had a great suspicion of institutions; at most they could serve as makeshift initiators of community, but they could not serve in place of genuine community. This separation of human from divine institution mirrors his dual understanding of the Church, which is both a human social arrangement and the living body of the Word of God. Heidegger's ideal community, the site of the genuinely political, is an emulation of this second vision; it is the divine word instituted as a community of saints who have been transfigured by the revelation of the word that is the meaning of being.

The thoroughgoing rejection of law and rule in Heidegger's thought, whether seen theologically in the turn to nominalism, metaphysically in the rejection of the principle of reason, or politically in the rejection of law in favor of leadership and authenticity, makes him out as an antinomian. His antinomianism was a particular theological-political project that owed much, as we have seen, to Lutheranism, particularly those post-Reformation radicals who radicalized Luther's preference of faith over reason and spirit over law into a revolutionary calling to transform human society here on earth. For such religious fanatics, the church or sect was the only just human society. This replacement of the polis by the church, which can also be seen as the sacralization of the public sphere, takes one of two paths. Either the political regime becomes a church through social revolution, or the church of believers withdraws from the greater society into small, self-contained sects potentially as small as the solitary individual. Heidegger chose the former course. The sacralization of the public sphere demanded a total political revolution.

This revolution, however, cannot succeed, principally because the attempt to found a politics upon this antinomian conception of authentic religiosity is an attempt to found a political regime beyond law. It is no accident that Heidegger's ideal *polis* is at heart a community of saints, for saints have no need of laws, and thus a community of saints is the only possible type of organization that corresponds to Heidegger's ideal of law-less or anarchic authenticity. There is little harm in viewing this ideal as the best and happiest of all possible worlds, but to measure large-scale societies by this ideal bespeaks an idealism dangerously close to madness. The contrast between Heidegger and Luther, whose ideal of Christian freedom and theology of the cross otherwise so influenced the former, is illustrative. While Luther argued that "because of the spirit and faith, the nature of all Christians is such that they act well and rightly, better than any laws can teach them, and therefore they have no need of any laws for themselves," he insisted in the next paragraph upon the necessity and legitimacy of secular rule, for unfortunately "scarcely one human being in a thousand is a true Christian."[1] One need not acquiesce to Luther's own quietist political commitments to recognize his simple practical wisdom: in the absence of universal saintliness, churches cannot replace states. Heidegger, like some of Luther's more radical Anabaptist followers, ignored this wisdom.

If Heidegger's antinomianism looked back to the radical Reformation, it also pointed forward to contemporary postmodernism. Heidegger's critique of modernity and the metaphysical tradition continues to exercise considerable influence over postmodernism, and if the connection I have demonstrated between a critique of metaphysics and political antinomianism holds for Heidegger, it may provide a useful tool for analyzing those influenced by Heidegger's critique. In fact, I want to suggest that much thinking that is characterized as antiliberal, whether or not it is directly influenced by Heidegger, is more truly understood as antinomian. The hos-

---

1. Luther, "On Secular Authority," 9–10.

tility to law and the state, the belief in an uncoerced unity of the people, the radical revolutionary millenarianism could equally describe Marxism, Russian nihilism, and anarchism. Heidegger's obvious religious impulse and the deep-rooted connections he drew between his theology, metaphysics, and politics merely make the underlying religious nature of this sort of politics manifest; Heidegger reveals the logic of antinomianism where it might be concealed.

Other current modes of political thinking share this antinomian logic. One could say that contemporary antinomianism is influenced by Heidegger, but it is perhaps more accurate to say that these movements are driven to antinomianism by much the same factors that drove Heidegger to it: a dissatisfaction with, and even hatred of, the bourgeois, liberal world. With Marxism, fascism, and anarchism consigned, at least for the time being, to the dustbin of history, contemporary antiliberalism turns more and more to antinomianism, whether it be the radical democrat's disdain for the state, or those who would celebrate the antistatism of a civil society that gives birth to peaceful revolutionary movements.

Postmodernism, in particular, is antinomian, especially those thinkers most influenced by Heidegger. Curiously, they exhibit their antinomianism all the more when they seek to distinguish themselves from Heidegger. The current mantra to "think with Heidegger against Heidegger" reveals itself to mean, "More antinomianism!" for postmodernists criticize Heidegger for neglecting his most profound thought, the difference of being that opens the space for the play and freedom of being. They criticize Heidegger, in short, for being insufficiently antinomian.

This criticism has long been present, albeit subdued, in postmodern thought. It became more prominent, however, in the battle over the meaning of Heidegger's political engagement, for it provided a means for so-called Left Heideggerians to maintain their Heideggerian legacy while also criticizing his Nazism.[2] The genuine Heideggerian thought for postmodernism is the critique of presence, a critique which subsumes a critique of reason and an antifoundationalism. "Presence" in this broad sense means all order and law. The critique of presence is at heart a critique of law. In

---

2. This is a fairly common strategy in recent years; see, for some instances, de Beistegui, *Heidegger and the Political*; Gianni Vattimo, *Beyond Interpretation: The Meaning of Hermeneutics for Philosophy*, trans. David Webb (Stanford: Stanford University Press, 1997); Derrida, *Of Spirit*; Lacoue-Labarthe, *Heidegger, Art, and Politics*; Schürmann, *Heidegger on Being and Acting*; and Caputo, *Demythologizing Heidegger*.

this guise, the antinomian critique of presence informs the postmodern understanding of the political. For postmodernists, the proper field of the political is the space beyond the law, whether that is thought as the anarchic economy, the mystical foundation of law, the empty signifier, the inoperative community, or "thinking without banisters." In each case, the name for the political stands opposed to law.[3] The postmodern concept of the political is fundamentally antinomian.

In effect, postmodernism's critique of presence repeats and radicalizes Heidegger's own attempt to purify fanaticism of its dogmatic tendency; postmodernism wants to purify Heidegger of the metaphysical residue in his thinking. As I have shown, the purifying logic of antinomianism has as its political conclusion a community of saints. Antinomianism includes two elements that make up its peculiar character as a thinking of the political: a rejection of coercive law in the name of a foundationless freedom and a community unified without law. Freedom (difference) and community (unity) are its hallmarks. The great value to studying Heidegger's political philosophy is that Heidegger illuminatingly exhibits these characteristics. Postmodernism wants to hold freedom against community and difference and plurality against unity; at most, a community of difference, which is to say, an anarchic community of plurality.

Can plurality and difference alone found the basis of a new thinking of the political or does the political necessarily involve unity? Unity is still central to Heidegger's concept of the political, which explains why he propagated a politics of order, albeit one without any consideration of human law and administration of difference. Postmodernism would push Heidegger beyond this residue of metaphysical unity to think the political as irreducibly plural. Is this last push to a nonmetaphysical politics possible? Does contemporary postmodernism indicate the path past Heidegger's error or does it exacerbate its antinomian failure?

These questions of unity and plurality in political life remain for us to consider in the wake of Heidegger. Heidegger sought the harmony of these principles in a spiritual *deus ex machina*, a beautiful community untouched by coercion, power, or individual difference—the beautiful community of

3. Schürmann, *Heidegger on Being and Acting*; Jacques Derrida, "Force of Law: The 'Mystical Foundation of Authority,'" in *Deconstruction and the Possibility of Justice*, ed. David Gray Carlson, Drucilla Cornell, and Michel Rosenfeld (New York: Routledge, 1992); Ernesto Laclau, *Emancipation(s)* (New York: Verso, 1996); Nancy, *Inoperative Community*; Arendt, *Life of the Mind*.

the religious fanatic unable to find the rose in the cross of modern life. The dissatisfactions with a modern liberalism founded upon the bedrock separation of church and state must be considered in light of the greater dissatisfactions incurred by Heidegger's unpolitical political religion. If politics is founded upon the necessity of law for human well-being, then one must conclude that Heidegger's great attempt to recast politics in the image of authentic Dasein was a failure in its most basic principle because it wanted to sidestep the inescapable nature of politics. The failure of his thought— the failure of all antinomian thought—is that he tries to redefine the political in a way that avoids the hard necessities of politics. His radical critique of the edifice of Western metaphysics, galvanized by his religious ideal of authenticity, is an attempt to transcend the limits of politics, which he mistook to be limitations of modern technical politics.

The failure of Heidegger's politics is more than the failings of an all-too-human person. It is the failure of his deepest and most radical principles, principles too radical, too religious, for the nature of politics. In laying a path to the root of modern existence, Heidegger passed by the political root which is the origin of all genuinely political thinking. If we are to learn anything from Heidegger, it must be that his path cannot be followed by real human beings: a conception of human being that does not genuinely take into account the essence of human political being, for all its profundity, cannot be the cure for our political crises.

Selected Bibliography

Adorno, Theodor W. *Negative Dialectics*. Translated by E. B. Ashton. New York: Continuum, 1990.

Arendt, Hannah. "For Martin Heidegger's Eightieth Birthday." In *Martin Heidegger and National Socialism: Questions and Answers*, ed. Günther Neske and Emil Kettering, 207–18. New York: Paragon, 1990.

———. *The Human Condition*. Chicago: University of Chicago Press, 1958.

———. *The Life of the Mind*. 2 vols. New York: Harcourt Brace Jovanovich, 1978.

———. *The Origins of Totalitarianism*. New ed. New York: Harcourt, Brace & World, 1966.

———. "What Is Existential Philosophy?" In *Essays in Understanding: 1930–1954*, ed. Jerome Kohn, 163–87. New York: Harcourt, Brace & Company, 1994.

———. "What Is Freedom?" In *Between Past and Future: Eight Exercises in Political Thought*, 143–71. New York: Penguin Books, 1968.

Aristotle. *Metaphysics*. Translated by Richard Hope. Ann Arbor: University of Michigan Press, 1960.

———. *The Nicomachean Ethics*. Translated by J.A.K. Thomson. New York: Viking Penguin, 1986.

Augustine. *Concerning the City of God against the Pagans*. Translated by Henry Bettenson. Harmondsworth, Middlesex: Penguin Books, 1984.

Barash, Jeffrey Andrew. "Heidegger's Ontological 'Destruction' of Western Intellectual Traditions." In *Reading Heidegger from the Start*, ed. Theodore Kisiel and John van Buren, 111–21. Albany: SUNY Press, 1994.

———. "Über den geschichtlichen Ort der Wahrheit: Hermeneutische Perspektiven bei Wilhelm Dilthey und Martin Heidegger." In *Martin Heidegger: Innen- und Außenansichten*, edited by the Forum für Philosophie, Bad Homburg, 58–74. Frankfurt a. M.: Suhrkamp, 1991.

Beistigui, Miguel de. *Heidegger and the Political: Dystopias*. New York: Routledge, 1998.

Berlin, Isaiah. "Two Concepts of Liberty." In *Four Essays on Liberty*. New York: Oxford University Press, 1969.

Bernasconi, Robert. *Heidegger in Question: The Art of Existing*. Atlantic Highlands, N.J.: Humanities Press International, 1993.

———. "Repetition and Tradition: Heidegger's Destructuring of the Distinction Between Essence and Existence in *Basic Problems of Phenomenology*." In *Reading Heidegger from the Start*, ed. Theodore Kisiel and John van Buren, 123–36. Albany: SUNY Press, 1994.

Bernstein, Richard J. *The New Constellation: The Ethical-Political Horizons of Modernity/Postmodernity*. Cambridge: MIT Press, 1992.

Blanchot, Maurice. "Thinking the Apocalypse." *Critical Inquiry* 15, no. 2 (1989): 475–80.

Blattner, William. "Existential Temporality in *Being and Time* (Why Heidegger is not a Pragmatist)." In *Heidegger: A Critical Reader*, ed. Hubert Dreyfus and Harrison Hall, 99–129. Cambridge, Mass.: Basil Blackwell, 1992.

Borgmann, Albert. *Technology and the Character of the Life-World: A Philosophical Inquiry*. Chicago: University of Chicago Press, 1984.

Bourdieu, Pierre. "Back to History." In *The Heidegger Controversy*, ed. Richard Wolin, 264–71. Cambridge: MIT Press, 1993.

———. *The Political Ontology of Martin Heidegger*. Translated by Peter Collier. Stanford: Stanford University Press, 1991.

Brogan, Walter. "The Place of Aristotle in the Development of Heidegger's Phenomenology." In *Reading Heidegger from the Start*, ed. Theodore Kisiel and John van Buren, 213–27. Albany: SUNY Press, 1994.

Caputo, John D. *Demythologizing Heidegger*. Bloomington: Indiana University Press, 1993.

———. "Heidegger and Theology." In *The Cambridge Companion to Heidegger*, ed. Charles Guignon, 270–88. New York: Cambridge University Press, 1993.

———. "Heidegger's Scandal: Thinking and the Essence of the Victim." In *The Heidegger Case: On Philosophy and Politics*, ed. Tom Rockmore and Joseph Margolis, 265–81. Philadelphia: Temple University Press, 1992.

———. *The Mystical Element in Heidegger's Thought*. New York: Fordham University Press, 1986.

———. *Radical Hermeneutics*. Bloomington: Indiana University Press, 1987.

———. "*Sorge* and *Kardia*: The Hermeneutics of Factical Life and the Categories of the Heart." In *Reading Heidegger from the Start*, ed. Theodore Kisiel and John van Buren, 327–43. Albany: SUNY Press, 1994.

Dallmayr, Fred. *Between Freiburg and Frankfurt*. Amherst: University of Massachussetts Press, 1991.

———. *The Other Heidegger*. Ithaca: Cornell University Press, 1993.

Deleuze, Gilles. *Nietzsche and Philosophy*. Translated by Hugh Tomlinson. New York: Columbia University Press, 1983.

Derrida, Jacques. *Aporias*. Translated by Thomas Dutoit. Stanford: Stanford University Press, 1993.

———. "Force of Law: The 'Mystical Foundations of Authority.' " In *Deconstruction and the Possibility of Justice*, ed. David Gray Carlson, Drucilla Cornell, and Michel Rosenfeld, 3–67. New York: Routledge, 1992.

———. "Heidegger's Silence." In *Martin Heidegger and National Socialism:*

Questions and Answers, ed. Günther Neske and Emil Kettering, 145–46. New York: Paragon, 1990.

———. "Interpreting Signatures (Nietzsche/Heidegger): Two Questions." In *Dialogue and Deconstruction: The Gadamer-Derrida Encounter,* ed. Diane P. Michelfelder and Richard E. Palmer, 58–71. Albany: SUNY Press, 1989.

———. *Of Spirit: Heidegger and the Question.* Translated by Geoffrey Bennington and Rachel Bowlby. Chicago: University of Chicago Press, 1989.

———. *Specters of Marx.* Translated by Peggy Kamuf. New York: Routledge, 1994.

Dreyfus, Hubert. "Heidegger's History of the Being of Equipment." In *Heidegger: A Critical Reader,* ed. Hubert Dreyfus and Harrison Hall, 173–85. Cambridge, Mass.: Basil Blackwell, 1992.

———. "Heidegger on the Connection Between Nihilism, Art, Technology, and Politics." In *The Cambridge Companion to Heidegger,* ed. Charles Guignon, 289–316. New York: Cambridge University Press, 1993.

———. "Mixing Interpretation, Religion, and Politics: Heidegger's High-Risk Thinking." In *The Break: Habermas, Heidegger, and the Nazis,* ed. Christopher Ocker, 17–23. Berkeley, Calif.: The Center for Hermeneutical Studies, 1992.

Ebeling, Hans. "Das Ereignis des Führers: Heideggers Antwort." In *Martin Heidegger: Innen- und Außenansichten,* edited by the Forum für Philosophie, Bad Homburg, 33–57. Frankfurt a. M.: Suhrkamp, 1991.

———. *Heidegger: Geschichte einer Täuschung.* Würzburg: Königshausen und Neumann, 1990.

Eckhart, Meister. *Deutsche Predigten und Traktate.* Translated and edited by Josef Quint. Munich: Carl Hanser, 1955.

———. *Meister Eckhart: German Sermons and Treatises.* Translated and edited by M. O'C. Walshe. 3 vols. London: Watkins, 1979.

Farias, Victor. *Heidegger and Nazism.* Translated by Paul Burrell. Philadelphia: Temple University Press, 1989.

Feher, Istavan. "Phenomenology, Hermeneutics, *Lebensphilosophie:* Heidegger's Confrontation with Husserl, Dilthey, and Jaspers." In *Reading Heidegger from the Start,* ed. Theodore Kisiel and John van Buren, 73–89. Albany: SUNY Press, 1994.

Fell, Joseph P. "The Familiar and the Strange: On the Limits of Praxis in the Early Heidegger." In *Heidegger: A Critical Reader,* ed. Hubert Dreyfus and Harrison Hall, 65–80. Cambridge, Mass.: Basil Blackwell, 1992.

Ferry, Luc, and Alain Renaut. *Heidegger and Modernity.* Translated by Franklin Philip. Chicago: University of Chicago Press, 1990.

Figal, Günther. *Martin Heidegger: Phänomenologie der Freiheit.* Sonderausgabe. Frankfurt a. M.: Hain, 1991.

Franzen, Winfried. "Die Sehnsucht nach Härte und Schwere: Über ein zum NS-Engagement desponierendes Motiv in Heideggers Vorlesung 'Grundbegriffe der Metaphysik' von 1929/30." In *Heidegger und die praktische Philosophie,* ed. Annemarie Gethmann-Siefert and Otto Pöggeler, 78–92. Frankfurt a. M.: Suhrkamp, 1989.

Fritsche, Johannes. *Historical Destiny and National Socialism in Heidegger's "Being and Time."* Berkeley and Los Angeles: University of California Press, 1999.

Funkenstein, Amos. *Theology and the Scientific Imagination from the Middle Ages to the Seventeenth Century*. Princeton: Princeton University Press, 1986.

Gadamer, Hans-Georg. "Back from Syracuse." *Critical Inquiry* 15, no. 2 (1989): 427–30.

———. "Heidegger und die Griechen." In *Hermeneutik im Rückblick*, vol. 10 of *Gesammelte Werke*, 31–45. Tübingen: J.C.B. Mohr, 1995.

———. *The Idea of the Good in Platonic-Aristotelian Philosophy*. Translated by P. Christopher Smith. New Haven: Yale University Press, 1986.

———. "Die Idee der Praktischen Philosophie." In *Hermeneutik im Rückblick*, vol. 10 of *Gesammelte Werke*, 238–46. Tübingen: J.C.B. Mohr, 1995.

———. "Martin Heidegger's One Path." In *Reading Heidegger from the Start*, ed. Theodore Kisiel and John van Buren, 19–34. Albany: SUNY Press, 1994.

———. "The Political Incompetence of Philosophy." In *The Heidegger Case: On Philosophy and Politics*, ed. Tom Rockmore and Joseph Margolis, 364–69. Philadelphia: Temple University Press, 1992.

———. "Die Religiöse Dimension." In *Neuere Philosophie: Hegel, Husserl, Heidegger*, vol. 3 of *Gesammelte Werke*, 308–19. Tübingen: J.C.B. Mohr, 1987.

———. *Truth and Method*. Translated by Joel Weinsheimer and Donald G. Marshall. 2d rev. ed. New York: Crossroad, 1990.

Garver, Eugene. *Aristotle's Rhetoric: An Art of Character*. Chicago: University of Chicago Press, 1994.

Gebert, Sigburt. *Negative Politik*. Berlin: Duncker & Humblot, 1992.

Gethmann, Carl Friedrich. "Heideggers Konzeption des Handelns in *Sein und Zeit*." In *Heidegger und die praktische Philosophie*, ed. Annemarie Gethmann-Siefert and Otto Pöggeler, 140–73. Frankfurt a. M.: Suhrkamp, 1989.

Gethmann-Siefert, Annemarie. "Heidegger und Hölderlin: Die Überforderung des 'Dichters in dürftiger Zeit.'" In *Heidegger und die praktische Philosophie*, ed. Annemarie Gethmann-Siefert and Otto Pöggeler, 191–227. Frankfurt a. M.: Suhrkamp, 1989.

Gillespie, Michael. *Hegel, Heidegger, and the Ground of History*. Chicago: University of Chicago Press, 1984.

———. "Martin Heidegger's Aristotelian National Socialism." *Political Theory* 28, no. 2 (2000): 140-66.

———. *Nihilism Before Nietzsche*. Chicago: University of Chicago Press, 1996.

Goldmann, Lucien. *Lukacs and Heidegger: Towards a New Philosophy*. Translated by William Q. Boelhower. Boston: Routledge & Kegan Paul, 1977.

Grondin, Jean. "The Ethical and Young Hegelian Motives in Heidegger's Hermeneutics of Facticity." In *Reading Heidegger from the Start*, ed. Theodore Kisiel and John van Buren, 345–57. Albany: SUNY Press, 1994.

Guignon, Charles. "History and Commitment in the Early Heidegger." In *Heidegger: A Critical Reader*, ed. Hubert Dreyfus and Harrison Hall, 130–58. Cambridge, Mass.: Basil Blackwell, 1992.

Haar, Michel. *Heidegger and the Essence of Man*. Translated by William McNeill. Albany: SUNY Press, 1993.

———. *The Song of the Earth: Heidegger and the Grounds of the History of Being*. Translated by Reinald Lilly. Bloomington: Indiana University Press, 1993.

Habermas, Jürgen. "Martin Heidegger: On the Publication of the Lectures of 1935." In *The Heidegger Controversy*, ed. Richard Wolin, 186–97. Cambridge: MIT Press, 1993.

———. *The Philosophical Discourse of Modernity*. Translated by Frederick G. Lawrence. Cambridge: MIT Press, 1987.

———. *Toward a Rational Society: Student Protest, Science, and Politics*. Translated by Jeremy J. Shapiro. Boston: Beacon Press, 1970.

———. "Work and Weltanschauung: The Heidegger Controversy from a German Perspective." In *The New Conservatism: Cultural Criticism and the Historians' Debate*, ed. Shierry Weber Nicholsen, 140–72. Cambridge: MIT Press, 1989.

Harries, Karsten. "Heidegger as Political Thinker." In *Heidegger and Modern Philosophy*, ed. Michael Murray, 304–28. New Haven: Yale University Press, 1978.

———. "Philosophy, Politics, Technology." In *Martin Heidegger: Politics, Art, and Technology*, ed. Karsten Harries and Christoph Jamme, 225–45. New York: Holmes & Meier, 1994.

Havas, Randall. "Nihilism and the Illusion of Nationalism." In *Martin Heidegger: Politics, Art, and Technology*, ed. Karsten Harries and Christoph Jamme, 197–209. New York: Holmes & Meier, 1994.

Hegel, Georg Wilhelm Friedrich. *Elements of the Philosophy of Right*. Translated by H. B. Nisbet. New York: Cambridge University Press, 1991.

———. *Phenomenology of Spirit*. Translated by A. V. Miller. New York: Oxford University Press, 1977.

Held, Klaus. "Heidegger und das Prinzip der Phänomenologie." In *Heidegger und die praktische Philosophie*, ed. Annemarie Gethmann-Siefert and Otto Pöggeler, 111–39. Frankfurt a. M.: Suhrkamp, 1989.

Herf, Jeffrey. *Reactionary Modernism: Technology, Culture and Politics in Weimar and the Third Republic*. New York: Cambridge University Press, 1984.

Herrmann, Friedrich-Wilhelm von. "Das Ereignis und die Fragen nach dem Wesen der Technik, Politik und Kunst." In *Kunst, Politik, Technik*, ed. Christoph Jamme and Karsten Harries, 241–59. Munich: Fink, 1992.

Hobbes, Thomas. *Leviathan: or the Matter, Forme and Power of a Commonwealth Ecclesiasticall and Civil*. Edited by Michael Oakeshott. New York: Macmillan, 1962.

Hoffman, Piotr. "Death, Time, History: Division II of *Being and Time*." In *The Cambridge Companion to Heidegger*, ed. Charles Guignon, 195–214. New York: Cambridge University Press, 1993.

Hölderlin, Friedrich. "In Lieblicher Bläue." In *Sämtliche Werke*, vol. 2/1, ed. Friedrich Beissner, 372–74. Stuttgart: W. Kohlhammer, 1951.

Horkheimer, Max, and Theodor W. Adorno. *Dialectic of Enlightenment*. Translated by John Cumming. New York: Continuum, 1972.

Ibañez-Noé, Javier. "Heidegger, Nietzsche, Jünger and the Interpretation of the Contemporary Age." *Southern Journal of Philosophy* 33, no. 1 (1995): 57–81.

Janicaud, Dominique. *The Shadow of That Thought: Heidegger and the Question of Politics*. Translated by Michael Gendre. Evanston: Northwestern University Press, 1996.

Janicaud, Dominque, and Jean-François Mattéi. *Heidegger from Metaphysics to Thought*. Translated by Michael Gendre. Albany: SUNY Press, 1995.

Jaspers, Karl. "Letter to the Freiburg University Denazification Committee (December 22, 1945)." In *The Heidegger Controversy,* ed. Richard Wolin, 144–51. Cambridge: MIT Press, 1993.

Jonas, Hans. "Heidegger's Resoluteness and Resolve." In *Martin Heidegger and National Socialism: Questions and Answers,* ed. Günther Neske and Emil Kettering, 197–203. New York: Paragon, 1990.

———. *The Phenomenon of Life*. New York: Harper & Row, 1966.

Jünger, Ernst. *Der Arbeiter: Herrschaft und Gestalt*. Stuttgart: Klett-Cotta, 1982.

———. "Total Mobilization." In *The Heidegger Controversy,* ed. Richard Wolin, 119–39. Cambridge: MIT Press, 1993.

Kant, Immanuel. *Critique of Practical Reason*. Translated by Lewis White Beck. New York: Macmillan, 1988.

———. *Critique of Pure Reason*. Translated by Norman Kemp Smith. New York: St. Martin's Press, 1965.

Kisiel, Theodore. *The Genesis of Heidegger's "Being and Time."* Berkeley and Los Angeles: University of California Press, 1993.

———. "The Genetic Difference in Reading *Being and Time*." *American Catholic Philosophical Quarterly* 69, no. 2 (1995): 171–87.

———. "Heidegger (1920–21) on Becoming a Christian: A Conceptual Picture Show." In *Reading Heidegger from the Start,* ed. Theodore Kisiel and John van Buren, 175–92. Albany: SUNY Press, 1994.

———. "Heidegger's Apology: Biography as Philosophy and Ideology." In *The Heidegger Case: On Philosophy and Politics,* ed. Tom Rockmore and Joseph Margolis, 11–51. Philadelphia: Temple University Press, 1992.

Klemperer, Klemens von. "Martin Heidegger's Life and Times: A Historian's View, Or: Heidegger and the Hubris of Philosophical Policy." In *Martin Heidegger: Politics, Art, and Technology,* ed. Karsten Harries and Christoph Jamme, 1–17. New York: Holmes & Meier, 1994.

Koepke, Wulf. "Das Wort 'Volk' im Sprachgebrauch Johann Gottfried Herders." *Lessing Yearbook* 19 (1987): 209–21.

Kozuma, Tadashi. "Technische Welt und anderer Anfang des Denkens." In *Destruktion und Übersetzung,* ed. Thomas Buchheim, 63–76. Weinheim: VCH Verlagsgesellschaft, 1989.

Krell, David Farrell. *Daimon Life: Heidegger and Life-Philosophy*. Bloomington: Indiana University Press, 1992.

———. *Intimations of Mortality*. University Park: Pennsylvania State University Press, 1986.

Laclau, Ernesto. *Emancipation(s)*. New York: Verso, 1996.

Lacoue-Labarthe, Philippe. *Heidegger, Art, and Politics*. Translated by Chris Turner. Cambridge, Mass.: Basil Blackwell, 1990.

———. "Neither an Accident nor a Mistake." *Critical Inquiry* 15, no. 2 (1989): 481–84.

———. "The Spirit of National Socialism and Its Destiny." In *Retreating the Political,* ed. Simon Sparks, 148–56. New York: Routledge, 1997.

———. "Transcendence Ends in Politics." In *Typography: Mimesis, Philosophy, Politics,* ed. Christopher Fynsk, 267–300. Cambridge: Harvard University Press, 1988.

Lang, Berel. *Heidegger's Silence.* Ithaca: Cornell University Press, 1996.

Levinas, Emmanuel. "As if Consenting to Horror." *Critical Inquiry* 15, no. 2 (1989): 485–88.

———. *Totality and Infinity: An Essay on Exteriority.* Pittsburgh: Duquesne University Press, 1988.

Losurdo, Domenico. "Heidegger and Hitler's War." In *The Heidegger Case: On Philosophy and Politics,* ed. Tom Rockmore and Joseph Margolis, 141–64. Philadelphia: Temple University Press, 1992.

Löwith, Karl. "European Nihilism: Reflections on the Spiritual and Historical Background of the European War." In *Martin Heidegger and European Nihilism,* ed. Richard Wolin, 173–234. New York: Columbia University Press, 1995.

———. "Heidegger: Thinker in a Destitute Time." In *Martin Heidegger and European Nihilism,* ed. Richard Wolin, 29–134. New York: Columbia University Press, 1995.

———. "My Last Meeting with Heidegger in Rome, 1936." In *The Heidegger Controversy,* ed. Richard Wolin, 140–43. Cambridge: MIT Press, 1993.

———. "The Occasional Decisionism of Carl Schmitt." In *Martin Heidegger and European Nihilism,* ed. Richard Wolin, 135–69. New York: Columbia University Press, 1995.

———. "The Political Implications of Heidegger's Existentialism." In *The Heidegger Controversy,* ed. Richard Wolin, 167–85. Cambridge: MIT Press, 1993.

Lukács, Georg. *History and Class Consciousness: Studies in Marxist Dialectics.* Translated by Rodney Livingstone. Cambridge: MIT Press, 1990.

Luther, Martin. "The Freedom of a Christian." In *Martin Luther: Selections from His Writings,* ed. John Dillenberger, 42–85. New York: Anchor Books, 1962.

———. "On Secular Authority." In *Luther and Calvin on Secular Authority,* ed. Harro Höpfl, 1–43. New York: Cambridge University Press, 1991.

———. "Sermons on the Catechism." In *Martin Luther: Selections from His Writings,* ed. John Dillenberger. New York: Anchor Books, 1962.

Margolis, Joseph. "Discarding and Recovering Heidegger." In *The Heidegger Case: On Philosophy and Politics,* ed. Tom Rockmore and Joseph Margolis, 405–22. Philadelphia: Temple University Press, 1992.

Marion, Jean-Luc. "The Essential Incoherence of Descartes' Definition of Divinity." In *Essays on Descartes' Meditations,* ed. Amélie Oksenberg Rorty, 297–338. Berkeley and Los Angeles: University of California Press, 1986.

———. *God Without Being.* Translated by Thomas A. Carlson. Chicago: University of Chicago Press, 1991.

———. "Heidegger and Descartes." In *Critical Heidegger,* ed. Christopher Macann, 67–96. New York: Routledge, 1996.

Marten, Rainer. "Heidegger and the Greeks." In *The Heidegger Case: On Philosophy and Politics,* ed. Tom Rockmore and Joseph Margolis, 167–87. Philadelphia: Temple University Press, 1992.

Martin, Bernd. "Martin Heidegger und der Nationalsozialismus." In *Martin Heidegger und das "Dritte Reich,"* ed. Bernd Martin, 14–50. Darmstadt: Wissenschaftliche Buchgesellschaft, 1989.

Marx, Karl. "Capital, Volume One." In *The Marx-Engels Reader,* ed. Robert C. Tucker, 294–438. New York: W. W. Norton, 1978.

———. "Wage Labour and Capital." In *The Marx-Engels Reader,* ed. Robert C. Tucker, 203–17. New York: W. W. Norton, 1978.

McCarthy, Thomas. "Heidegger and Critical Theory: The First Encounter." In *Martin Heidegger: Politics, Art, and Technology,* ed. Karsten Harries and Christoph Jamme, 210–24. New York: Holmes & Meier, 1994.

Meinecke, Friedrich. *Cosmopolitanism and the National State.* Translated by Robert B. Kimber. Princeton: Princeton University Press, 1970.

Milchman, Alan, and Alan Rosenberg, eds. *Martin Heidegger and the Holocaust.* Atlantic Highlands, N.J.: Humanities Press, 1996.

Mitchell, Joshua. *Not by Reason Alone: Religion, History, and Identity in Early Modern Political Thought.* Chicago: University of Chicago Press, 1993.

Mörchen, Hermann. *Adorno und Heidegger: Untersuchung einer philosophischen Kommunikationsverweigerung.* Stuttgart: Klett-Cotta, 1981.

Müller, Max. "Ein Gespräch mit Max Müller." In *Martin Heidegger und das "Dritte Reich,"* ed. Bernd Martin, 95–117. Darmstadt: Wissenschaftliche Buchgesellschaft, 1989.

———. "Martin Heidegger: A Philosopher and Politics: A Conversation." In *Martin Heidegger and National Socialism: Questions and Answers,* ed. Günther Neske and Emil Kettering, 175–97. New York: Paragon, 1990.

Nancy, Jean-Luc. *The Birth to Presence.* Translated by Brian Holmes et al. Stanford: Stanford University Press, 1993.

———. *The Experience of Freedom.* Translated by Bridget McDonald. Stanford: Stanford University Press, 1993.

———. *The Inoperative Community.* Translated by Peter Connor, Lisa Garbus, Michael Holland, and Simona Sawhney. Edited by Peter Connor. Minneapolis: University of Minnesota Press, 1991.

———. "Of Being-in-Common." In *Community at Loose Ends,* ed. Miami Theory Collective, 1–12. Albany: SUNY Press, 1990.

Neske, Günther, ed. *Erinnerung an Martin Heidegger.* Pfullingen: Neske, 1977.

Nietzsche, Friedrich. *The Birth of Tragedy and The Case of Wagner.* Translated by Walter Kaufmann. New York: Vintage Books, 1967.

———. "On the Uses and Disadvantages of History for Life." In *Untimely Meditations,* ed. R. J. Hollingdale, 57–123. New York: Cambridge University Press, 1983.

———. *Thus Spoke Zarathustra.* Translated by Walter Kaufmann. New York: Viking Press, 1966.

———. *The Will to Power.* Translated by Walter Kaufmann and R. J. Hollingdale. Edited by Walter Kaufmann. New York: Vintage Books, 1968.

Oberman, Heiko. "Martin Luther: Forerunner of the Reformation." In *The Reformation: Roots and Ramifications,* trans. Andrew Colin Gow, 23–52. Grand Rapids, Mich.: William B. Eerdmans, 1994.

Ott, Hugo. "Biographische Gründe für Heideggers 'Mentalität der Zerrissenheit.'" In *Martin Heidegger—Faszination und Erschrecken: die Politische Dimension einer Philosophie,* ed. Peter Kemper, 13–29. New York: Campus, 1990.

———. "Heidegger's Catholic Origins: The Theological Philosopher." In *Martin Heidegger: Politics, Art, and Technology,* ed. Karsten Harries and Christoph Jamme, 18–33. New York: Holmes & Meier, 1994.

———. "Martin Heidegger und der Nationalsozialismus." In *Heidegger und die praktische Philosophie,* ed. Annemarie Gethmann-Siefert and Otto Pöggeler, 64–77. Frankfurt a. M.: Suhrkamp, 1989.

———. *Martin Heidegger: Unterwegs zu seiner Biographie.* New York: Campus, 1992.

Petzet, Heinrich. *Encounters and Dialogues with Martin Heidegger: 1929–1976.* Translated by Parvis Emad and Kenneth Maly. Chicago: University of Chicago Press, 1993.

Pippin, Robert. *Modernism as a Philosophical Problem.* Cambridge, Mass.: Basil Blackwell, 1991.

———. "Nietzsche, Heidegger, and the Metaphysics of Modernity." In *Nietzsche and Modern German Thought,* ed. Keith Ansell-Pearson, 282–310. New York: Routledge, 1991.

Pöggeler, Otto. *Der Denkweg Martin Heideggers.* 3d ed. Pfullingen: Neske, 1990.

———. "Destruction and Moment." In *Reading Heidegger from the Start,* ed. Theodore Kisiel and John van Buren, 137–56. Albany: SUNY Press, 1994.

———. "Destruktion und Augenblick." In *Destruktion und Übersetzung,* ed. Thomas Buchheim, 9–29. Weinheim: VCH Verlagsgesellschaft, 1989.

———. *Heidegger in seiner Zeit.* Munich: Fink, 1999.

———. "Heidegger, Nietzsche, and Politics." In *The Heidegger Case: On Philosophy and Politics,* ed. Tom Rockmore and Joseph Margolis, 114–40. Philadelphia: Temple University Press, 1992.

———. "Heideggers politisches Selbstverständnis." In *Heidegger und die praktische Philosophie,* ed. Annemarie Gethmann-Siefert and Otto Pöggeler, 17–63. Frankfurt a. M.: Suhrkamp, 1989.

———. *Neue Wege mit Heidegger.* Munich: Alber, 1992.

———. "Nietzsche, Hölderlin und Heidegger." In *Martin Heidegger—Faszination und Erschrecken: die Politische Dimension einer Philosophie,* ed. Peter Kemper, 178–95. New York: Campus, 1990.

———. *Philosophie und Politik bei Heidegger.* 2d ed. Munich: Alber, 1974.

———. "'Praktische Philosophie' als Antwort an Heidegger." In *Martin Heidegger und das "Dritte Reich,"* ed. Bernd Martin, 62–92. Darmstadt: Wissenschaftliche Buchgesellschaft, 1989.

———. *Schritte zu einer Hermeneutische Philosophie.* Munich: Karl Alber, 1994.

Ringer, Fritz. *The Decline of the German Mandarins.* Hanover: University Press of New England, 1990.

Rockmore, Tom. *Heidegger and French Philosophy: Humanism, Antihumanism, and Being.* New York: Routledge, 1995.

———. *On Heidegger's Nazism and Philosophy.* Berkeley and Los Angeles: University of California Press, 1992.

Rorty, Richard. "Taking Philosophy Seriously." *The New Republic,* 11 April 1988, 31–34.

Rose, Gillian. *The Broken Middle: Out of Our Ancient Society.* Cambridge, Mass.: Blackwell Publishers, 1992.

———. *Dialectic of Nihilism.* New York: Basil Blackwell, 1984.

———. *Mourning Becomes Law: Philosophy and Representation.* New York: Cambridge University Press, 1996.

Rosen, Stanley. *Nihilism: A Philosophical Essay.* New Haven: Yale University Press, 1969.

———. *The Question of Being: A Reversal of Heidegger.* New Haven: Yale University Press, 1993.

Rousseau, Jean-Jacques. "Social Contract." In *The Collected Writings of Rousseau,* vol. 4. Edited by Roger D. Masters and Christopher Kelly. Translated by Judith R. Bush, Roger D. Masters, and Christopher Kelly. Hanover: University Press of New England, 1994.

Safranski, Rüdiger. *Ein Meister aus Deutschland: Heidegger und seine Zeit.* Munich: Hanser, 1994.

Sartre, Jean-Paul. "The Humanism of Existentialism." In *Essays in Existentialism,* ed. Wade Baskin, 31–62. New York: Citadel Press, 1993.

Shirmacher, Wolfgang. *Ereignis Technik.* Vienna: Passagen, 1990.

———. *Technik und Gelassenheit: Zeitkritik nach Heidegger.* Munich: Alber, 1983.

Schmidt, Gerhart. "Heideggers Philosophische Politik." In *Martin Heidegger und das "Dritte Reich,"* ed. Bernd Martin, 51–60. Darmstadt: Wissenschaftliche Buchgesellschaft, 1989.

Schmitt, Carl. *The Crisis of Parliamentary Democracy.* Translated by Ellen Kennedy. Cambridge: MIT Press, 1985.

Schürmann, Reiner. "Anti-humanism: Reflections of the Turn towards the Postmodern Epoch." *Man and World* 12, no. 2 (1979): 160–77.

———. "A Brutal Awakening to the Tragic Condition of Being: On Heidegger's *Beiträge zur Philosophie.*" In *Martin Heidegger: Politics, Art, and Technology,* ed. Karsten Harries and Christoph Jamme, 89–105. New York: Holmes & Meier, 1994.

———. *Heidegger on Being and Acting: From Principles to Anarchy.* Translated by Christine-Marie Gros. Bloomington: Indiana University Press, 1987.

———. "Riveted to a Monstrous Site: On Heidegger's *Beiträge zur Philosophie.*" In *The Heidegger Case: On Philosophy and Politics,* ed. Tom Rockmore and Joseph Margolis, 313–30. Philadelphia: Temple University Press, 1992.

Schwan, Alexander. "Heidegger über das 'Wesen der Freiheit.'" In *Philosophie und Poesie: Otto Pöggeler zum 60. Geburtstag,* ed. Annemarie Gethmann-Siefert, 9–36. Stuttgart: Friedrich Frommann, 1988.

———. "Heideggers 'Beitäge zur Philosophie' und die Politik." In *Kunst, Politik, Technik,* ed. Christoph Jamme and Karsten Harries, 175–202. Munich: Fink, 1992.

———. *Politische Philosophie im Denken Heideggers.* 2d ed. Opladen: Westdeutscher Verlag, 1989.

———. "Zeitkritik und Politik in Heideggers Spätphilosophie." In *Heidegger und die praktische Philosophie,* ed. Annemarie Gethmann-Siefert and Otto Pöggeler, 93–107. Frankfurt a. M.: Suhrkamp, 1989.

Scott, Charles E. *The Question of Ethics: Nietzsche, Foucault, Heidegger.* Bloomington: Indiana University Press, 1990.

Seubold, Günther. *Heideggers Analyse der neuzeitlichen Technik.* Munich: Alber, 1986.

Sheehan, Thomas. "How (Not) to Read Heidegger." *American Catholic Philosophical Quarterly* 69, no. 2 (1995): 275–94.

Shelley, Percy Bysshe. "On Life." In *Prose,* vol. 6 of *The Complete Works of Percy Bysshe Shelley,* ed. Roger Ingpen and Walter Peck, 194–97. New York: Charles Scribner's Sons, 1929.

Sikka, Sonya. *Forms of Transcendence: Heidegger and Mystical Theology.* Albany: SUNY Press, 1997.

Sluga, Hans. "The Break: Habermas, Heidegger, and the Nazis." In *The Break: Habermas, Heidegger, and the Nazis,* ed. Christopher Ocker, 1–16. Berkeley, Calif.: The Center for Hermeneutical Studies, 1992.

———. *Heidegger's Crisis: Philosophy and Politics in Nazi Germany.* Cambridge: Harvard University Press, 1993.

Smith, Gregory. *Nietzsche, Heidegger and the Transition to Postmodernity.* Chicago: University of Chicago Press, 1996.

Strauss, Leo. *Studies in Platonic Political Philosophy.* Chicago: University of Chicago Press, 1983.

Taminiaux, Jacques. "Heidegger and *Praxis.*" In *The Heidegger Case: On Philosophy and Politics,* ed. Tom Rockmore and Joseph Margolis, 188–207. Philadelphia: Temple University Press, 1992.

Taylor, Charles. "Engaged Agency and Background in Heidegger." In *The Cambridge Companion to Heidegger,* ed. Charles Guignon, 317–36. New York: Cambridge University Press, 1993.

———. *The Ethics of Authenticity.* Cambridge: Harvard University Press, 1992.

———. *Sources of the Self: The Making of the Modern Identity.* Cambridge: Harvard University Press, 1989.

Taylor, Mark C. *Erring: A Postmodern A/theology.* Chicago: University of Chicago Press, 1984.

Tertulian, Nicolas. "The History of Being and Political Revolution: Reflections on a Posthumous Work of Heidegger." In *The Heidegger Case: On Philosophy and Politics,* ed. Tom Rockmore and Joseph Margolis, 208–27. Philadelphia: Temple University Press, 1992.

Thiele, Leslie Paul. *Timely Meditations: Martin Heidegger and Postmodern Politics.* Princeton: Princeton University Press, 1995.

Thucydides. *The Peloponnesian War.* Translated by Richard Crawley. New York: Modern Library, 1951.

Troeltsch, Ernst. *Die Sozialphilosophie des Christentums.* Zurich: Verlag Seldwyla, 1922.

———. *The Social Teaching of the Christian Churches.* Translated by Olive Wyon. 2 vols. Vol. 2. New York: Macmillan, 1949.

Tugendhat, Ernst. "Heidegger's Idea of Truth." In *Critical Heidegger,* ed. Christopher Macann, 227–40. New York: Routledge, 1996.

van Buren, John. "The Ethics of *Formale Anzeige* in Heidegger." *American Catholic Philosophical Quarterly* 69, no. 2 (1995): 157–70.

———. "Martin Heidegger, Martin Luther." In *Reading Heidegger from the Start,* ed. Theodore Kisiel and John van Buren, 159–74. Albany: SUNY Press, 1994.

———. *The Young Heidegger.* Bloomington: Indiana University Press, 1994.

Vattimo, Gianni. *Beyond Interpretation: The Meaning of Hermeneutics for Philosophy.* Translated by David Webb. Stanford: Stanford University Press, 1997.

———. *The End of Modernity.* Cambridge: Polity Press, 1988.

Vietta, Silvio. *Heideggers Kritik am Nationalsozialismus und an der Technik.* Tübingen: Niemeyer, 1989.

Villa, Dana. *Arendt and Heidegger: The Fate of the Political.* Princeton: Princeton University Press, 1996.

———. "The Banality of Philosophy: Arendt on Heidegger and Eichmann." In *Hannah Arendt: Twenty Years Later,* ed. Larry May and Jerome Kohn, 179–96. Cambridge: MIT Press, 1996.

Vogel, Lawrence. *The Fragile "We": Ethical Implications of Heidegger's Being and Time.* Evanston: Northwestern University Press, 1994.

Volpi, Franco. "*Being and Time*: A 'Translation' of the *Nicomachean Ethics?*" In *Reading Heidegger from the Start,* ed. Theodore Kisiel and John van Buren, 195–211. Albany: SUNY Press, 1994.

———. "Dasein as *Praxis*: The Heideggerian Assimilation and Radicalization of the Practical Philosophy of Aristotle." In *Critical Heidegger,* ed. Christopher Macann, 27–66. New York: Routledge, 1996.

Walzer, Michael. *The Revolution of the Saints: The Origins of Radical Politics.* Cambridge: Harvard University Press, 1965.

Weber, Max. *Economy and Society.* Edited by Guenther Roth and Claus Wittich. 2 vols. Berkeley and Los Angeles: University of California Press, 1978.

———. *The Protestant Ethic and the Spirit of Capitalism.* Translated by Talcott Parsons. New York: Charles Scribner's Sons, 1958.

White, Stephen. *Political Theory and Postmodernism.* New York: Cambridge University Press, 1991.

Wolin, Richard. "French Heidegger Wars." In *Labyrinths: Explorations in the Critical History of Ideas,* 142–61. Amherst: University of Massachussetts Press, 1995.

———. "Karl Löwith and Martin Heidegger—Contexts and Controversies: An Introduction." In *Martin Heidegger and European Nihilism,* ed. Richard Wolin, 1–25. New York: Columbia University Press, 1995.

———. *The Politics of Being: The Political Thought of Martin Heidegger.* New York: Columbia University Press, 1990.

———, ed. *The Heidegger Controversy.* Cambridge: MIT Press, 1993.

Yack, Bernard. *The Longing for Total Revolution: Philosophic Sources of Social Discontent from Rousseau to Marx and Nietzsche.* Princeton: Princeton University Press, 1986.

Young, Julian. *Heidegger, Philosophy, Nazism.* New York: Cambridge University Press, 1997.

Zimmerman, Michael. *Contesting Earth's Future: Radical Ecology and Postmodernism.* Berkeley and Los Angeles: University of California Press, 1994.

——. "Heidegger and Marcuse: Technology as Ideology." *Research in Philosophy and Technology* 2 (1979): 245–61.

——. *Heidegger's Confrontation with Modernity: Technology, Politics, and Art.* Bloomington: Indiana University Press, 1990.

——. "*L'affaire* Heidegger." *Times Literary Supplement,* 7–13 October 1988, 1115–17.

——. "Ontological Aestheticism: Heidegger, Jünger, and National Socialism." In *The Heidegger Case: On Philosophy and Politics,* ed. Tom Rockmore and Joseph Margolis, 52–89. Philadelphia: Temple University Press, 1992.

Zuckert, Catherine. "Martin Heidegger: His Philosophy and His Politics." *Political Theory* 18, no. 1 (1990): 51–79.

Index

administration, administrators, 229, 230,
    233, 248–49, 251–52, 261
    Weber on, 230–32
Adorno, Theodor W., 76, 139 n.15, 148, 179
aisthēsis, 54
alētheia, 17, 33, 44–47, 94, 122, 123 n. 3,
    158, 160–61, 199
alētheuein. See alētheia
alienation, 63, 71–73, 78, 80, 87, 116,
    236–37
antinomianism, 3–4, 10–11, 266, 269,
    270–73
    relation to postmodernism, 271–72
anti-Semitism, 220–21 n.70. *See also*
    racism and National Socialism
anxiety, 87–89, 94, 97, 111
apocalypsism, millennialism, 263, 265, 269
Aquinas, Thomas, 14, 16, 19, 21, 29 n.18,
    64, 169 n. 49
archē, 47–48, 55, 217
Arendt, Hannah, 18 n.7, 94 n. 33, 120, 179
    on Heidegger's politics, 9 n. 7, 103,
    182–83
    on Heidegger as pure thinker, 45 n. 27,
    241
    on racism, 192 n. 35
Aristophanes, 239
Aristotle, 10, 40–41, 157, 266–67
    dianoetic virtues, 32–34, 44
    on labor, 119–20
    metaphysics, 140, 215
    modes of *alētheuein*, 17–19, 23 n. 14

order of being, 29 n. 18
phronēsis contrasted with *deinotes*,
    61–62, 254
on practical wisdom, 57–59; and leader-
    ship, 225
on *praxis*, 51–52, 98
rhetoric, 241
on *technē*, 122–23, 172
art, 159, 184 n. 18, 20. *See also poetry* and
    poisēis
    as authentic action, 122
    and authentic being of Dasein, 163
    as brought into being by *technē*, 161
    concretion of the gods in works of, 170
    as enduring presencing of historical
    truth, 161
    modern view of, 159
    poetic moments of, 160–61
    preservation of the mystery of being in a
    work of, 165
    revelatory nature of, 122
    Romantic view of (the state as a work
    of), 159–160, 163 n. 42, 184, 187
    world opened up by a work of, 161–64
Augenblick. See moment of vision
Augustine, 41–42, 68–69, 97–98, 102, 258
authenticity, 237, 241, 269. *See also*
    phronēsis
    as antinomianism, 3–4
    and art, 163, 165
    and being, 122, 151–157, 160, 165–66,
    215–16, 218–19

www.ingramcontent.com/pod-product-compliance
Lightning Source LLC
Chambersburg PA
CBHW021851020426
42334CB00013B/284